Intelligence: Multiple Perspectives

Intelligence: Multiple Perspectives

Howard Gardner

Mindy L. Kornhaber

Warren K. Wake

Harcourt Brace College Publishers

Fort Worth   Philadelphia   San Diego   New York   Orlando   Austin   San Antonio
Toronto   Montreal   London   Sydney   Tokyo

Publisher	Ted Buchholz
Editor in Chief	Christopher P. Klein
Assistant Editor	Linda Wiley
Project Editor	Publications Development Company
Senior Production Manager	Ken Dunaway
Cover Design	Sue Hart
Book Design	Publications Development Company
Photo Researcher	Sue Howard

Cover illustration by Warren K. Wake, based on a drawing by Abraham Bosse © 1645, from *Manière Universelle de Mr. Decaragues,* Vol. 1.

ISBN: 0-03-072629-8
Library of Congress Catalog Card Number: 95–79342

Address for Editorial Correspondence: Harcourt Brace College Publishers, 301 Commerce Street, Suite 3700, Fort Worth, TX 76102.

Address for Orders: Harcourt Brace & Company, 6277 Sea Harbor Drive, Orlando, FL 32887-6777. 1-800-782-4479, or 1-800-433-0001 (in Florida).

Printed in the United States of America
7 8 9 0 1 2 3   039   9 8 7 6 5 4 3 2

For our children

Preface

No psychological topic is of greater interest to the general public, and to the discipline of psychology as a whole, than intelligence. Laypeople argue at length about who is intelligent, how to become smarter, and what difference IQ makes. Psychologists and other scholars debate the definition of intelligence, the best ways to measure it, and the relation between intelligence and other social virtues, like creativity, or social vices, like criminal behavior. Much controversy has surrounded the study of intelligence, but few would dispute Richard Herrnstein's claim that the study of intelligence has been one of the greatest successes of 20th-century psychology.

Given the interest in and accessibility of the topic, it is hardly surprising that hundreds of books and thousands of articles—both scholarly and popular—have been written about intelligence in the past few decades. What is surprising indeed is that, until this time, no introductory textbook has focused on intelligence. Those who want to master the material on intelligence must read more advanced books, written primarily for graduate students and scholars; distinctly "pop" books, whose authority and coverage are open to question; or introductory books written from the point of view of one or another theorist. An even less palatable alternative is to skim dozens of general texts, in the hope of gaining a sense of how the field thinks about intelligence today—or, more probably, how the field conceived of intelligence some years ago.

The book that you have begun to read confronts this situation in a clear and comprehensive way. Within one volume, we have surveyed the major approaches to intelligence that have evolved since the scientific study of intelligence began, about a century ago. Contemporary work on intelligence is viewed in the light of its philosophical origins, the earliest attempts to measure intelligence, and the findings obtained from disciplines ranging from anthropology to computer science to neuroscience. Each of the major positions is presented fully and fairly, though not uncritically. In addition, the educational, societal, and political implications of research on intelligence are considered.

A textbook is not the place to wave one's own theoretical banner, and we have avoided the temptation to favor one line of work over another. Still, the subject of intelligence is highly controversial, and there is probably no way to write a textbook that will satisfy everyone to the same extent. To put our own cards on the table, we believe that the final word on intelligence has not yet been spoken by the scientific community and that it is important to review a range of positions and perspectives. In doing so, we use a sequence of topics that, we believe, makes sense. We begin by considering conceptions of intelligence in different cultures and historical eras. We then explore intelligence as it is usually conceived of—as a psychological and biological property of the individual. Next, we present alternative conceptions of intelligence. Finally, we investigate intelligence as it plays out in broader contexts, such as the school and the workplace.

In addition to the usual textbook accoutrements, this book has a number of special features and accents that deserve mention. It provides full descriptions of four recent theories of intelligence (Chapter 7). It looks at intelligence across time and cultural settings (Chapters 1, 2, 8, and 9). It integrates the topic into mainstream developmental and cognitive research (Chapters 4 and 6, respectively). We hope that these diverse explorations will enable readers to gain a multifaceted understanding of intelligence.

September 1995

Acknowledgments

Books on complex and controversial topics frequently have more than one parent. A word about the authorship in this case: Major responsibility for drafting the book was shared by Mindy Kornhaber and Howard Gardner. Warren Wake prepared Chapter 6 and numerous illustrations for that and other chapters.

We wish to thank Christina Oldham, Eve Howard, Nancy Marcus Land, and Chris Klein for their editorial support. We thank Nira Granott who worked on the early phases of this project. We are grateful to Stephen Ceci, Raymond Fancher, Earl Hunt, John Klein, John Kounios, Robert Sternberg, William Tucker, and Irwin Waldman for providing tough and useful critiques of earlier versions of the manuscript.

We also thank librarians and staff members of the Harvard University Library System, especially those at Countway, Gutman, Harvard-Yenching, and Widener. With their help, we were able to locate and draw upon the wide range of materials needed for a thorough exploration of this topic.

During 1994–1995, we were aided immeasurably by Melissa Brand. Melissa tackled a diverse array of responsibilities—from tracking down footnotes to finding apt illustrations to securing permissions—enabling us to bring this book to completion. She brought to this demanding work keen organizational skills and unfailing good spirits, all too frequently compensating for the authors' shortcomings in these areas. She has our heartfelt thanks. We would also like to thank Lewis Burke Frumkes for his generous support of our research on intelligence. We extend our thanks as well to Sandi Watson for logistical assistance during the writing process, to Lisa Bromer for generously helping with proofreading, and to Daisy Scott for her thorough reading and thoughtful suggestions. We are also grateful to friends and colleagues at Harvard Project Zero whose interest and support sustained us throughout this project.

HG
MLK
WKW

September 1995

Contents

Chapter 4
The Developmental Perspective: Piaget and Beyond   97

Chapter 5
Biological Perspectives   135

Chapter 6
The Cognitive Perspective   161

Chapter 7
Recent Perspectives   195

Chapter 8
From the Perspective of School   246

Chapter 9
From the Perspective of the Workplace   266

Chapter 1

Historical and
Cultural Perspectives

Introduction

It is often helpful to anticipate an experience. Before you travel to a foreign country, it's a good idea to imagine yourself in the setting, and, if you have time, to talk with others who have been there. Before meeting with people you don't know well, it is sometimes useful to think about questions you may have for them and what you and they will say.

This approach is also worthwhile when you begin studying something. It is intriguing to think about (and even to write down) what you might already know about the topic, along with your questions, expectations, and hopes. As you delve further into the topic, it can be instructive to return to these earlier thoughts and see the ways in which your own thinking has changed and, in the best instance, to realize how your understanding has deepened.

By now you have probably anticipated where we are headed. At this point, as you are beginning a book on intelligence, but before the authors have played their cards, it is a good idea to sit back and think about what intelligence means to you. In doing so, you might ask yourself: What do I think intelligence is? Is it one ability? Many abilities? Is it a property of the individual's brain? Can intelligence be changed? If so, how? Who is intelligent? Why do I think this? In what ways might my ideas about intelligence be similar to, and different from, those of other people?

To begin to explore these questions, let's take a brief guided tour of the term. Your conception of intelligence may be similar to conceptions held by many Western psychologists, namely that intelligence involves the ability to carry out abstract problem solving (Sternberg, 1986a, 1990). Lewis Terman, an American psychologist who helped to devise some of the first standardized intelligence tests, is typical in this regard. Terman argued: "*An individual is intelligent in proportion as he is able to carry on abstract thinking . . .*" (Terman, 1921, p. 128).

Abstract thinking also defies exact definition, but it is reasonable to view it as the ability to grasp relationships and patterns, especially those not readily detected by the senses. While one can see colors or hear tones just by using one's senses, abstract thinking is likely at work in solving the kinds of problems found in Box 1.1.

Although Terman (1921) argued that "intelligence is the ability to think in terms of abstract ideas" (p. 129), he also acknowledged that others viewed intelligence differently than he did:

> . . . it is frequently intimated that the individual who flounders in abstractions but is able to handle tools skillfully, or play a good game of baseball, is not to be considered necessarily as *less* intelligent than the individual who can solve mathematical equations, acquire a huge vocabulary, or write poetry. The implication is that the two individuals differ merely in having different *kinds* of intelligence, neither of which is higher or better than the other. (p. 128)

Terman went on to say that "it is difficult to argue with anyone whose sense of psychological values is disturbed to this extent" (p. 128).

Terman's notion of intelligence as abstract problem solving has predominated among Western psychologists; nevertheless, there are many dissenters. Using a variety of methods, numerous psychologists have argued that intelligence goes beyond the ability for abstract thinking. As we will see in Chapters 3 and 7, to these investigators, intelligence incorporates abilities that enable people not only to use tools skillfully but also to carry out a wide range of other tasks, from sailing to singing.

Additional arguments against intelligence as abstract problem solving have come from anthropologists and psychologists studying other cultures. They assert that this conception of intelligence might be parochial. For example, researchers who have studied traditional cultures in Africa, the Pacific islands, and elsewhere have found that social ability is often the marker of good thinkers. For example, among the Puluwat Islanders of Micronesia, those who are moderate and diplomatic in behavior are deemed the best thinkers. Such individuals are considered even more intelligent than Puluwat navigators who, until recently, were trained to sail among scores of widely scattered islands in wooden boats without benefit of written maps and largely without navigational tools (Gladwin, 1970).

That differing conceptions of intelligence exist across individuals and cultures reflects a fact aptly described by social psychologist Jacqueline J. Goodnow:

> We do not simply learn to solve problems. We learn also what problems are considered worth solving, and what counts as an elegant rather than simply acceptable solution. (Goodnow, 1990, p. 259)

Box 1.1
Examples of Problems Drawing
on Abstract Thinking

Verbal analogies, such as the following, are often posed to test abstract thinking:

Thermometer is to temperature as barometer is to: (a) blood pressure, (b) wind speed, (c) atmospheric pressure, (d) blood alcohol.

Chicken is to duck as cat is to: (a) mouse, (b) seal, (c) penguin, (d) cow.

Abstract thinking may also be tapped using logical reasoning problems. A now-classic example of such a problem was posed by Wason (1969, p. 471):

Each card depicted below has a triangle on one side and a circle on the other. Which of the cards do you need to turn over to know whether the following sentence is true: Every card with a red triangle on one side has a blue circle on the other.

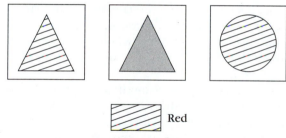

Raven's Progressive Matrices, an intelligence test that relies on figural reasoning, also draws on abstract problem solving. An example of it can be found on page 82.

The Answers: (c), (b), the red triangle and the red circle.

Thus, whether you regard intelligence primarily as abstract problem-solving ability, adept social behavior, some combination of both, or something else entirely, it is useful to step outside your own view. In doing so, it is possible to gain both an understanding of others' conceptions as well as an ability to see your own notions in perspective.

In this chapter, we first investigate briefly some dimensions along which to consider how diverse definitions of intelligence are formulated. Then, taking our cue partly from Terman (1921), who argued that all societies are ruled and shaped by their most intelligent members (in his view, those who were best at abstract thinking), we survey how those in other times and cultures have selected people for complex or central tasks. What were the bases on which important roles in various societies were filled? What behaviors were taken as indicators of an ability to assume complex tasks? How were young people helped to develop their abilities and to assume key roles in their respective cultures? Such questions prod us to think about intelligence in the context of what various cultures have considered important. Finally, we consider issues pertaining to the comparison of intelligence across cultural groups.

Dimensions on Which Diverse Conceptions of Intelligence Depend

The preceding remarks lead to some fundamental issues surrounding the study of intelligence. Because intelligence is a concept without an agreed-on definition, what counts as intelligence depends on whom you ask, the methods the respondents use to explore the topic, the level of analysis of their investigation, and the values and beliefs they hold.

Whom you ask yields notions of intelligence that vary among cultures. Furthermore, answers vary even within the same culture. For instance, contemporary intelligence experts in the United States associate intelligence more closely with academic behaviors like verbal and problem-solving abilities, whereas laypersons associate intelligence with practical problem solving, personal character, and interest in learning. Both groups believe intelligence is related to social competence (Sternberg, 1990).

Definitions vary even within the same discipline of study. Thus, among psychologists, the link between intelligence and abstract thinking has been asserted most strongly by psychometricians (those who devise intelligence tests and other "mental measurements"). However, social psychologists, such as Jacqueline Goodnow, quoted above, are more likely to link intellectual functioning to social interactions, practices, and values.

Similarly, conceptions of intelligence vary within the discipline of anthropology. At one end of the spectrum are scholars like Claude Levi-Strauss. He maintained that there is a single kind of human intelligence, which is expressed differently in different cultures (Gardner, 1981). For example, all human beings classify objects into categories. Unschooled traditional peoples tend to classify on the basis of sensory properties: sharks and dolphins may be categorized together because they look reasonably alike. However, schooled Westerners tend to classify less on the basis of appearance and more on underlying anatomical and evolutionary differences. They would place sharks and dolphins in separate categories.

Anthropologists at the opposite end of the spectrum hold that universals are an illusion; thinking is specific to a given culture. According to such researchers, each culture affords those within it different physical environments, different patterns of experience, and different opportunities to develop and demonstrate skills. Therefore, intelligence differs from culture to culture (Berry, 1974; Berry & Irvine, 1986; Sternberg, 1990), with some cultures valuing logical reasoning; others, powers of persuasion; and yet others, good listening.

In between these two poles are anthropologists and other researchers who maintain that cultures with similar practices and social organization yield similar patterns of intellectual abilities (Berry, 1984, 1988; Cole & Scribner, 1974; Murdoch, 1986; Sternberg, 1990). Thus, societies that value literacy and provide universal schooling would tend to have similar views on, and patterns of, intelligence. These conceptions would differ from those in societies where most youngsters are raised to attend to the natural landscape, hunt animals, and gather food (Berry, 1974; Sternberg, 1990).

The methods for studying intelligence vary both within and across disciplines and help shape definitions of intelligence. For much of the past 100 years, psychometricians' methods relied on statistical analyses of results from intelligence tests. Such methods fostered a notion among some psychologists, and other researchers as well, that performing well on intelligence tests was a sign of intelligence. To quote Edwin Boring, a renowned psychologist, a "narrow definition" of intelligence is that "Intelligence is what the [intelligence] tests test" (cited in Jenkins & Patterson, 1961, p. 210).

Anthropologists' methods rarely emphasize testing nor do they adhere to experimental designs preferred by psychometricians and many other psychologists. Instead, anthropologists observe people functioning in their everyday environments; they record, study, and often participate in the practices of a culture; and they try to come to an understanding of local people's own views. Anthropologists' responses about matters of intelligence often focus on local people's definitions and on competence in the performance of a culture's tasks and roles (Cole & Scribner, 1974).

The distinct testing and experimental methods of psychology and the participant-observation methods of anthropology are still used. However, an increasingly large middle ground draws on both fields. A growing number of psychologists are adopting an *ecological* perspective—placing individual intelligence in the context of social interaction, resources, and cultural forces (Bronfenbrenner, 1979; Ceci, 1990). An example of an ecological perspective can be found in the work of psychologist Jean Lave. Lave has found that Western adults may fail "scholastic math" tests of fractions. For example, they may have difficulty calculating $\frac{1}{2} \times \frac{3}{4}$ when they encounter the problem on a paper-and-pencil test. Yet, the same adults can successfully solve a tangible version of this problem when measuring and manipulating food as part of a weight-loss program (Lave, 1990).

The level of analysis on which the inquiry focuses further complicates responses to questions concerning intelligence. Intelligence can be studied at many levels, ranging from the neuron, to the individual, to socioeconomic systems. If intelligence could be studied within a single discipline at a single level, it might be easier (though still not simple) to agree on a single definition. However, no one discipline or subdiscipline has "cornered the market" on studying intelligence. Therefore, any genuine attempt to understand intelligence must grapple with several disciplines and at least some of the levels within them.

Finally, *values and beliefs* shape the views of intelligence that different people hold. For example, many American parents believe innate mental abilities account for their children's intellectual performance. In contrast, many parents in Japan and other parts of Asia are more likely than their American counterparts to believe that hard work (or lack thereof) accounts for intellectual performance (see Chapter 8). Thus, to get a more complete portrait of intelligence, we must look not only into the heads of those being studied and those who are studying them, but also at the range of concepts and capacities honored within and across cultures.

Selecting People for Important Roles in Various Cultures and Eras

Traditional Cultures and Ascriptive Selection

For most of human history, people lived in what are described as traditional cultures. It is not possible to do justice here to the vast array of customs and practices exhibited by these cultures—even those still found throughout the world today. Such cultures include hunter-gatherers, nomadic herders, stable fishing communities, and agricultural peoples (Denny, 1988; Murdoch, 1988).

The common thread among these cultures is that the great majority of their people are engaged in providing for their subsistence needs, such as food and shelter. Formal schooling is rare because subsistence needs are time-consuming. Instead, young people acquire knowledge and skill for adulthood while working alongside their elders. Where schooling does exist, it is limited to a few individuals. Formal learning may consist of orally transmitted knowledge. Typically, where there is a written language, few who are not formally schooled become literate (LeVine & White, 1986).

Traditional people may admire literacy, but they do not usually define intelligence in terms of literacy skills. Instead, as the Puluwat Islanders and African tribes reveal, an ability to deal wisely with others is often regarded as a mark of intelligence among people in traditional cultures. This focus makes a great deal of sense, especially since these cultures depend on cooperative efforts of many people to secure their own basic needs.

Just as the types of problems deemed challenging and important among traditional people differ from those problems valued among many psychologists, so, too, do behaviors associated with problem solving (Sternberg, 1990). Industrialized North Americans, within and outside academic environments, may associate intelligence with speedy answers (Sternberg, 1988). However, in traditional cultures, patient and sensible behaviors that are deliberately in line with social norms are often seen as markers of intelligence. For example, rural members of the Baganda tribe of Uganda think of intelligence, or *obugezi,* "as slow, careful, active, straight-forward and sane" (Berry, 1984, p. 347). In Zimbabwe, the Mashona tribe's word for intelligence, *ngware,* is applied to a person who exercises prudence and caution, especially in social interaction. The Kispsigis of Kenya use the word *ngon* to indicate both intelligence and social responsibility (Berry, 1984).

Despite the association found between wisdom or intelligence and social skills within many traditional cultures, selection of individuals for key roles in such societies is rarely, if ever, determined by a formal test of social abilities. Instead, intelligence of this sort is widely acknowledged and expected among those who are "older and wiser." This expectation is sensible: In the absence of widespread literacy, elders' experience-based knowledge is the most likely source of information that others need. Thus, leaders in such cultures are typically elders—the heads of families or clans.

In some cultures, certain families and clans become identified as producing leaders. Edward Sapir, an anthropologist and linguist who studied Native American cultures in the early 20th century, described such a phenomenon among the Indians of the American Northwest and Canada's British Columbia. He found that the highest chief exercised authority "not so much because of his individual rank as such, as because the house group that he represents is, for one reason or another, the highest in rank in the community" (Sapir, 1915, p. 473).

Within a given clan, particular forms of inherited leadership may be common. The "eldest son of the eldest son" was the basis for determining the next

Ascriptive selection of leaders is common in traditional societies and also occurs in industrialized nations. One such example is the investiture of His Royal Highness, Prince Charles, as the Prince of Wales on July 1, 1969.

emperor within Chinese dynasties. It has also been the preferred means for designating monarchs throughout Europe.

The appointment of a leader on the basis of a person's position within a social hierarchy is known as *ascriptive* selection. As with royal families in Europe, ascriptive selection often depends on one's birth order and gender. In contrast, *meritocratic* selection is said to rest on an individual's achievements or ability, rather than coincidences of birth. Meritocratic selection often rests on the quality of a person's work or his or her performance on a test.

Traditional ascriptive modes may coexist alongside meritocratic selection modes, even in unlikely places. For example, in the United States, there is no formal tradition of inherited leadership or aristocracy. Nevertheless, political and social leadership has been an occupational role associated with certain families, such as the Adamses, Roosevelts, Kennedys, and Rockefellers. Thus, even in our own merit- and test-oriented society, not only ability but ascriptive characteristics matter in selecting leaders.

Selecting leaders on the basis of family membership has certain strengths that have enabled this mode to endure within both traditional and industrialized societies. The strengths of ascriptive leadership sometimes lie in an historic popular regard for the family as a whole, such as that held for the Kennedys in the United States, the Nehrus and Gandhis in India, or the imperial family in Japan. Where inheritance is an accepted principle, leadership passes from one generation to the next in a predictable, stabilizing fashion. In addition, kings or other clan-based leaders, though they vary in their political and interpersonal skills, can attract very capable advisers who are loyal to the clan as a whole or to "the office." Traditionally, such advisers have also been members of the aristocracy or leading clan (Weber, 1947).

Meritocratic Selection Within an Apprenticeship System

Just as social and political leadership is often inherited within certain clans, other clans may become pre-eminent in other kinds of work. Thus, every clan does not produce the full array of needed household goods; instead, some clans produce pottery, others produce cloth, others still may buy and sell certain commodities. Here again, the elders are commonly regarded as the most knowledgeable and skilled persons.

When a trade or craft is inherited within families, children begin acquiring skills for their future work at a very young age. They learn at first by watching the activities of their elders and listening to their conversation. Often, as soon as they are able, children in families of tradespeople or artisans are called on to assist in small but necessary work-related tasks. For example, daughters of Mayan midwives learn about delivering babies by hearing about their mothers' work and by observing their mothers providing prenatal and postnatal care. They may also help their mothers by gathering medicinal herbs with them.

The system of learning that is carried out through informal means within families often becomes formalized into an apprenticeship system. In such a system, adults who are highly skilled in a given craft are recognized as masters. The masters become responsible for teaching their craft to young apprentices.

Puluwatans maintain both informal and formal systems for learning highly prized navigation skills. Very young Puluwat boys learn navigation skills informally by being taken on long voyages. On board, the master navigator is not the stern sea captain of Western lore. Instead, he shares his thoughts and talks freely about his work "especially if he has a son or other student navigator aboard who

Puluwat children watching a canoe come in from a trip. Most Puluwat boys gained navigation skills through informal apprenticeship.

can learn from his example" (Gladwin, 1970, p. 57). The informal system continues as boys learn to maneuver any number of freely available small boats in and around the local waters. Most of the island's men gain functional navigation skills through this informal system. They learn to recognize where a reef is by the color of the sea, and to steer and handle the sail under normal weather conditions (Gladwin, l970).

However, if a boy is seen as having a knack for acquiring these skills, he may be among the few encouraged to enter a formal apprenticeship in navigation. In nearly all cases, the youngster is apprenticed to a master who is closely related to him. Usually, the master is the apprentice's father. In a few cases, a master will accept a steep payment to teach his valued skill to an apprentice who is not part of his extended family.

Apprentice navigators on Puluwat memorize a vast amount of information. They memorize star courses—patterns of stars on the night horizon that mark the routes between any two of the many islands that have been sailed by Puluwat navigators. They memorize reef locations and shapes, and the landmarks of numerous islands as they appear from diverse vantage points. Apprentices also acquire techniques for sailing in storms, for steering by the feel of the waves, and for estimating their location after being adrift (Gladwin, 1970).

The time between starting an apprenticeship and achieving the status of master navigator on Puluwat is about 20 years. The end of this study is marked by a final

Puluwat apprentices learning from the master navigator.

trial sail—a long interisland voyage undertaken by the apprentice with a crew that includes his master. However, fewer than half of those who begin the navigator's apprenticeship ultimately undertake this test. Of those who do, many are still not seen as having skills fully adequate to handle the longer sailing trips. The best practicing navigators are readily acknowledged. Yet, even they consult their own, often retired masters, whose vast storehouse of knowledge is widely appreciated.

Similarities exist between the apprenticeships on Puluwat and those that came into prominence during the late Middle Ages and the Renaissance in Europe. As on Puluwat, typically only boys were apprenticed. The term of apprenticeship was also lengthy (traditionally, seven years in England). In addition, the master was often a boy's father. Where the master was not related, the boys' parents paid the master a fee to secure his services. The master then acted *in loco parentis,* assuming duties ordinarily carried out by the boy's parents, as well as teaching him the "art and mystery" of his craft. That is, he would train the youngster in the skills and special techniques of his trade (Scott, 1914; Rorabaugh, 1986). Just as on Puluwat, in order for a young man to become a master, he undertook a final trial. The European apprentice was required to produce a "master piece" or to demonstrate his craft in an examination before members of a guild. The guilds set standards for controlling the apprenticeship system and judging merit (Scott, 1914).

Craft guilds in Europe existed not only to regulate quality, but also to limit the quantities of goods that could be produced. This stranglehold on the market in turn enabled them to set prices for the goods. In the 16th century, when the guilds were undermined by middlemen and traders, so was the apprenticeship system. Traders gave less skilled workers raw materials, did not supervise their work, and paid them fees for finished goods. These goods could be produced and sold below the cost of guild-supervised work (Scott, 1914), and the trader could make a handsome profit.

The growth of trading, wage labor, and capital in Renaissance Europe created a demand for new skills. Historian Fernand Braudel (1982) has noted that a young Renaissance merchant:

> . . . had to be able to establish buying and selling prices, to calculate costs and exchange rates, to convert weights and measures, to work out simple and compound interest, to be able to cast up a simulated balance sheet for an operation, and to handle the various instruments of credit. This was by no means child's play. (p. 408)

In the West, the rise of commerce has been associated with the rise of secular schools. The training of merchants included schooling to foster notation-based skills, such as writing, arithmetic, and accounting. Some of those intending to become merchants studied law and then served apprenticeships in foreign consulates, especially in those countries containing important markets and major trade routes (Braudel, 1982; Csikszentmihalyi, 1990).

Schooling, Written Examinations, and Leadership Selection

Leadership by virtue of age, heredity, craft expertise, or any other means operates in a social system that sustains that type of leadership. As illustrated by the medieval guilds, when the surrounding social system changed, standards of quality and forms of education set by guild officials could no longer be maintained.

Changes in the social system also affect political leadership. If the level of expertise required to manage various realms of government exceeds the abilities of the inherited leadership, the ruling power's legitimacy may be questioned. The need for expertise in tax collection, trade, defense, and other government work, and the need to bolster legitimacy are two reasons why merit-based civil service tests have been adopted (see Weber, 1947).

The Civil Service Examination System in China

By far the most long-lived civil service examination system was the one used in China from the 7th century into the early 20th century. The examination system's structure underwent many changes in its long history. Yet, throughout its existence, the system was guided by the philosophical doctrines set forth by Confucius about 500 B.C. Key principles of Confucian social thought are that a good society is harmonious and that harmony is maintained through hierarchical organization. Confucius also promoted the idea that leaders within the hierarchy should be selected and rewarded on the basis of superior moral behavior, which, he said, all men are capable of achieving through education (Cleverley, 1985; Lee, 1985).

For much of its history, selection into the Chinese civil service was determined by several levels of examinations, each of which contained numerous grueling exercises. The first level was administered in local districts, the next in the provincial capitals, and the final and highest level in the national capital. For some levels, as many as 20,000 men would be housed in individual cells within an examination hall. There, under the surveillance of soldiers, they were left to answer questions from before dawn one morning into the evening of the following day (Ishisada, 1974).

The examination questions required the candidates to compose traditional forms of poetry and to write essays in a highly formalized style on topics drawn mostly from classical Chinese philosophy and history. For example, a question drawing on the *Analects* of Confucius could read: "There are three things that a gentlemen fears." The candidates would then have to write an essay identifying and explaining the importance of these three things: "the will of heaven," "great men," and "the words of the sages" (Ishisada, 1974, p. 15).

Examinees who succeeded at such tasks on the highest level of the examinations could anticipate great status and honors. Such men often served as key advisers to the emperor and lived in material comfort. But even success at the lowest

Chinese examination hall and civil service candidate.

level could mean a life somewhat shielded from the more extreme hardships of imperial China.

Because so much was at stake in the examinations, preparations for them sometimes began even before birth (Ishisada, 1974). Expectant mothers in the upper classes avoided strange foods, listened to poetry, and attended assiduously to posture—practices that were believed to produce especially capable sons. More direct preparation for the examinations began when boys were still toddlers. By age 3, they began learning to write a traditional 1,000-character poem that served as a primer. Slightly older boys often studied in private academies or with tutors.

In line with Confucius' notion that all men could learn (as well as with political concerns for legitimacy), the government did not leave the education of future officials solely in the hands of private, wealthy families. In most localities, it sponsored schools where poorer families could send their sons beginning at about age 7. Yet, few poor families could afford to part with the needed labor their sons provided. Thus, an entire village might band together to support the schooling of one or two of the most promising youngsters.

Whether rich or poor, students preparing for the examinations were required to memorize Confucian works and other classics line by line. When these books had been completely absorbed, the boys might memorize commentaries on the books. They also practiced writing poetry and writing responses to potential exam questions. It has been estimated that a boy of 15 who completed this education would have memorized more than 430,000 characters of Chinese text. Such young men were commonly known as *dúshūrén,* "people who read books" (Ishisada, 1974).

The civil service examinations were meant to select capable government officials, and their accessibility was supposed to legitimate the government's power. However, this exam system may have worked in contradiction to those goals (Lee, 1985). Some historians have asserted that rather than providing access, the system excluded as many people as possible from government (Ishisada, 1974; Lee, 1985). Huge numbers of potentially able individuals could not even enter the system: no women were permitted to take the test, and the majority of the people were poor and could ill afford to educate their sons. For each man who passed the first, district-level exam, perhaps a hundred others would fail. Of the men who passed the district-level exam, only roughly one in 3,000 succeeded on the highest level, the palace examination (Ishisada, 1974; Lee, 1985).

Some scholars have questioned the success of the system in selecting morally superior individuals for leadership. It appears that the extreme competition of the system actually fostered less than ideal moral behavior. Despite threats of harsh punishment, examinees were known to cheat. Tiny model-answer books were often found in examination halls. Excavations under examination compounds have even uncovered tunnels connecting exam cells to the outside world (Ishisada, 1974)!

One might ask whether the tests' content made sense. Why select government officials on the basis of their ability to write poetry and to identify obscure passages from ancient texts? Such tests are quite unlike the required final masterpiece in an apprenticeship system. The masterpiece is meant to demonstrate an aspiring master's high-level accomplishment in the same field or discipline that he will work in. In contrast, the civil service exam didn't ask examinees to show how they would deal with tax collection, with people seeking redress from injustice, or with other official duties.

One explanation for the content of the Chinese exams is that the writing and memorization they required were seen as signs of superior moral behavior. After all, such skills demanded a great deal of disciplined study over many years, and Confucius had asserted that education was believed to be the path to moral behavior. Another possible reason is that the acquisition and reward of such knowledge secured dedicated civil servants, because their knowledge was useless outside the realms of government or of preparing others for government exams (Lee, 1985). Unlike the practical lore of the Puluwat apprentice, or the skills acquired by aspiring Renaissance merchants, Chinese scholars' storehouse of classics often rendered them out of touch with the worldly problems they were supposed to manage.

Many debates and test reforms were undertaken to try to make the exams a better instrument for selecting talented government officials. Yet, the core of classical texts was retained through the last examinations in 1905, when the imperial hierarchy had nearly staggered to its close.

Civil Service Examinations in Britain

Given the dilemmas of the Chinese examinations, it may seem odd that British visitors to imperial China were quite impressed with them. Yet, the British government was confronting difficulties not unlike those of imperial China. Britain had grown to be a vast and complex empire that was spread around the globe. Furthermore, industrialization within England had led to a migration of the population from the countryside to the cities, creating an onslaught of housing, poverty, and sanitation problems (Russell-Smith, 1974). Mayors in these rapidly growing cities had little expertise in dealing with such difficulties. City officeholders were appointed largely via patronage and advanced with seniority. Appointments had little to do with competence.

By the mid-19th century, the situation in London and other major cities had reached crisis proportions. In its search for capable administrators who could manage these pressing problems, Britain, like China, adopted a civil service examination system. The two systems shared much more than similar motivating impulses. Like the Chinese version, the British examination was a punishing exercise. The British were concerned about staffing their bureaucracy with moral individuals. Their exam was open to all young men "subject only to evidence of good character and health" (Russell-Smith, 1974, p. 17). Yet, as in the Chinese system, wide-open access was somewhat illusory. The small number of "superior" posts could only be filled by men whose families could support them through years of the best education. The first British civil service examinations, held from roughly 1870 through 1925, drew on the curriculum of Oxford and Cambridge. Like the Chinese system, the examination tested the applicant's writing ability on traditional subject material. However, it also included some questions dealing more directly with government work (Russell-Smith, 1974).

Despite its flaws, the British examination very effectively tested "a candidate's capacity to deal with masses of paper under conditions of stress; successful candidates afterwards found that a good life in the Civil Service consisted in doing just that" (Russell-Smith, 1974, p. 21). Synthesizing information from a large number of documents is common to bureaucrats in all parts of the world. Using this information and their experience, they must prioritize new tasks assigned in the documents. They must know the regulations and procedures governing any task or assignment. This knowledge helps them decide whether they should respond on their own or whether others above or below them in rank need to be involved. If so, they write memos to these others about the task.

Digesting documented information and organizing activities around it are crucial elements of a bureaucrat's work.

According to the influential sociologist Max Weber, and as the cases of China and Britain demonstrate, bureaucratic control cannot be sustained by people appointed on the basis of wealth or aristocratic title. Rather, bureaucracy is the exercise of control on the basis of technical training and knowledge gained in the office (Weber, 1947).

Given that industrialization and international trade create a need for armies of able bureaucrats, it is not surprising that meritocratic examinations eventually spread from China and Britain to much of the rest of the world. These have become an important marker in the lives of many people inside and outside of government, because both public and private employers want capable managers. In Chapter 9, we will again take up the issue of job selection based on tests.

College Entrance Exams

As all students know, employers are not alone in attempting to secure applicants on the basis of meritocratic examinations. Such exams are also a prominent feature of the educational landscape. This method of school admission may have also originated in China. In imperial China, the district-level exams served to select a small proportion of men to enroll at a school that qualified them to take higher-level examinations.

In the United States, the motivation for college admission exams came from a group of leading colleges seeking an agreed-on means to select the members of their relatively small freshman classes. Members of this group hoped that a meritocratic test would identify capable people who might not otherwise come to the colleges' attention. However, college and high school educators also wanted an exam system to provide some guidelines to high schools that were preparing students for college admission.

Between the colonial era and the mid-19th century, students in America, like students in China, were tested largely on classical subjects. Each college in America had its own separate set of admission tests, but each tested applicants on roughly the same set of subjects: Latin, Greek, ancient philosophy, the Bible, mathematics, and rhetoric. As in China, the model of a learned person was one who was steeped in the knowledge of the ancients; as in China and Britain, there was also a belief that those schooled in classics would be better prepared for leadership roles. Many faculty members of the leading colleges in the United States believed the classical curriculum provided "mental discipline"; that is, traditional subjects were thought to develop general faculties of reasoning and memory better than the study of modern languages or the sciences.

The classical curriculum gave way in a tide of technological innovation that swept over America around the time of the Civil War. Business leaders were not thrilled with the diet of classics fed to college students. The industrialist and philanthropist Andrew Carnegie expressed a popular view: "In my own experience I can say that I have known few young men intended for business who were not injured by a collegiate education" (Callahan, 1962, p. 9). He was grateful that "a new idea of education" had taken hold, one that placed more emphasis on theoretical and applied sciences, social sciences, and business.

By the late 19th century, changes were also occurring in high schools, which now had a larger and more diverse body of students. Very few of these students completed high school, and even fewer went on to college. Rather than continuing to teach all students the classical curriculum, high schools introduced vocational education, modern languages, and other subjects regarded as more appropriate for the majority of students.

Once the high school curricula expanded, the academic basis for college admission was no longer quite so clear. Should colleges continue to rely on tests of the classics? If so, they would be excluding young people who were capable of college work but who had studied other subjects. Should they add tests of the newer subjects? If so, which ones? What subjects did high schools have to teach to prepare students for college?

In contrast to most nations, the United States has no central authority that determines high school requirements and university admission standards. Therefore, leaders of colleges and secondary education had to work together over a period of years to iron out some of these questions. Eventually, they decided that various colleges should use the same entry tests to assess applicants in a diverse range of subjects. The College Entrance Examination Board was launched in 1900 to develop these examinations. Colleges were still free to accept whomever they wished. However, they now had a more coordinated and uniform basis for admissions decisions.

Although the early College Entrance Examination Board tested various areas of the curriculum, the tests emphasized students' ability to synthesize information and to convey their ideas coherently and powerfully (Rudy & Brubacher, 1976, p. 246). (See Box 1.2). These are skills that college students need, especially in the more demanding colleges.

To assess these skills, the College Board hired knowledgeable exam readers drawn from college and high school faculties. The readers were instructed to judge students' exams holistically: ". . . if a mistake has been made . . . the readers are not necessarily to mark on an exact mathematical basis, but from a study of the [exam] book to judge whether a candidate is prepared to undertake college work and to mark accordingly" (Farrand, 1926, p. 26). Thus, the College Entrance Examination Board readers went beyond determining simply whether an answer was correct. They tried to find out whether a student had some understanding of the subject as a whole. However, largely because of considerations of efficiency and of perceived fairness, this practice of testing and scoring gave way to questions whose answers could readily be judged as simply right or wrong; eventually, the test answers were left to machines to score.

**Box 1.2
Sample Questions From the 1905 College
Entrance Examination Board**

The first College Entrance Examination Board developed tests that required students to express their ideas coherently in writing and in other ways. Tests were scored by knowledgeable readers.

From the botany exam:

Describe the internal structure of a typical leaf, stem and root, illustrating your answer by a drawing of a cross-section of each.

Explain the use of water in the higher plants; also how water is taken in; also how it is given off. Describe experiments illustrating the two latter subjects.

From the physics exam:

Make a diagram showing a concave mirror, an object and an image formed by light coming from the object. Explain your construction.

A covered kettle boils much more quickly than an open kettle. Account for the heat which is saved, in various ways, by the cover.

Psychological Testing of U.S. Army Recruits

A change in college testing practices was spurred by efforts all over the world—in China, Britain, the United States, France, and elsewhere—to discover more efficient ways to select people for jobs and education. Such efforts helped to launch psychological tests of intelligence.

The first intelligence tests intended for schoolchildren were developed in France by Alfred Binet and Théodore Simon between 1904 and 1911. These tests were individually administered to determine whether a youngster needed remedial education. Binet's method involved giving a child a variety of brief practical tests (like counting coins, and naming body parts), to see whether he or she could learn in a regular classroom. (We discuss Binet's work in some detail in the following chapter.)

The move to easily scored, short-answer tests for college admissions in the United States was promoted by a small group of American psychologists who were interested in testing and measuring intelligence in the manner Binet had devised. Lewis Terman, one of these psychologists, had adapted Binet's tests for American schoolchildren. H. H. Goddard, another of the psychologists, had used Binet's tests on people in a large mental institution in New Jersey.

At the beginning of World War I, these and other psychologists, led by Harvard professor/Army Major Robert Yerkes, offered to help the military make more efficient personnel decisions by testing the intelligence of army recruits (Kevles, 1968). After a few months' effort, Yerkes' group had organized the Army Alpha Examination. This and the Army Beta Examination (for non-English speakers and illiterate recruits) were administered to 1.75 million soldiers under the authority of the Committee for Classification of Personnel in the Army (Yerkes, 1921).

DIFFERENCES BETWEEN THE ARMY TESTS AND OTHER EXAMINATIONS

Like the other tests and selection measures discussed so far, the Army examinations were meant in part to help identify able leaders (Kevles, 1968). However, the tests were unlike attempts to plumb the Puluwat navigators' ability, the craft of the medieval apprentice, the breadth of classical philosophy of future Chinese or British bureaucrats, or the writing skills of American college applicants: the Army exams did not require individuals to organize and present extended examples of their thinking. Furthermore, unlike the means to designate skilled people discussed so far, there was no necessary connection between doing something well in a culturally valued area (like behaving diplomatically, navigating oceans, writing essays, or, in this case, leading soldiers) and ultimately being identified as a capable or intelligent person. The Army tests stemmed largely from Binet's brief and practical tests of schoolchildren. Therefore, they did not try to determine whether an individual soldier had any in-depth skill or knowledge of the work he was supposed to do in the military.

Yerkes, Terman, and the other testers believed that evidence from extended tasks in particular disciplines was not necessary to ascertain intelligence. Instead, as Terman later wrote, intelligence could be determined "by sinking shafts, as it were, at a few critical points" (Terman, 1919, p. 1). The Army mental tests thus used a "shotgun approach." The tests presented many different short tasks—mazes to solve, pattern-matching tests for numbers, picture and sentence completion problems, general information questions, analogies, and other puzzles. (Box 1.3 gives some examples.) Recruits' answers, recorded with a single mark, were believed by psychologists to reveal the examinees' intelligence or mental ability.

Because these tests were efficient and said to be scientific, they became an extremely popular model for testing. After World War I, Yerkes and Terman together produced the National Intelligence Test—an intelligence test for schoolchildren that could be mass-administered. Terman later produced a number of other intelligence tests. Carl Brigham became chairman of the College Board's Commission on New Tests. He recommended short-answer tests as "an aid in problems of admission and in other matters of educational administration" (Angier,

MacPhail, Rogers, Stone, & Brigham, 1926, p. 45). The result was the first Scholastic Aptitude Test (SAT).

The popularity of the Army tests and their offspring encouraged defining the concept of "intelligence" in terms of performance on short-answer exams that were not grounded in any area of expertise. In the United States performance on short-answer tests came to represent intelligence, much as Chinese candidates' memorization of Confucian texts came to represent moral behavior and aptitude for governing.

Box 1.3
Examples From the World War I U.S. Army Examinations

The Army Alpha test (for literate examinees) asked questions requiring knowledge that not all literate examinees would possess, such as:

Information Questions:

Dioxygen is a
disinfectant
food product
patent medicine
toothpaste

"Eventually—why not now?" is an "ad" for a
revolver
cleanser
flour
automobile
(Yerkes, 1921, p. 234)

Practical Judgment Questions:

We see no stars at noon because
they have moved around to the other side of the earth
they are so much fainter than the sun
they are hidden behind the sky

If a drunken man is quarrelsome and insists on fighting you, it is usually better to
knock him down
call the police
leave him alone
(Yerkes, 1921, p. 229)

Analogies:

Washington—Adams :: first—president   second   last   Bryan

esteem—friends :: despise—forsake   detest   enemies   people

(Yerkes, 1921, p. 233)

Box 1.3 (Continued)

The Army Beta examination (for non-English speakers and illiterate recruits) consisted of various kinds of mazes, puzzles, and picture completion problems. It required not only problem-solving abilities, but knowledge of particular aspects of culture to which some recruits would not have been exposed.

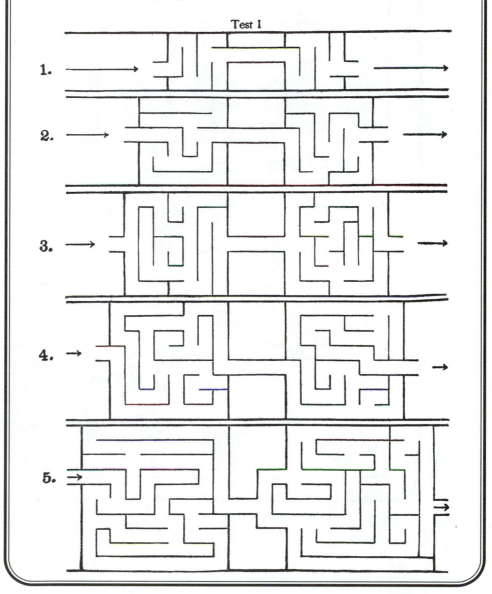

Test 1

Box 1.3 (Continued)

Test 6

FINDINGS OF GROUP DIFFERENCES IN THE ARMY EXAMS

Another key point about the Army tests for this discussion of intelligence and culture is that published analyses of the test data found that cultural and racial groups differed in their level of achievement on the tests. These findings are not surprising. It was evident from the Army's report that groups differed with respect to education, health, English language skills, and familiarity with American culture (Yerkes, 1921). Each of these differences could affect test performance. Nevertheless, the Army psychologists believed their tests measured an innate and inherited trait and therefore asserted that the main reason the scores differed among groups was that the groups differed in their levels of intelligence.

The psychologists' view was not unusual. At the time of the Army tests, scholars in Europe and the United States, as well as many laypeople, subscribed to theories of racial superiority that put those of Northern European ancestry at the top and Africans at the bottom (Gould, 1981; Hofstadter, 1944/1955; Kevles, 1985).

The debate in America that raged around these and later findings of group differences in test scores flares up periodically until this day. The controversy over Herrnstein and Murray's *The Bell Curve* (1994) is the most recent example. We take up this debate in more detail in Chapter 3. For now, we use the report of the Army test findings to help illuminate methodological issues that must be considered in any discussion of cultural differences in intelligence.

Methodological Issues Surrounding Findings of Cultural Differences in Intelligence

The Army examinations are a good place to begin exploring assertions of group differences in intelligence (Gould, 1981), because they illustrate a number of important problems that occur in comparing the intelligence of people across cultures, age groups, or other categories. But before discussing the particular problems of the Army examinations, it is worth exploring what scientific studies generally attempt to do. The reason this is important is that Yerkes, Terman, Brigham and others involved in comparing groups' performance on intelligence tests claimed their findings had a scientific basis.

Scientific studies attempt to find causal explanations for certain phenomena or behaviors. To investigate the behavior (or "outcome"), scientific researchers use experimental and statistical methods that allow them to isolate and test a suspected cause (or "predictor"). To isolate the suspected cause and rule out other possible causes, researchers who work with animals or physical materials often try to ensure that these are as similar as possible. When humans form the pool of subjects, researchers try to assign individuals on a random basis into groups. In random assignment, extraneous factors not related to the predictor usually "cancel each other out."

Box 1.3 Answers

Army Beta Test 6 answers (see page 22 for test), in case you had trouble finding the missing parts (and some of the authors did!).

1.	Mouth.	11.	Trigger.
2.	Eye.	12.	Tail.
3.	Nose.	13.	Leg.
4.	Spoon.	14.	Shadow.
5.	Chimney.	15.	Ball (in hand).
6.	Ear.	16.	Net.
7.	Filament.	17.	Forearm.
8.	Stamp.	18.	Horn.
9.	Strings.	19.	Arm (in mirror).
10.	Rivet.	20.	Diamond.

The goal of these methods is to create conditions in which "all other things are equal." When all other things are equal, experiments can proceed to test whether a given predictor is responsible for a given outcome. For example, if a scientist suspects that the hippocampus plays a role in rats' learning, she can remove the hippocampus from the brains of the rats in her sample. If she carries out this procedure deftly, and only the rats on which she operated later fail to learn how to run a maze, to push a pedal in their cage for a bit of cheese, or perform other tasks, she is justified in thinking that the hippocampus, or connections between it and other parts of the brain, plays a part in learning. If another researcher wants to show that 6-year-olds who are actively coached over 2 weeks can learn to juggle, he will coach one group of randomly assigned children and will let another group of randomly assigned children play uncoached over 2 weeks with balls, clubs, and other juggling props. Then, if the coached 6-year-olds juggle and their untutored agemates don't, it's reasonable for the experimenter to conclude that the coaching makes a difference.

When these methods are followed, a study's findings can be *replicated*: other investigators, using the same materials and test procedures, can repeat the initial study and get the same results. When different investigators observe the same results, this helps to show that the findings are *reliable* rather than unpredictable. Such procedures, and any replications of them, enable researchers to say that what they have found is *valid*: the relationship between the predictor and the outcome they found represents something "real," a situation that obtains in the world outside the experimenter's laboratory. For example, an intelligence test that actually identifies individuals who are successful in school can be said to be valid. In contrast a so-called intelligence test that features many items that probe rote memory might not actually identify those individuals who succeed in today's scholastic environment (where sheer memory is not as important as it used to be).

If all other things are equal in their sample, the researchers can also make *valid inferences* about their findings; that is, it is reasonable for them to infer that what they've discovered in their study occurs elsewhere. For example, if other experimenters replicate the results on the rats' hippocampus, researchers can infer that all rats need a hippocampus to learn new things. (They can't validly infer the same thing about other animals or people until analogous studies are done on those populations. They can only hypothesize that the hippocampus plays this role in other species.)

The preceding paragraphs help to point out where difficulties crop up in many scientific studies. Problems include finding and using comparable materials or samples, isolating a suspected cause, using careful procedures to test the relationship between predictors and outcomes, and making valid inferences. Studies that compare group differences in intelligence have further complications. According to Michael Cole, a psychologist who has carried out comparative cognitive research since the 1960s, these problems involve both cognition and comparison (Cole & Means, 1981).

First, let's consider problems in the sphere of cognition. Researchers studying other phenomena have several advantages over researchers studying intelligence or other matters related to thinking. The study of other kinds of phenomena usually involves fairly well-defined events or evidence. Descriptions of a rat learning to run through a maze can be agreed on to a large extent. But human intelligence is a whole other story. As discussed earlier, within the same society, and even within the same discipline of study, there is not always agreement about which behaviors are intelligent.

Furthermore, many scientists work with phenomena that are readily and clearly measurable. In maze running, the experimenter sees that the distance between the gate and the cheese is 4 meters long, the route contains 9 right angles, and half the rats learn to find the cheese in under 20 seconds after 3 trials. The study of intelligence is quite different. Without agreement on what behaviors are intelligent, the tools used by some researchers to measure any such behaviors may not be measuring intelligence at all, according to other investigators' standards.

A related difficulty in research on human intelligence is that it is quite challenging to tie any particular behavior to the ability to perform a particular cognitive process. Behaviors that are observable and measurable to some degree may stem from the same unobservable process; but then again, they may not. For example, two people may write the answer "132" to the question "$11 \times 12 = ?$". But we don't know from this alone whether both respondents multiplied 12 by 10 and added another 12, or multiplied 11×10 and added another 22; or spat out a memorized answer, copied from a neighbor, or used some wholly different approach like a calculator. Similarly, if both give incorrect answers, we do not know whether they fail to understand multiplication, understand multiplication but are careless, understand multiplication but can't read the problem, or simply aren't interested in taking our little test.

Now we can add the second area of difficulty, namely the problems of comparing different cultural groups. As discussed above, scientists studying physical phenomena try to make use of materials or subjects whose differences are minimized. This tack enables the researchers to make valid inferences regarding other beings or materials that resemble those they've studied. For example, because the rodents they use are often genetically identical and raised in the same environment, researchers can be sure that the careful procedures they perform on one rat will likely have the same effect if performed on another rat. But people taking intelligence tests are only identical if they came from the same zygote. Therefore, it is very hard to know whether the same test materials and procedures are even understood—let alone answered—in the same way by people who are taking them.

A further wrinkle: cross-cultural researchers try to understand outcomes using *two groups* that are *different* to start with. As Cole and Means (1981) put it, "Because the two comparison groups differ in a host of ways, it will be logically impossible even to maintain that the researcher's treatment is psychologically identical for both" (p. 11). Thus, when comparing two groups from two different cultures:

> . . . the inferential difficulties we face are extremely serious. None of the all-other-things-equal assumptions that we could use to avoid a lot of work in non-comparative research is available to us. We cannot assume that all subjects understand instructions in the same way; we cannot assume that the stimuli within the experiment proper are equivalent for all of them (that is, equally familiar, equally easy to tell apart, or equally associated with one another). Most important, we cannot assign our subjects at random to the relevant experimental conditions and then assume that these kinds of nonequivalences apply equally to all groups.
>
> In short, we are in trouble. (Cole & Means, 1981, p. 63)

Cole and Means go on to detail ways of conducting studies so as to reduce "the risk of inferential nonsense." One way is to adapt materials so that they are, in some sense, "psychologically equivalent" to the different groups involved. So, for example, if we want to show that people are capable of answering multiplication problems, even though not all of them read, it may be necessary to give some respondents paper and pencils, and give others various objects to manipulate and cluster. Or, we could acknowledge that the groups differ not only on a particular variable of interest—like multiplication techniques or intelligence—but in a whole host of ways. These differences must then be documented and considered as possible causes for the outcomes that occur.

Let's return now to the Army tests, to see how they fared as scientific research.

Within-Group Differences

It might be argued that the Alpha and Beta tests provided psychologically equivalent examinations for two different types of recruits, literate and illiterate (or non-English speakers), respectively. However, each group still contained men who had markedly different levels of literacy and different levels of familiarity with test materials. Within the group of Alpha test takers, some were native English speakers who had earned a high school diploma. Others were native speakers who had only completed the first few years of elementary school. Still others had been in the country for a very short period of time and had acquired only very basic literacy skills in English.

Even if recruits from various cultures could read English equally well, there were likely differences in experience with the test materials. For example, on the sentence completion tests (see Box 1.3), people who were quite literate might have large disparities in their grasp of American culture.

The group that took the Beta exam also varied in literacy and in familiarity with test materials. Some spoke or wrote little English, but might have been literate in their own language. Others were native English speakers who went to school but never mastered reading. Others never went to school in the United States or elsewhere. Some of these men had never even used a pencil (Kevles, 1968). Such men probably never encountered the kind of problems they were being asked to solve. On the other hand, those who had been to school abroad but who were not literate in English might have been somewhat familiar with picture completion tasks that were set before them. (See Box 1.3 for an example of picture completion tasks.)

Nonstandardized Procedures

The procedures for assigning men to one group or another varied among the many Army camps in which the tests were administered. Different camps used different standards to gauge whether recruits were literate enough to take the Alpha test (Yerkes, 1921, p. 665). Assignment to one test group or another also varied within the same camp. For example, if the number of men waiting to take the Beta test got too large, some men initially assigned for the Beta were reassigned to take the Alpha test (Gould, 1981).

Another procedural problem surrounds the instructions. Consider this example from the Army Alpha test instructions:

> Attention! Look at 7. Notice the three circles and the three words. When I say "Go" make in the *first* circle the *third* letter of the *first* word; in the *second* circle the *first* letter of the *second* word; and in the *third* circle the *first* letter of the *third* word—Go! (Yerkes, 1921, p. 126)

Such instructions were read aloud in 10 seconds, often in large, noisy rooms. Questions about the instructions were not permitted. Thus, some men might have done badly because they understood the directions but couldn't do the task. Others might have done badly because they didn't understand the directions; if they had, they would have fared well. Others might have failed because they couldn't—and apparently didn't—hear what they were supposed to do (see Gould, 1981).

It should now be apparent that recruits were not grouped randomly, procedures for testing men were not carefully followed, instructions were not clear to all, and materials were not psychologically equivalent. Thus, the *design* of the Army tests did not create conditions in which all other things were equal. Therefore, it was not reasonable for Yerkes and other psychologists to attribute differences in the test outcomes of cultural groups to a single underlying cause, namely intelligence.

The *analysis* of the data might have also made it difficult to argue that mental ability was responsible for group differences in test scores. The Army psychologists did find relationships between test scores and other variables, such as amount of education, education in one U.S. state or another, the health of the recruit, and the number of years spent in the United States (Yerkes, 1921). However, such relationships were largely dismissed. Instead, Yerkes' report asserted that the differences between groups were ultimately due to underlying differences in intelligence, or "the sort of ability that is measured by these two examinations" (Yerkes, 1921, p. 425).

Why? The Army psychologists, just like Puluwatans or residents of imperial China, viewed intelligence in ways that were influenced by a given time and place. Their report largely reflected then-current notions that intelligence was inherited and varied by race and class. They asserted this even though the data could—and did—lead others to conclude that test results varied with schooling, language skills, and familiarity with test materials. These different interpretations shed light on an important point:

> Science, since people must do it, is a socially embedded activity. It progresses by hunch, vision, and intuition. Much of its change through time does not record a closer approach to absolute truth, but the alteration of cultural contexts that influence it so strongly. Facts are not pure and unsullied bits of information; culture also influences what we see and how we see it.
>
> This argument, although still anathema to many practicing scientists, would, I think, be accepted by nearly every historian of science. In advancing it, however, I do not ally myself with an overextension now popular in some historical circles: the purely relativistic claim that scientific change only reflects the modification of social contexts, that truth is a meaningless notion outside cultural assumptions, and that science can therefore provide no enduring answers. As a practicing scientist, I share the credo of my colleagues: I believe that a factual reality exists and that science, though often in an obtuse and erratic manner, can learn about it. (Gould, 1981, pp. 21–22)

It is this journey of science to uncover some factual reality regarding intelligence that we will trace in the next chapter.

Summary

In this chapter, we have pointed out that notions about intelligence vary over time, across cultures, and even within cultures. Definitions of intelligence depend on whom you ask, their methods and levels of study, and their values and beliefs. Definitions are associated with the needs and purposes of different cultures. In various traditional cultures, intelligence, or "using one's mind well," is often linked to skill in dealing with other people. Such definitions make a great deal of sense because traditional cultures typically rely on cooperative efforts of many people to meet their subsistence needs. Among Western designers of intelligence tests, definitions have emphasized an ability to solve abstract problems.

Because cultures' values and needs vary, their means of selecting people to perform complex and skilled tasks may also vary. Ascriptive selection—by birth and social position—is found in many cultures, from the most traditional to the most technological. In some cultures—for example, on Puluwat—the identification of future navigators rests in some part on social position but also on the perceived abilities of a youngster. Meritocratic selection involves systematic efforts to identify individuals based on ability. Yet, as we discussed, the civil service examination systems used in China and Britain still favored those who came from the upper classes.

The Chinese, British, and Puluwatan efforts are distinct from selections made by the Army tests in that they called on people to demonstrate extended efforts in domains of knowledge valued by their culture. For example, British civil service candidates had to know the classics of their culture, write essays, and, in the process, demonstrate their ability to handle masses of paper in a relatively efficient way. In contrast, selections on the basis of Army intelligence tests were independent of any in-depth knowledge or skill. They used a "shotgun" approach developed by Binet.

The education and development of abilities also vary within and across cultures. In traditional cultures, where subsistence needs are pressing, there is commonly no formal schooling and no formal writing system. Learning usually occurs at the feet of one's elders, who are widely believed to be the wisest members of the community. Apprenticeships are a formal system for gaining skills and knowledge from an elder or "master." The extent of one's knowledge and skills is not just assumed to increase with age. Instead, the apprentice's level of knowledge and ability must be demonstrated before a master or guild members. In places and eras where literacy has grown increasingly important to the culture, apprenticeships have been included in the training of young merchants, along with formal schooling. In modern industrialized countries, much information can be captured in printed materials. Nevertheless, the highest reaches of many valued domains of knowledge, ranging from music to surgery, are still best acquired and evaluated in apprenticeship situations.

Finally, in this chapter, we tried to shed light on difficulties that arise in comparative studies of intelligence. In a scientific study, to attribute an outcome (such as a test score) to an underlying cause (such as intelligence), requires that "all other things are equal"—it is difficult to achieve that condition in studies of intelligence. First, researchers do not agree on what intelligence is and therefore what tasks might be used to assess it. Second, it is hard to know whether those taking the tests are using the same underlying psychological processes. Third, when attempting to compare two different cultural groups, test materials and procedures are unlikely to be psychologically equivalent. Comparative studies need to be scrutinized for their design and analysis, and such studies must also be considered in light of the cultural contexts of their authors.

Suggested Readings

Cole, M., & Means, B. (1981). *Comparative studies of how people think: An introduction.* Cambridge: Harvard University Press.

Cole, M., & Scribner, S. (1974). *Culture and thought: A psychological introduction.* Cambridge: Harvard University Press.

Gould, S. (1981). *The mismeasure of man.* New York: Norton.

Sternberg, R. J. (1990). *Metaphors of mind: Conceptions of the nature of intelligence.* Cambridge: Cambridge University Press.

Stigler, J. W., Shweder, R. A., & Herdt, G. (1990). *Cultural psychology: Essays on comparative human development.* Cambridge: Cambridge University Press.

Chapter 2

Origins of the Scientific Perspective

Introduction

In 399 B.C., Socrates was convicted and sentenced to death by a jury of some 500 fellow citizens. His crimes were failing to believe in the gods of the city-state, and corrupting the youth of Athens. In his self-defense, Socrates denied both charges and claimed he was following a line of inquiry inspired by the gods. The Oracle at Delphi had told Socrates' friend that no man was wiser than Socrates. Socrates argued that the activities for which he was being tried were simply his attempts to understand what the Oracle meant. These attempts involved questioning statesmen, poets, playwrights, and craftsmen to see whether they were wiser than he. Often, though, these inquiries took place in the presence of bystanders:

> . . . young men, those who have most leisure, sons of the most wealthy houses, follow me of their own accord, delighted to hear people being cross-examined; and they often imitate me, they try themselves to cross examine, and then, I think, they find plenty of people who believe they know something, when they know little or nothing. So in consequence those who are cross-examined are angry with me instead of with themselves. . . . (Plato, *The Apology,* 1956, p. 429)

Ancient Philosophy: Why Begin With This?

Why begin an historical overview of scientific investigations of intelligence with the *Apology?* For several reasons: Socrates and other ancient Greek philosophers left to later generations a legacy of questions concerning the nature of intelligence. They began to elaborate methods of investigation. In addition, they presented a model of human intelligence against which others have been compared.

Topics for Inquiry

The dialogues of Plato (which featured his teacher, Socrates), and the writings of Aristotle form some of the earliest systematic efforts to explore fundamental questions concerning intelligence. For example, as we saw above, Socrates said he wanted to know who was wisest and tested others' knowledge to help him answer his question. As noted in Chapter 1, attempts to test people and determine their ranking have continued through the 20th century.

Another central issue that can be traced back to Greek philosophers concerns the links between the intellect and the body (Plato, 1949). Defining the areas of the brain that are associated with various kinds of problem solving, and grappling with the relationship between the mind and body, are topics that have occupied philosophers and scientists for centuries and are still being investigated today.

The role of sense perception in intelligence was another topic explored by Socrates, Plato, and others in their circle (Plato, 1956c). As we will see in this chapter, some of the first mental tests attempted to determine intelligence using sensory perception tasks.

Questions about the kinds of abilities people are born with play an important role in the contemporary study of cognitive development and linguistics. Yet, the origins of such modern questions can be traced to the Greeks as well. For example, Socrates hypothesized that individuals have inborn, or innate knowledge (Plato, 1956b).

In addition, more than two millennia ago, Socrates argued that individuals are born with different capacities and these differences are typically inherited (Plato, 1956b). The notions of inborn differences in intelligence and the heritability of such differences are studied and debated by scientists and scholars through the current moment.

These and other topics first investigated by the Greeks will concern us in this and subsequent chapters.

Socrates.

Methods of Inquiry

A second reason this overview begins with Socrates is that the ancient Greek philosophers were the first to elaborate systematic methods for exploring the questions they posed.

Greek philosophers, especially Plato's student Aristotle, developed a formal system of logic to test hypotheses and make deductive inferences. This method drew on inductions from particular examples—those visible to the senses (for example, "This creature is furry"). However, it placed greater emphasis on universal truths (e.g., "All mammals have fur"). The route to achieving knowledge about the particular often employed deductive, syllogistic reasoning from universals: "All mammals have fur. This creature is a mammal. Therefore, this creature has fur." Aristotle placed great importance on universals: "Knowing the universal also gives knowledge of the particular, but knowing the particular does not involve knowing the universal" (Aristotle, 1963, p. 195). The search for universal laws that can explain a variety of particular instances is a common feature of scientific work.

The Greeks' Influence on Notions of Intelligence

A third reason to begin with the Greeks is that they have helped to shape a prevalent view about what intelligence is, namely, abstract reasoning in language and mathematics (see Chapter 1). Skill in logic, geometry, and disputation were central aims of the schools established by Plato, Aristotle, and other Greek philosophers. This educational tradition was maintained and expanded over some two millennia and was still influential when scientific psychology was launched in the latter part of the 19th century. Thus, initially, those most concerned with studying intelligence were educated in a system whose model of an intelligent person was someone who had mastered the subjects and skills first formalized by the Greeks (Donald, 1991; Gardner, 1985).

The Transition to Scientific Investigation

The Debate Between Rationalists and Empiricists

About 20 centuries after Socrates, philosopher-scientists began to explore some of the questions first posed by the Greeks. Soon thereafter, a debate arose between two groups who held different views of the mind and of the origins of knowledge. This debate continues among their intellectual descendants today.

Contemporary *rationalists* trace their views to the 17th-century French philosopher, mathematician, and scientist, René Descartes. (Hence, they are also known as *Cartesians*.) Descartes argued that the mind is the source of our most certain knowledge—of our own existence and of mathematics. To Descartes, and the rationalists who followed him, some forms of knowledge were inborn or innate. Because Descartes' method to establish such truths was based on an examination of his own thoughts, he is sometimes referred to as an *introspectionist* philosopher.

Descartes, a devout Catholic, believed the mind or soul (the French word *l'âme* conveys both) was God-given and immortal. It was also without physical attributes (nonmaterial) and, thus, was separate and distinct from the body. This notion of separation of mind and body is known as *dualism*.

René Descartes.

In contrast to the mind, Descartes regarded the bodies of men and animals as automata, or "moving machines" built of nerves, bone, blood vessels, and muscle (Descartes, 1637/1969, p. 138). Nevertheless, Descartes realized that "light, sounds, smells, tastes, heat and all other qualities pertaining to external objects are able to imprint on it [the mind] various ideas by the intervention of the senses" (p. 137). This state of affairs created a dilemma: if the mind and body were separate, one material in nature and one not, how did they interact? How did events affecting the automata-body inform the mind's ideas? How did the ideas originating in the mind direct the automata-body to speak or otherwise communicate its ideas?

Descartes' Challengers

Descartes' ideas were challenged on several fronts from his day forward. Descartes' contemporary, the British philosopher, Thomas Hobbes, argued that the mind was "something corporeal" (Hobbes, 1969, p. 246). He and others who maintain that the mind has a physical basis in the body are called *materialists*.

John Locke, another British philosopher, objected to Descartes' assertion of innate knowledge. Locke claimed that anyone who observed a young infant "will have little reason to think him stored with plenty of ideas . . ." (Locke, 1690/1939, p. 250). Instead of containing any Cartesian "original ideas," Locke said the human mind is originally blank, a "white paper" (p. 248).

Locke is regarded as the father of British empiricist philosophy, a philosophy that has had a powerful impact within scientific psychology. *Empiricists,* in contrast to rationalists, argue that experience is the basis of knowledge.

John Locke.

Locke argued that ideas come from two sources. Most ideas—notions like "yellow, white, heat, cold, soft, hard, bitter, sweet"—come from sensory information transmitted by the nerves to the brain (Locke, 1690/1939, p. 248). The other source of ideas is *reflection* or "the notice which the mind takes of its own operations . . ." (p. 249). According to Locke's doctrine of the association of ideas, complex thoughts and abstract reasoning abilities grow from combining and relating ideas obtained from reflection and sensation.

Locke's empiricism and associationism were pursued by British philosophers during the 18th and 19th centuries. "Associationist" philosophers and psychologists of the 19th century, including James Mill, John Stuart Mill, and Herbert Spencer, devised a kind of chemistry of the mind. Complex thoughts ("compounds") were built of simpler elements. Associations were formed according to regular principles, such as the co-occurrence of elements or their regular sequence. Locke's empiricism also served as an intellectual foundation for 20th-century behaviorism, which claimed that behavior consists of responses to environmental stimuli. (We pursue behaviorism in more detail later in this chapter.)

Kant's Reconciliation of Empiricism and Rationalism and His Challenge to a Science of Psychology

Empiricist views and rationalist views of the mind were seemingly incompatible. Empiricists argued that thoughts arise from experience and sensory information. In contrast, rationalists maintained that the mind had certain types of innate knowledge, independent of experience and sensory information. Nevertheless, a reconciliation of these two opposing views was forged by the German philosopher, Immanuel Kant.

In his *Critique of Pure Reason* (1781/1958), Kant argued that there is an intrinsic nature to the intellect that exists prior to experience. According to Kant, the human mind comes furnished with given "categories," such as relation, unity, and quantity, and given "modes of appearance," such as time and space. Thus, like Descartes, Kant maintained some rationalist notions: The mind has certain innate properties that are independent of the experiences detected by our senses.

At the same time, Kant argued (as had the empiricists) that in order to acquire knowledge, humans depend in part on sensory experience. But the knowledge that we acquire about the world through our senses is not highly individualistic or subjective. Rather, in Kant's view, the human mind cannot help but perceive the sensory world in ways that are innately determined. Human minds are organized to see the world as arrayed in the modes of space and time, with perceptions organized into categories like causality (or other types of relations), quantity, and quality. Mediating the world of sensory information and the mind's innate categories and modes are *schemata,* which are now often termed mental representations.

Kant devised the schema as part of his effort "to relate the physical world . . . to the world of the inborn mental architecture" (Gardner, 1985). Kant's effort was seminal for various branches of psychology and cognitive science. For example, Jean Piaget, for 60 years the leading researcher in developmental psychology, explored how children construct their understanding of time, space, causality, and other of Kant's categories (see Chapter 4).

Yet, Kant maintained there could be no science of the mind. Like the Cartesians, he argued that the mind lacked a material basis. Thus, experimentation on the mind was impossible. Furthermore, he felt that, unlike a bodily organ, the mind did not sit still under examination. In effect, the mind was a moving target: it was changing even as it was being studied. Finally, Kant was gloomy about scientific study of the mind because science relied on mathematics, and he did not foresee a way to quantify what occurred in the mind (Gardner, 1985).

Immanuel Kant.

The Beginnings of a Scientific Psychology

Contributions From Anatomy, Physiology, and Medicine

Despite Kant's prognosis, within Kant's lifetime (1724–1804) and shortly thereafter, research in various disciplines chipped away at each of his objections to a scientific study of the mind. For example, as we'll see in Chapter 5, investigations of the anatomy and physiology of the nervous system began to uncover links between portions of the brain and specific human abilities. In the early 19th century, Franz Gall, a German anatomist and phrenologist, argued that human functions were linked to specific parts of the brain. (Phrenologists incorrectly believed it was possible to know a person's mental "faculties" by feeling the bumps on a person's skull.) Gall's anatomical studies indicated that the massive development of the cerebral cortex in man and mammals was responsible for their capabilities compared to other animals (Changeux, 1985). In addition, physicians and scientists in Europe, such as Marc Dax, Paul Broca, and Carl Wernicke, found relationships between specific sites of brain damage and such capabilities as speech production and comprehension.

Investigations into the nervous system helped counter Kant's claim that there was no mathematical underpinning to support a science of mental activity. It had been widely believed that nerve impulses were too fast to measure. Like the immaterial mind or the immortal soul, these impulses were regarded as unrelated to material bodies and their mechanistic activity. However, Hermann von Helmholtz and later experimental scientists showed that nerve impulses were rather slow. Helmholtz's experiment required subjects to hit a button as soon as they felt a stimulus touch different parts of their leg. From these experiments, Helmholtz calculated that nerve impulses did not travel at a divine speed, but at a comparatively earthly rate of under 100 meters per second (Changeux, 1985).

Complications From Astronomy

Another of Kant's objections—that the mind could not study itself—was undermined when astronomy furnished an impending scientific psychology with questions and methods that more objectively studied an individual's perceptions. Evidence from astronomy indicated that individuals' perceptions and responses to the same events varied. Astronomers had found that when two individuals recorded the time of the same stellar transit, their estimates often differed. The astronomers' technique for determining when a star had crossed a given point involved two sensory systems: sight and hearing. The astronomers observed a star as it approached a cross that was marked on the telescope. While they observed this encounter, they listened to the ticking of a clock. Their task was to estimate how much time had elapsed since the last tick of the clock, at the instant they saw the star reach a line of the cross. Such discriminations were supposed to be accurate to one- or two-tenths of a second. However, it was found that the observers' estimates could differ by almost one whole second (Boring, 1950).

"Complication" tasks—those that made use of two or more sensory systems—soon became a vehicle for the study of higher mental processes. Complications were believed to reveal more about higher mental processes than single stimuli events used to detect nerve speed. This was because subjects were required to compare one event to another and arrive at a judgment.

The Dutch physiologist, F. C. Donders, believed that complications could be used to measure how long it took for a human mind to carry out the "operation of discrimination." In the late 1860s, he made use of Helmholtz's finding that an individual's *reaction time* to a single sensory stimulus could be measured. By subtracting an individual's reaction time to a single stimulus from the time it took that person to solve a complication task, Donders calculated how long it took to make a discrimination.

Early Experimental Psychology

From the 1860s into the 1890s, experiments involving complication tasks, reaction times, and the subtractive procedure were widely used. Such research was pursued in what was, arguably, the world's first experimental psychology laboratory, established by Wilhelm Wundt in Leipzig, Germany, in 1879. Work in this lab, using complication tasks and other procedures, led Wundt to propose that a number of basic processes or "elements" were necessary to solve complications. Among these elements were reflex, perception, cognition, judgment, and voluntary action (Boring, 1950).

Wundt's effort to study the elements and associations of sensory perceptions was clearly in line with Locke's philosophy. However, rather than relying on philosophical examinations of the mind, Wundt made use of a careful and systematic form of introspection. His experimental subjects were people trained to report as accurately as possible on their conscious experiences in perceiving various stimuli and carrying out tasks.

In laboratory work that went on for decades, Wundt attempted to explore conscious experience as systematically as physicists studied the external world. As a reflective pioneering scientist, he also produced many publications detailing methods and findings. In addition, he attracted researchers from all over Europe and North America who transplanted these methods when they returned home.

Exploring Cultures in the Search for Other Origins of Higher Mental Processes

Despite the successes of Helmholtz, Wundt, and other experimentalists in building a scientific basis for the study of the mind, these investigations were not wholly satisfactory even to some of their proponents. Many believed it was possible to understand thinking processes in terms of basic elements, but it was clear to some that "higher mental processes" could not be completely explained by these methods. It was hard to imagine how epic poetry could be written or steam engines could be invented just through the association of simple psychological elements. Could language, could religion actually be built of such stuff?

Wundt, who is sometimes caricatured as a compulsive German professor, argued that there was much to be learned by studying human achievements outside of the laboratory—in human societies. Wundt's efforts in this area yielded a 10-volume work *Folk Psychology: An Investigation into the Developmental Principles of Language, Myth, and Custom.* (Wundt, 1901). In it, he attempted to explain how religion, language, and custom came to exist. The explanation he advanced on these matters was analogous to his laboratory findings that thought was built of simple elements. To Wundt, the achievements of culture also grew from smaller units—in this case, individuals. Individuals form the link or association between one culture and the next: the contributions of individuals in earlier, simpler cultures give rise to later, more differentiated, and more advanced cultures (Haeberlin, 1916).

Herbert Spencer, a British philosopher and a contemporary of Darwin, was also concerned with demonstrating that cultures, like thought, grow from simple elementary structures to great, highly differentiated complexes. Spencer argued that *evolutionary forces* could explain growth from simple, homogeneous states to more complex, differentiated ones. To Spencer, evolution was a natural force at play in individuals, in species, in geological changes, in bodies of knowledge, and in societies.

Spencer and many other philosophers and scientists asserted that evolution yielded progress in all things (Mayr, 1982). This made it possible to rank all things from lowest to highest in development. One could rank members of species and cultures on an array of characteristics, including intelligence. Not surprisingly, any such ranking of human beings was headed by those doing the ranking: Western European men of the upper economic classes (see Gould, 1981). Spencer's ranking of industrialized Western societies and the upper classes over all other cultures and classes is typical in this regard.

Contributions From Natural History: Evolution and the Impact of Darwin's Theory

Spencer, and many other thinkers between the mid-18th and the mid-19th century, were striving to devise coherent ideas about evolution. However, the British naturalist, Charles Darwin (1809–1882), is generally credited with the first convincing theory of evolution. He began formulating his views in about 1837, soon after returning from his famous five-year voyage around the globe on the *HMS Beagle.* The theory, put forth in his book, *On the Origin of Species* (1859/1964), had a profound impact on the study of intelligence. To understand this impact, it is first necessary to consider the theory's claims.

According to Darwin's theory, three features of biological life account for evolutionary change: *variation* within species, *natural selection* from among these variations, and *inheritance* of variations that enable adaptation to environments. Darwin's argument for his theory began by noting that individuals within species varied greatly. Breeders made use of this variation to create more desirable plants and animals. Darwin noted that variation in species of plants and animals was also found in nature. He then asked how these variations came to exist and thereby to enable a given species to adapt to its "conditions of life," including the "struggle for existence" because of the "high rate at which all organic beings tend to increase" (Darwin, 1859/1964, p. 63).

> Owing to this struggle for life, any variation . . . if it be in any degree profitable to an individual of any species . . . will tend to the preservation of that individual, and will generally be inherited by its offspring. The offspring, also, will thus have a better chance of surviving, for, of the many individuals of any species which are periodically born, but a small number can survive. I have called this principle, by which each slight variation, if useful, is preserved, by the term Natural Selection, in order to mark its relation to man's power of selection. (p. 61)

Darwin asserted that current species descended over many generations on the basis of these evolutionary forces from older or extinct species. So, for example, it was possible that a single, extinct carnivore could have given rise to many existing carnivores, such as dogs, foxes, weasels, and cats (Darwin, 1859/1964; Mayr, 1982).

Darwin's theory was greatly at odds with prevailing religious and philosophical views (helping to account for the 15-year delay between formulation and publication of his theory). In Darwin's time, it was widely held that existing species reflected God's creation or plan. Species therefore had distinct, God-given, "essential" natures (Mayr, 1982).

Furthermore, it was widely held that human beings occupied a unique position in God's creation. Man was created by God in his image and endowed with a rational mind. Given this view, it is not surprising that, in *Origin,* Darwin's arguments for evolution relied on numerous examples of wild and domesticated

Charles Darwin.

animals and plants. He barely mentioned human origins. This discussion was delayed until Darwin published *The Descent of Man* (1871).

In *The Descent of Man,* Darwin asserted quite boldly that the same factors that affect change in other species—variation, natural selection, and inheritance—have been at work on human beings. Furthermore, he argued that just as domesticated animals can be bred for certain kinds of dispositions, evolutionary forces operated not only on the human body but also on human mental abilities: "mental aptitude, quite as much as bodily structure . . . appears to be inherited" (Darwin, 1871, p. 256).

Implications of Darwinian Evolution

Darwin's work has had several powerful implications for the study of intelligence. For example, it paved the way for comparative studies of human and animal intelligence: ". . . the difference in mind between man and the higher animals, great as it is, certainly is one of degree and not of kind" (Darwin, 1871, p. 460). Thus, if we were descended from and still closely related to primates, there was much that could be learned about intelligence from studying other animals.

In 1882, Darwin's friend and disciple, George Romanes, published the first comparative psychology book, *Animal Intelligence,* which, in part, considered animals' mental abilities and motivations. Other comparative psychologists focused on how animals learned new skills. As we will see below, Edward Thorndike, and others who did comparative research, later applied lessons from animal learning to human learning.

Darwin's assertion that evolution acted on both body and mind also encouraged studies of comparative anatomy. One could look at the nervous systems of other species and begin to form hypotheses about the development and functions of nervous system structures in humans.

In addition, Darwin asserted that intelligence, like other characteristics, was inherited. Darwin did not know how inheritance per se was accomplished. (He had not read Gregor Mendel's then-obscure research on the genetics of trait inheritance in pea plants (Mayr, 1982).) To some extent, Darwin argued for Lamarckian inheritance; that is, in *The Descent of Man,* Darwin claimed that abilities acquired during the lifetime of an adult can be inherited by the next generation. He cited investigations that claimed children of English manual laborers are born with larger hands than are children of the gentry, and that children of excellent Eskimo seal catchers grow up to be excellent seal catchers, even if their fathers die when the children are too young to be taught this skill (Darwin, 1871). Lamarckianism has been discredited, but Darwinism sparked, and continues to spark, numerous studies on the degree to which intelligence is inherited and the extent of environmental influences on intelligence.

Another line of inquiry in the field of intelligence stemmed from the importance Darwin placed on individual variation of diverse characteristics: some plants had better yields than others, and some Eskimos were better seal catchers than others. Darwin's theory thus helped paved the way for the study of individual differences in intelligence (Joynson, 1989), a huge area within psychology, which we will explore in Chapter 3.

Early Efforts to Study the Inheritance of Intelligence

Galton's Effort to Breed Brighter Humans

Darwin lived during a period of great social and technological change. As discussed in Chapter 1, British industrialization encouraged people to leave agriculture and migrate to the cities. The growth of cities and industries created a great need to identify and train individuals who were capable of managing the new social and economic challenges.

A variety of routes were pursued to encourage the development and training of highly capable individuals: Efforts were made to broaden schooling, to study how children learn, and to test and select people on the basis of merit. Yet another option was inspired by Darwin's work and proposed by Darwin's energetic half-cousin, Francis Galton. Galton argued that the key was eugenics—enhancing the human race's mental capacities by improved, selective breeding:

The processes of evolution are in constant and spontaneous activity, some pushing towards the bad, some towards the good. Our part is to watch for opportunities to intervene by checking the former and giving free play to the latter. . . . It is earnestly to be hoped that inquiries will be increasingly directed into historical facts, with the view of estimating the possible effects of reasonable political action in the future, in gradually raising the present miserably low standard of the human race. . . . (Galton, 1892, p. xxvii)

In *Hereditary Genius* (1869), Galton documented his own investigation into historical facts, in order to support his claim that intelligence is inherited.[1] Galton's investigation consisted of selecting, or having others select, the names of the most eminent men from books containing biographies of accomplished people in diverse realms. These included judges, statesmen, military commanders, writers, artists, and leading mathematics students at Cambridge University.

Francis Galton.

Galton then explored the family trees of these eminent men. He found that many of the relatives of the eminent were also well-known and accomplished people. Furthermore, according to Galton's analysis, across these various groups, eminent fathers were more likely to have eminent sons, as opposed to eminent nephews or other, more distant eminent relatives. Because those nearest in relation to the eminent men were more likely to become well known, Galton asserted that intelligence was inherited.

Note that it would certainly be possible to argue for an environmental explanation for the same phenomena: that sons were more eminent because they were raised in the households of eminent men, while nephews were not. However, Galton hoped to rule out environmental influences to the greatest extent possible. He foreshadowed a long line of research involving adopted twins in claiming that "had [the eminent] been changelings when babies, a very fair proportion of those who survived . . . would, notwithstanding their altered circumstances, have equally risen to eminence" (Galton, 1869, p. 38). (We discuss twin and adoption studies in Chapter 5.)

---

[1] The cross-pollination that occurred in the work of Darwin and Galton is worth noting. Each made claims that drew on the other's work. For example, Galton wrote *Hereditary Genius* 10 years after *On the Origin of Species* was published, but noted that his ideas were supported by direct praise from Darwin. Darwin then drew on Galton's work in claiming intelligence was inherited when he wrote in *The Descent of Man*: ". . . we now know, through the admirable labours of Mr. Galton, that genius, which implies a wonderfully complex combination of high faculties, tends to be inherited; and, on the other hand, it is too certain that insanity and deteriorated mental powers likewise run in families." (Darwin, 1871/1984, pp. 252–253).

Galton also tried to rule out environmental influence by defending his use of reputation as a proxy for underlying ability. He claimed reputation was a good measure of ability. It did not simply represent social position or influence since, according to Galton, all able individuals can attract the notice and high regard of others (Galton, 1869).

Galton's Application of Statistics to the Study of Intelligence

While it is possible to fault Galton for his reluctance to entertain alternatives to inheritance of genius, there is no doubt that Galton's work was revolutionary in its application of mathematics to the study of intelligence. Galton asserted:

> There is a continuity of natural ability reaching from one knows not what height, and descending to one can hardly say what depth. I propose . . . to range men according to their natural abilities, putting them into classes separated by equal degrees of merit. . . . (Galton, 1869, p. 26)

Using the developing field of statistics, Galton argued that natural ability could be arrayed according to "the law of deviation from an average" (Galton, 1869, p. 28). According to this law, any kind of recurring trait or event that is subject to the same set of conditions forms the same pattern—what we now commonly call a bell curve or normal distribution. For example, the weight of individual beans harvested from bean plants grown in the same soil, with the same sunlight, water, and fertilizer, would form a bell-shaped distribution. The accuracy of shots fired at a target by marksmen who are of equal skill, and are all equipped with the same rifles and bullets, will also form a bell-shaped distribution. (See Figure 2.1.)

FIGURE 2.1
Diagram of normal distribution with standard deviations. Percentages indicate how much of the total distribution is contained between standard deviations.

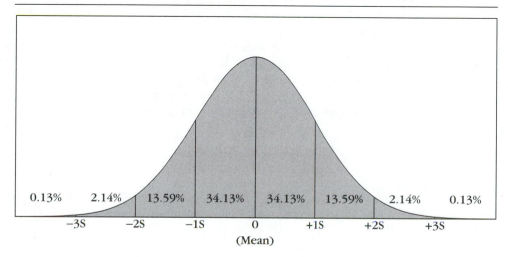

Within this distribution, most events or traits will tend to have an average value (the "mean" value). However, an important property of this distribution is that it is easy to calculate the proportion of the population that is contained within given distances (or deviations) from the mean. Today, we commonly divide such a distribution into standard deviations.[2] The standard deviation provides a handy rule of thumb for estimating how much of the distribution is contained within a particular distance from the mean (see Figure 2.1).

Because Galton viewed intelligence as a natural ability that was not related to differentially occurring conditions such as education or class, he argued that intelligence followed the law of deviation from an average. Thus, the greatest number of people would have about average intelligence. Galton divided the distribution of intelligence of the British male population into 14 classes. Seven of these ranged from slightly above average ("class A") to extraordinary eminence ("class G"), and seven ranged from slightly below average ("class a") to extremely low intelligence ("class g"). Galton divided the distribution into 14 classes so that the numbers of men rated the highest and lowest in ability were in accord with his calculations about the rate of occurrence of eminence (class G) and "imbecility" (class g) in Britain (roughly 250 men per million in each of these 2 classes) (see Figure 2.2).

Years later, after an effort to gather data from human subjects (which we'll describe below) rather than from biographies, Galton discovered that people who are particularly intelligent (or short or tall or strong) tend to have children who are not quite as intelligent (or short or tall or strong) as their parents. This tendency for an extreme value in one generation to move toward the average value in the next generation is known as *regression to the mean.* It is the typical pattern of events, over time, for a wide range of phenomena, from the performance of sports teams (which usually do not land in first or last place year after year), to the height of people, to the weight of beans over generations. Thus, contrary to notions of Spencer and others who maintained evolution was progressive, Galton's analysis revealed that characteristics tended over generations to hover around the average.

Regression toward the mean frustrated Galton's hope of breeding brighter human beings. Without extreme intervention on a scale that human cultures have not yet tolerated over generations, eugenics cannot yield more intelligent humans. (Nevertheless, as we will see in Chapter 3, eugenically oriented programs and policies were undertaken in various countries.)

---

[2] Technically, the standard deviation is a measure of variability that is calculated by taking the square root of the average of all the individual squared deviations from the mean that are contained in a distribution.

Figure 2.2

This table and the caption below it are from Francis Galton's *Hereditary Genius* (1869). In this table Galton's classes F and G or f and g, when added together, summed to roughly the proportions of "eminence" or "imbecility" that he found in his empirical investigations (Galton, 1869).

Grades of Natural Ability, Separated by Equal Intervals		Numbers of Men Comprised in the Several Grades of Natural Ability, Whether in Respect to Their General Powers, or to Special Aptitudes							
Below Average	Above Average	Proportionate, viz. One in	In Each Million of the Same Age	In Total Male Population of the United Kingdom, viz. 15 Millions, of the Undermentioned Ages:—					
				20—30	30—40	40—50	50—60	60—70	70—80
a	A	4	256,791	651,000	495,000	391,000	268,000	171,000	77,000
b	B	6	162,279	400,000	312,000	246,000	168,000	107,000	48,000
c	C	16	63,563	161,000	123,000	97,000	66,000	42,000	19,000
d	D	64	15,696	39,800	30,300	23,900	16,400	10,400	4,700
e	E	413	2,423	6,100	4,700	3,700	2,520	1,600	729
f	F	4,300	233	590	450	355	243	155	70
g	G	79,000	14	35	27	21	15	9	4
x all grades below g	X all grades above G	1,000,000	1	3	2	2	2	—	—
On either side of average			500,000	1,268,000	964,000	761,000	521,000	332,000	149,000
Total, both sides			1,000,000	2,536,000	1,928,000	1,522,000	1,042,000	664,000	298,000

The proportions of men living at different ages are calculated from the proportions that are true for England and Wales. (Census 1861, Appendix, p. 107.)

Example—The class F contains 1 in every 4,300 men. In other words, there are 233 of that class in each million of men. The same is true of class f. In the whole United Kingdom there are 590 men of class F (and the same number of f) between the ages of 20 and 30; 450 between the ages of 30 and 40; and so on.

Measuring and Testing Individual Differences

Galton's Effort to Measure the Intelligence of Individuals

In *Hereditary Genius,* Galton assumed that reputation was a reasonable measure of ability. Given this assumption, he felt that biographical encyclopedias provided information adequate enough for him to assert that intelligence was inherited. But Galton ultimately decided that, in order to get a better grasp of the human variability on which selection and inheritance operated (the fundamental information for a eugenics program), he needed to gather some new empirical data. Toward this end, he established the Anthropometric Laboratory in 1884. The lab was housed for 6 years at the Kensington Science Museum. There, for a fee of a few pence each, 9,300 museum patrons participated in Galton's effort to study human physical and mental characteristics (Kevles, 1985).

Poster for Galton's Anthropometric Laboratory.

Galton gathered data about people's weight, height, hand strength, breathing power, head size, and various psychophysical characteristics. The latter were obtained by measuring reaction times and individuals' abilities to make fine sensory discriminations.

Recall that reaction time measurements and sensory discrimination tasks were also components of the psychophysical laboratories of Wundt and other investigators. However, Wundt's aim was to get a *general* picture of human mental activities. Toward that end, Wundt and others relied on data from a few trained introspectionists. These individuals carefully examined and reported their own mental processes, and what they reported was considered representative of human thinking processes.

In contrast, Galton wanted to know about the variability or *individual differences* of the characteristics he studied. To get a grasp of this variability, Galton needed a great deal of data from a large number of people. In order to gather such data, Galton invented "the *mental test,* an experimental method of measurement which is characterized by its brevity . . ." (Boring, 1950, p. 484).

Galton's mental tests measured such things as the highest pitch a person could hear, and how well he or she could distinguish small differences in weights, colors, smells, tactile stimuli, and the lengths of lines. The tests focused on sensory skills, in line with the tradition of the British empiricists and associationists who believed that information was transmitted to the mind by the senses. It follows from this tradition that those with greater sensory perception had more information to work with and greater powers of discrimination. They were likely more intelligent.

Although Galton invented the mental test, and with it the scientific study of individual differences in intelligence, Galton's tests were soon rejected for their seeming lack of external validity. An American follower of Galton's work, the psychologist James McKeen Cattell, developed a battery of 50 mental tests akin to those used by Galton. Clarke Wissler, a student in Cattell's lab at Columbia University, then explored whether high scores on the Cattell battery were associated with high academic achievement. In 1901, he announced that they weren't. In fact, Columbia students' grades bore hardly any relationship to their scores on tests from the Cattell battery. Wissler's work, though it suffered from experimental design flaws (described in Chapter 3), undermined the notion that perceptual speed and sensory discrimination were underlying abilities on which intelligent behavior depended (Sternberg, 1990; Wissler, 1901/1961).

The Work of Alfred Binet

At about the same time Galton was using psychophysical tests to explore individual differences in intelligence, the French psychologist Alfred Binet was beginning to investigate these differences from another perspective:

> It seems to us that in intelligence there is a fundamental faculty, the alteration or the lack of which, is of the utmost importance for practical life. This faculty is judgment, otherwise called good sense, practical sense, initiative, the faculty of adapting one's self to circumstances. To judge well, to comprehend well, to reason well, these are the essential activities of intelligence. (Binet & Simon, 1916/1973, pp. 42–43)

Binet's notion of intelligence led him to explore "comprehension, judgment, reasoning, and invention" (Binet & Simon, 1916/1973, p. 40) and other higher-order skills, as opposed to the sensory skills that Galton tested. Throughout much of the

Alfred Binet.

1890s, Binet and his colleagues investigated such skills in normal and retarded children. Binet examined sensory discrimination skills as well, but placed limited emphasis on them.

Binet's investigations into judgment coincided with the growth of mass education in France, a trend which created new challenges for schools. In the past, most of the children who attended school had come from well-to-do families and had received training in social and intellectual skills even before formal education. However, with the advent of mass education, schools had to educate a new, far more diverse group of children. Some of these youngsters had little exposure to the sort of information that teachers would expect of the privileged children. Some were able to learn readily, others were not. Some behaved well, others were unruly.

Given students' disparate backgrounds and dispositions toward learning, it became hard to know which children were capable of learning but difficult to teach, and which children had genuine learning difficulties. To help resolve such issues, in 1904 the French Ministry of Public Instruction asked Binet to devise a test to identify those children who truly "were unable to profit . . . from the instruction given in the ordinary schools" and would benefit from remedial education (Binet & Simon, 1916, p. 9).

Alfred Binet and Théodore Simon published their first mental tests in 1905. Their methods, like those of Cattell and Galton, relied on brief tests. However, unlike their predecessors, Binet and Simon focused on tests of practical and everyday knowledge. Children were asked to follow simple instructions, such as to be seated or to pick up something from the floor. Among other tasks, they were asked to name familiar objects presented to them in pictures, to copy geometric forms, to count objects, and to repeat sentences and strings of numbers of varying length. (See Box 2.1.)

Binet and Simon argued that it was important to ask children to do a variety of different tests: "Every child has his individuality; one succeeds best in test 'A' and fails in test 'B'; another, of the same age, fails in 'A' and on the other hand succeeds in 'B.'" (1916/1973, p. 243). Binet and Simon believed that different tests called on different abilities, which could develop unequally in different children. Thus, they asserted:

we can determine the intellectual level of a child only by the sum total of the tests. Success in many different tests is alone characteristic. The mark of intelligence is therefore not made nor can it be made as one measures height. For the height, it suffices to have a table of average measurements for that age. . . . It is altogether different for the measure of intelligence. (Binet & Simon, 1916, p. 243)

Box 2.1
Sample Tests From Alfred Binet and Théodore Simon's "Measuring Scale of Intelligence" (1911 Revision)

Binet and Simon organized their test questions in graded levels of difficulty for children of different ages.

Four Years
Name key, knife, penny
Repeat three figures
Compare [the length of] two lines

Six Years
Distinguish morning and evening
Copy diamond
Count thirteen pennies

Eight Years
Compare two objects from memory
Count from twenty to zero
Repeat five digits

Ten Years
Place five weights in order
Copy a design from memory
Place three words [e.g., Paris, fortune, and stream] in two sentences

Twelve Years
Give more than sixty words in three minutes
Define three abstract words
Comprehend a disarranged sentence

Having already studied children's judgment for many years, Binet knew that children of different ages could solve different kinds of problems. Binet's breakthrough in intelligence testing was to organize his test questions in graded levels of difficulty for children of different chronological ages. If a 12-year-old child passed most of the questions appropriate for 12-year-olds, then the child was said to have a *mental age* of 12. If an 8-year-old passed the tests intended for a 12-year-old, then this young child also had a mental age of 12. Using this system, Binet could gauge whether a youngster was working at, above, or below the level of his or her classmates. Typically, a child's mental age would be noted with an indication of the difference between the child's mental age and chronological age.

William Stern (1912/1965), a German psychologist, found the mental age system adequate for comparing children of the same chronological age. He noted, however, that similar disparities between chronological and mental ages had different implications for children of different chronological ages. For example, a 12-year-old whose mental age is 10 is not likely to experience difficulties in learning as severe as those of a 5-year-old with a mental age of 3, even though both are 2 years behind their agemates.

To have a better sense of the mental functioning of children of different ages, Stern devised what was later termed the intelligence quotient or IQ. This was calculated by dividing the mental age (MA) of a child by the child's chronological age (CA). Later, to remove the decimal point, the result was multiplied by 100.

Using this formula (MA/CA $\times$ 100), a child functioning at a mental age equal to the chronological age would have an IQ of 100. However, the 12-year-old with a mental age of 10 (mentioned above) would have an IQ of 83, somewhat below the expected average of 100. The 5-year-old child with a mental age of 3 would have an IQ of 60, quite a bit below the expected average of 100. The differences between the expected average and the actual scores on IQ tests are typically measured in standard deviations. For many IQ tests, the standard deviation is ±15 points. Thus, the first child's IQ of 83 is about 1 standard deviation below the mean. This score falls within the low-normal range. The second child's IQ of 60 is 2.67 standard deviations below, which falls within the range of retarded.

Because a single number could be assigned to a child's performance on the Binet–Simon tests, it was easy to forget that this number was never intended to represent a single underlying capacity or quantity. An IQ score or mental age is not a doctor's scale, informing us about such physical characteristics as height or weight. However, many people, including intelligence testers, have reified the score: they have come to see the score as a measure of a distinct, quantifiable "thing" inside a person's head (see Gould, 1981).

Intelligence—once reified—could lend support to eugenic efforts (see Gould, 1981). When reified, intelligence came more to look like a breedable trait, like height in Clydesdales or weight in hogs. However, not only were Binet's tests different from Galton's, so were his purposes. Recall that Galton wanted to improve the mental ability of the human race through eugenic programs. For Galton, it was important to get data on the variability of intelligence in order to begin to devise programs that encouraged or discouraged certain people from having children. In contrast, Binet studied individual differences because he was interested in the development of thinking in children. He undertook to measure ability because he believed that better educational decisions could be made with such information. Binet felt strongly that assignment to remedial education could enhance the mental ability of retarded children. Though he assigned a number to a child's performance, Binet (unlike Galton) never believed intelligence was an unchanging or fixed attribute of a person, and he did not argue that intelligence was inherited (Binet & Simon 1916/1973; Gould, 1981).

The Influences of Binet and Galton

Both Galton and Binet died in 1911, leaving large areas of investigation to be pursued by other scientific researchers. Galton endowed a laboratory and professorship at University College, London, to foster research in eugenics and the inheritance of intelligence. Galton's life and legacy also spurred the development of statistics and its application in studying inheritance of mental and physical qualities. Soon, researchers devised factor analysis, a statistical method that has been used to investigate whether one or more types of ability account for IQ test results. (Factor analysis is discussed further in Chapter 3.)

Binet's research impelled work in the development of mental tests of reasoning, judgment, and related abilities. These tests were readily adopted, especially in the burgeoning area of mass education. It is worth noting that, because Galton's tests of sensory discrimination were discredited, it was typical for the data from Binet-style tests to be used both by researchers interested in education and by those pursuing eugenics. Thus, many later researchers combined the test methods of Binet with the purposes of Galton (Fancher, 1985).

This combination is evident in the work of the Army psychologists, whom we encountered in Chapter 1. One of the Army psychologists, Lewis Terman, adapted Binet's tests for use by American schoolchildren. In line with Galton's ideas, he wrote, "The children of successful and cultured parents test higher than children from wretched and ignorant homes for the simple reason that their heredity is better" (Terman, 1916, p. 115). Cyril Burt, Britain's leading educational psychologist, felt similarly. He concurred that "backward" children often came from impoverished homes and suffered from ill health and physical defects. Nevertheless, he argued, their condition was due to "a general inferiority of intellectual capacity, presumably inborn, and frequently hereditary" (quoted in Hearnshaw, 1979, p. 76). In the United States, Binet's intelligence tests played a part in determining eugenic issues such as whether prison inmates, the mentally handicapped, and other "defectives" would be sterilized (Degler, 1991; Gould, 1981; Kevles, 1985).

The topics of mental testing, inheritance of intelligence, eugenics, and factor analysis are enormous, and each is associated with many controversies. We discuss them in greater detail in Chapter 3. Before we do, it is important to consider other strands of scientific research that have helped to shape our understanding of intelligence.

Scientific Investigations Affecting the Study of Intelligence

Behaviorism/Learning Theory

Within a few years of Binet's effort to devise mental tests of judgment, a coup was brewing that would divert much of psychology away from the study of higher mental processes, such as judgment and reasoning. The official launching of the movement is usually set as 1913. In that year, an American psychologist, John Watson, attacked psychological investigations that relied on introspectionist methods. In reality, the revolution attributed to Watson was simmering for some time among a number of people. Like Watson, other investigators, especially in the United States and Russia, felt the introspectionists' reports were subjective; one person's consciousness could not be observed by others, and one's own testimony about the workings of one's own mind was simply not reliable. These researchers believed data from psychological experiments ought to be objective and verifiable in the way that physicists' or chemists' data were. They argued that the way to make psychology a rigorous, truly scientific discipline was to avoid the study of such fuzzy notions as plans, images, consciousness, schemata, thoughts, ideas, and the mind. Instead, psychology should investigate observable behaviors, and build a science of the laws that governed these behaviors (Gardner, 1985).

From about 1920 through the 1940s, experimental psychology, especially in the United States, focused on the way behaviors were acquired or learned. Experiments by Watson, B. F. Skinner, and numerous other behaviorists sought to train organisms to give a particular, measurable response (R) to a particular, measurable stimulus (S) in a given situation. In "S–R" theory, behaviors were not the result of thought, plans, will, or the like; they were reactions to events in the environment. Activities often thought of as being driven at least in part by mental processes were redefined in terms of observable S–R patterns. Even language, the means by which thoughts and plans are often formulated and expressed, was reduced to "biosocial stimuli": "Any object or event which is socially important is given a name which becomes a substitute stimulus for the objects or the events." This stimulus provokes other language in a "biosocial response" (Weiss, 1930/1973, p. 303).

Like the empiricists and associationist psychologists, behaviorists emphasized that the environment was the key to determining human capabilities. Unlike John Locke, however, they shunned the notion that the "mind" has ideas. In fact, they viewed the mind not as a "white paper" on which information could be written, but as a "black box," about which little could be revealed.

Behaviorist theory had an impact on ideas about intelligence and education. Edward Thorndike, perhaps the leading educational psychologist in the United

States during the first half of this century, had been conducting experiments in animal learning using behaviorist methods since about 1900. One of his findings from comparative learning experiments with animals was that "exercise" or repetition increases the rate of problem solving.

Thorndike (1913) applied his idea of repetition to classroom learning for children. He argued that, to help students learn language, they should encounter the same words as frequently as possible; to help them learn mathematics, books should be revised to emphasize common calculations and eliminate any needless words. Many popular school textbooks were written and revised along these lines. These and other insights from behaviorist research may have encouraged the notion that intelligence can be measured by speedy correct responses. At a minimum, it de-emphasized the role of thoughtful judgment and reflection (see Chapter 8).

Biological Investigations

Behaviorists were determined to produce environmentally based laws that governed learning and intelligent activity. In contrast, eugenically oriented designers and users of intelligence tests believed human biology governed intelligence. However, while these two groups were at work, biologists and psychologists were undertaking a range of investigations that indicated neither biology nor environment alone was usually adequate to explain intelligence.

Eugenicists' arguments in favor of policies directing human breeding may be understood in part from their inadequate knowledge about heredity. As noted earlier, when Darwin wrote *On the Origin of Species* and *The Descent of Man,* he was unaware of Gregor Mendel's work in genetics. Because Darwin did not have a mechanism to explain how variations were inherited, he often adopted Lamarckian language. Lamarck's ideas of inheritance were only put to rest in 1889 by August Weismann. By amputating the tails of mice, breeding them, and then amputating the tails of their offspring over many generations, Weismann demonstrated that acquired characteristics were not inherited. Only the genetic material contained in the "germ plasm" was (Degler, 1991).

In the wake of this revealing experiment, Mendel's work was rediscovered and came to dominate thinking about inheritance. Mendel, an Austrian monk, bred some 30,000 pea plants over 7 years and studied how various characteristics, such as the plants' height and seed texture, were inherited from one generation to the next. Mendel came to conclude that, among pea plants, two "elements" governed the characteristics he studied, much like sperm and egg provide the characteristics of offspring in animals (Kevles, 1985; Mayr, 1982).

Mendel found that two tall pea plants would produce tall plants. Two short plants would produce short plants. But a tall plant, when cross-fertilized with a short plant, also produced tall plants. Thus, the element for tallness was "dominant." The element for shortness was "recessive." Given this pattern, it becomes possible to predict mathematically which elements and appearance will be inherited by the offspring (see Figure 2.3).

FIGURE 2.3

Inheritance patterns for recessive and dominant genes that Mendel studied mathematically can be predicted mathematically. The matrix below shows the results of a cross between two heterozygous tall pea plants. In the early part of the 20th century, patterns Mendel found in pea plants were popularly—and *incorrectly*—applied to the inheritance of intelligence and other human characteristics.

	T	t
T	TT 25%	Tt 25%
t	Tt 25%	tt 25%

T = Tall (Dominant)
t = Short (Recessive)

50% Heterozygous Tall (Tt)
25% Homozygous Tall (TT)
25% Homozygous Short (tt)

Mendel knew that inheritance among pea plants was simple, and that the pattern he found might not be true for other plants (Mayr, 1982). Nevertheless, inheritance of a trait via the single Mendelian element or "unit character" posited for pea plants became a popular way of explaining a whole host of characteristics, including human intelligence. Even Henry Goddard, a World War I Army psychologist, and a skeptic with regard to intelligence as a unit-character, wrote that feeblemindedness was "a condition of mind or brain which is transmitted as regularly and surely as color of hair or eyes" (quoted in Kevles, 1985, p. 79).

The ideas Mendel derived from pea plants remained popular at least through the 1920s, but as early as 1905, many scientists recognized these were too simplistic (Mayr, 1982). Geneticists realized that few visible characteristics are governed by the straightforward principles that applied to pea plants. The genetic base of most characteristics is governed polygenetically—by many genes.

Alongside the recognition that many genes contribute to most observable characteristics, geneticists acknowledged and emphasized the distinction between genotype and phenotype. The genetic inheritance of an organism (genotype) can be expressed in a variety of ways (phenotype). The phenotypical expression of a characteristic need not, and often does not, represent genes alone;

rather, it represents some combination of genes and environmental factors. The notions of phenotype and polygenetic control countered the eugenicists' notion that there was a simple equation between genetic input and intellectual destiny.

Work With Mentally Impaired Individuals

Other findings that mitigated against straightforward environmental or genetic explanations for intelligence came from investigations with mentally impaired individuals. For example, in 1931, a British researcher, Lionel Penrose, began a massive investigation of 1,280 "defectives" in the Royal Eastern Counties' Institution in Colchester. Penrose's study was aimed at understanding the causes of the deficits in each of the institution's patients (see Kevles, 1985).

Penrose found that various causes of mental impairment were commonly at work in the same patient. For example, a patient could have some inherited illness like Huntington's disease, which affects thinking, alongside an acquired disease like syphilis, which also impairs thinking, and might, in addition, suffer from the stresses of living without adequate food and shelter. In only roughly 25% of the cases studied did Penrose find heredity alone at work (Kevles, 1985).

A number of other clinicians and researchers associated with mental institutions found that mental abilities—as measured by IQ scores—could be enhanced. Given a stimulating environment, such as the opportunity to work in the home of one of the institution's staff, institutionalized children's IQs rose, and they could become functional outside the institution (Bronfenbrenner, 1979, for a personal account; Kevles, 1985).

Studies of mentally impaired people have not only shed light on intricate interrelationships of heredity and environment in intelligence, but have also shown complex relationships among intelligent activity, IQ, and the human brain. As noted earlier, intelligence has frequently been reified. Thus, IQ scores are seen as measuring some "thing" that enables people to do abstract intellectual work. But studies of brain-damaged patients, undertaken in the 1930s and 1940s by D. O. Hebb, underscored that the relationship between IQ scores and the ability to plan or act intelligently is not at all straightforward. Damage to the brain's frontal lobes can severely hamper a person's ability to organize his or her behavior in space and time and to devise new approaches to solving a problem. Patients with extensive frontal lobe damage appear quite impaired. Yet, Hebb demonstrated that they commonly show no loss in IQ (Hebb & Penfield, 1940)—another indication that measured intelligence is not a readily interpretable quality.

Technology

No review of scientific advances in the study of intelligence is complete without at least an acknowledgment of the crucial role that technological discoveries have played. For example, the ability to generate and measure electrical current enabled Helmholtz to track the speed of nerve impulses. The development of statistics facilitated the study of the inheritance of intelligence. It also supported the rigorous construction and analyses of intelligence tests, which we will discuss in Chapter 3. Electroencephalograms (EEGs) enable the recording of the brain's electrical activity. Powerful microscopes have allowed researchers to explore cell division and the structure of neurons. The use of X rays and advanced imaging technologies have made it possible to see and understand the brain and its structures. As Chapter 6 details, the invention and development of computers have provided researchers with a means to model human thinking and to analyze massive amounts of information. In Chapter 5, we discuss how computers, in conjunction with advanced imaging techniques, are finally allowing researchers to do what the behaviorists believed too difficult: get an external, verifiable picture of the brain in the process of problem solving.

Summary

An attempt to summarize 2,400 years in the development of anything—let alone the origins of scientific thought about intelligence—necessarily involves choices. We have highlighted the questions and methods that generations of thinkers have used to explore intelligence. These should provide a framework for thinking about the scientific investigations that will be covered in later chapters.

We began by discussing the Greek philosophers, who probed issues fundamental to later investigations. Among these issues were the inheritance of intelligence, the ranking of people by their intelligence ("wisdom"), the role of the senses, and the idea that knowledge may be innate. The Greeks also began to elaborate methods for systematically investigating questions and building up knowledge.

Two later philosophers, Descartes and Locke, proposed alternative conceptions of the intellect that have been drawn on by later thinkers and researchers. Descartes, a rationalist philosopher, maintained that humans have innate knowledge. A proponent of dualism, he argued that the mind and body were separate. The latter, having a material basis, could be studied; the former, divine in nature, could be known only through introspection. In contrast, Locke, an empiricist, argued that we are not born with knowledge. We acquire knowledge through our sensory experiences of the world and our capacity to reflect on our own mental operations. As a materialist, he maintained the mind was made of matter and thus could be studied.

Nineteenth-century scientists such as Donders, Helmholtz, and Broca exploited the material nature of the body to illuminate the workings of the mind. These researchers uncovered relationships between the senses and the nervous system, as well as between the brain and such human skills as language production and comprehension. Laboratory work of introspectionists and associationists proved limited in explaining higher mental processes: It is hard to derive an understanding of the accomplishments of human civilization from sensory and perceptual processes. Thus, Wundt also advocated studies of cultural phenomena such as religion, language, and custom.

The theory of evolution had a potent impact on the study of intelligence. It gave way to Galton's eugenic endeavors and his study of the inheritance of intelligence using statistical methods. Evolution's emphasis on variation also paved the way for the study of individual differences by Galton, Binet, and later generations of intelligence testers. We study individual differences in detail in the following chapter.

Suggested Readings

Burtt, E. A. (Ed.). (1939). *The English philosophers from Bacon to Mill.* New York: Modern Library.

Changeux, J. P. (1985). *Neuronal man.* (Laurence Carey, Trans.) New York: Pantheon Books.

Degler, C. (1991). *In search of human nature.* New York: Oxford University Press.

Gardner, H. (1985). *The mind's new science.* New York: Basic Books.

Wilson, M. D. (1969). *The essential Descartes.* New York: New American Library.

Chapter 3

The Psychometric Perspective

Discussions concerning the theory, nature, and measurement of intelligence historically have resulted more in disagreement than in agreement, more in smoke than in illumination.

—Hans J. Eysenck (1986, p. 1)

Introduction

In the previous chapter, we introduced the work of Francis Galton and Alfred Binet, both of whom were concerned with the study of individual differences in intelligence. In this chapter, we trace the work of their intellectual descendants: psychometricians who have explored variations in intelligence among individuals by constructing psychological tests and carrying out statistical analyses of test results.

The study of individual differences is notable for technical developments in test construction and statistical analyses, and is renown for social and scientific controversy. To some, the discovery of g[1] and the statistical analyses related to g are the most compelling findings and contributions of psychology (e.g., Anderson, 1992; Herrnstein, 1991, personal communication; Herrnstein & Murray, 1994; Jensen, 1980, 1987; Kline, 1991). To these psychologists, intelligence tests and statistical analyses of their results may help shed light on the organization or "structure" of the intellect: whether one or many abilities account for intelligence, and the relationship of these abilities to each other (e.g., Cattell, 1987; Gustafsson, 1984, 1988; Thurstone, 1938; P. E. Vernon, 1950, 1956). As

---

[1] g (general intelligence) as defined by psychometricians is unrelated to Galton's intellectual "class g," introduced in Chapter 2.

we discuss in Chapter 5, such research also helps reveal contributions of genetics and of various environments to mental functioning (Bouchard, 1990, 1991; Plomin, 1986, 1988; Scarr, 1989). In addition, psychometric tests have been seen by some as a tool for meritocratic selection, permitting recognition and advancement of capable individuals from diverse social circumstances, based on an objective measure (Herrnstein, 1973; Jensen, 1980).

Other psychologists, educators, and scientists have been critical of the study of individual differences from the psychometric perspective. Some critics cast a harsh eye toward the tests' construct validity. They argue that such tests don't measure "intelligence" but rather only a narrow and somewhat idiosyncratic range of human abilities (e.g., Gardner, 1983). Furthermore, critics assert that intelligence tests do not necessarily measure the experience, knowledge, and other matters that enable people to function well and solve problems in their daily lives (e.g., Ceci, 1990; Gardner, 1991a; Wiggins, 1989). Not unlike the claims leveled against the Chinese civil service exams (see Chapter 1) have been critics' charges that psychometric tests have resulted in harmful educational practices, such as rote learning and separate, tracked classes (e.g., Fredericksen & Collins, 1989; Gardner, 1991b; Neill & Medina, 1989; Oakes, 1985). Psychometric tests have also been seen as undermining social justice, rather than promoting it, especially when such tests have been used to advocate eugenic ends (Gould, 1981; Kevles, 1985). Perceived and real abuses have even led to demands that intelligence tests be banned (Allen, 1992; Reschley, 1981). (See also discussion of *Larry P. v. Wilson Riles,* later in this chapter.)

In this chapter, we explore both scientific and social issues surrounding individual differences in intelligence. We begin with "the idea of general intelligence." First proposed by Charles Spearman, general intelligence (*g*) is regarded by many as the key to intelligence. After this, we look at alternatives to Spearman's formulation. We introduce factor analysis and the structure of human intelligence according to various factor analysts. We also consider the construction of tests on which factor analyses are based, and we review some of the controversies in testing that have arisen in the social realm. Finally, we consider a few more recent efforts to measure intelligence, which some psychometricians claim are free from the cultural influences that have made performances on traditional psychometric tests difficult to interpret.

The Idea of General Intelligence (*g*)

The work of Binet and of Galton had tremendous influence on later investigators. Charles Spearman was particularly affected and intrigued by Galton's work. Early in the 20th century, Spearman, an English military engineer turned psychologist, decided to carry out some studies of his own (Fancher, 1985). In one study, Spearman gathered various measurements from 24 children at a local village school. The measurements included an assessment by their teacher of the children's

Charles Spearman.

"cleverness in school," ratings by other students of the children's "common sense out of school, and assessments of their ability for sensory discrimination of light, weight and pitch" (Spearman, 1904). In another study, Spearman collected exam scores in classics, languages, and music from 33 children in an upper-class preparatory school.

At the village school, Spearman found positive relationships among all the different measures, even between sensory discrimination tasks and evaluations of students' academic ability. This finding stood in direct contradiction to Clark Wissler's research (discussed in Chapter 2), which Spearman did not know about when he conducted the two studies.

At the preparatory school, Spearman found that there was a strong relationship among the exam results in different subjects (see Figure 3.3 on page 65). He even found strong relationships between academic subjects like Latin and music, "a faculty that is usually set up on a pedestal entirely apart" (Spearman, 1904).

Spearman argued that the various relationships he found within and among all these different sensory tasks and academic subject matters could be explained by a "two-factor" theory (Spearman, 1904, 1923, 1927). The first factor was "General Intelligence" or *g* (Spearman, 1904). Spearman argued that *g* was a factor used to some extent in all intellectual tasks. The second he called "Specific Intelligence," specific factors, or "*s.*" Spearman said that *s* described whatever ability was unique to carrying out a given task and that such specific factors were unrelated across tasks (Spearman, 1904, 1927).

Spearman believed that *g* measured a neurologically based "power" or "energy" that drives the ability to do intellectual work (Spearman, 1923, p. 5). Across diverse kinds of problem solving, such work consisted of the "eduction of relations and correlates." Basically, this is the ability to draw out and apply logical relationships between elements. Spearman called such elements "fundaments." In the eduction of relations, two fundaments are given—for example, "hot" and "cold"—and the task is to determine the relationship between them (e.g., "opposite"). In the eduction of correlates, a fundament and a relationship are given, and the task is to educe a second fundament, which is related to the first by the given relationship. For example, "hot" and "opposite" are given, and the fundament that is educed is "cold" (Spearman, 1923).

Correlation

How did Spearman derive the idea that *g* supported all reasoning? To understand Spearman's work, we need to consider correlation, a statistical tool that Galton had earlier applied to the study of individual differences. Correlation was initially termed by Galton as "co-relations," (Galton, 1888/1961). As that name indicates, correlation is a measure of the extent to which two variables are associated. Another way of thinking about correlation is the degree to which two variables, such as height and weight, or wealth and school achievement, vary together.

A correlation coefficient (or r) is a measure that ranges from −1 to +1. The coefficient gives two pieces of information: the *direction* of the relationship and its *magnitude.* The sign in front of the number indicates the direction of the relationship. A positive sign reveals that as one variable increases, the other variable also increases. A negative sign reveals a negative, or inverse, relationship: as one variable increases, the other variable decreases (see Figure 3.1).

The number indicates the magnitude of the relationship, that is, the degree to which one variable is associated with another. The more closely the two variables are associated, the closer the coefficient will be to 1 (or −1, in an inverse relationship). If there is no linear association between two variables, the coefficient will be zero (Figure 3.1 (c)). Magnitude and direction of relationship are illustrated in Figure 3.1.

Uses of Correlation

EXPLAINING VARIANCE

Another way to think about correlation is in terms of *variance.* As the term indicates, any variable—for example, height, income, or IQ scores—varies. The variance is described as a spread (or distribution) of scores. In the normal curve, discussed in Chapter 2, most of the scores hover around the middle. Yet, a distribution of scores extends downward from the middle, or central, point. This dispersion of scores from one end of a distribution to the other is known as *variance.* The more spread out the scores are, the larger the variance. Variance is represented as s^2 or σ^2, the square of the standard deviation. (Mathematically, variance is the arithmetic average of the squared deviations of all individual scores from the mean of the distribution.)

Squaring the correlation coefficient (r^2) indicates the proportion of variance the variables have in common. For example, a correlation of .7 reveals that nearly half (49%) of the variance is shared by the two variables. The same notion is often expressed: "Half the variance in x can be explained (or accounted for) by y." But, because correlation alone does not indicate causality in the relationship, one can also say correctly, "Half the variance in y can be accounted for by x."

FIGURE 3.1

Correlation: A correlation coefficient provides two pieces of information. The sign (+ or −) indicates the direction of the relationship. The number indicates the magnitude of the relationship. Examples of hypothetical correlations: (1) Positive correlation (e.g., r = +1); (2) Negative correlation (e.g., r = −1); (3) Absence of linear correlation (e.g., r = 0).

(1)

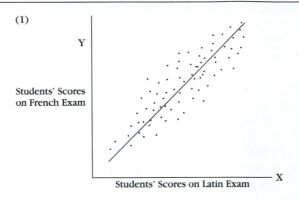

(2)

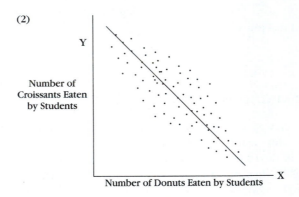

(3)

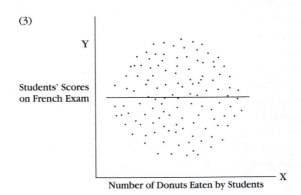

PREDICTION

One of the key uses of correlation is for *prediction*. Given knowledge of the direction and magnitude of a relationship, it is possible to use either variable to approximate the level of the other variable. For example, as we'll discuss in Chapter 5, a long line of psychometric research focuses on the high correlations in IQ between monozygotic (identical) twins and on the lower IQ correlations between other kinds of siblings. Correlations between sets of twins enable researchers to predict or estimate IQ scores for one twin based on knowledge of the other's. Differences or similarities in predicted IQ scores for mono- and dizygotic twins help researchers generate theories about environmental and hereditary influences in IQ scores (Plomin, 1986, 1990; see also Chapter 5).

Limits of Correlation

CORRELATION AND CAUSATION

An *essential* point to remember about correlation is that, though it allows prediction, a correlation between two variables does not imply a causal relationship between them. A correlation (or, if it's helpful, the proportion of shared variance) between two variables may stem from a number of phenomena. Three hypothetical examples illustrate this point.

1. We may find that between 1965 and 1995 there was a decrease in the average size of miniature French poodles and an increase in the average height of professional basketball players. A computer could plot the relationship on a pair of axes and calculate a correlation coefficient for these two variables. However, it is entirely unlikely that either of these two variables affects the other.

2. We may find that as candy prices change, so does the cost of pastries. Despite this relationship, there's little reason to believe that more expensive candy causes more expensive pastries, or vice versa. Instead, the two variables may have a third variable in common—the cost of sugar, or general inflation—which has led to an increase in both.

3. Even if there appears to be a relationship between two variables, the directionality of the relationship may be unclear. As a traditional example, happy mothers are usually found to have happy babies. But who is making whom happy?

It is possible to begin building a causal argument from correlations, but, to do so, other forms of evidence beyond statistics must be brought to bear. For example, arguments that a positive correlation between smoking and lung cancer is a causal relationship rely on, among other things, theories of biological mechanisms causing cancer, and studies over time of the lungs of smokers and nonsmokers.

ACCURACY OF A CORRELATION

Another crucial point about correlation is that the size of the correlation can be affected by several things. A lower correlation coefficient will be obtained in a study that uses a narrow sample (or *restricted range*) of the population, because a narrow sample is unlikely to reflect the variation in a broader sample (see Figure 3.2). One example of this comes from Wissler's study, mentioned earlier.

FIGURE 3.2
Restricted range lowers correlations. This illustration reveals how a narrow sample of the population may not detect a correlation that exists in the wider population. Across the sample as a whole there is a positive correlation between variables x and y. Yet in each of the three narrow samples (enclosed in the boxes) no correlation appears.

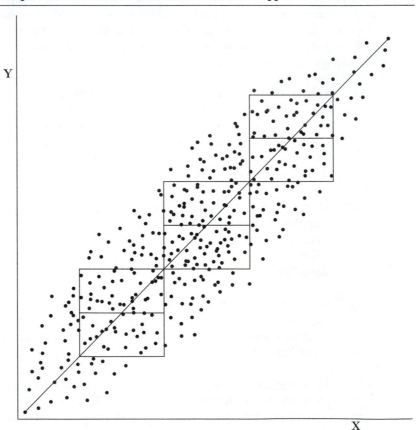

Wissler (1901/1961) claimed there was little relationship between psychophysical tests of intelligence and academic performance. However, his data drew on tests of Columbia College students, who were very likely in the upper range of academic performance. Spearman (1904) argued that the low correlation between psychophysical and academic tests stemmed from the fact that Columbia students are too highly specialized; that is, their range of academic performance is narrow and thus not representative of a larger, more heterogeneous population. Later investigators have studied Wissler's data and agreed that the correlations Wissler reported between psychophysical tests and academic performance are lower than would be expected in a broader, more representative sample of the population (Jensen, 1980; Sternberg, 1990).

Various sources of error also affect correlation. We do not obtain absolutely consistent results even when we use the best instruments properly. Because our measurements waver, so will correlations between measurements.

SPEARMAN'S USE OF CORRELATION TO THEORIZE ABOUT INTELLIGENCE

One way to grasp the relationships among a number of variables is to construct a table or "matrix" of correlation coefficients. After Spearman gathered his data from school children and calculated the various correlation coefficients, he put the results in a matrix of correlations. When Spearman looked at the correlations among various tests of the preparatory school boys, he saw that all the tests correlated positively with each other, and that some tests correlated more highly than others. (See Figure 3.3)

Reading down the first column, we see a stronger correlation between exam scores in classics and French than between those in classics and music. Spearman maintained that the different correlations between measures reflected differences in the degree to which particular tasks drew on (or were "saturated with") *g*. Differences in the extent to which test scores correlated with each other also led

FIGURE 3.3
This is the table of correlations Spearman (1904) constructed from his investigation of students in a British prepatory school. Because all the measures in these diverse areas were positively correlated in this and other research, Spearman asserted that there was one factor common to all intellectual tasks. He called this factor General Intelligence, or *g*.

	Classics	French	English	Math	Pitch	Music
Classics	—	.83	.78	.70	.66	.63
French	.83	—	.67	.67	.65	.57
English	.78	.67	—	.64	.54	.51
Math	.70	.67	.64	—	.45	.51
Pitch discrimination	.66	.65	.54	.45	—	.40
Music	.63	.57	.51	.51	.40	—

FIGURE 3.4
According to Spearman (1904), activities or performances in some areas drew more heavily upon *g* than activities in other areas. Thus, for example, performance in classics was highly correlated with *g*, while discriminating weights was not.

Activity	Correlation With General Intelligence	Ratio of the Common Factor to the Specific Factor	
Classics	0.99	99 to	1
Common sense	0.98	96	4
Pitch discrimination	0.94	89	11
French	0.92	84	16
Cleverness	0.90	81	19
English	0.90	81	19
Mathematics	0.86	74	26
Pitch discrimination among the uncultured	0.72	52	48
Music	0.70	49	51
Light discrimination	0.57	32	68
Weight discrimination	0.44	19	81

Spearman to assert that there is a "Hierarchy of the Intelligences," with ability in classics leading the way, followed by common sense, and, lagging far behind, the ability to make discriminations in different weights (see Figure 3.4).

The Pluralists

Factor Analysis and the Assault on Spearman's Two-Factor Theory

Spearman argued that a single, physiologically based entity, *g,* could explain intellectual performances of various types, but others found fault with Spearman's analysis. The debates among Spearman and his fellow psychometricians centered on two points: the actual existence of *g* and the number of entities or factors representing intelligence. A fellow British psychologist and factor analyst, Sir Godfrey Thomson, argued that, though Spearman might calculate correlation coefficients and find a hierarchical order among them, there was no evidence that such findings represented an underlying entity in the nervous system. Thomson claimed most tests measured a mixture of different underlying processes, rather than any sort of "pure 'factor'" (Thomson, 1939, p. 4). Along with Thomson, a number of other, later researchers have also criticized the notion that *g* measures anything pure (e.g., Humphreys, 1971) or any one thing truly inside the head (Cronbach, 1990; Gould, 1981).

Another round of criticism leveled against the two-factor theory concerned the number of factors needed to explain the correlations among different measures of cognitive ability, and, by inference, intelligence. These criticisms drew largely on findings from factor analysis.

Factor analysis is complex mathematically; outside readings are necessary to get a more detailed introduction to the topic (see Kline, 1991; McDonald, 1985; Sattler, 1992). Factor analysis builds on the idea of multiple correlations. These are correlations between a given variable and two or more others—for example, between an overall IQ score and a test involving verbal tasks as well as a test involving spatial tasks.

Factor analysis is a set of statistical methods "in which variations in scores on a number of variables are expressed in a smaller number of dimensions or constructs" (Kline, 1991, p. 10). These dimensions are called factors. Psychometricians often derive factors from a very large number of intercorrelations in a group of tests given to many people. The factors are meant to represent an ability common to a group of tests. To help explain factor analysis, Gould (1981) has used the analogy of factoring in algebra, "where you simplified horrendous expressions by removing common multipliers of all terms . . ." (p. 245).

It's not possible to graph on a two-dimensional page the many correlations that go into a factor analysis: graphing correlations involving three variables requires three dimensions. With four variables, we need to exercise our visualization skills and imagine four planes of data in "hyperspace."

To get a graphical sense of how factor analysis works, we'll launch backward from hyperspace (where factor analysis is most used) into three dimensions, which can be more readily visualized (Gould, 1981; Manni, Winikur, & Keller, 1984). Suppose you have given three tests to several hundred people and have plotted the results. You might get something that looks like Figure 3.5.

At first, the model may seem to be only a mob of data points shaped like a blimp. However, it's possible to draw, lengthwise through the middle of these points, one line that best represents the average distance between all the points. This line, which, in essence, averages the variance in the test results, is called *the first principal component.* Among psychometricians, it is often said to represent the *general factor,* or *g,* in a group of tests (Jensen, 1980).

The first principal component explains the most variance, but other lines could be drawn that would also represent average distances between the data points. These other lines would explain some of the remaining variance. For example, a second line could be drawn across the widest or middle part of the whole blimp. This line would lie at 90 degrees to the first line, and it too would represent a great deal of information. This is the *second principal component.* Yet a third line, at right angles to the other two, could be drawn in the plane coming out from the page.

With larger numbers of tests and larger correlation matrices, the task becomes considerably more complicated. Many more factors can be extracted from a set of 25 tests. However, having 25 different factors hardly serves the task of simplifying and explaining the variation in test results, especially when each successive factor accounts for less and less of the variance.

FIGURE 3.5
Model of three-dimensional scatterplot of correlations among scores on three tests, with first and second principal components.

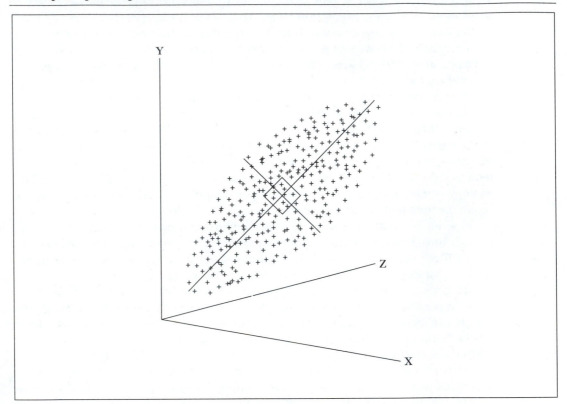

THE PLURALISTS' DEBATES: HOW MANY FACTORS? HOW ARE THEY ORGANIZED?

The Idea of Group Factors. Given that it is feasible to extract more than one factor from a correlation matrix of several tests, it is not surprising that later psychometricians not only debated Spearman's two-factor theory but differed with each other. The differences surrounded both the number and the organization of factors that were being extracted using factor analysis. As we will see below, some argued that there are several factors of equal importance (e.g., Guilford, 1967; Thurstone, 1938). Others agreed that there were factors besides *g*, but said that *g*, or some form of it, was still at the top of the hierarchy (Cattell, 1987; Gustafsson, 1984; Horn & Cattell, 1966; P. E. Vernon, 1950, 1956).

Both proponents and critics of *g* agreed that factor analyses needed to incorporate *group factors.* These are factors that are associated with particular groups of tests. For example, factors associated with vocabulary tests, reading comprehension tests, and tests of antonyms and synonyms might be clustered together as a group and called a *verbal* or *language* factor. Factors associated with tests that require people to rotate shapes in space, to imagine how a flat piece of paper would look if folded along certain lines, and to recognize objects from partial representations might be clustered together and labeled a mental *visualization* or *spatial* factor. As we'll detail below, different psychometricians argued for different group factors.

Rotation.   Some of the debates about group factors arise from the fact that there are defensible and reasonable ways to proceed in factor analysis, but there is no single mathematically correct solution to a factor analysis. Typically, most factor analysts don't base their analyses on the original component factors that are discussed above and are illustrated in the blimp (Figure 3.5). Instead, they rotate the factors. In the course of rotation, some factors become more highly associated, or correlated, with variances from some tests or subtests than with others (see Figure 3.6).

The correlation between variables (such as tests of spatial abilities) and a particular factor (for example, spatial visualization) is called a *factor loading.* The goal of most factor analysts is to rotate factors to approach *simple structure* (Kline, 1991). In simple structure, the factors are rotated to achieve many near-zero loadings and a few high loadings. That is, many variables are highly associated with one factor and not associated with the others. To many in the field, this yields the simplest or clearest picture of factors.

However, not all factor analysts follow the same rotation techniques. For example, in Figure 3.6, factors are kept orthogonal (at 90°) and rotated. However, many factor analysts assert that factors should not be orthogonal. Instead, factors

FIGURE 3.6

Simplified model of orthogonal rotation of factors. Dots are various tests. Rotation of factors F_A + F_Z "load" tests onto factors.

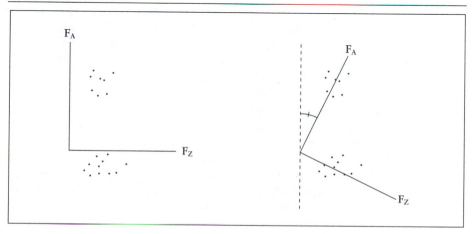

need to be at oblique angles to account for as much of the variance as possible. Different factor analytic methods, as well as differences in the kinds of tests on which the factor analyses were based, helped to create some of the models of intelligence detailed below.

NONHIERARCHICAL THEORIES OF INTELLIGENCE BASED ON FACTOR ANALYSIS

Louis L. Thurstone and Primary Mental Abilities.   One of the first major alternatives to Spearman's two-factor theory was offered by Louis L. Thurstone. Thurstone (1938) sought to identify "separate and unique mental abilities" (p. 92), which he termed primary mental abilities. To identify these primary mental abilities, Thurstone administered a battery of 56 diverse tests to 240 Chicago-area college students who volunteered to take them. Using factor analytic methods on the resulting correlation matrix, Thurstone argued that seven independent primary abilities explained intellectual functioning better than one general factor (Thurstone & Thurstone, 1941).

The primary abilities Thurstone identified were verbal comprehension (the ability to understand verbal information); verbal fluency (the ability to produce verbal material rapidly); number (the ability to do arithmetic rapidly and to solve arithmetic word problems); memory (the ability to remember different types of material, such as letters, words, numbers, and images); perceptual speed (the speed at which letters, numbers, and objects are recognized); inductive reasoning (grasping general ideas from specific instances); and spatial visualization (the ability to rotate objects, solve visual puzzles, and visualize shapes) (Thurstone & Thurstone, 1941). Though Thurstone's primary abilities did not include *g,* later factor analyses by other researchers indicated that *g* could be extracted from the primary abilities, a finding Thurstone himself acknowledged (Anderson, 1992; Cattell, 1987).

J. P. Guilford and the Structure of Intellect Model.   Another American theorist whose factor analyses veered away from the importance of *g* was J. P. Guilford. The theory of intellect put forth by Guilford postulated 120 separate factors (Guilford, 1967). The factors were organized along 3 dimensions or "categories." Guilford proposed 4 types of *content categories,* on which 5 types of *operation categories* operate. In addition, there were 6 types of *product categories,* in which information occurred. Multiplying the numbers of types in each category (4 contents × 5 operations × 6 products) leads to the theorized 120 separate factors or abilities, which are usually displayed in a cube (Figure 3.7). In later writings, Guilford spoke of 150 separate factors.

Using Guilford's model of the Structure of Intellect in Figure 3.7, one example of a factor is the cognition of figural units. This factor is linked to the ability to recognize individual pictorial representations. For these and other factors, Guilford employed various tests to measure the ability. A test of cognition of figural units might call on people to identify shapes.

FIGURE 3.7
Guilford's Structure of Intellect Model (1967) postulated 120 factors.

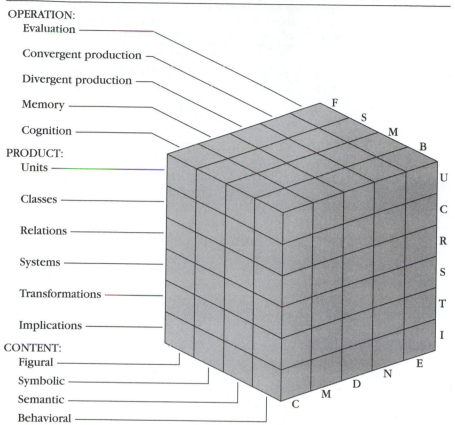

OPERATION:
  Evaluation
  Convergent production
  Divergent production
  Memory
  Cognition
PRODUCT:
  Units
  Classes
  Relations
  Systems
  Transformations
  Implications
CONTENT:
  Figural
  Symbolic
  Semantic
  Behavioral

HIERARCHICAL THEORIES BASED ON FACTOR ANALYSIS

P. E. Vernon.   With some notable exceptions such as Guilford and Thurstone, most factor analysts have tended toward analyses that yield a hierarchical pattern of group factors. In hierarchical models that include *g*, *g* explains part of the variance in all of the tests. In contrast, group factors explain variance in particular tests and not in others. Philip E. Vernon, a British psychologist, has provided a clear visual representation of the distinction between an analysis such as Thurstone's original one, where group and specific factors alone explained the data, and hierarchical factors in which general, group, and specific factors explain the data (P. E. Vernon, 1956). (See Figure 3.8.)

Vernon's own hierarchical theory (see Figure 3.9) encompasses two major group factors under *g*. One group factor, *v:ed,* is extracted from "verbal intelligence tests, together with other tests depending on manipulation of words," which generally involve "an education factor." The other factor, *k:m,* is associated

FIGURE 3.8
P. E. Vernon's (1956) representation of (I) hierarchical models;
(II) group and specific factors, as in Thurstone's model; and
(III) a pattern representing Spearman's (1904) model in which
only *g* and specific factors were proposed.

I. BI-FACTOR PATTERN

Test	General Factor	Group Factors				Specific Factors
		A	B	C	D	
1	X	X				X
2	X	X				X
3	X	X				X
4	X		X			X
5	X		X			X
6	X			X		X
7	X			X		X
8	X			X		X
9	X			X		X
10	X				X	X
11	X				X	X
12	X				X	X

II. MULTIPLE-FACTOR PATTERN

Test	Common Factors				Specific Factors
	A	B	C	D	
1	X		X		X
2	X				X
3	X	X			X
4		X			X
5	X	X		X	X
6			X		X
7		X	X		X
8	X		X		X
9			X		X
10				X	X
11		X		X	X
12			X	X	X

III. UNI-FACTOR PATTERN

Test	General Factors	Specific Factors
1	X	X
2	X	X
3	X	X
4	X	X
5	X	X
6	X	X
7	X	X
8	X	X
9	X	X
10	X	X
11	X	X
12	X	X

FIGURE 3.9
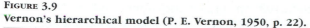
Vernon's hierarchical model (P. E. Vernon, 1950, p. 22).

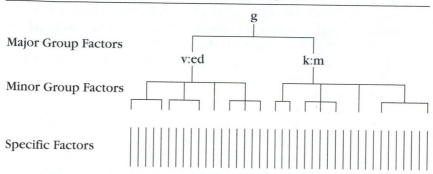

with tests of "mental manipulation of shapes" and tests of mechanical ability (1956, p. 144). Under each of these major group factors are minor group factors, such as verbal and numerical abilities under *v:ed,* and spatial ability and manual ability under *k:m.* At the lowest rung are specific factors, which are drawn on by particular tests.

Vernon felt that including tests that loaded on *k:m* would make test batteries more useful in educational and vocational guidance of students. He argued that such tests would give a broader perspective on the abilities of the mentally ill (1972, p. 145).

Horn and Cattell. Like Vernon, Raymond B. Cattell and John Horn, two psychologists working in the United States, also proposed a hierarchical theory in which there are two important broad factors. These they called fluid ability (Gf) and crystallized ability (Gc) (Horn & Cattell, 1966). In addition, there are three other "second order" factors:

1. General visualization (Gv) (involving figural-based problem solving);

2. General fluency (Gr) (involving the recognition and recall of labels for cultural concepts);

3. General speediness (Gs), which relates to quickness in dealing with problems presented in words, numbers, or pictures.

Under each of these are narrower group abilities and, at the lowest rung again, specific abilities.

Fluid ability (Gf) is akin to Spearman's notion of *g,* though *g* itself is not used in this model. Recall that Spearman considered intelligence, and his measure for it (*g*), to be the "eduction of relations and correlates" (Spearman, 1923). Similarly, Gf "appears to operate whenever the sheer perception of complex relations is involved" (Cattell, 1987, p. 115). Cattell found that tests that load on fluid ability are (a) seriation and classification tests and (b) analogies in which the material is either nonverbal or nonrepresentational figures. Tests in which any verbal or representational materials are completely familiar, and thus require only deciphering of the relations between them, also test fluid ability (for example, up:sky as down:ground). In this model, it is thought that Gf measures a biologically based capacity for thinking.

In contrast, crystallized ability (Gc) concerns diverse skills and knowledge that are acquired in a culture. Among the tests that load on Gc are tests of numerical ability, mechanical information and skills, and vocabulary.

Crystallized and fluid abilities are positively correlated. Cattell has offered the *investment theory* to explain this finding. Crystallized ability skills depend in part on investment of fluid ability in learning experiences found in the culture. Though Cattell (1987) asserted that schooling can't really change intelligence, he acknowledged that levels of crystallized ability stem from schooling as well as from investment of fluid ability:

> From Oxford to the Chinese literati, cultures have explicitly or implicitly set up definitions of intelligence entirely in their own image. What is more, they probably create in the *actual* mental structure of a generation, a detectable, broad, factor pattern—Gc—in the image of their culture. (p. 345)

Arguments for Gf and Gc come not only from tests but also from evidence that the two factors show different patterns of development and decline. Performance on tests that load on fluid intelligence peaks at about the age of 18. Performance on tests that load on crystallized intelligence continues to improve through most of the adult years (Cattell, 1987).

Jan-Eric Gustafsson.   Gustafsson, a Swedish psychometrician, has devised a hierarchical model that is compatible in structure with most of the models previously mentioned (Gustafsson, 1984, 1988). In Gustafsson's model, *g* appears at the top of the hierarchy. Underneath this are three broad factors reminiscent of others already introduced: Gv, Gf, and Gc. However, in his factor analyses, Gustafsson has ascertained that Gf is basically the same as *g* and that Gc is a narrower ability from the Gc described by Cattell and Horn. Gv is a factor that loads on tests involving figural problem solving. Beneath these three broad factors are more primary factors akin to those discussed by Thurstone and Guilford.

John Carroll.   The most extensive effort to understand the structure of intellect has resulted in John Carroll's recent "three-stratum" theory (Carroll, 1993). Carroll reanalyzed over 450 correlation matrices of tests of cognitive abilities. The correlation matrices were gathered from studies in the United States and several other countries, published between 1927 and 1987. The studies included people diverse in age, occupation, and measured ability. All told, they represented data from more than 130,000 individuals.

Carroll's reanalysis of these data sets has led him to propose a hierarchical theory. At the highest level (Stratum III) is *g*. Below this (at Stratum II) are eight broad abilities: fluid and crystallized intelligence, learning and memory processes, visual and auditory perception, facile production, and speed. At the base of the hierarchy, and below each of the Stratum II factors, are several narrow Stratum I factors.

As the factor theorists illustrate, factor analysis proposes ways to think about how various intellectual abilities are organized, but it reveals no single answer. As Cattell observed (1987), whatever structure is determined cannot be considered universal across different cultures and populations (see also Kline, 1991). The structure will vary depending on who is tested and the cultures they come from. In arriving at a structure, much also depends on the kinds of tests that are used to establish the initial correlation matrices and the kind of factor analytic methods that are used to extract factors from the matrices. Whether a factor analyst adopts one model versus another is determined in some part by his or her own prior conceptions (Anderson, 1992) and by certain societal traditions. For example, many British factor analysts, like P. E. Vernon, follow in the British tradition of Spearman and have a model in which *g* is prominent. In the United States, researchers like Thurstone, Guilford, and Horn and Cattell, seem to adopt models where narrower factors appear adequate to explain patterns of test performance and the importance of *g* is diminished (Gustafsson, 1988).

That *g* need not materialize in a factor analysis raises a fundamental question: Is *g* only a mathematical finding? If *g* is not a statistical artifact, is it "real?" We return to these questions in the summary of this chapter.

Construction of Intelligence Tests

Factor analyses, in the context considered here, are based on correlations among intelligence tests of various types. What do these tests look like? How are they constructed? How well do the tests correlate with, and predict, performances on other measures besides intelligence tests—for example, with academic success and job success?

Intelligence tests fall into two broad categories:

1. *Individually administered tests* occur in one-on-one situations. These are usually given to an examinee by a psychologist trained in test administration. The tests are individually scored and interpreted in light of information about the individual and his or her level of effort, attention, and comfort during the testing.

2. *Group tests* are taken by a number of examinees at the same time. The tests are often scored by a machine and interpreted according to established guidelines. Unlike individually administered tests, in a group test situation, the test administrator can rarely assist the individual examinee by probing for further understanding or by providing encouragement (Cronbach, 1990).

Test Characteristics

Test instruments have evolved a long way since the time Spearman went about collecting exam grades, teachers' and students' opinions, and measures of sensory discrimination. Current, commonly used tests of intelligence seek to eliminate biases of the sort that may appear in teachers' and peers' judgments. Scrutiny of tests for other forms of bias is an ongoing effort for test developers (see Sattler, 1992). In addition, modern tests are intended to be highly *reliable* and *valid* for their intended purposes. Although we have discussed these terms in Chapter 1, we delve into each in somewhat more detail here.

The *reliability* of a test concerns the degree to which the test gives consistent results. In reliable tests, unsystematic variation in test results is minimized. If a test is highly reliable, the score can be interpreted as measuring the performance of an individual on the test, rather than random events unrelated to the individual's performance.

In reality, no test is perfectly reliable. Therefore, according to psychometric theory, an intelligence test's actual or *observed score* reflects two pieces of information. The first is an estimate of the individual's theoretical *true score,* the amount of the score dependent on the intelligence of the individual. The second is an *error score,* the amount of the score due to unsystematic variation. A test's *reliability coefficient* is based on results from testing a group of people. It is a ratio of the variance in estimated true score over the variance in observed score.

Reliability coefficients range from 0 (no reliability) to 1.0 (perfect reliability). Reliability coefficients, often written as r_{tt}, are usually obtained by establishing correlations between (a) a test and itself or (b) equivalent, alternate forms of the test. In *test–retest reliability,* a sample of people is given the same test twice, usually after a brief intervening period. This procedure helps to indicate whether the test gives consistent results over time. In *parallel form reliability,* two versions of the same test are both given to one sample group of examinees. During a single test administration, half the sample takes one version of the test ("Form A") and the other half takes a second, equivalent version ("Form B"). If the test is reliable, the means and variances of the two test forms should be the same, and the scores from the two should correlate highly. *Internal consistency reliability* seeks to determine whether the tests' questions, or sections of a test, are consistent with each other. Split-half reliability is one way of ascertaining internal consistency. In split-half reliability, a test is generally divided by its even and odd questions into two alternate forms. The forms are given in a single administration. If the test reliably measures a particular characteristic, the two forms of the test should be highly correlated (Sattler, 1992).

Tests are more likely to prove reliable if the interval between test administrations is short. When the interval is short, intervening events outside the test situation are fewer, and changes in test takers are likely to be small. Reliability will also be greater if the sample of those taking the test is heterogeneous. This typically yields a wide range of scores, so no one score will have a big effect on the overall correlation. In addition, reliability is enhanced with longer tests. The more items on a test, the less impact any one item can have on the overall correlation (Sattler, 1992).

Reliability is also affected by testing conditions (Sattler, 1992). The intelligence tests given by the U.S. Army, discussed in Chapter 1, illustrate some conditions that reduce reliability: a lack of understanding of test directions, frustration on the part of those being tested, or the assignment of inappropriate groups to take a given test (see Fancher, 1985; Gould, 1981; Yerkes, 1921).

Validity has traditionally referred to the idea that a test measures what it is intended to measure (Messick, 1989; Shepard, 1993). If a test measures what it is supposed to, it becomes possible to draw inferences from performance on the test to circumstances beyond the testing situation.

A number of psychologists have emphasized that validity is not an inherent part of any test. Instead, the validity of a test must be established for *the particular use* to which it is put (Messick, 1989; Shepard, 1993). For example, a test that is found to be valid in predicting high school performance should not be considered valid for predicting performance in college or on the job until its validity for such purposes has been demonstrated. When establishing the validity of an intelligence test, or other tests, one should rely on integrated arguments from three related forms of investigation (Cronbach, 1990).

Criterion validity, the first form, is investigated by comparing test scores for a particular test with a standard outcome or *criterion* external to the test. One example of this is *concurrent validity,* which entails an effort to ascertain validity by comparing a test against a criterion that is current—such as recent school grades or tests of academic achievement. *Predictive validity* seeks to establish a correlation between a current test and a future performance. For example, Jensen (1980) argues that IQ tests taken in childhood have predictive validity when measured against such criteria as total years of formal education or grades in graduate school.

The second source of argument is known as *content validity.* Establishing content validity involves examination of the test to see whether the test items represent the content area that the test is designed to measure. For example, if a test is supposed to measure crystallized intelligence, it should include a variety of questions that draw on skills and knowledge that are acquired in a culture, such as vocabulary, numerical ability, and mechanical skills.

Finally, *construct validity* concerns a test's relationship with the theoretical "construct," or quality, it is supposed to measure. Intelligence is one such

construct (other examples include aggression and creativity). Construct validation is a process that seeks to support or refute the construct by using, in part,
predictable or systematic differences in test scores that are supposed to measure
the construct. For example, if a theory of intelligence argues that people with
high intelligence will be good at abstract problem solving, and people who turn
out to be good at such problem solving score high on tests of intelligence, this
correlation validates the claim that the test measures the construct intelligence
(Cronbach, 1990).

More recently, some psychologists have argued that a reformulated version of
construct validity should be the basis, or "unifying conception," for validity studies of tests (Messick, 1989; Shepard, 1993, p. 423). According to these researchers,
construct validation must demonstrate that a test both measures the construct
that it is intended to measure, and is valid for a particular purpose. Construct validation must also investigate how particular values and assumptions shape the interpretation of the test. For example, what sort of treatments follow from a given
test, if the test is seen as measuring reading readiness instead of IQ? (Shepard,
1993). Finally, construct validation must investigate both the positive and the ad-
verse social consequences of the test (Messick, 1989; Shepard, 1993).

For such investigations, validation needs to be based on the structure of the
test itself as well as on the relationship between the test and the variables external
to it. In addition, validation must consider and rule out competing hypotheses. For
example, if a test is supposed to measure mathematical ability but has strict time
limits, which prevent many test takers from finishing it, it is not clear that the test
has measured the real math ability of the examinees or largely the speed at which
they take the test (Shepard, 1993). Validation should not only rely on correlational
data (for example, the relationship between one test of mathematical ability and
another), but should also draw on experimental studies when needed. An experimental study might be designed to have subjects who are matched for math ability; subjects solve the same set of problems under timed and untimed conditions.
Such an experiment could confirm or disconfirm the validity of a speeded math
test in measuring mathematical ability.

Like reliability, correlations obtained for validity can be affected by whether
the test is used with appropriate subgroups, whether the sample of people taking the test is heterogeneous, and how great a time has elapsed between the administration of any tests being compared. The criterion against which a test is
measured, and how well the criterion can be measured, also affect a test's validity.

Reliability and validity are linked. Reliability is necessary for validity: it would
be impossible to know whether a test was measuring what it claimed to be, if the
test results were inconsistent. The more reliable a test is, the higher its validity
can be. However, reliability alone can't establish validity. For example, a test that
asks people to recall strings of nonsense syllables might be highly reliable, but it
may not turn out to be a valid measure of vocabulary size or of memory for meaningful materials. The various forms of validation mentioned above are needed to
claim that a test is valid for a particular purpose (Cronbach, 1990).

Norms

In Chapter 1, we emphasized the importance of establishing standardized proce-dures in testing. When a test is given in a standardized fashion, that is, when test instructions, materials, and other test conditions are as identical as possible for all test takers, it is possible to establish a norm for the test (Cronbach, 1990). A norm is a distribution of scores for a particular test group (sometimes called the stan-dardization group). Norms allow comparisons between an individual's test score and the standardization group. The norm against which an individual is compared should be based on a group of test takers with similar, relevant characteristics. For example, a 12-year-old's performance on a vocabulary test should be com-pared against the performance of other 12-year-olds. Furthermore, it is important that test norms be kept current. Current performances of an individual (or group) should not be compared against norms derived many years ago, when, for exam-ple, conditions of schooling were very different.

A Closer Look at Intelligence Tests

Having outlined some of the general properties that modern-day psychometri-cians and test publishers strive for, let's look at a few of the tests that have actu-ally been produced.

The Wechsler Scales are individually administered intelligence tests that are among the most frequently given. The scales were first introduced by David Wechsler in 1939. Wechsler had been chief psychologist at New York's Bellevue Hospital. He had also served as a test administrator for the U.S. Army during World War I. The Wechsler Scales reflect Wechsler's experiences with the Army Alpha and Beta tests: roughly half of the Wechsler Scales (the "Verbal" portions) draw on lan-guage and knowledge gained through experience, like the Alpha test. The remain-ing part (the "Performance" portions) draws more heavily on pictorial representations and puzzlelike activities, and is less language-dependent, as was the Beta examination (Fancher, 1985; George, 1983). Compared to the Verbal por-tions, the Performance portions are thought to be a more direct measure of fluid ability (Sattler, 1992).

Wechsler believed intelligence involved persistence, motivation, and moral and aesthetic values, among other things (Wechsler, 1971). Thus, Wechsler was clear that he did not think his tests reflected "intelligence":

> . . . the abilities called for to perform these tasks do not, per se, constitute intel-ligence or even represent the only ways in which it may express itself. They are used and can serve as tests of intelligence because they have been shown to cor-relate with otherwise widely accepted criteria of intelligent behavior. (Wech-sler, 1971, p. 52)

Basically, Wechsler did not seek to determine the amount of an individual's intelli-gence. Rather, he sought to design an intelligence test that would allow individuals to demonstrate a fuller range of their strengths and weaknesses than the Army tests and other, earlier intelligence tests had allowed. To do this, he devised a test with several individual subtests for Performance and Verbal tasks. Each subtest was normed to allow for comparisons in ability (Fancher, 1985). His original test, the Wechsler-Bellevue Intelligence Scale—Form I, was intended for adults. Since that time, the test has been revised several times. In addition, Wechsler tests for children, similar in structure to the adult form of the test, have been created and revised.

The most recent version of the Wechsler tests includes two tests designed for children. The Wechsler Preschool and Primary Scale of Intelligence—Revised (WPPSI-R) is intended for young children, roughly ages 3 to 7. The Wechsler Intelligence Scale for Children, Third Edition (WISC-III) is used for older children, generally ages 6 through 16. The Wechsler Adult Intelligence Scale—Revised (WAIS-R) is intended for people ages 16 and above. Tests for the various age groups include 5 to 7 subtests each in the Verbal and Performance categories. (See Box 3.1 for simulated examples from the WAIS-R subtests.)

Each full administration of the WAIS-R yields a Verbal IQ, a Performance IQ, and a Full Scale IQ. Rather than using the old formula of mental age/chronological

---

Box 3.1
Simulated WAIS-R Questions

The WAIS-R, intended for adults ages 16 and over, contains 6 Verbal subtests and 5 Performance subtests. The following simulate WAIS-R subtest questions.

General Information

1. How many wings does a bird have?
2. How many nickels make a dime?
3. What is steam made of?
4. Who wrote *Tom Sawyer*?
5. What is pepper?

General Comprehension

1. What should you do if you see someone forget his book when he leaves a restaurant?
2. What is the advantage of keeping money in a bank?
3. Why is copper often used in electrical wires?

Box 3.1 (Continued)

Arithmetic

1. Sam had three pieces of candy and Joe gave him four more. How many pieces of candy did Sam have altogether?

2. Three women divided eighteen golf balls equally among themselves. How many golf balls did each person receive?

3. If two buttons cost 15¢, what will be the cost of a dozen buttons?

Similarities

1. In what way are a lion and a tiger alike?

2. In what way are a saw and a hammer alike?

3. In what way are an hour and a week alike?

4. In what way are a circle and a triangle alike?

Vocabulary

This test consists simply of asking, "What is a _____?" or "What does _____ mean?" The words cover a wide range of difficulty.

Picture Arrangement

(Simulated items courtesy of the Psychological Corporation)

age × 100, the Wechsler and all other modern tests yielding an IQ score use "deviation IQs." These scores are derived by comparing an individual's scores to those of a reference group of persons who are the same age as the individual. The mean score for a Full Scale deviation IQ is 100, and the standard deviation is 13.

Comparisons between Verbal and Performance scores, along with other knowledge about an examinee, can help in the interpretation of a person's intellectual functioning. For example, if a person has a significantly better Performance IQ than Verbal IQ and comes from an impoverished background, the lower Verbal IQ may be due to limitations in educational experiences. Depending on the individual examinee, such differences might also be explained in terms of difficulties in processing verbal information or relatively better motor coordination than verbal skills (Sattler, 1992).

Raven's Progressive Matrices was the name given to a test first produced by John Raven, a student of Charles Spearman. It elaborates on Spearman's notion of intelligence as "the eduction of relations and correlates" (Spearman, 1923). Raven's test, first published in 1938, requires examinees to apprehend and apply relations using visual representations. The test items all call on examinees to analyze, compare, and solve analogies based on abstract figures arranged in a matrix pattern (Raven, 1938). (See Figure 3.10 for examples.)

Raven's Progressive Matrices is a test that can be administered either to a group or on an individual basis. No time limit is prescribed, though the test is generally completed within an hour. Like the Wechsler Scales, the Raven's test appears in several forms intended for use by people of different ages. For 5–11-year-olds, there is a 36-item Coloured Progressive Matrices test that uses colors to maintain children's interest. For 6–17-year-olds, there is a 60-item Standard Progressive Matrices. This test can also be used for adults of roughly average ability. For those about 17 and older and for adults of better than average ability, there

FIGURE 3.10
Two examples (figures A4 & A5) from Raven's Standard Progressive Matrices.

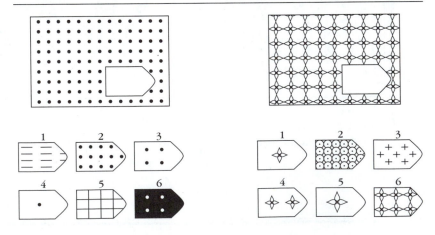

is a 48-item test, the Advanced Progressive Matrices (Sattler, 1992). Most of the tests are grouped into sets of 12 items. Within each set, the matrices are arranged in order of progressive difficulty—hence the test's name.

Results from Raven's Progressive Matrices are generally reported in the form of percentile rankings. An individual's raw scores on the test, based on the number of matrix problems answered correctly, are compared with the scores of others of the same age in a norm group. The percentile score for an individual examinee is based on the percentage of those in the norm group distribution with raw scores lower than the individual's score. For example, on the Standard Progressive Matrices, a 10-year-old who correctly answers 49 of the 60 items has scored at the 99th percentile: a score of 49 is higher than 99% of other 10-year-olds.

Because the test consists solely of nonrepresentational figures, it is said to be less dependent on formal education and cultural experience. Thus, it is described as "less culturally loaded." Like the Performance sections of the Wechsler Scales, the Raven's test is often considered a measure of "fluid intelligence" (Carpenter, Just, & Shell, 1990; Hunt, 1987). Because it does not involve language, it is sometimes a preferred test for young children, elderly people, and those with language difficulties (Sattler, 1992). Since it relies on abstract figures, it has also been widely used in cross-cultural studies (Jensen, 1980).

RELATIONSHIP OF INTELLIGENCE TESTS TO OTHER VARIABLES

School Achievement.   The Wechsler tests, especially the Wechsler Verbal IQ score, have been shown to correlate strongly with achievement in elementary school (see Jensen, 1980) and grade point averages of high school and college students (Cronbach, 1990; Jensen, 1980). Raven's Progressive Matrices predict school grades less well than the Wechsler Scales. This is not surprising, since it is more a measure of fluid rather than crystallized intelligence. It does not draw on the language, mathematical, and information tasks that schools focus on (Jensen, 1980).

Job Status.   Though the Wechsler Scales may help to predict grades, the Wechsler and other intelligence tests fare less well in predicting whether a person who scores around the average will enter a profession or unskilled work (Cronbach, 1990). Such tests are better at predicting job status for those who score either above or below average. For example, on average, those who score high on intelligence tests generally have higher status jobs in fields such as science or law. On average, those who score low tend to have less prestigious occupations (Cronbach, 1990; Jensen, 1980). As the words "on average," should indicate, within occupations there is still a wide range of intelligence test scores among individuals (Jensen, 1980).

Job Success.   Although intelligence test results may help predict occupational status, such scores are less able to predict success within a particular career (Cronbach, 1990; Jensen, 1980). Job success depends on many variables, such as motivation and the ability to interact well with others, which standardized intelligence tests do not explore (see Chapter 9).

Because selection for jobs and school programs has crucial ramifications for an individual, it is vital to remember the words of Lee Cronbach (1990): "almost never should a test score by itself determine what will be done by or for the person" (p. 4). Other information, including evaluations beyond tests, can play an important role in placement and selection of individuals (Gardner, 1991a; Klitgaard, 1985; Kornhaber & Gardner, 1991).

Uses of Intelligence Tests

The Wechsler Scales and Raven's Progressive Matrices illustrate an important point about the use of intelligence tests. Not all intelligence tests are equally useful for all purposes. For example, the Wechsler Scales, especially those subtests used in measuring Verbal IQ, correlate better with scholastic performance than does the Raven's test (Jensen, 1980; Sattler, 1992). On the other hand, if one were conducting research into the nature of *g,* and seeking to uncover cognitive processes associated with it, or if the examinee had language difficulties, the Raven's test might be a more useful instrument. Wechsler geared his tests to tap several abilities; Raven's "measures g and little else," (Jensen, 1980, p. 646).

These observations do not make either test inherently better than the other. Provided a test meets contemporary psychometric standards for reliability and validity, has been scrutinized for various forms of bias, and uses updated norms, it is difficult to label *the test itself* a "bad" test.[2]

Because modern intelligence tests are generally carefully scrutinized, problems with tests arise for reasons outside of the testing instrument itself—namely, in the interpretation and use of test results. Test use has implications not only for individuals, who may seek diagnosis and counseling, but for identifiable groups of individuals within a society. Psychometricians not only measure differences among individuals, but they also analyze test results to study differences among various groups: old and young, men and women, rich and poor, the retarded and the gifted, as well as Blacks, Whites, Asians, Hispanics, and other identifiable groups (Anderson, 1992). It is especially when considering *group differences,* and in the oft-related area of the inheritance of intelligence, that controversy has been abundant (see Herrnstein & Murray, 1994).

---

[2] To help educators, psychologists, and others select tests that meet such standards, and to use these tests well, guidelines have been published by various organizations. Among the most prominent of these publications is the *Standards for Educational and Psychological Testing* (American Educational Research Association, American Psychological Association, and National Council on Measurement in Education, 1985).

Controversies Involving Test Use

Early Use of Tests for Eugenic Ends

The association of different ethnic groups and races with different levels of intelligence has a long and often ugly history predating testing (see Degler, 1991; Gould, 1981). Once measurement of differences became more systematic, via the use of tests and quantifiable scores, differences in mean test scores of groups were sometimes harnessed to arguments that some groups were less intelligent than others (e.g., Brigham, 1923; Goddard, 1912; Terman, 1916).

Even before the U.S. Army Mental Tests (see Chapter 1), early intelligence testers made use of tests to foster the eugenic breeding of humans described by Galton (discussed in Chapter 2). Henry Goddard, an American psychologist, was the first to use the Binet–Simon tests in the United States. While working at the Training School for Feeble-Minded Boys and Girls in Vineland, New Jersey, Goddard used the Binet–Simon tests to explore whether "feeblemindedness" ran in families. After testing youngsters at the school, he investigated intelligence among their relatives who lived nearby. He published his results concerning one such family in a widely influential, and now thoroughly discredited book, *The Kallikak Family: A Study in the Heredity of Feeble-mindedness* (Goddard, 1912).

According to Goddard, Martin, the founding father of the Kallikaks, had a sexual encounter with a tavern girl. The 480 descendants of this liaison included many criminals as well as feebleminded and diseased individuals. After this affair, Martin married a respectable woman. Almost all of the 496 descendants from this marriage were decent citizens of average or better intelligence.

Goddard also gave intelligence tests to prison inmates, juveniles in reformatories, and residents of "homes for wayward girls." Among each of these groups, he found high rates of "feeblemindedness." Goddard's work was used to support the view that low intelligence was found more among the poor and criminals and that the "condition" was inherited.

Lewis Terman, who adapted the Binet–Simon tests and normed them on a group of 400 adults and 2,300 children of average social class (1916), also found differences among groups.

Lewis Terman.

He believed these differences were genetic in origin. In a fusion of Binet's methods with Galton's aims (Fancher, 1985), Terman advocated both educational and eugenic measures. In 1916, he wrote:

> . . . it will be wiser to take account of the inequalities of children in original endowment and to differentiate the course of study in such a way that each child will be allowed to progress at the rate which is normal to him, whether that rate be rapid or slow. (Terman, 1916, p. 4)

However, Terman, unlike Binet, believed separate educational programs could not improve the mental functioning of those who tested poorly. Rather, Terman recommended educational programs to make the less intelligent child fit for some modest occupation, and to lessen taxpayers' costs by preventing slow students from repeating a school year (Terman, 1916, 1922).

At the same time, Terman asserted that his intelligence tests provided a way to identify the "feebleminded." These, he argued, were more prominent in some groups, for example, "Spanish-Indian and Mexican families of the Southwest and also among negroes [sic]" (1916, p. 91), than in others.

Terman (1916) argued that the use of tests to identify feeblemindedness

> . . . will bring tens of thousands of these high-grade defectives under the surveillance and protection of society. This will ultimately result in curtailing the reproduction of feeble-mindedness and in the elimination of an enormous amount of crime, pauperism, and industrial inefficiency. (pp. 6–7)

Goddard and Terman were among the small group of psychologists who developed the U.S. Army Mental Tests. As discussed in Chapter 1, the Army used intelligence testing to help classify soldiers for service in World War I, and the tests included questions that were clearly biased. Furthermore, the tests were often administered using nonstandardized procedures, and test results were interpreted with race and ethnicity foremost in mind. (See Box 3.2 for a famous controversy involving the Army exams.)

The work of Goddard and Terman and other test developers was used both before and after World War I to fuel laws permitting eugenic sterilization of prison inmates and residents in homes for the retarded. By 1911, 6 states had passed laws allowing forced sterilization of the "feebleminded" and others. By 1928, 9,000 such sterilizations had occurred; by the late 1930s, 20,000 had been performed (Kevles, 1985).

Sterilization decisions were often made on the basis of intelligence tests. In 1927, the U.S. Supreme Court, in an 8–1 decision, upheld the right of states to sterilize those who scored poorly on intelligence tests. The 1927 case is known as *Buck v. Bell.* John Bell was the superintendent of the Virginia Colony for Epileptics and Feebleminded. Carrie Buck was a 17-year-old White woman who bore an infant daughter out of wedlock. Both mother and daughter were suspected of

Box 3.2
The Lippmann–Terman Debate

In 1922–1923, a series of magazine articles debating the findings and implications of the U.S. Army intelligence tests was published in *The New Republic* and *Century Illustrated.* On one side of the debate stood Lewis Terman, a professor at Stanford University, who had helped to develop a number of intelligence tests, including the Army's Alpha and Beta examinations. On the other side of the debate was Walter Lippmann, a Harvard-educated journalist and "public philosopher" (Schlesinger, 1959; Steel, 1980).

Both men shared a "progressivist" view that was common in the early part of the 20th century—namely, that science could help guide social policy. However, scientific facts do not lead directly to policy. Lippmann (1922/1976) came to realize that the ability of politicians, and of the wider public, to access scientific information is the end result of a long, selective process in which experts play a crucial rule.

In the debate, Lippmann set himself up to monitor and interpret the claims made by Terman and other experts in the field of intelligence testing. During the course of seven essays and a letter to the editor, Lippmann pointed out a number of flaws in the claims made by intelligence testers and their supporters in the eugenics movement. For example, it had been widely reported that the average mental age of the Army examinees was 14 and that only 5% of the army test-takers were "A" men—men smart enough to be considered for officer training school. Such findings led eugenicists to argue that the United States was threatened by the presence of so many intellectually inferior individuals.

However, Lippmann (1922/1976) made several important counter-arguments. For example, he noted that the mental age score norms that were used for the Army exam were established by testing a relatively small group of Californians. That group could not serve as a standardization group for 1.75 million Army recruits. In addition, he took aim at the content of the tests, which appeared to measure only "the type of mind which is very apt in solving Sunday newspaper puzzles . . ." (p. 15). He argued that whether such "stunts" actually test intelligence, "Nobody knows" (p. 10). Lippmann also pointed out that it was not odd that the tests determined that only 5% of recruits were "A" men. He noted that the Army tests were designed to select roughly 5% of the recruits—the "A" men—for officer training. They did this, in part, by timing the tests in such a way that no more than 5% could finish the whole exam (p. 12).

Continued

Box 3.2 (Continued)

Lippmann also took exception to claims by Terman and other test developers that their instruments measured innate intelligence. Lippmann claimed that, because testing began only when a child was several years old, education and environment already had a vast impact on test performance (Lippmann, 1976, pp. 24–25, 26–27). Finally, Lippmann argued that intelligence tests had great potential for misuse. This stemmed from assertions by intelligence testers that their instruments measured an inherited and fixed human trait. When used in school settings, such tests could amount to "stamping a permanent sense of inferiority upon the seal of a child" (p. 19).

Terman responded to these blows with one essay and one letter to the editor. However, his effort was not markedly successful: Terman certainly had more technical understanding of the tests and measurements (see Cronbach, 1975), but Lippmann was more polished in writing and rhetoric (Samelson, 1979). In his essays, Lippmann mixed reasoning and evidence with some sarcasm; Terman took the opposite tack, mixing a large amount of sarcasm with limited amounts of evidence and reasoning. For example, on the issue of whether the tests measure inherited intelligence or might be altered by early childhood experience, Terman wrote, in 1922, "It is high time that we were investigating the IQ effects of different kinds of baby talk, different versions of Mother Goose, and different makes of pacifiers and safety pins" (quoted in Block & Dworkin, 1976, p. 37). Finally, on the issue of the potential abuse of test results, Terman was similarly dismissive and demonstrated some naïveté about test use (Samelson, 1979). Terman claimed that it was "one of the recognized rules of the game" that mental tests should not be used to mark a child as permanently inferior. He asserted that Lippmann's fear of such a possibility is only evidence of what "an excited brain can conjure up" (quoted in Block & Dworkin, 1976, p. 35).

One of the ironies of the Lippmann–Terman debate is that Lippmann's better arguments did little to halt the escalation of testing in the United States. As powerful as Lippmann's arguments may have been, they were simply arguments; they offered no clear solution to the educational and other selection issues that tests were designed to handle (White, 1990, personal communication). In contrast, the tests, though imperfect and subject to misuse, offered a concrete, efficient, and inexpensive means for measuring individual differences.

being "feebleminded." Not long after the birth, Carrie was committed to the Colony, where her mother also lived. The Board of the Colony wanted Carrie sterilized. After considering the case, Justice Oliver Wendell Holmes, writing for the majority, declared:

> We have seen more than once that the public welfare may call upon the best citizens for their lives. It would be strange if it could not call upon those who already sap the strength of the State for these lesser sacrifices. . . . The principle that sustains compulsory vaccination is broad enough to cover cutting the Fallopian tubes. . . . Three generations of imbeciles are enough (quoted in Kevles, 1985, p. 111).

In its day, the court's decision in *Buck v. Bell* raised little outcry (Kevles, 1985). However, by the mid-1940s and for 25 years thereafter, claims about genetic bases for the mental inferiority or superiority of various groups were rarely tolerated. Three reasons are likely. First, the Nazi eugenic program, which ultimately led to the extermination effort against Jews and other minority groups during World War II, made such debates morally and politically unacceptable. Second, at least in the United States, the group of test designers and others knowledgeable about testing became more heterogeneous. Originally comprised largely of well-established descendants of Northern European families, this group expanded to incorporate those from Southern and Eastern European backgrounds. Finally, the notion that IQ was inherited in as straightforward a manner as height in pea plants had long been discredited within the scientific community and was becoming discredited in popular circles as well (Degler, 1991; see Chapter 2). Thus, from World War II until the late-1960s, arguments about group differences focused on environmental explanations and largely ignored biological underpinnings of intelligence.

RENEWED ARGUMENTS FOR INNATE GROUP DIFFERENCES

In 1969, arguments for biological bases of group differences in intelligence were reawakened. The rekindling spark was a lengthy article by Arthur Jensen, a professor of psychology at the University of California at Berkeley (Cronbach, 1975). The article was entitled "How Much Can We Boost IQ and Scholastic Achievement?" (Jensen, 1969).

Jensen (1969) began his article with the statement, "Compensatory education has been tried and it apparently has failed" (p. 2). The programs Jensen referred to were aimed largely at minority and poor youngsters. These programs sought to narrow the gap in achievement between minority and majority youths. IQ tests were used as a measure.

Jensen (1969) noted that evaluations of the programs revealed the IQ gap had not markedly narrowed. The reason for the programs' failure, according to Jensen, was that the programs were based on incorrect premises. The programs' designers believed differences were due to environmental factors, to "social, economic, and educational deprivation and discrimination" (p. 2). Jensen argued that the programs "failed" because they sought to raise IQ scores. These, he said, were largely genetically based. Jensen wrote:

> The current literature on the culturally disadvantaged abounds with discussion . . . of how a host of environmental factors depresses cognitive development and performance. . . . But the possible importance of genetic factors in racial behavioral differences has been greatly ignored. . . . (p. 80)

Jensen's article drew wide popular protests and was rebutted by leading scholars (e.g., Cronbach, 1969; Hunt, 1969; Kagan, 1969). A frequent critique of Jensen's article revolves around the notion of heritability (Anderson, 1992; Cronbach, 1969; Hunt, 1969; Kagan, 1969). Heritability ("h^2") is a statistic that indicates what proportion of the variance in IQ scores (or other variables, like height or shyness) *within a population* is attributable to heredity. (You can think of it here as the percent of intelligence attributable to genetics.) Because heritability is a population statistic, it does not explain what proportion of intelligence is due to heredity within an individual (see Chapter 5).

An easily confused point about heritability is that the heritability of IQ (or some other variable) calculated from one group cannot be attributed to another group. This point is well illustrated by Robert Plomin, a leading behavioral geneticist, who offers the following hypothetical example: differences *among* people in verbal ability may be largely explainable in terms of genetic differences; however, average differences *between* men and women in verbal ability may be largely due to environmental features (Plomin, 1988).

Though it is not valid to make inferences about heritability from one group to another, Jensen was prepared to take this step. He assumed that because a large proportion of the variance in Whites' IQ scores could be explained by heredity, IQ scores among minorities were also largely attributable to heredity (even though he recognized that the extent to which IQ was heritable in non-White populations had not been adequately studied). The implication was that because mean IQs in the Black population are roughly one standard deviation lower than mean IQs of Whites, genetic differences were responsible at least in part (Jensen, 1969).

Like Terman and Goddard before him, Jensen (1969) questioned the desirability of allowing low-IQ people to have children, and he expressed concern about the effect of such people on "Our National IQ" (p. 93). He called for "eugenic foresight" in devising welfare policies (p. 95). He also argued that the education of Black youngsters should emphasize memorization and rote teaching and learning, rather than abstract problem solving.

Not surprisingly, Jensen's comments met fierce criticism. In recent years, his work has steered clear of social policy. Instead, he has focused on understanding neurophysiological bases for *g* (see below and Chapter 5).

History repeats itself. In 1994, precisely a quarter century after Jensen's controversial article, psychologist Richard Herrnstein and social analyst Charles

Murray published *The Bell Curve,* a book that completely reopened the discussions that surrounded Jensen's earlier article. Drawing heavily on data from a longitudinal study of over 10,000 American youths, Herrnstein and Murray argued that the case for *g* was solid; that *g* is highly heritable; and that there is little chance to change one's IQ significantly. More provocatively, the authors maintained that group differences in IQ were a primary cause of increasing social divisions within American society. They attributed a whole raft of social conditions, ranging from poverty to out-of-wedlock children to the incidence of crime, in significant measure to the larger number of individuals of lower psychometric intelligence in the general American population. *The Bell Curve* sold more copies and generated more controversy than any recent social scientific book.

Most of the initial reactions to the Herrnstein–Murray book were negative (Fraser, 1995; Gould, 1995; Jacoby & Glauberman, 1995; Sternberg, 1995). Some critics agreed that the case for *g* is now stronger than it has been in years past; others disputed even this claim. Many critics pointed out that IQ has in fact gone up in recent years, and the IQ differences between racial and ethnic groups have been reduced. Both of these facts call into question the claims about the relative immutability of measured intelligence. Few individuals defended the Herrnstein–Murray claim that social ills are linked to psychometric intelligence; there are too many other intervening variables that influence intelligence, and too many other factors that are related to poverty and crime, for psychometric intelligence to emerge as a significant contributor.

CURRENT CONTROVERSIES INVOLVING EDUCATION

Intelligence test scores, from Binet's time on, have been widely used for placement of children in remedial education. Because minority children score lower on average on such tests, disproportionate numbers of minority children have been subject to remedial classes (Manni, Winikur, & Keller, 1984). Often, in these classes, little in the way of stimulating or challenging material is presented, and rote learning is common (Oakes, 1985).

The disproportionate representation of Black children in remedial classes has led to a number of court challenges in the United States. Perhaps the most famous of these is *Larry P. v. Wilson Riles.*[3]

Larry P. was a Black student placed in remedial education, and Riles was the state superintendent of education in California. In 1972, a California district court judge ruled that intelligence tests resulted in overrepresentation of Black students in classes for the educable mentally retarded (IQs of 55–70). He stated that these classes were not beneficial to the children and that they were not designed to help children develop skills needed to return them to regular classrooms. Furthermore, the court ruled that IQ tests were not valid for Black students, because they were normed on a White population.

---

[3] 343 F. Supp. 1306 (N.D. Cal. 1972) (preliminary injunction), *affirmed,* 502 F.2d 963 (9th Cir. 1974), *opinion issued,* No. C-71-2270 RFP (N.D. Cal. Oct. 16, 1979), 793 F.2d 969 (9th Cir. 1984).

This decision was challenged by a Black parent, Mary Amaya, in 1988. Amaya was trying to find out why her son was having learning difficulties. However, diagnosis precluded an IQ test: she was told her son could not be given an IQ test because he was Black. Along with several other Black parents, she sued California for illegally barring Blacks from being tested while allowing Whites and other minority groups to be tested. Amaya and her fellow plaintiffs were granted a preliminary injunction enabling their children to have IQ tests (Allen, 1992).

As this case and the Jensen (1969) article illustrate, the use and interpretation of intelligence testing for educational or other social policy purposes is far from a straightforward matter (see Allen, 1992; Anderson, 1992; Gardner, 1991a; Gottfredson, 1986; Jensen, 1980; Kornhaber, Krechevsky, & Gardner, 1990). This state of affairs is renown despite advances in statistical methods and test development. In part, we believe that controversies remain because, though the tests yield scores, and these scores may be reliable and valid, the interpretation of tests and their use is played out against an ever changing social and political landscape. Even if *g* measures something real, as many scientists now believe, it provides no sure guide for realizing individuals' abilities in the surrounding society.

Contemporary, Laboratory-Based Studies of Individual Differences

One of the many dilemmas associated with standardized intelligence tests is that they often measure an unclear mixture of things, from test-taking skills, to knowledge, to some possible biological substrate like *g* (Eysenck, 1986; Horn, 1989). In an effort to explore intelligence free from such confounding influences, some researchers are using laboratory tasks somewhat reminiscent of the basic psychophysical tasks first proposed by Galton. At this point, such tasks have had little impact in applied realms such as educational placement and job selection. They remain largely confined to experimental work that seeks to explore biological underpinnings of individual differences in *g*.

Reaction Time Studies

Reaction time experiments, in which subjects are asked to respond to a particular stimulus and their response time is measured, have a long history (see Chapter 2). A more complex, modern version of this technique has been advocated by Jensen (1980, 1991).

Jensen's choice reaction time experiments require a subject to sit in front of a panel on which several buttons are arranged in an evenly spaced semicircular pattern. Above each button is a small light. All are equidistant from a "home button" aligned at the center of the base of the semicircle (see Figure 3.11).

When a light goes on above one of the buttons, the subject must move his or her index finger from the home button to the button below the illuminated light.

FIGURE 3.11

Experimental equipment used by Jensen (1980) for reaction time studies. A subject keeps an index finger on the home button at the center of the base until one or more lights (crossed circles) are illuminated. The subject then moves his or her finger as quickly as possible to one of the push buttons beneath the illuminated lights.

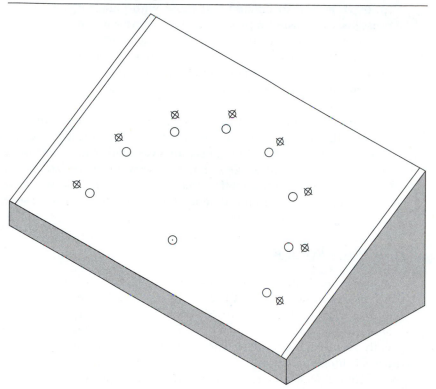

The reaction time (RT) is the time it takes for the subject to remove the finger from the home button after the light is illuminated (Jensen, 1980). This is separately measured from movement time (MT), the time it takes the subject to move the finger from the home button to the button below the light. The more lights illuminated, the greater the choice (measured in bits[4]) and the greater the complexity of the task.

Results of reaction time studies indicate a negative correlation between RT and IQ. The correlation varies (depending in part on the measures used) but

---

[4] Jensen explains a bit in the following way: A bit reduces the "amount of uncertainty of choice by one-half." No choice, i.e., one button, is measured as 0 bits of information conveyed by the stimulus. Two lights have 1 degree of uncertainty, and thus one bit; "four lights convey 2 bits, and eight lights 3 bits of information" (Jensen, 1980, p. 692).

rarely reaches beyond −.4. In other words, reaction time explains no more than 16% of the variance in IQ.

Jensen (1980) has found that the disparity in performance between lower and higher IQ groups widens as the number of bits of information increases. As he put it, "a task correlates more highly with *g* as the task's complexity is increased" (p. 695). Jensen speculated that those with higher IQs do better on the task because they are faster in processing bits of information than those with lower IQs. To Jensen, IQ and RTs are correlated because both rely on processing speed (Anderson, 1992; Jensen, 1991). Hans Eysenck, a British researcher, maintains that neural efficiency explains superior performance in such tasks. Individuals better at performing on RT tasks have less error or "noise" in the transmission of information (Eysenck, 1986).

Jensen and others have argued that choice reaction time tasks are basically culture-free and are a rather direct measure of speed in some neural activity. However, others have said the task involves motivation, control over visual search and attention, and strategies that may vary from person to person (Anderson, 1992; Ceci, 1990; Longstreth, 1986). Thus, though the tasks are less culturally loaded than traditional intelligence tests, they may not represent only neural activity, as Jensen has claimed.

Inspection Time Studies

A less complicated measure aimed at exploring individual differences in *g* involves inspection time (IT) tasks. In these tasks, subjects are presented with a simple stimulus for a very brief period of time. The typical stimulus consists of a short horizontal line with two parallel lines of different length extending vertically from each end of it. The subject must indicate which of the two vertical lines is longer.

The IT measures the shortest stimulus exposure time at which the subject performs without error. Lower ITs are correlated with higher IQs, leading to estimates of a moderate negative correlation of approximately −.5 (Anderson, 1992; Nettelbeck, 1987). That is, IT may explain about 25% of the variance in IQ.

Although IT correlates more with IQ than does RT, IT studies are subject to some of the same criticisms as RT studies. Thus, some critics claim that more than speed is involved in solving these tasks. For example, different subjects may use different approaches to solving the task (Anderson, 1992). It is also possible that the differing motivations of subjects to excel on an apparently meaningless task calls the results (and the interpretations) into question. However, the simplicity of this task, as well as research aimed at undermining the "different approach" criticism make such explanations more difficult to accept than in the case of the RT studies (see Brody, 1992). Whether speed, neural efficiency, or some other physiological cause explains the IT–IQ correlation awaits further research.

As with factor analytic studies, debates about the meaning of correlations between intelligence test scores and IT and RT may also be seen in light of historical views about intelligence. For those who follow in the biologically focused traditions of Galton and Spearman—Jensen and Eysenck are prominent among them—RTs and ITs provide persuasive evidence that basic physiological processes are at the heart of intelligence. For those who follow more in the tradition of Binet, in which reasoning and judgment are primary, findings based on responses to brief stimuli are interesting and possibly important but do not address the higher-order thinking skills that matter most to them. Among the theorists of intelligence who have attempted to synthesize these traditions are Mike Anderson, Howard Gardner, and Robert Sternberg (see also Perkins, 1995). Their work is discussed in Chapter 7.

Summary

In this chapter, we have introduced scientific and social issues related to the study of individual differences in intelligence. Regarding social issues, we have considered how early tests were used toward eugenic ends against particular groups. Consideration of the work of Terman and Jensen, as well as the *Larry P. v. Wilson Riles* case, provided some insights into controversies involving intelligence tests and educational placement. We noted that intelligence tests, however reliable and valid they are, do not alone provide answers for individuals (see Cronbach, 1990) or for the wider society.

On the scientific front, we introduced correlation, factor analysis, and test construction. We considered how various factor analysts conceptualized the structure of intellect. In addition, we looked at two intelligence tests and noted how these tests can be useful in different circumstances and for different populations. We also looked into recent research intended to explore physiologically based differences in intelligence.

We return here to questions associated with g. As we noted in the introduction to this chapter, g is regarded by many researchers to be one of psychology's most compelling discoveries. Yet, as we mentioned in the section on factor analysis, it is not clear from factor analysis whether g is a statistical artifact or something beyond this—something "real."

Some researchers continue to argue that factors extracted from mental tests merely represent correlations among intelligence tests (Kamin, 1981). However, in recent years, it has become more and more difficult to maintain that g is just a statistical jack-in-the-box popping up here or there, depending on factor rotation.

Arguments supporting g come from various sources. Psychometricians, from Spearman's time on, have argued that even without factor analysis, mental tests are positively correlated. To such researchers, this correlation indicates that mental tests measure something in common (e.g., Herrnstein & Murray, 1994; Jensen, 1993). Furthermore, IQ scores, taken to represent g, correlate with other intelligence-related measures, such as achievement test scores, years of school completed, and status of occupation.

Going beyond psychometric measures, laboratory measures reveal relationships between relatively straightforward discrimination tasks (for example, IT) and IQ. Defenders of *g* therefore argue that *g* is not only a statistic but has some neurological basis (Eysenck, 1986; Jensen, 1993a, 1993c).

In addition, the biological basis of *g* has been supported by twin studies. Even when reared apart, so that the influence of similar environment is ruled out, identical twins have very highly correlated IQ scores (see Chapter 5).

The nature of *g* is still not resolved by these arguments. Though it is reasonable to assert that *g* is not merely a statistical artifact, whether *g* reflects speed, efficiency, or some other property or combinations of properties is not yet clear. Further connections between intelligence and biology will be explored in Chapter 5. In the meantime, we turn away from the often contentious study of individual differences to consider next the ways in which the development of intelligence occurs across human beings. In the study of cognitive development, all roads lead to the eminent Swiss biologist-turned-psychologist, Jean Piaget.

Suggested Readings

Cronbach, L. (1990). *Essentials of psychological testing* (5th ed.). New York: Harper & Row.

Fancher, R. E. (1985). *The intelligence men: Makers of the IQ controversy.* New York: Norton.

Jensen, A. (1980). *Bias in mental testing.* New York: Free Press.

Sattler, J. (1992). *Assessment of children* (Rev. & Updated 3rd ed.). San Diego: Jerome M. Sattler, Publisher.

Chapter 4

The Developmental Perspective: Piaget and Beyond

Introduction

Great psychologists put forth complex and intricate theories, but they are often remembered best for a striking demonstration. The founding behaviorist, Ivan Pavlov, showed that dogs can be conditioned to salivate at the sound of a bell. The founding psychoanalyst, Sigmund Freud, demonstrated that unconscious wishes—for power, for sexual satisfaction—are reflected in ordinary dreams or slips of the tongue. And Jean Piaget (1896–1980), the most important student of intellectual development, showed that young children are not able to conserve quantities, such as liquids.

Consider a typical Piagetian demonstration (Figure 4.1). The child is presented with two identical beakers (A1, A2), each containing the same amount of liquid. The child confirms that there is the "same amount of water" in both beakers. Then, in front of the watchful eyes of the child, an experimenter pours the contents of beaker A1 into a new beaker (B), which is taller and slimmer. Naturally, the water reaches a greater height in this narrower

Jean Piaget.

FIGURE 4.1
The conservation of liquid.

The experimenter shows the child
two containers filled with equal
amounts of liquid (A1 and A2).

The experimenter then pours the
liquid from one of these containers
into a taller, thinner glass (B).

The experimenter asks the child,
"Is there more juice in this cup
(A1) or in this glass (B)?" The
child, not yet conserving liquid in
Piaget's scheme, indicates that now
there is more liquid in the taller,
thinner glass.

container. Now the crucial question. The experimenter turns to the child and says, "Is there more water in this beaker (A2) or in this beaker (B)?"[1]

For an older child—say, a child of 8 or 9 years—the answer to the question is self-evident. The 8-year-old watches the demonstration and says, "Well, there's the same amount in both, because you didn't add any or take any away." Indeed, the 8-year-old seems somewhat surprised that the question has been posed at all.

For a typical 4-year-old, however, the question elicits an entirely different response. A child this age watches the same demonstration and declares, "There's more water in this one (B)." Asked why, the child replies, "The water goes much higher here—so there has to be more."

What of the typical 5- or 6-year-old? A child that age may well puzzle over a correct answer. Initially, when asked about the amount of water, the child will think for a minute and then, echoing the 4-year-old, will point to beaker B. But the experimenter, following common Piagetian practice, then challenges the child. "Yesterday, one of your classmates was here, and pointed to this beaker (A2). She said that there was more water in it (A2) because that beaker (B) is so skinny." Now the child appears generally conflicted and may say, "I'm just not sure. That one (B) is taller, but this one (A2) is fatter."

To any adult, as to the 8-year-old, questions about conservation of liquid (technically: conservation of continuous quantities) appear trivial. After all, the crucial question is whether the amount of water has been changed, by adding or subtracting liquid. The history of pouring from one container to another is irrelevant. It was Piaget's great genius not to take this assumption for granted. Instead, working with his long-time collaborator, Bärbel Inhelder, Piaget let young children reveal that they had formulated an entirely different view of the world.

The young child—in Piaget's phrase, the "preoperational child" or, in this case, the "nonconserver"—brings an entirely different perspective to the world. For the young child, what counts is not whether water has been added or taken away. Rather, the child looks at appearances and, in particular, at the height reached by the water. If the water reaches a greater height, the child assumes that there must be more of it. Or, alternatively, if the child happens to be struck by the greater width of the original beaker, he or she may declare that there is more water in the original beaker. What is crucial is that the child lacks a sense that *the amount of liquid* remains constant, independent of the appearance of the vessel that contains it, so long as there has been no addition or subtraction of liquid.

Most of us are struck by the demonstration of nonconservation of liquids because the finding is counter-intuitive. Piaget presented many such surprises. Young children prove incapable of conservation, period. In conservation of substance studies, young children will look at two identical balls of clay. Then, the experimenter will take one ball and squash it into a pancake shape. This action has no effect on the response of the conserver, who once again asserts that the

---

[1] In actual studies with children, experimenters typically point or use concrete names, like "the one over there."

pancake has the "same amount of clay" as the ball did. But the nonconserver, struck by the greater area of the pancake form, is likely to declare that it has "more clay" than the original ball.

Conservation of number presents a similar pattern. In the classic form of the experiment, the child observes two arrays of six beads each. The beads are carefully aligned in one-to-one correspondence of one row with the other. The child confirms that the same number of beads appears in each array. Then the experimenter places the beads in array 2 much farther apart than in array 1 (or, in a variant, the beads in array 2 are placed touching each other). By now, the results of the experiment should be predictable. The conserver is unaffected by the appearance of the arrays ("It's the same, of course. You didn't add or take away any beads.") But the nonconserver, struck by the appearance of array 2, responds that there are now more beads in array 2, because the array's physical expanse is so much greater.

Among nonpsychologists, Piaget is most famous for these striking demonstrations of the differences between the minds of the young child and the older child. The conservations function like Pavlov's salivating dogs or Freud's symbol-filled dreamers. But in the world of psychology, Piaget stands out because he was the foremost student of children's thinking in our time. Not only did Piaget understand children's minds in a far more sophisticated way than did his predecessors, but he also put forth a picture of the developing child—a set of terms, an overall framework, and a series of stages that outlined the development of the child's mind from infancy through adolescence.

Because Piaget is the most important student of children's thinking—of children's intelligence—it is appropriate that we begin our survey of the development of intelligence with a review of Piaget's work. However, although the study of children's minds essentially began with Piaget's research, it certainly has not ended there. Therefore, after introducing Piaget's principal ideas, we offer a critique of his approach. Then, later in this chapter, we examine several of the most important lines of thought that have grown up in the aftermath of Piaget's contributions. Some later theorists have been frankly critical of the Piagetian approach; others, the so-called neo-Piagetians build on Piaget's approach; and a few recent researchers have attempted to synthesize the most robust features of both the Piagetian and the non-Piagetian approaches.

Piaget: The Man and the Methods

As an adult, Piaget studied the minds of ordinary children; as a child, he was himself a prodigy. Like many precocious young scientists, Piaget began with a strong interest in the natural world. His first paper, published when he was 11 years old, was a description of an albino sparrow that he had spied in his native Switzerland. Moving quickly through school, Piaget was 22 when he attained his doctoral degree in biology. By then, he had published many articles and even a novel. He thought that he would spend his life as a biologist, specializing in how living organisms gain knowledge of the external world. He hoped to one day write a *magnum opus* on the topic of "Biology and Knowledge" (1967/1974).

Gifted young scholars often undertake postdoctoral studies. Piaget became convinced that, as a budding student of knowledge, he ought to learn something about the nature of intelligence. With that intent, he went to Paris to work in the laboratory of Théodore Simon, who had developed the first intelligence tests with the famous Alfred Binet. Piaget's job was to help standardize tests so that one could know how a given child compared to his or her age-mates. While recording right and wrong answers, however, Piaget had a crucial insight. It was important to know whether a child got the right answer, but it was far more revealing to know *how* the child reasoned.

Suppose, for example, a child was told the comparative heights of three individuals, and was asked which was the tallest. (A sample problem: If Beth is taller than Alice, and Beth is shorter than Fran, who is the tallest?) It was useful to know that a child might give the answer, "Beth," but it was even more important to know *why* the child gave that answer. If, in conservation-of-number tasks, a child points to the dispersed array as more numerous, what does that tell about the mind of the child?

As Piaget liked to relate, he was a student of biology and knowledge who took a brief detour to look at what was known about the development of intelligence in children. That detour, he would admit, lasted a lifetime. Not until 1967, when Piaget was 71 years old, did he actually publish his major book on *Biology and Knowledge*. In the meantime, he had fundamentally altered our understanding of how children think, and, indeed, of what thinking is all about.

Piaget felt comfortable talking about his work as the study of intelligence. Several books he authored use the term "intelligence" in the title. It is important to stress, therefore, that Piaget used the term in a somewhat different sense than is common among other scientists. For most of the individuals whose work is reviewed in this book, intelligence is a comparative term, and the study of intelligence is a study of *differences in intelligence.* As a scientist, however, Piaget, was fundamentally uninterested in the differences among human beings (though, of course, he recognized that they exist). Instead, he was interested in the principles of mental development that obtained across *all normal human beings.* For him, intelligence was a property of the species—just like language or depth perception or, for that matter, puberty. One should study intelligence in a way analogous to the way that one would study any universal property of humankind.

Piaget brought to the study of children the same methods of the naturalist that he had learned as a young biologist. He watched children—his own children, the children of his native Switzerland, the children enrolled in the school at the institute that he directed—and he described what they did and, by inference, how they were thinking. He then developed more general models about the nature of thought and intelligence.

Sensitive adults have long observed children, and, since the time of Charles Darwin, scientifically oriented adults have kept careful "baby biographies" in which they chronicled the milestones of their own and other children. Piaget differed from other observers of his time in two fundamental respects.

First, he conjured up many interesting problems and puzzles for children to tackle. Thus, watching his infants, he hid an enticing object under a pillow, then moved the pillow to a new location. He waited to see whether—and if so, where—the infants searched for the desired object. Or, working with somewhat older children, he asked them who was more at fault: a child who broke a single dish while stealing a cookie; or a child who broke a stack of dishes while trying to help his mother clean the kitchen.

Second, Piaget conceived of these puzzles and problems in terms of broader scientific and theoretical issues. When hiding the objects and then moving them, he was not just playing "hide and seek": he was trying to determine the child's understanding of what an *object* is, and whether an object continues to exist even when it is out of sight. When asking children about fault and blame, he was trying to tease out the factor of *intentionality*: at which point does a child begin to take into account the *motivation* of an actor, as opposed to the sheer *consequences* of an action that has been carried out?

In formulating these studies, Piaget developed a *clinical method* that has become very influential. In earlier studies, investigators either had treated every child in an identical fashion, no matter how the child reacted, or, committing the opposite sin, had "led" the child to a desired answer. Piaget sought to avoid these perils. He took the child's interests and reactions seriously and tried to be responsive to them; at the same time, he took scrupulous care not to push the child's behavior or response in one or another direction. As indicated earlier, he would even challenge a child's answer, just to see how firmly the child would stick to the first response. Because of his skill at clinical interviewing, Piaget was able to discover what was really on the child's mind, thereby going beyond the expectations of the adult experimenter or theorist.

Storming the Piagetian Fortress

It would have been optimal if the most important theorist of children's intelligence had developed a vocabulary and a framework that were easy to describe and remember. But, although he was a brilliant observer and a deep thinker, Piaget was not a particularly clear expositor of his ideas; his books do not make easy reading. Moreover, his entire theoretical edifice is far too complex to summarize here. (For fuller treatments, see Gardner, 1981; Ginsburg & Opper, 1988; Piaget, 1983.) Still, before turning to Piaget's actual claims about the stages of children's development, it is important to introduce some of his most important concepts. This section represents a modest attempt to break through the thicket of terminology and the fortress of frameworks erected by Piaget over a 60-year period of research.

Every psychological theorist has certain building blocks. Pavlov spoke of conditioned reflexes; Freud recognized unconscious wishes. Piaget's favorite units or elements were "schemes" and "operations." He referred to any organized pattern of behavior as a scheme. For example, all infants have schemes of sucking; they suck all manner of objects, ranging from nipples to fingers to toys, that are introduced into their mouths. Individuals of all ages have numerous schemes. Presumably, as you are reading these words, you are currently employing schemes of reading, note taking, underlining, finger tapping, yawning, grinning, and the like. Human beings combine schemes in various ways to attain various goals; for example, you may read, underline, and rehearse the material in this chapter so that you will be able to answer a question in class or on an examination.

Piaget was not interested in the accidental properties of a particular scheme as it happened to be enacted on a particular occasion. He was interested in the underlying structures of schemes—their core properties and organization, stripped of specific enactments. Piaget therefore concentrated on what is common to all variants of a particular scheme, or the processes common to all instances of a scheme-in-action—for example, to *all* sucks of the nipple, or to *all* underlinings of key words. These schemes, in turn, combine to yield "structures of knowledge." The child comes to know the world better over the years as the result of the *differentiation of schemes* (the various patterns by which one can ingest liquid and food become gradually differentiated from one another) and the *integration of schemes* (the various schemes, like sucking and looking, come to work together with increasing smoothness and flexibility).

Piaget recognized the existence of schemes throughout life, but he used the term "operation" to characterize the most important structures of knowledge in later life. In infancy and early childhood, schemes are enacted in the visible physical world. Later on, children do not have to carry out actions publicly; they can carry them out privately, implicitly, in the confines of their own minds. These "internalized" or "interiorized" actions are called operations.

As an example, in figuring out how many objects are in an array, and which of a pair of arrays is more numerous, a child can use the scheme of counting. But the child can also carry out mental operations in which he or she can reverse an action—for example, pushing a widely dispersed array back closely together once again, or pouring the water from the taller, thinner beaker back into the original, squatter one. Like schemes, operations can be thought of without reference to the particular objects involved. The operation of placing two arrays of objects in one-to-one correspondence, or the operation of returning continuous quantities to an original container represents universal mental operations. They can be carried out with reference to clay balls, water jars, or even an abstract entity named "Z."

Building on his work as a biologist, in which he was intent on describing how organisms operate, Piaget developed a vocabulary that describes the use of schemes, operations, and other structures of knowledge. He termed the key processes "assimilation" and "accommodation." As Piaget described it, any activation of a scheme inevitably involves both assimilation and accommodation. In assimilation, the accent falls on treating the external world so that it fits into the already existing schemes; in accommodation, the accent falls on the organism's modifying its schemes so that it conforms to the external world.

Let's make these terms more palpable. The infant sucks nearly every object that is placed in or near its mouth. Sometimes, the child treats every object—independent of size, shape, taste—as if it were identical, using the same mouth and tongue movements. In this case, the processes of assimilation predominate, and diverse objects are forced into preexisting schemes. At other times, the child modifies the sucking scheme, so that it is appropriate for the particular contours of an object; thus, the child sucks smoothly and rapidly when drinking milk but sucks irregularly and slowly when exploring a rattle. In the latter activities, the child is accommodating to the properties of specific objects in the external world.

The same pair of processes is invoked in all cases where the child is exploring or coming to know the world. In the experiment of conservation of liquids, for example, the nonconserver assimilates the taller, thinner beaker (B) to earlier experiences, where amount has been linked to perceived height. The scheme—"in determining quantity, attend to height"—has dominated this encounter. However, with some prompting, the child might come to realize that the failure to add or subtract quantity is relevant to the situation; in that case, the child is accommodating to the particular facts of the current situation and may modify his or her response accordingly.

As noted, all experiences contain aspects of assimilation and accommodation. They differ primarily in terms of which process is dominant. In play, for example, assimilation dominates: the child treats objects not in terms of their actual features but as occasions for exercising favored schemes, like tossing or squeezing. In imitation, accommodation dominates: the child suppresses favored schemes of the moment in order to reproduce some element of the external world.

Piaget looked with favor on occasions where assimilation and accommodation are roughly in equilibrium: the child both honors current ways of behaving and takes into account the particular facts of an occasion without surrendering to them. But Piaget also recognized value in disequilibrium, or what he called *disequilibration*. When schemes are not in accord with one another, when the balance between assimilation and accommodation is in disarray, cognitive progress is likely to occur. Suppose a child thinks that an object always remains in its original locus, but then no longer finds it there (because it has been hidden). This disequilibrium would stimulate the child to revise his or her notion of the behavior of objects. Or, suppose a child thinks that there is now more liquid in beaker B, but finds that, when the water is poured back into A2, it is exactly at the same height as in A1. The resultant disequilibrium might result in the child's becoming a conserver of liquids.

Piaget's terms—accommodation, assimilation, and equilibrium—provide a convenient and powerful way of describing all of human knowing, from the infant's exploration of objects in a crib to the theorist's evaluation of alternative hypotheses. In that one sentence, we summarize the strength and the weakness of Piaget's terminological fortress. Its strength is that a great variety of behaviors can be "assimilated" to the same terminological and analytic framework. Its weakness is that it is so general that the particular, idiosyncratic occasions of knowing may not be well accommodated by this overly inclusive vocabulary.

The Four Stages of Development

In medieval paintings, children are typically depicted as if they are small adults (Ariès, 1962). That is, the ratios between their heads and various parts of their bodies resemble the ratios observed in adults; the child is simply smaller. According to Piaget, most previous researchers had seen children as small adults. Children were acknowledged to be shorter and to have less information, but, fundamentally, their thought processes were assumed to be the same as those of adults.

Piaget changed this view of children for all time. According to Piaget, infants were born without substantive knowledge but with definite means for coming to know the world. Their initial schemes of sucking, listening, and looking, and the fundamental processes of assimilation and accommodation, were the building blocks on which children constructed their knowledge. The image of construction was crucial for Piaget. Children never simply imitated others; they were always seeking to make sense of the world, through trying out schemes, combining them in various ways, constructing miniature theories of the world, and seeing the ways in which the theories were or were not adequate.

All together, Piaget's studies yielded a clear-cut picture of the child. The child is a problem solver, constantly testing strategies and experimenting in an attempt to make sense of the world. A certain model of the world emerges and is then revised as a result of further experimentation, with its attendant feedback. For Piaget, the young child resembled what Piaget himself was like in his youth—a kind of scientist-in-knickers.

Piaget devoted many years to observing children, posing problems for children to solve, and noting their behaviors and explanations. From his enormous collection of research, he developed accounts of the steps that children passed through, first in infancy and then in later childhood. These accounts were supported by two contrasting scholarly disciplines and looked in two directions: toward biological sources of behavior, and toward logical (algebra-style) descriptions of how this behavior was structured. As a result of this work, Piaget proposed that children passed through four major stages of intellectual development. This portrait, much investigated and much critiqued, remains the most ambitious effort to date to describe the growth of intelligence in all children. Against this effort, all subsequent work has come to be judged.

Stage 1:   The Sensory-Motor Stage

In this stage (Piaget, 1952b), the task of the infant is to come to know the physical world and the social world through the use of sensory systems (primarily, vision and audition) and the use of motor systems (primarily, the use of hand and mouth to explore the world). The chief objects of the physical world are food and toys; the chief objects of the social world are caretakers, particularly parents. Piaget's description of infancy relies heavily on descriptions of what children do in these encounters and explorations. But, as a philosophically oriented investigator, Piaget is never content just to describe sucking or looking for toys.

Rather, he portrays the child's intellectual growth in terms of an understanding of objects and time, space, and causality.

Piaget saw infancy as divided, roughly, into six substages. The shift from one substage to the next is subtle, but by the time all six have passed, the child has become an entirely different kind of mental creature, and is thinking about the world in fundamentally different ways. Let's consider these substages briefly.

SUBSTAGE 1: USES OF REFLEXES

The newborn is a collection of basic reflexes, such as sucking, swallowing, crying, making gross bodily motions, and the like. At first, these actions are performed in completely instinctual fashion. But after the first few weeks of life, the child begins to accommodate to the features of particular objects and sights; he or she is no longer assimilating everything to the same precise scheme.

SUBSTAGE 2: ACQUIRED ADAPTATIONS AND PRIMARY CIRCULAR REACTIONS

The second stage begins when the child is able to coordinate two behavioral patterns, such as bringing a hand up to the mouth during sucking. When the child constantly repeats a behavioral pattern so that it becomes smoothed and mastered, the child is exhibiting a primary circular reaction. An infant of two months will systematically grasp a sheet and let it go, grasp a sheet and let it go, until the set of movements has achieved autonomy and flexibility.

SUBSTAGE 3: PROCEDURES TO MAKE INTERESTING SIGHTS LAST

During the middle of the first year of life, the child becomes capable of secondary circular reactions. Instead of being practiced for their own sake, the circular reactions are executed for specific goals, such as the maintenance of a desired display. After an adult drums on a cushion in an enticing manner, for example, a child will continue to arch its head and shake its arm in a certain way. While the head-arching and arm-shaking do not themselves produce the drumming motion, the child is using all available procedures in order to achieve, in almost magical style, a desired goal.

SUBSTAGE 4: COORDINATION OF SECONDARY ACTIONS

Toward the end of the first year of life, the child enters an enigmatic new stage. For the first time, a child is not restricted to repeating an action in order to gain a goal; rather, the child can combine schemes (coordinate secondary circular reactions) in an effort to obtain a new goal. For example, when the child is presented with a bell placed on a cushion, the child first strikes the cushion, repeating the activity done before. Then, the child is able to carry out a new action—depressing the cushion with one hand while grasping the bell with the other hand—in order to obtain the goal.

At this time, the child also reveals an incomplete understanding of the concept of an object. If an object has been hidden at location A, the child learns to look for it there. Then, in front of the child, the experimenter moves the object to location B and hides it there. Despite witnessing this movement of the object to a new location, the child returns to search at location A. The existence of the object cannot yet be dissociated from its customary location.

SUBSTAGE 5: TERTIARY CIRCULAR REACTIONS—NEW MEANS THROUGH EXPERIMENTATION

In the fifth stage, the child is not only able to combine schemes but can actually solve problems. It develops new means through active experimentation. At age 14 months, Piaget's daughter Jacqueline found that a certain movement of her fingers led to a tilting of a box. She then varied the conditions of the movement, keeping track of her discoveries, until she arrived at an effective way of tilting the box. In this activity, the child no longer relies on familiar schemes; rather, drawing on all of the actions in its repertoire, the child attempts to devise a solution adequate to the demands of the new situation.

SUBSTAGE 6: INVENTION OF NEW MEANS THROUGH MENTAL COMBINATION

Toward the latter part of the second year of life, the child reaches the high point of sensory-motor intelligence and begins the transition to the second major stage of cognitive development. The substage 6 child is able for the first time to devise means for solving problems through internal or mental combinations. Rather than having to try out steps overtly, the child will pause and appear to consider alternatives via an inner exploration of ways and means. When she was 20 months old, Jacqueline Piaget found herself at a closed door with a blade of grass in each hand. Earlier, she might have been stymied or simply dropped the grass. Instead, after some moments of thought, she placed the blades of grass in a way that would allow her to retrieve them after she had passed through the door.

By the end of the first major period of intelligence—the sensory-motor stage—the child's reaction to hidden objects is entirely different. Not only does he or she go immediately to location B, after seeing an object being hidden there, but even more impressively, the child can imagine the trajectory of an object after it has been hidden from sight, and can compute its likely location. The child clearly has gained a full-blown sense of objects. Rather than linking objects to particular sites, or believing that an object out of sight no longer exists, the child has a theory that objects continue to exist and have their own locations and trajectories, regardless of whether one is able to observe them.

A child traverses an enormous mental landscape in less than two years. Once a bundle of reflexes with little flexibility, the child gains the ability to solve problems not just through exploration of schemes but even through mentally imagining what might be done under various circumstances. No one has taught the child this knowledge; rather, it has been built up, step-by-step, as a result of constantly experimenting with schemes and scrupulously observing the consequences of different experiments. In the process, says Piaget, the child has built up the staples of the physical world: an appreciation of the way in which objects exist and of the nature of spatial and temporal constraints. In addition, although this sphere was of lesser interest to Piaget, the child has built up knowledge of the social world. The 2-year-old understands that humans continue to exist even when they are absent from the scene. He or she becomes sad when a parent leaves the scene, but there is now full expectation of the parent's return.

Stage 2: The Semiotic (Symbolic) Stage and the Preoperational Child

Like other observers of children, Piaget noted that the child of 2, 3, 4, or 5 years inhabits a world quite different from that of the infant. Not only can the child walk, run, and jump; far more important from an intellectual point of view, the child is able to talk and to use other kinds of symbols, such as drawings, gestures, or numbers, in order to refer to and make sense of the world.

To capture these important milestones, Piaget designated a stage in early childhood as the semiotic or symbolic stage. The child is now capable of representational thought; he or she can use words, pictures, and other kinds of symbols, mentally or in the world, to refer to entities that exist in the world. Moreover, in Piaget's view, a whole ensemble of capacities grows out of this ability to represent—to use one thing to stand for another. Piaget saw that the playing child could use a stick to refer to a horse; the talking child could give a name to that stick-horse; the dreaming child could conjure up experiences in his or her imagination; the imitating child could use a present or even an absent model as a way of stimulating his or her own behavior. The activities that children used to do overtly could now be done inside their minds; an image was a kind of deferred imitation that could be performed in the theater of the mind's eye.

To speak of a symbol-using child is to speak of the 3- or 4-year-old in a positive way. Piaget was keenly aware of the many things that a child of this age can still not accomplish. Recall that because the young child is not able to carry out important mental operations, he or she is unable to conserve liquids, or substance, or number. In Piaget's view, the preoperational child was dominated by the physical appearances of displays; faced with the denser array or the taller beaker, the child assumed that it contained more entities. The child could not reason about the relation between dimensions—height and width, density and spareness. More crucially, the child was not able to perform a mental operation (like pouring the water back, or rearranging the objects in the array) in order to appreciate the fundamentally unchanged nature of the amount.

In a famous characterization, Piaget described the preoperational child as being "egocentric." By this he meant not that the child was conceited but rather that the child was able to apprehend a situation only from his or her point of view. In the classic Piagetian demonstration of egocentrism, a child is seated at a table in front of a model of three mountains, each painted a different color and otherwise distinctive in appearance. The child is asked how the model would look to a person or doll seated at a different spot, elsewhere at the table, and (as a result) apprehending the model of the mountains from a different angle. Typically, the child is presented with three photos or sketches and asked to match each with the perspective of a viewer seated at another point around the table.

Children younger than 6 or 7 years characteristically select a picture that represents precisely the same view that they see. Their own perspective is simply universalized. But children of 8 or 9 years find this problem no more difficult than the conservation tasks. They are able to place themselves in the eyes of another, to "decenter" from their own perspective, and to anticipate how the same scene would appear to individuals who could behold the three-mountain display from a variety of vantage points.

Stage 3:   Concrete Operations

Shortly after beginning regular school, children become capable of operational thinking. They can perform mental operations in their heads, and then undo these operations, again working in their heads. Lest one conclude that operational thinking is a consequence of school, however, consider the opposite possibility. Perhaps school begins, the world over, around the age of 6 or 7 precisely because children are no longer tied to their physical activities or to simple forms of symbolic reference, but can now consider the implications of actions without having to carry them out. This, indeed, is what Piaget maintains.

We have already encountered the operational child in the descriptions of those who succeed at conservation tasks. Although the responses of the preoperational child are virtually dictated by the physical appearance of the arrays, the operational child brings to bear a fundamentally different frame of mind: he or she observes the manipulation by the experimenter but realizes that the manipulation itself does not affect quantity. The reason that the child recognizes this is because he or she is able to perform mentally a compensatory or "reversing" mental operation; the child knows that if the liquid were poured back or the beads were reassembled into their original configuration, the amounts would not have changed. By the same token, the operational child is not tied to his or her own view of the mountain. Mentally, the child is able to transport himself or herself to the vantage point of another person and to see how the world looks through that person's eyes.

Piaget uses the plural ("concrete operations") because the child becomes capable of a *set* of operations at this time. We have witnessed the operation of "reversibility" (pouring the liquid back) and the operation of "decentering" (moving to someone else's position). One other example—typically called "class inclusion"—also illustrates operations at work. A preoperational child is shown 7 beads;

5 are white and 2 are black. Asked whether there are more "white beads" or more "beads," the child will insist that there are more white beads because there are only two black ones. The child will resist the necessary comparison of the whole set of beads, including black and white, with one subset of beads, all white.

What is going on here? According to Piaget, the preoperational child is unable to maintain a simultaneous awareness of a whole and a part. The preoperational child can compare white beads with black beads if both kinds are visible, because this task involves merely a perceptual discrimination. However, the same child cannot compare the class of all beads with the class of white beads because it is impossible to compare a set *physically* with its subset. Two groups, one consisting of all the beads, the other of all the white beads, cannot be conceived simultaneously because the white beads would have to belong to two groups and hence be in both places at the same time. For such a comparison to be executed, a mental operation is required. And so, the analysis runs, the child is compelled to reinterpret the question as a comparison of black and white beads and come up with the wrong answer. But the operational child is able to create groups mentally, and, under these circumstances, a comparison of white beads and all beads poses no problem at all.

Stage 4: Formal Operations

Just as concrete operations coincide roughly with the onset of formal schooling, formal operations coincide roughly with the onset of secondary schooling. The formal operational child is able to think comfortably about a hypothetical world, a world that is constructed not by objects but by propositions or theories and the statements that comprise them. The concrete operational child is comfortable solving problems mentally, but these problems deal with concrete entities, like balls of clay or the perspective of paper maché mountains. The formal operational child—or, more properly, youth—is comfortable thinking about a world that is made up of thoughts, ideas, and concepts.

The reading that you are doing is a typical formal operational undertaking. You are reading about the claims that Piaget is making—for example, that intellectual development consists of four major stages. Later, you will have to compare that theory with others that question the appropriateness of stage analyses. There are no physical stages in the world to measure, or reverse, or imagine; these are theoretical constructs to be debated, and this enterprise can only be meaningfully joined by formal operational thinkers.

It is not difficult to get a mental image of the formal operator. He or she is comfortable in a scientific laboratory. Indeed, most of Piaget's examples of formal operational tasks come from the physics or chemistry laboratory. In scientific experiments, a theorist lays out a hypothesis—for example, what causes the period of a pendulum, or what causes a substance to change color under certain conditions, or what causes a billiard ball to bounce at the angle that it does. Various experiments are then carried out to see which theoretical explanation is the most adequate. Any child older than a toddler can try out various experiments. What distinguishes the formal thinker is his or her ability to figure out which variables are crucial and which ones are not. This kind of thinking can be done only if one can create propositions (the change in color is caused by factors A and B, while C, D, and E are irrelevant) and then systematically vary factors to see whether the proposition is in fact correct or whether it has to be altered in some way.

A famous demonstration devised by Bärbel Inhelder and Jean Piaget gives a feeling for the development of formal operational thinking. In the balance-scale problem (Figure 4.2), the child is provided with a lever or balance scale, consisting of a fulcrum and a beam (see Gardner, 1982). In one variant of this problem, 8 pegs are arrayed, equally spaced apart, with 4 on each side of the fulcrum. Five equal weights are on the balance. Three are on the right side of the scale, all on the third peg away from the fulcrum, and 2 are on the left side of the scale, both on the fourth peg from the fulcrum. The question is: Which way will the scale tilt?

The typical preoperational child does not know what to make of this task. He or she would like to play with the scale to see what happens. But the child's response will be tied to the particular dimension on which he or she happens to alight. If the child notes that there are more weights on the right side of the scale, he or she will say the right side will tilt; if the child notes, instead, that the weights on the left side of the scale are farther from the fulcrum, he or she will say that the left side will tilt. If either prediction turns out to be wrong, the child will just shrug and will offer no further possibilities.

Given the same problem, the typical concrete operational child is in a quandary. The child knows that two variables are relevant to the problem: (1) the number of objects and (2) the distance from the fulcrum. Moreover, the child has a rough-and-ready sense that the two variables pull in opposite directions. Mentally, he or she knows that if the two weights are placed farther from the fulcrum, they will "carry more weight." But the child is not able to figure out the relationship between these two variables either mentally or through experimentation. Whenever the variables of weight and distance point in opposite directions (as they do in this problem), the child is stuck.

FIGURE 4.2
The balance scale problem.

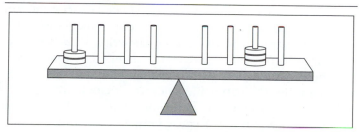

The formal operational child is also aware that the two variables are in conflict with one another. Unlike the concrete operational child, however, he or she is able to go beyond this simple appreciation of the relevant variables. The child can develop a theory about the relative contribution of number (one more or one fewer weight on a peg) and distance from the fulcrum (one unit away, two units away); and, equally importantly, the child can then proceed to test this theory. By varying the "weights" of these variables one at a time, the child gradually comes up with a solution. Moreover, the solution not only pertains to this particular array of weights and distances, but can also be used to predict the results of any configuration of weights and distances. In the logic-based terms of formal operations, the child has appreciated compensation (weight compensates for distance), inverse relations (the connection between adding a weight and removing a weight), and the connections between the operations of compensation and inverse relations. (Piaget typically states the understanding in terms of a logical calculus.) This integrated theoretical framework allows an individual to appreciate scientific theories, whether they obtain to balance beams or to the development of children's cognition.

Piaget's theoretical edifice is quite magnificent. It extends from the first concrete movements of the infant to the most sophisticated moves of the theory-oriented adolescent. It stipulates that all children pass through the same sequence of stages in the same order, and that each later stage subsumes crucial features of the earlier stages. It covers the territory of three separate disciplines: (1) psychology (the thinking process of the child), (2) biology (the underlying processes of assimilation, accommodation, and equilibrium), and (3) logic (the logical structures that are presumed to underlie the thinking of the child). It encompasses fascinating empirical demonstrations, such as the emerging object sense of the infant and the conservation problems of the young child, and it puts forth a powerful set of theoretical statements about ways in which the child differs from the adult, and the universal set of stages that allow one to advance from one status to the next.

Piaget's Theory: Some Critical Perspectives

Any ambitious theory will surely gain attention and, ultimately, criticism, and Piaget's theory has had more than its share of both (see Brainerd, 1978; Piattelli-Palmarini, 1980). Most of Piaget's basic demonstrations have been replicated, so long as the conditions of the original experiments were rigorously followed; but almost everything else that Piaget has written has been challenged, and much of the magnificent edifice has been dismantled by the succeeding generation of researchers. It should be added, right away, that nearly all scientific theories have a brief half-life; the better the scientific theory, the more research it stimulates, and the new research generated almost always shakes many of the initial claims. Piaget is important not because he got it all right, but because he was the first person to portray children's intellectual development in detail and because people continue to address the questions that Piaget himself first raised.

Each of the emphases that Piaget introduced has been questioned. Piaget sees the child as a scientist who solves problems that are posed; but some researchers feel that "scientist" is not the best way, or the only way, to think of children's thought. After all, only a few cultures have developed science, and yet, all over the world, children surely think. Perhaps the artist or the politician or the salesperson constitutes a better model of the human mind.

Others feel that Piaget is too much in awe of neighboring disciplines. They feel that his biological terminology does not really add anything to his analyses, and that the claims for underlying logical structures (such as reversibility or compensation) cannot be sustained. Indeed, it is fair to say that succeeding researchers have taken Piaget's stage claims and his empirical demonstrations very seriously, but almost no one outside his immediate circle has continued to use the biological and logical lenses on which he himself was so dependent.

Piaget's view of intelligence is limited in other ways. As far as he was concerned, intellectual development stops at adolescence. Various researchers have suggested that there may be stages beyond formal operations (Arlin, 1984, 1989; Demetriou, 1990; Getzels & Jackson, 1972; Labouvie-Vief, 1990; Richards & Commons, 1984). Perhaps adults are capable of finding new problems (as well as solving old ones), of conceptualizing theories on their own, of systematizing or synthesizing knowledge, of appreciating relativity or irony in ways that most adolescents are not. Highly creative individuals need to master a domain—a task that takes upward of a decade (Gardner, 1993; Gruber, 1984; Hayes, 1985). No wonder there are almost no creative geniuses among teenagers!

Piaget was interested in intelligence as it was observed in all human beings; he focused on the universals of the mind. For this reason, he understandably neglected two facets: (1) the differences among individuals within a culture and (2) the differences across cultures. But the question can be raised: Is there such a thing as the "pure" or the "universal" mind? Perhaps each culture features its own areas of thinking and its own forms of thinking (see Chapter 1), and the search for the universal is therefore misguided, or at least inadequate. By the same token, although all individuals may attain the object concept or conservation, this fact precisely makes these demonstrations of little interest. Many scientists, including most of those represented in this book, feel that the important questions about intelligence have to do with the *differences* among human beings, and Piaget had almost nothing to say about them.

Piaget also ignored the question of how to make individuals more intelligent or how to speed their cognitive development. Indeed, Piaget did not like this question, terming it the "American Question" because he was so often asked about training and acceleration on visits to the United States. Piaget felt development takes place at its own optimal rate; it is at best unproductive and at worst dangerous to challenge that rate. Piaget was skeptical that development could actually be accelerated. One might cajole a nonconserver into giving a conservation response;

but as soon as one stopped giving hints, or introduced another kind of conservation problem, the child's genuine nonconserving persona would again come to the fore.

Piaget was essentially uninterested in the questions of context. He did not think that it mattered whether a child was raised in the wilds of Africa or the cities of Europe, nor even whether the child attended school. Development might occur a bit more slowly in the latter case, but eventually the species characteristics would emerge in the predictable order. Moreover, the particular materials that one used were not important: conservation was conservation whether one looked at water, clay, or beads. However, a whole school of intelligence has developed, focusing on the importance of context—the culture in which one lives, the values of one's family, the nature and kind of schooling one receives, the particular objects and environments that one encounters (Ceci, 1990; Cole & Scribner, 1974; Resnick, 1991; Rogoff, 1990). We touched on such issues in Chapter 1 and we will return to them in Chapters 7 and 8.

The most severe challenge has been mounted against the most central claims in Piaget's framework. Scientists now question Piaget's claims that there are four stages through which all children pass. The most extreme critics wonder whether the designation of stages makes sense at all. Perhaps development is far smoother, with few if any qualitative shifts along the way.

Equally strong challenges have been directed against the claim that specific cognitive operations exist and can be activated irrespective of the nature of the content toward which they are directed. A mild version of this critique claims that children will appear more or less precocious, depending on the kinds of content and the problems that are posed. A strong version of this critique suggests that there may not be a single intelligence, rooted in logical-mathematical structures. Rather, human beings are capable of a number of different kinds of intellectual operations, using diverse content like music, language, or spatial information. The portrait of one kind of intelligence may bear little resemblance to the portrait of other kinds, including the logical-mathematical variety that proved of particular interest to Piaget (Gardner, 1993b).

Powerful Challenges

Piaget would have gained neither attention nor criticism had it not been for the compelling nature of the particular demonstrations that he carried out with children. As noted, his precise operationalizations have proved robust; when people do just what Piaget did with children, they obtain his results. However—and this has proved most damaging to the Piagetian enterprise—when one begins (in the manner of a good formal operator) to vary some of the factors of the experiments, a different picture of development emerges.

Consider what has happened when other scholars have looked at the following Piagetian phenomena but have approached them in other ways.

THE OBJECT CONCEPT

As early as 3 months after birth, infants register surprise when an object disappears behind a screen and comes out in a different form. They are surprised when an object appears to pass through a wall. They understand that objects undergo continuous motion, and that two objects cannot occupy the same space at the same time. They have expectations that objects have solidity, unity, and clear boundaries, and that they retain the same appearance even when they are removed from sight (Baillargeon, 1987; Carey & Spelke, 1994; Leslie, 1988). By 7 or 8 months after birth, infants are capable of appreciating that an object has moved to a new location, so long as they do not have to remember that location. It appears that the child's lack in sensory-motor substage 4 (p. 106) is in the area of memory rather than in an object sense. Moreover, the child's growing appreciation of a sense of object appears to depend on the maturation of certain structures in the prefrontal cortex, and not on the history of prior explorations and experiments in earlier substages (Diamond, 1991).

CONSERVATION OF NUMBER

Some years ago, Gelman and Gallistel (1978) showed that youngsters as young as 2 or 3 years are able to appreciate conservation of number. They exhibit their full powers when participating in a magic game. A magician either shifts the orientation of an array without changing the number of elements, or surreptitiously adds or deletes an item from an array. A youngster playing the game wins a prize if he or she can indicate which array has more items, even when the arrangement of the items has been altered. Nearly all toddlers succeed at this game.

Building on the Gelman paradigm, Wynn (1992) has shown that even infants can appreciate the difference between small numbers, like 3 and 4 (see also Starkey, Spelke, & Gelman, 1990). Infants are habituated to an array that has a certain number of elements. As in the Gelman magic paradigm, the infants pay little attention when the items in the

Rochel Gelman.

array have been rearranged spatially, but they register surprise when an item has been added or deleted. The basic operations of conservation of number are clearly available well before the beginning of the school years. The greater difficulty experienced by children on the classical Piagetian paradigm seems to stem from the wording of the questions ("Which has more now?") and from the peculiarities of the actions of spreading out or scrunching together.

EGOCENTRISM

After Piaget published his initial studies, it was thought that preschoolers could not assume the perspective of another individual. This claim has been greatly modified by subsequent researchers. Children as young as 2 years will reorient displays when they are showing them to others, clearly indicating that these children know that the displays will not look the same to other persons. The "three-mountain problem" has been shown to be alien to children. When children are asked to hide a ball so that a police officer cannot see it, they can do so well before school age (Donaldson, 1978). And when familiar figures like Grover (from "Sesame Street") are used, once again youngsters appear nonegocentric. As early as 3 or 4 years, they can tell how a scene will look to Grover at different points on a railroad trip (Borke, 1978). Maybe Piaget and his associates were egocentric in selecting a task and a set of conditions (difficult-to-read photographs) that fell outside the interests and experiences of children.

CLASS INCLUSION

Even a task thought to be impossible for preoperational children can be solved, if the experimenter is ingenious. McGarrigle, Grieve, and Hughes (1978) showed that the form of the original question was destined to confuse children. In their clearer version, a child is shown a picture of sleeping cows, of which only some are black, and is asked, "Are there more black cows or more sleeping cows?" According to a strict Piagetian interpretation, this question should elude children because they are being asked to compare a subclass (black cows) with the class of which it is a part (sleeping cows). However, children are able to answer this question at ages when they are thought to be preoperational. According to the experimenters, the descriptor "sleeping" helps the child to attend to the whole class. When the question "Are there more black cows or more cows?" is posed, the child naturally assumes that the comparison is between black cows and nonblack cows. The class inclusion question itself turns out to be far trickier than the operation of comparing subclasses with their superordinate classes.

FORMAL OPERATIONS ON THE WANE

The entire concept of formal operations has been strongly attacked. Experimenters have shown that the concept does not really discriminate among youths.

When the tasks are defined rigorously, very few adolescents in any culture can perform the kinds of comparisons of variables and the assessment of propositions demanded by Piaget (Capon & Kuhn, 1979; Grinder, 1975; Neimark, 1975). Indeed, the classical tests of formal operations seem to be tests of how much laboratory science one has had. Conversely, if formal operational thought is defined loosely—for example, as the ability to deal with hypothetical entities or to engage in a discussion about various propositional claims—then much younger children are able to handle the tasks as well. After all, even youngsters have no difficulty in dealing with the world of fiction; and any 8-year-old is able to argue quite persuasively with his or her parents about why he should not have to clean his room.

It appears, then, that most of Piaget's strong claims rested on the artifacts of his particular experiments, rather than on deep truths about what youngsters can and cannot do at specific ages. When the conditions of the task are simplified or changed, youngsters readily handle what appeared to be impossible.

Almost no one defends Piaget's precise claims anymore. Instead, this set of results has led to two different outcomes. Some harsher critics question the viability of the entire superstructure constructed by Piaget; they say that it no longer makes sense to think of youngsters as passing through discrete stages (Brainerd, 1978; Fodor, 1975). Others continue to maintain that there is some sense in the general progression put forth by Piaget, and that it is better to build on what Piaget has shown than to start from scratch. It is to the work of these new (or neo-) Piagetians that we now turn.

The New Piagetians

A number of scholars have taken as their task the preservation of the central aspects of Piaget's theory: they have been termed "neo-Piagetians" or "New Piagetians." The best known are Robbie Case and Kurt Fischer. These scholars have undertaken similar courses. While developing their own particular vocabularies, they have preserved broad stages, reminiscent of the four major Piagetian stages. They have added fine detail, including substages, and have developed precise methods for determining the stage(s) or level(s) at which a child is performing. In that sense, they have been more Piagetian than Piaget.

On the other hand, Case and Fischer have modified Piaget in various respects. To begin with, they have looked more broadly than Piaget, taking into account aspects of social and emotional development, as well as the development of intelligence, à la Piaget. For Case and Fischer, intelligence is more than logical problem solving. Second, both scholars have been sensitive to the possibilities of training, or advancing from one stage (or substage) to another; they have been more interested in educational issues than Piaget ever was. Perhaps most important, each scholar has emphasized the importance of context and of content. Rather than taking an extreme Piagetian position—that an individual is "at a stage," period—they recognize that individuals may be at one stage with materials that are familiar, and

Robbie Case.

at a lower developmental stage with respect to materials or contexts that are unfamiliar.

Each of these scholars has put forth a specific image, which guides his perspective on cognitive development. For Case, the essence of intelligent behavior is problem solving. In conceptualizing the human mind, Case relies on the image of a computer (or its programs) that has a problem to solve. The program receives data as input, holds on to the data, processes the data in various ways, and arrives at a more-or-less satisfactory solution.

For every problem situation, Case defines a goal or objective, and a series of steps, or strategies, that must be undertaken in order to proceed from the initial statement of a problem to the ultimate achievement of a goal. The child (often conceptualized as "an Executive") is aided in the pursuit of the goal by a steady increase, over the years, in the capacity of short-term memory (sometimes called "M space")—the amount of information that can be retained in the mind during the process of solving the problem. The increase in memory storage capacity is a joint product of biological maturation and the attainment of greater automaticity, as the result of extensive practice.

As an example of Case's approach, consider the familiar balance-scale problem. The 4-year-old appreciates a single goal: determining which side of the beam will go down. The child's strategy is restricted to noting which side looks like it bears more weight, and then predicting that the weightier side will fall. For the older child, the overall goal of predicting the final state of the beam can be broken down into a series of subgoals (figuring out which side has the most units, or which side has the weighted pegs farthest from the fulcrum). The child can then set up strategies for dealing with each of these goals (counting the number of weights on each peg, comparing the numbers across pegs and sides, and so on). The possession of enhanced working memory allows the older, more developed child to "compute" with these various strategies and to combine them to get a more refined and comprehensive answer to the balance-scale problem.

The central concept for Fischer is that of a skill; he terms his approach "skill theory." A skill can be either acted out physically or evidenced as a mental skill or operation. Fischer describes an extensive set of stages (called tiers) that encompass the organization of skilled behavior at various levels of sophistication,

Kurt Fischer.

ranging from single sensory-motor sets (at 3 to 4 months) to a system of abstract systems (at 24 to 26 years of age) (Fischer & Pipp, 1984b). There are specific algebraic transformation rules about how specific skill structures can be transformed into more power and more integrated structures. Over the years, the number of hypothesized tiers and levels has increased, and Fischer has found evidence relating them to changing brain structures (Fischer & Rose, 1994).

Fischer recognizes that the amount and type of experience that a child has with a certain skill will determine the tier level of that skill; therefore, a child may be at a higher level with respect to one skill (or set of skills) than with another. "Unevenness in development is therefore the rule, not the exception" (1980, p. 480), Fischer has declared. He also emphasizes that a child's apparent level of sophistication will be affected by the amount of environmental support that is available. It is possible to determine the child's optimal level of performance, as well as his or her more normal performance, when these supports have been removed.

Fischer's favorite examples are taken from the social domain. In one line of study he requests stories about events that involve some people who are nice and others who are mean, and then asks the subjects to act out stories using dolls. Fischer then analyzes the skills that are involved in understanding such social interactions.

At an elementary level, called "single sets," the child is simply able to understand one doll's behavior as nice (for example, doll A gives a present to doll B), and the other's as mean (for example, doll B hits doll A). At the next level, called "mapping" (or "representational mapping"), a child can portray relations between two such behaviors, "mapping them" on one another. Doll A says mean things to doll B, and doll B reciprocates by hitting doll A. At a third level, two mappings are coordinated to yield a system: the youth can connect relations to one another. For example, doll A declares that she wants to be a friend with doll B but at the same time hits doll B; doll B is insulted; doll A then apologizes, offers a present to doll B, and the two ultimately befriend one another. Finally, at the most sophisticated level (system of systems), the youth or adult is able to coordinate these various systems into a single overarching system. Each doll is capable of nice and of mean intentions, and these can be changed, with reciprocal interactions on the part of the other doll in the relation. The result is an abstraction: human behavior is seen and understood by the person as a set of interactions in which both nice and mean motivations are constantly invoked.

The Computer as Model for the Development of Mind

The neo-Piagetians (particularly Case) have been influenced by the invention of the computer, but they have not made it central to their work. In this respect, they differ from a set of scholars who consider the problem solving of a child as directly analogous to the problem solving that is executed on a computer. These scholars have been inspired particularly by the team of Herbert Simon and Allen Newell at Carnegie-Mellon University. Simon and Newell have argued that intellectual activity can *all* be conceptualized as problem solving, and that simulation on a computer provides the most convincing evidence of how problem solving actually takes place, on a moment-to-moment, step-by-step basis (see Gardner, 1985; Newell & Simon, 1972; and Chapter 6 of this book).

Followers of Newell and Simon have often used Piagetian tasks as a way of carrying through their own work with children. One of the first scholars to take this "information processing" approach was Robert Siegler, now at Carnegie-Mellon University. We can gain a feeling for Siegler's approach by reviewing his analysis of the balance-scale problem.

Siegler has isolated four rules that children might follow in solving balance-scale problems. The rules are stated in ascending order of complexity.

1. The child bases judgments on a single dominant dimension—specifically, the number of weights. If the number of weights on both sides is equal, the child simply guesses, because he or she is unable to attend to two dimensions simultaneously.

2. The child attends to the values on the dominant dimension when those values are unequal; but when the values or the dominant dimensions are equal, the child also considers a subordinate dimension. Invoking this rule, the child will select the side with more weights, irrespective of their distance from the fulcrum. If the dominant clue of weight provides no help, however, the child will take the subordinated dimension of distance into account.

3. The child is able to take into account both the dominant and the subordinate dimensions. When both dimensions point to the same side, the child responds correctly. But when one dimension favors one side (e.g., more weights on the right) and the other dimension points to the other side

(e.g., greater distance on the left), the child lacks a consistent rule for resolving the conflict: Hence, the child just guesses.

4. The child not only takes into account both dimensions but is also able to weigh the contributions of each one. In the balance-scale problem, children know that they must multiply the torques on both sides (number of weights × distance from the fulcrum) in order to make an accurate prediction.

As a straightforward description of increasingly sophisticated rules, Siegler's work seems reasonable but not notably different from that undertaken by Case and, indeed, by Inhelder and Piaget themselves. In fact, however, Siegler's analysis goes beyond that of the other scholars in a number of ways.

The standard Piagetian account is a description of what students do. Siegler claims to be able to predict youngsters' responses on particular problems. In his research, he gave students six kinds of problems, only some of which placed the dimensions in conflict. By positing that a particular child was able to follow one rule but not another, Siegler was able to predict which problems that child could solve, which problems that child could not solve, and the reasons for the failures. For example, a 5-year-old would follow rule 1, and all the successful and unsuccessful responses could be predicted on that basis. A college student would adhere as rigidly to rule 4, with consequent successes. Moreover, success did not always match with age; sometimes, a simpler rule, rather than a more sophisticated rule, was more likely to produce accuracy on certain problems. As a convinced information processing scientist might say, this line of Piagetian research, which began with description and after-the-fact explanation, has moved to prediction and an explanation for the success of the prediction.

Siegler's task-analytic method provides a finer-grained understanding of what a child is doing in approaching a balance-scale task. One could program a computer to mimic the child's handling of the task at each level of development. Such finer-grained understanding may also be necessary for successful training. Having shown that the youngest subjects did not, on their own, focus on the dimension of distance from the fulcrum, Siegler trained them to do so; accordingly, the performance of 70% of the subjects improved on those tasks where invocation of rule 1 alone got them into difficulties (Siegler, 1991).

In this early work, Siegler was influenced by the computational approach but did not literally simulate the work of students on the computer. In more recent work concerned with the acquisition of the ability to count, Siegler has in fact defined strategies with precision and developed computer models of how children master this important skill (Siegler & Shipley, 1995). In the actual construction of computer programs, Siegler was following the path first introduced with respect to Piagetian tasks by his colleagues at Carnegie-Mellon, David Klahr and J. G. Wallace.

Klahr and Wallace (1976; see also Klahr, 1984) have looked at the conservation-of-number task. On their analysis, in order to appreciate that x elements are always the same in number as x elements, independent of how the x elements happen to be arranged in space, the child has to compile a mental record of all previous encounters of x elements. The child records each experience on a time line, which can be analogized to an entry in a computer program. The computer system—whether human or mechanical—retains all these entries and can scan all previous encounters of x elements. If this survey reveals that spreading out, crunching together, stacking, and so on, always retains the same number x, then the computer can generalize that x elements always remain the same, irrespective of their spatial array. Moreover, through a process called *redundancy elimination,* the system can form a more sophisticated rule: spreading (or crunching together) never affects the numerosity of a display.

In approaching conservation in this way, Klahr and Wallace seek to make a number of points—in dialogue, so to speak—with Piaget. First, one can go beyond mere description and even beyond the use of the computer as a metaphor; it is actually possible to describe behavior with such specificity that one can write a computer program and observe it at work. Second, one does not need to invoke "grand concepts" like stages or mental operations; one can detail particular experiences and the lessons derived from them. This approach sticks very close to the data; recognizing that individual youngsters have different experiences, it keeps open the possibility that youngsters may develop different rules, or draw different generalizations—as indeed they will. Finally, the Klahr–Wallace approach deals with the problem of developmental change by positing that the rules (or, in their terms, production systems) followed by children can change; hence, their cognitive system is self-modifying. Rather than development remaining a mysterious, biological process that is restricted to human beings, it has been elucidated in a step-by-step fashion and can be simulated on an electromechanical device.

As in many areas of study, the computer has wrought a revolution in our understanding of mind. Not only are computers routinely used for all sorts of scientific work, but many scientists in cognitive development believe that the computer provides a viable model of human thinking. It is therefore important to bear in mind that only certain kinds of problem solving have lent themselves to simulation on computers, and that the actual computer model changes as human beings redesign the kinds of computers that we use. For example, the Carnegie-Mellon team has been influenced chiefly by serial computers that carry out one step at a time. Recently, however, the greatest advances in computing have been realized with parallel distributed systems, which, like the human brain, can carry out many operations simultaneously (see Chapter 6). It will be many years before we know whether the computer is simply the latest in a series of convenient metaphors for the mind (the steam engine, the telephone switchboard) or the "one best metaphor."

Modules of Mind: Beyond Universals

Piaget put forth the strong position that all thinking during a specific developmental stage reflects the same underlying mental operations. Whether one is dealing with space, time, number, or language, the child is at a certain operational level and carries out the same operations with respect to diverse content. Other scholars have not pushed his point with the same degree of fervor; yet, by and large, they have directed their attention to the kinds of logical-mathematical, scientific, and numerical problems that Piaget himself favored.

In recent years, a number of scholars, influenced particularly by cultural considerations and stimulated by an interest in education, have argued that Piaget focused on only one among a number of different uses of mind. A more comprehensive view of cognition can be obtained only if one looks well beyond the kinds of logical problems that Piaget scrutinized. Particularly, one must consider capacities that can only develop if one lives in certain kinds of cultures and is exposed to certain kinds of educational systems.

A central figure in this movement is David Feldman. In *Beyond Universals in Cognitive Development* (1994), Feldman argues that Piaget set his sights too narrowly by focusing on the Kantian categories of time, space, and number, which can be assumed to be encountered universally and to develop independent of cultural settings. Feldman points out three additional kinds of domains that deserve analysis:

1. *Cultural domains* are those that all individuals living within a culture are expected to master. For example, in our culture, all human beings are expected to read and write. In another culture, literacy may not be required, but all individuals might be expected to master certain rituals or to be able to hunt, fish, or farm. The educational structures of such societies are constructed so that these lessons are taught and learned, and within those societies, domain practices may even be thought (erroneously) to be universal. The fact that relatively few individuals within our society actually perform formal operations indicates that this is by no means a universal capacity; at most, it might someday become a cultural universal in the West.

2. *Discipline-based domains* are those that can be mastered over a number of years within a culture. In our own culture, one might include the academic disciplines, like American history or biology, as well as avocational pursuits, such as chess or sailing. There is no requirement that every individual in the society master such domains, though some mastery might be expected within certain subgroups in the culture. Still, there exist established routines for acquiring such expertise. At the far end of the discipline-based domains are those that Feldman calls *idiosyncratic*: these are new or odd pursuits that only selected individuals may actually confront. Playing the contrabassoon, being a Civil War buff, or creating hypermedia programs are possible idiosyncratic pursuits.

3. *Unique domains* feature skill and ability areas that have been pursued and mastered so far by a single individual. Typically, unique domains are

not of much interest to others and might be thought to be deservedly unique: perhaps Mindy can invent more new uses for a brick than anyone else; in all likelihood, Howard is the only person who can find a letter that has been misplaced in his files. But occasionally—and this occurs particularly in academic disciplines—an individual's invention can come to affect one's culture. When Newton and Leibnitz both invented the calculus at the end of the 17th century, they created a set of practices that eventually became a recognized domain. At first, only a few idiosyncratic souls mastered the calculus. But now, 300 years later, the calculus is a discipline-based domain, having moved quite a distance from its initial, unique status. It is even possible to envision a society where mastery of the calculus, like ordinary literacy, might achieve the status of a cultural universal.

An important line of evidence in support of Feldman's program is the existence of prodigies. Feldman and Goldsmith's (1986) definition of a prodigy is: an individual who performs in a domain at an adult level, while he or she is still a child. There may be prodigies in operational thinking à la Piaget, and there may be a few prodigies who excel across the disciplinary board. For the most part, however, prodigies turn out to have quite discipline-specific strengths. Feldman and Goldsmith describe one prodigy who composes music at age 6; another who plays competitive chess at age 8; a third who can write novels and plays at age 5. These individuals stand out in these particular domains. However, when examined in other domains, or when given standard tests of operational thinking, they appear much more like their age-mates than like prodigies in other areas. Studies of expertise in other areas—for example, learning about various kinds of dinosaurs—confirm that young individuals can achieve adult-level skills through practice, but these skills remain remarkably restricted to the particular contents through which they were developed (Chi, Glaser, & Farr, 1988; Ericsson & Smith, 1991). In general, profiles of accomplishment are uneven rather than uniform.

Such studies constitute a crucial input to theories of multiple intelligences (see Chapter 7). Piaget and most other theorists of intelligence have placed on a pedestal a set of capacities that are logical-mathematical and/or linguistic in nature. A child is seen as smart if he or she is skilled in mathematics, skilled in language, or, better yet, skilled in both domains. Youngsters with skills in sailing, music, drawing, athletics, dance, or knowledge of self or of others, may be seen as talented but they are rarely acknowledged as intelligent. A focus on the various domains offered in a culture, and an examination of the areas in which children excel, yields a quite different perspective on the intellect.

In this pluralistic or modular view, human beings have evolved to be able to carry out a number of different kinds of operations on a number of different kinds of content. Nearly all human beings can find their way around a spatial terrain, master a dance, detect when someone is deceiving them, or reproduce a melody; but in each of these cases, some individuals master these skills much more rapidly and advance to a much higher plane than others. The avenues pursued and the heights attained are always a joint product of innate endowment, cultural opportunities, and amount of practice and motivation. Such an analysis does not deny the importance of the kinds of problems and domains investigated by Piaget and his circle, but it construes them as a few areas drawn from a much larger universe, rather than as a privileged set of competencies that alone merit the phrase "intelligent."

Those investigators who take a modular view of mind are distinguished from the mainstream Piagetian research community by several factors. First, they attend not only to those capacities that all humans can accomplish but also to those that are featured in certain cultural settings. Second, they focus on those educational settings that inculcate high levels of skill, and they also look at those individuals who have achieved great (even adult-level) competence while still in childhood. Additionally, they question the notion of *general* structures or competencies, à la Piaget; in their analyses, youngsters can be at one degree of sophistication with one content, but at a far higher (or lower) degree of sophistication with another kind of content.

They continue to see themselves as developmentalists in the Piaget tradition in two respects: (1) they focus on the same issues of the development of knowledge that were first articulated and pursued by Piaget, and (2) they believe that some kind of stage-and-transition approach ought to be pursued within each domain of knowledge. At the same time, they remain open to the possibility that the nature of stages and transitions observed with reference to one content (for example, spatial knowledge) might prove quite different from that observed with reference to another content (like musical or personal knowledge).

Constraints on Knowing

One of the most influential social scientists of the 20th century is Noam Chomsky, a linguist who has worked for many years at the Massachusetts Institute of Technology. Chomsky began his studies with an attempt to write a "grammar" for language—indeed, for all languages. As he saw it, the job of the linguist was to specify the rules that allow individuals to produce sentences that are grammatical and that allow listeners to judge which sentences follow those rules of grammar and which do not. This may seem like a simple task, but it has, in fact, never been carried out completely. Grammar books continue to be loaded with exceptions and ad hoc explanations (Chomsky, 1957, 1980; Gardner, 1995a).

From this seemingly arcane pursuit, Chomsky went on to develop a set of strong views about human cognition. They have had enormous influence throughout academe, especially among those who study intellectual development. As Chomsky sees it, language skills come about because humans have a "language faculty." Just as human beings have organs that allow their bodies to function well, the human mind consists of a number of abilities or "mental organs" that follow prescribed rules. Children the world over learn to speak language(s) easily, not because their parents are good teachers but rather because they already possess abstract rules and principles that allow them (1) to make sense of the language that is spoken around them and (2) to produce and understand acceptable sentences in that language.

Chomsky and his associates, particularly the philosopher Jerry Fodor (1975, 1983), believe that the mind is best thought of as a collection of mental organs or modules, each with its own sets of rules and constraints. The language faculty features its own set of principles; they allow parsing of sentences in terms of noun and verb phrases, and conversion of statements into questions and vice versa. By analogy, a faculty of face recognition, allows us to distinguish one face from another, even when those faces have changed over the years. (The face faculty works only on right-side-up faces; humans and other primates are poor at recognizing faces when they are seen upside down.) Chomsky and his associates speculate that there are faculties dealing with music, spatial perception, understanding of other people's minds, and so on (Pinker, 1994). This suggestion makes their claims similar to those put forth by Feldman, Gardner, and others who believe in multiple intelligences.

Chomsky began to establish his reputation in the late 1950s, when he challenged the influence of B. F. Skinner, the leading psychological behaviorist of his day. Chomsky convinced many scholars—especially the soon-to-be-influential younger scholars—that Skinner's approach to language and behavior was largely circular and that human capacities could be explained only if one attributed (to human beings) complex systems of rules and transformations that were represented in the mind. In similar fashion, Chomsky, Fodor, and others challenged Piaget explicitly in 1975, when several scholars gathered outside Paris for a meeting on language and learning (Piattelli-Palmarini, 1980).

Piaget was prepared to be gracious and to find points of agreement, but Chomsky would have none of it. He challenged most of the major claims put forth by Piaget and other developmentalists. From his perspective, there is no such thing as "general knowledge" or "underlying general operations of thought"; rather, each mental faculty, and each domain of knowledge, has its own rules and principles. What explains the human capacity for language has little relevance to what explains music, mathematics, or facial recognition.

Chomsky was equally scornful about the notion of stages of development or learning. For Chomsky, what is most important is the knowledge that is built into the human mind at birth—knowledge that is often called "innate." We cannot begin to understand human beings unless we factor in those initial states of knowledge that we possess by virtue of our species membership. The analogy of constructing knowledge through assimilation and accommodation was rejected in favor of built-in knowledge that is essentially triggered by the environment. The infant acquiring language resembles a squirrel that already knows how to bury nuts. The image of a blank slate on which the knowledge of the community has to be etched or constructed was rejected.

The Piagetian program of research was not derailed by the Chomskian attack, but it certainly was thrown for a loop. Chomsky had both critiqued the major posts of support for the Piagetian program and put forth a competing model: the mathematically oriented analysis of language that he and his colleagues had engaged in as they identified the rules and principles undergirding succeeding versions of grammars. Perhaps, indeed, more progress could be made in the study of children's intelligence if one looked at domains one by one, and if one tried to establish the knowledge present at the beginning of the infant's life and the ways that successive layers of knowledge were "triggered" in order to produce adult levels of competence.

This approach to the study of cognition has come to be called the "constraints" approach (Carey & Gelman, 1991; Hirschfield & Gelman, 1994). Constraints is not used in a negative sense; rather, it relates to the conditions that allow learning and development to take place. Individuals who adhere to the constraints approach seek to discover the initial forms of knowledge that are present at birth or soon afterward: Which hypotheses and expectations are favored by children as they grow older? How can the ways in which initial knowledge changes over time best be described? What is the form of the final, adult level of knowledge? In this enterprise, they are helped particularly by the construction of formal models that represent levels of knowledge, and by the careful study of the kinds of behaviors and errors that children never issue, presumably because their mental structures are constrained so as to minimize the possibility that such behaviors or errors will ever occur.

We have already encountered some work that fits comfortably into the constraints point of view. Many scholars, unconvinced by Piaget's portrait of infancy, have attempted to sketch the kinds of knowledge of the physical world that the infant already has. Elizabeth Spelke (1991) shows that, in most respects, the infant is born with a sense of an object. The infant knows that objects are solid, follow certain trajectories rather than others (objects fall rather than rise), and do not change in fundamental ways (shape, solidity) without clear-cut manipulations. Changes over time, in this sense of object, are far fewer and less substantive than Piaget suggested. By the same token, scholars like Wynn, Starkey, and Gelman have shown that infants already have a basic sense of number: they can detect alterations in the numerosity of a display. Gelman goes on to show that children as young as 2 years already possess an ensemble of basic principles that regulate their approach to counting. Among these are the notion that each item in an array gets a separate word or tag; the order of tags remains stable; the order in which the items are tagged is irrelevant, so long as each is tagged only once per count; and so on (Gelman, 1979). These principles serve as constraints that determine how the child goes about mastering counting, and which mistakes he or she is unlikely to make (e.g., touching the same item twice) or likely to make (e.g., confusing the order of number words).

Frank Keil has helped to illustrate the power of the constraints approach. According to his analysis, one can see constraints at work in each of the major domains of cognition. Chomsky and his associates show us the constraints that operate in the realm of language. Gelman and her colleagues show us the constraints that operate in the realm of number. We can note that these constraints do not bear any obvious relationship to one another—we can say that each set is domain-specific.

Keil's own work has focused on ontology—the study of what exists. Keil approaches this complex philosophical territory by studying the kinds of objects that youngsters can detect, and the ways in which they preferentially group them. Even very young children appreciate the difference between objects that are living (plants and animals) and those that are not (toys, machines). They reject displays (or queries) in which a living entity is converted into a nonliving one (say, a dog into a bowl) or a nonliving entity into a living one. More interestingly, although they make far fewer distinctions than do older individuals, there are certain kinds of constraints that they honor in their groupings. Thus, they will not say of a nonliving object that it sleeps or is angry or has an idea, just as they will not say of a living object that it takes place over time or that it was made by a machine. Because it is most unlikely that youngsters are taught these *ontological distinctions* in any formal way, it makes more sense to infer that young minds are so constructed that they readily make some distinctions while not readily being able to make others.

Some workers in the constraints tradition have gone beyond studying classifications of objects to examining the child's development of theories (Carey, 1985; Carey & Spelke, 1994; Hirschfield & Gelman, 1994; Keil, 1991). In their view, the young child parses the world into broad domains—the living, the human, the inanimate—and develops theories about these domains. The child is seen as having a theory of life (all objects that move are alive, all objects that don't move are dead); a theory of matter (matter is composed of little bits, which one can see; heavier objects fall more rapidly than lighter ones); and a theory of mind (all humans have minds; those that look like you have a mind that resembles yours). These theories constrain which objects children notice, which explanations they readily adopt, which cultural understandings (e.g., that mass does not determine acceleration) are difficult to master. Some of these theories are sensible; others are not, and need somehow to be revised. Just how these theories change, if they do, is a subject of keen interest to these investigators of children's theories; where they agree is that Piaget's stage-and-structure explanations do not suffice. In diametric opposition to Piaget, some theorists believe that these early conceptions (and misconceptions) endure with great tenacity, even in the face of development and formal education (Gardner, 1991; see also Chapter 8).

Although some constraints theorists might be tempted to remark that their work refutes that of Piaget, this would be too strong a conclusion to draw. For one thing, the entire interest in children's theories can be traced back to Piaget's early writings on children's conceptions of the world (1929). Even specific lines of work, such as investigation of children's minds, replicate work done by Piaget nearly 70 years ago. Moreover, much of this research depends on demonstrations devised by Piaget and concepts introduced by Piaget, even if the conclusions drawn are often quite different.

It makes more sense to think of these new lines of work—in information processing, in modules of minds, in constraints—as plausible reactions to the Piagetian enterprise. Because Piaget emphasized description of children in relatively natural settings, information processors try to model the behaviors with a computer. Piaget stressed the unitary nature of knowledge, so modularists try to show the differences among various domains. Because Piaget showed the child constructing knowledge essentially from scratch, constraints theorists try to show what knowledge is present at birth and which factors constrain the way in which that knowledge develops thereafter. Constraints theorists actually differ greatly among themselves on the status of stages or major developmental reorganizations; the sources of these changes; and the extent to which it continues to be useful to speak of development and learning, as opposed to "mere" triggering or the lifelong persistence of youthful misconceptions.

Attempts at Synthesis

In analyzing the dialectics of thought, the 19th-century German philosopher Hegel pointed out that sequences follow a familiar pattern: first, there is a thesis; then, there is a contrasting antithesis; and finally, there are attempts at synthesis, in which the strongest portions of thesis and antithesis are mined to produce a position that is more coherent and cogent than any of its rivals. In the first part of this chapter, we reviewed Piaget's main claims; next, we surveyed the various responses to Piaget. Here, we examine three recent attempts to synthesize the strongest themes in the work of the past half-century.

1. Robbie Case has proposed the existence of *central conceptual structures* (1992). In his description, children's cognitive development can be described in terms of a small number of structures that govern performance on an ensemble of tasks. One such structure, which proves particularly important for performances on Piagetian tasks, centers around the knowledge of number. A second structure deals with social cognition, particularly the appreciation of intention and motivation. There may well be other conceptual structures dealing with domains like spatial knowledge and motor action.

For each of these structures, analogous changes occur as the child develops. All of these comparable structures are subjected to certain more general developments, such as changes in speed of processing or changes in working memory. By positing this new concept, Case hopes to be able to preserve the general explanatory framework favored by Piaget, Fischer, and himself. At the same time, he recognizes the accumulating developmental data indicating that processing of number is not the same as processing of other kinds of information; and that there are stronger ties among the family of numerical tasks than there are between tasks that involve number and those that feature other kinds of content.

2. While Case reaches out from the Piagetian base to encompass more modular kinds of findings, Gardner and Wolf (1983) begin from the opposite vantage point. Their study of early symbolic development revealed that development of competence in one symbolic domain, such as music or storytelling, follows a developmental path that is distinctive from development in other symbolic domains—for example, drawing or numerical sophistication. Indeed, they speak of disparate "streams" of development. In this sense, their work is faithful to the modular, non-Piagetian position.

Yet, further analysis of the data on symbolic development has revealed a more complex picture. Most events in symbolic development seem to respect the "banks" of specific streams, but others seem to overflow, in "wavelike" fashion, across several symbolic domains. In describing the broad spectrum of symbolic development, Gardner and Wolf (1983) isolate four Piaget-style major waves of development, each occurring at approximately yearly intervals.

As an example, consider the wave of "event-structuring" that occurs at the age of 18–24 months. Children come to appreciate the basic event structure of a narrative: that an agent does something with certain consequences. This knowledge shows up, predictably, in early language and pretend play. However, more surprisingly, one also sees evidence of this wave in children's early drawing. Asked to draw a truck, the 2-year-old child will seize the marker and make "vroom, vroom" sounds while pushing the marker, in trucklike fashion, back and forth across the paper. Hence, the skill of event-structuring is transported, as a general symbolic vehicle, to the less evident domain of graphic depiction.

A similar story can be told about each of the subsequent waves. A wave of "topological mapping" at age 3 begins with an appreciation of analog relations in the graphic sphere but is imported to other domains, like music or storytelling. The same thing happens with a wave of "digital mapping" at age 4, and a wave of "notational (or second order) symbolization" at the age when school commences.

The important point here is that an examination of one crucial aspect of child development cannot be subsumed neatly under a pro-Piagetian or anti-Piagetian perspective. Certain "streamlike" aspects of symbolization give aid and comfort to a modular perspective; but the rival "wavelike" aspects are more congenial with a Piagetian perspective. A Hegelian synthesis needs to incorporate relevant portions from each point of view.

3. In a bold theoretical synthesis, Annette Karmiloff-Smith seeks to venture "beyond modularity" and to present a "developmental perspective on cognitive science" (1992). Once a student of Piaget, with a particular interest in language, Karmiloff-Smith has found much that is attractive in the modular position. In particular, she feels that Piaget's disavowal of any form of innate or early knowledge,

insistence on general stages across all kinds of content, and specific theoretical vocabulary cannot be sustained in the light of subsequent research. She concedes the existence and import of separate domains of knowledge, each with its own rules and constraints. At the same time, Karmiloff-Smith continues to believe in the Piagetian view of the child as an active constructor of knowledge; she believes that it is important to tell the story of child development because, as she insists, "children do develop"; and she feels that knowledge in the young is not as insular and modularized as claimed by the chief critics of Piaget.

Karmiloff-Smith's particular attempt at synthesis grows out of careful examination of five separate domains of knowledge: language, number, notation (drawing), understanding of the physical world, and understanding of the social-psychological world (theory of mind). In each

Annette Karmiloff-Smith.

domain, she concedes that there exist certain issues and problems that are unique to that domain, and she makes no claim that these domains develop at the same speed.

Karmiloff-Smith attempts to show, however, that children pass through the same general phases with respect to each of these domains. Specifically, each child begins with implicit knowledge—with the capacity to perform tasks, admittedly in a rigid and inflexible "programlike" fashion. Over time, with practice and feedback, the child's knowledge becomes more flexible. Then the child begins to develop more explicit forms of knowledge—in Karmiloff-Smith's terms, the child passes through a cycle of "representational redescriptions." The child becomes explicitly aware of what he or she is doing, can reflect upon it, and ultimately can talk and even theorize about it. As Karmiloff-Smith conceptualizes it, children are drawn to revise their current descriptions so that they can deal with contradictions that arise and so that they can understand the world, and their own thinking, in a more comprehensive way.

This sequence of events occurs in each domain and with respect to each kind of content. In that sense, it is universal and stagelike, in the best Piagetian tradition. Using familiar examples, one sees the sequence at work as one learns to play a passage on the piano, solve a Rubik's cube, master a rule of language, or draw a person. Yet, because the timing of this process, and the extent to which it is ultimately achieved, is not lockstep, aspects of individual differences and modularity are recognized as well.

Summary

In this chapter, we surveyed the work of Jean Piaget, the most important theorist of children's intelligence. We then examined a number of lines of work that were carried out in reaction to Piaget. Although Piaget's interest in the mind was piqued by his work on intelligence tests, his view of intelligence differs from that of most other individuals reviewed in this book. Piaget is interested not in differences in intellectual capacities across human beings but rather in those properties of mind, of intelligence, that are found throughout the world, by courtesy of our membership in the human species.

Piaget's accomplishment is most impressive. He developed clinical methods for studying children, ranging from his own three infants to schoolchildren throughout the world. He made a number of amazing and counterintuitive discoveries, such as infants' difficulties in appreciating the permanence of objects and preschoolers' difficulties in appreciating conservation of substance and number. Most importantly, he described a set of stages of cognitive development through which all normal children are supposed to pass, and he developed a vocabulary—rooted in biology and in logic—for describing the ways in which cognitive development actually proceeds.

When Piaget's tasks are replicated with precision, researchers obtain the same results that he did. But when changes are made in the operationalization, children typically reveal much greater understanding of key concepts and operations. In retrospect, it appears that Piaget depended too much on complex verbal instructions and questions; used displays that were unnecessarily complex and often unfamiliar to children; and did not separate out the core or basic competence from more sophisticated expressions of that competence. As a result, children's development now seems to be smoother, less stagelike, and, in some ways, far more precocious than Piaget had envisioned.

Piaget's shadow is so vast that it has dominated work in the past 30 years, both by those who are sympathetic to the Piagetian project and those who are motivated to prove him wrong. Neo-Piagetians like Case and Fischer agree with the broad outlines of Piaget's theory. Case has been partial to the computer model of problem solving; Fischer, to the analysis of skills and their interrelations and development. These neo-Piagetians have provided far more detail about stages and sequences. They recognize that Piaget's project focused on some uses of mind, rather than on others, and that his strongest claims about stage sequences and universality cannot be sustained.

More influenced by computer science and information processing approaches, developmentalists like Siegler, Klahr, and Wallace have sought to move from description to explanation. Either literally or metaphorically, they write the programs that children are presumed to follow when they attempt to understand the operation of a balance scale or to conserve number. These studies yield extremely fine-grained analyses of behavior and can make strong predictions about which problems will be mastered and why. However, it remains an open question whether the computer is the single best model for children's thought.

The Piagetian perspective on universalism has been critiqued from a number of points. Feldman and Gardner point to the existence of different domains of knowledge and competence, many quite removed from the logical-mathematical issues that have concerned Piagetians. Moreover, they provide evidence that development of one intelligence, in one kind of domain, has only superficial relations to development of other intelligences in other domains, and that strength or weakness in one area does not predict strength or weakness in other areas.

Strongly influenced by the linguist Chomsky, those operating as "constraints researchers" begin with an acknowledgment of the existence of separate domains, like language, music, or face perception, each with its own brain structure and rules of organization. The constraints theorists attempt to describe the initial knowledge state as well as the constraints that determine which paths are followed, which errors are made, and which errors are almost never observed. Constraints theorists differ from one another on whether children's thought simply unfolds from an initial nucleus, is "triggered" by certain environmental events, or undergoes some stage changes of a Piagetian flavor.

Finally, in response to the Piagetian thesis and the post-Piagetian antithesis, a few theorists are attempting to synthesize the strongest lines of work of the past half-century. Robbie Case and associates posit the existence of central conceptual structures, which have one foot in the Piagetian camp, one foot in the modularity camp. Gardner and Wolf analyze symbolic development in terms of Piaget-like "waves" that cut across disparate content, and modularlike "streams" that reflect only the operation of one symbolic system. Finally, in the most ambitious synthesizing effort to date, Karmiloff-Smith portrays a broad sequence of steps, from implicit knowledge to explicitly stated propositional knowledge, which characterizes the growth of human knowledge in five important domains. A task that lies ahead is the integration of the study of intelligence as a universal human property with the study of intelligence as a factor that distinguishes one human being from another.

Until this point in the book, we have focused almost exclusively on the human individual as an isolated psychological creature—at first, a young child with certain initial intellectual proclivities and abilities; later, an adult who can perform at a determinable level on tasks of consequence to the culture. Whatever their many differences, both the psychometric and the developmental approaches direct their attention to the individual in relative isolation from other persons and institutions of the society.

In the last three chapters of this book, we turn our attention directly to the human being as he or she is embedded in a social context—such as school and the workplace—and as these entities help to form and to guide the human mind. In entering this realm, we encounter the work of Lev Vygotsky, a Russian born in the same year as Piaget, whose analysis of human cognitive development extended well beyond the skin of the individual. Vygotsky and his contextualist followers laid out in detail the supportive—indeed, constitutive—role played by humans, like parents and teachers, and by inventions of the culture, such as physical tools, notational systems, and systems of interpretation and meaning.

Both Piaget and Vygotsky wrote as psychologists, but they were aware of the relevant disciplines that extend beyond psychology—biology, anthropology, and technology, for example. Each of these disciplines, and others as well, is necessary if we are to realize our goal of a full understanding of intelligence. Intelligence may be a psychological construct, but its explication requires that we don the hats of other kinds of investigators and try to integrate their varying perspectives.

Accordingly, in Chapter 5, we approach the topic of intelligence through the lenses of investigators trained in biology—brain scientists, geneticists, and others with a biological orientation. In Chapter 6, we approach intelligence from the perspective of those who work primarily with computers, and we consider the nature of intelligence in its computational as well as its human form.

Suggested Readings

Cole, M., & Cole, S. (1993). *The development of children* (2nd ed.). New York: Scientific American Books/Freeman.

Flavell, J. H., Miller, P. H., & Miller, S. A. (1993). *Cognitive development* (3rd ed.). Englewood Cliffs, NJ: Prentice-Hall.

Ginsburg, H., & Opper, S. (1979). *Piaget's theory of intellectual development* (2nd ed.). Englewood Cliffs, NJ: Prentice-Hall.

Kagan, J. S. (1994). *The nature of the child.* New York: Basic Books. (Original work published 1984)

Karmiloff-Smith, A. (1992). *Beyond modularity: A developmental perspective on cognitive science.* Cambridge, MA: MIT Press.

Siegler, R. S. (1991). *Children's thinking.* Englewood Cliffs, NJ: Prentice-Hall. (Original work published 1986)

Sternberg, R. J. (1988). *Mechanisms of cognitive development.* Prospect Heights, IL: Waveland Press. (Original work published 1984)

Chapter 5

Biological Perspectives

Introduction

Einstein's Brain

In 1955, the man widely considered to be the greatest scientist of his era, Albert Einstein, died peacefully in his sleep. Arrangements were made to remove his brain from his skull: there was considerable curiosity about whether this man—supremely intelligent by almost any definition—might have possessed a brain that differed in instructive ways from the brains of other individuals of his time and station in life.

For 20 years, Einstein's brain remained in a jar that was stored in a doctor's office in the American Midwest. Then, in the early 1980s, two well-known neuroanatomists, Arnold Scheibel and Marian Diamond, studied Einstein's brain carefully. They found that, in comparison with a control group of 11 elderly men, Einstein's brain had a significantly larger number of oligodendroglia cells.[1] Additionally, the brain exhibited a smaller ratio between neuronal and glial cells in the left inferior parietal lobe, an area of the brain thought to be important for verbal associations and conceptualization (Altman, 1991).

Interest in Einstein's brain reflects a long-standing belief among many scientists and laypersons that people of extraordinary intelligence or intellectual achievement may differ in some physical or physiological way from the rest of the population. Perhaps brighter people have brains that are larger (or smaller); that feature more (or less) electrical activity during periods of problem solving; that contain more or deeper fissures in the cortex.

---

[1] These are cells located near nerve cell bodies that support the central nervous system.

Let us assume that one could, indeed, establish some kind of physical differ-ence between the brain of Einstein (or Isaac Newton, or Marie Curie), on the one hand, and the brains of some control population on the other. Many questions would still remain. Were these scientists-to-be born with different kinds of ner-vous systems? Were their brains initially indistinguishable from those of other in-dividuals, but, for some reason, developed in a different way during the opening decade or two of life?

Possibly, Einstein's brain would look just like other individuals' brains but might function differently. Perhaps Einstein used his brain more often, or more efficiently, or perhaps he drew in combination on an unusually diverse set of neural centers when he was doing his most challenging work. It is even possible that Einstein's brain looked different from that of other individuals, but the par-ticular variation in appearance did not in itself contribute to his genius. After all, Einstein's hairstyle has seldom been duplicated—hence his immediate recogniz-ability when an image of his head is emblazoned on sweatshirts—and yet few would attribute his genius to the fact that his flowing white locks were singularly unkempt.

In this chapter, we consider the evidence that intelligence—in its most com-mon scientific and lay definitions—may reflect a biological property of men and women. Specifically, we focus on the most likely possibility: that specific proper-ties of the human nervous system, and particularly of the human brain, contribute significantly to the intellectual powers (or intellectual limitations) of individual human beings. We (the authors) do not believe that biological evidence is privi-leged over other kinds of evidence; but there is little question that many—perhaps most—observers are particularly impressed when one can point to an area of the brain, or a set of genes, and declare "Here lies intelligence!"

Four Distinct Biological Pathways

One promising approach is to consider what is known about the structure of the human brain; after all, few would dispute the claim that intellect is first and fore-most a reflection of the three-pound gray mass located within the skull.

A second approach is to look at indexes that measure some aspect of the func-tioning of the brain. Intelligence is not a static property; it is brought to bear when individuals are puzzling over a problem, engaged in invention, or attempt-ing to survive in a challenging environment. Thus, many scientists have looked for indexes of the "brain at work."

A distinctly different tack on intelligence is taken by those who are interested in human genetics. From their perspective, it is worth figuring out to what extent human intelligence is a function of genetic endowment, or, to use the common terminology, to what extent intelligence is "heritable." Comparisons of identical and fraternal twins are particularly useful for approaching these issues.

A final biological lens on intelligence considers the processes of human development. Scientists interested in development use information about the brain and about genetics. But rather than thinking of these sources as fixed, they focus on the ways in which the nervous system develops, or fails to develop, over a long period of time; and they consider the ways in which genes express themselves, or fail to express themselves, at various points in the course of development.

None of these approaches in itself solves the problem: What *is* intelligence? Indeed, for the most part, researchers in the biological tradition have accepted the definitions of intelligence used by other researchers—for example, scores on tests of intelligence, or the society's decision that someone (like Einstein, or the founding Soviet leader, V. I. Lenin) is highly intelligent. Thus, biologically oriented researchers have looked for correlations between test scores, on the one hand, and such factors as the size of the brain, the electrophysiological functioning of the nervous system, or the person's genetic heritage, on the other. But *if* their program of research succeeds fully, they will no longer need to depend on such external measures: instead, the biologically oriented researchers will be able to read intelligence directly by examining the brain-wave record or the genetic endowment.

The Organ Called the Brain

We now take it for granted that human knowledge, perception, consciousness, and, for that matter, ambition, jealousy, and courage are all functions of the human brain. One cannot proceed as a biological scientist unless one believes that the human brain, along with its extensions throughout the nervous system, is the site of all mental life and experience. It is therefore worth recalling that the special functions of the human brain were not appreciated in classical times, and that as recently as the time of the influential philosopher René Descartes (1596–1650), the interaction of the soul and the body was assumed to occur via the pineal gland at the base of the brain (see Chapter 2).

Only in the past two centuries have scholars directed their interest in the human mind to the organ called the brain. The beginning of the 19th century witnessed the rise of *phrenology*, a line of study engaged in by such outstanding anatomists as Franz Joseph Gall and Johann Kaspar Spurzheim. These individuals believed that important clues to human intellect came from the size and the shape of the human skull (which supposedly reflected the brain that was housed within). They measured many regions of the skull, and the ratios among those regions, and sought correlations to intelligence, wisdom, wit, criminality, love of family, love of animals, and various other human virtues and vices (Gardner, 1975) (see Figure 5.1).

The 19th-century form of phrenology was eventually discredited because its means of assessing human attributes were not any more developed than its primitive means of measuring relevant parts of the skull. Once it was known, for example, that an outstanding writer like Anatole France had one of the smallest recorded brains ever (weighing about 1,000 grams), and that many otherwise dull individuals have large brains, it was hard to accept the more simpleminded forms of phrenology.

Yet, in retrospect, the program of the phrenologists deserves to be honored for two reasons (Fodor, 1983). First, these researchers were attempting to look as carefully as their methods permitted at what the human brain was actually like. Second, they were attempting to relate what they discovered about the size and construction of the brain to specific aspects of human behavior and thought. These two missions are continuing, unabated, today.

The Organization of the Brain

A great deal of knowledge about the human brain has been acquired since the time of Gall and Spurzheim. For gross anatomical purposes, the brain can be divided into two large sections, or cerebral hemispheres—popularly known as the "left brain" and the "right brain." (See Figure 5.2.) Spreading across those hemispheres, 40 or 50 easily delineable regions (and hundreds of smaller but still recognizable areas) can be identified. Many of these regions subserve readily identifiable functions; for example, within the visual cortex, in the occipital lobes, are 30 to 40 distinct areas that are involved in different aspects of the recognition of shapes, as well as areas that relate visibly perceived objects to other sensory properties (like sound or touch), to names, and to meanings. Other areas of the brain have not been as intensively studied, but similar divisions of labor occur within the auditory cortex (in the temporal lobe) and the somaesthetic cortex (in the parietal lobes).

Until the 1960s, the functions of these parts of the brain were established by rather gross methods. One could identify the functions of left and right hemispheres by providing signals simultaneously to both halves of the brain, and then comparing the speed and accuracy of the individual's responses to those competing signals. In one such technique, called dichotic listening, subjects are equipped with earphones that transmit contrasting signals at the same time, and are simply asked to report what they hear; their responses indicate which parts of the brain are "dominant" for certain kinds of information. Such studies have revealed, for example, that, in right-handed individuals, the left hemisphere is "dominant" for linguistic signals, and the right hemisphere has comparable "dominance" for musical and other nonverbal auditory sounds (Kimura, 1973; Milner, 1967; Sperry, 1974). In other words, in most individuals, most linguistic processing occurs in the central regions of the left cortex, particularly in those regions called Broca's area and Wernicke's area. Processing of music and noise occurs in comparable regions of the right hemisphere. Left-handed individuals present a more complex picture: most of them have the same cortical representations as right-handers. But about one-third of left-handers present the opposite picture: they process linguistic sounds primarily

FIGURE 5.1
Phrenologists attempted to link specific aspects of human behavior and thought to specific areas in the brain. Lacking methods to study the brain itself, phrenologists inferred from the size and shape of the skull the functions of underlying brain areas.

Phrenological, Chart

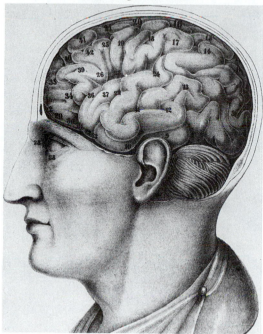

By Dr. N. Wheeler and C. G. Burleigh Jr.
Approved by L. N. Fowler

1. Amativeness: connubial love, attachment to the opposite sex.
2. Parentiveness: love of one's own offspring, of children and pets.
3. Adhesiveness: love of friends and society, attachment, sociability.
4. Union for Life: exclusive love of one sexual mate for life.
5. Inhabitiveness: love of home, desire to dwell in one place.
6. Concentrativeness: close application to one thing at a time.
7. Love of Life: clinging to life, sense and dread of death.
8. Combativeness: resistance, courage, bravo, defence, resolution.
9. Destructiveness: severity, force, indignation, instinct to destroy.
10. Alimentiveness: appetite and relish for food, hunger, thirst.
11. Acquisitiveness: love and accumulation of property, frugality.
12. Secretiveness: conceals the thoughts and feelings, policy, restraint.
13. Cautiousness: carefulness, fear, solicitude, watchfulness.
14. Approbativeness: love of character, fame, praise, display.

15. Self-Esteem: self-respect and confidence, dignity, independence.
16. Firmness: decision, stability, perseverance, fixedness.
17. Conscientiousness: love of justice, truth, morality, duty, equity.
18. Hope: anticipation, expectation of future good.
19. Spirituality: intuition, spiritual revery, faith, prophecy, credulity.
20. Reverence: religious fervor and love of worship, respect.
21. Benevolence: kindness, pity, goodness, charity, generosity.
22. Constructiveness: mechanical ingenuity, making things.
23. Ideality: imagination, fancy, taste, refinement, purity, love of poetry.
24. Sublimity: love of grandeur, the sublime and the magnificent.
25. Imitation: copying, patterning, representing, describing, acting out.
26. Mirthfulness: wit, fun, jocoseness, smiling, laughing, playfulness.
27. Individuality: to observe, know, examine, individualize.
28. Form: recollection of shape, faces, countenances, looks of things.

29. Size: measuring length, breadth, space, height, bulk, by the eye.
30. Weight: balancing, climbing, shooting, horsemanship, equilibrium.
31. Color: judgment of colors, their various shades, tints.
32. Order: system, arrangement, every thing in its proper place.
33. Number: mental arithmetic, cyphering, reckoning in the head.
34. Locality: desire to travel, recollection of places, direction.
35. Eventuality: memory of events, history, facts, news, stories.
36. Time: chronology, recollection of time, dates, ages, beat in music.
37. Tune: sense of sound, melody, musical taste and talent.
38. Language: command of words, disposition and ability to talk easily.
39. Causality: reason, thought, ideas, traces out causes and effects.
40. Comparison: comparing, illustrating, analyzing, criticising.
41. Human Nature: perception of motives and character.
42. Agreeableness: pleasantness, winning, suavity, persuasiveness.

Entered according to Act of Congress

FIGURE 5.2
Four views of the human brain.

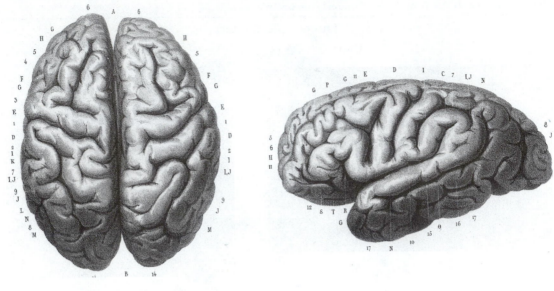

Dorsal View   Lateral View

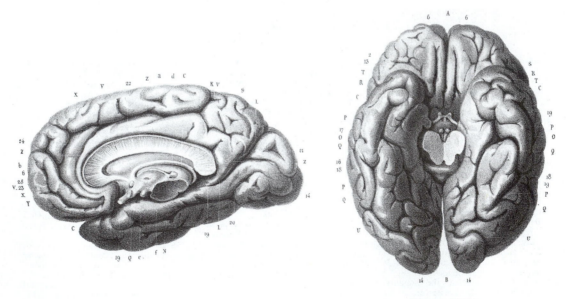

Medial View   Ventral View

in their (dominant) right hemisphere, and nonlinguistic sounds primarily in their left (nondominant) hemisphere.

Until the past few decades, the functions subserved by more focal regions of the brain were established by inference, the chief ally being the study of once-normal individuals who had suffered strokes or other kinds of brain disease. If, for example, individuals with damage to the superior part of the left temporal lobe were able to hear linguistic sounds but not to understand what those sounds meant, it was inferred that this region of the brain was crucial for the processing of word and sentence meaning.

The study of brain-injured patients led to the discovery of many surprising syndromes (Gardner, 1975; Geschwind, 1974). For example, in the condition called alexia without agraphia (or, less technically, word blindness), individuals lose the ability to read but can still write and spell. However, these individuals are not blind. They can recognize and name visually presented objects, read numbers, and even trace the contours of words that they cannot read. Curiously, however, they cannot name colors.

Careful study of syndromes like alexia without agraphia helps us to understand how information is represented in the brain. The cluster of symptoms just described suggests, for example, that visual information is readily associated with tactile information (as in object recognition) and named on that basis; for these patients, there is impairment in decoding purely on the basis of visual information. (That is presumably why the reading of words and the recognition of colors is so difficult: there are few if any tactile associations to such visual information.) Moreover, existence of this syndrome challenges facile categorization of functions: this syndrome supports the counterintuitive notions that verbal symbols are processed differently from numerical symbols, and that numerical symbols actually share more in common with objects that can be recognized and named.

Thanks to the pioneering work of David Hubel, Torsten Wiesel, and their colleagues (Hubel, 1979; Hubel & Wiesel, 1962), technology that allows for far more specific determination of brain functions has been developed. Using microelectrode recording from single cells in the visual cortex, these investigators have established that there exist specific cells, and columns of cells, that respond not to whole objects, but rather to such particular properties of objects as their color, shape, orientation, and movement in space. Cells in other parts of the cortex have similarly specific responses to particular properties of sound and of bodily sensation; other "hypercomplex" kinds of cells appear to be dedicated to specific appearances: they register reliably and only in the presence of facial configurations, tongue shapes, or handlike configurations. Most of these electrical recording studies, it is true, have been carried out with animals, particularly cats and monkeys; but it is assumed without controversy that the nervous system of human beings is similarly wired with respect to these perceptual capacities, though not with respect to more conceptual abilities.

Determination of the quite amazing specificity of the nervous system has constituted an important scientific advance. Earlier beliefs (Lashley, 1950; Lenneberg,

1967) that any part of the nervous system could carry out any function, or that all parts of the nervous system function similarly or equivalently, have been seriously challenged (Geschwind, 1974). When it comes to understanding human behavior, it is more important to know *where* in the nervous system a lesion has occurred than to know the size of the lesion or its cause. Yet, the determination of specificity harbors a paradox.

Put simply, the nervous system does not function as a set of thousands of isolated centers which "go off" at will. Rather, the nervous system is quite superbly orchestrated, so that responses rarely interfere with one another. Human behavior is organized, purposive, and integrated; the individual does not feel as if he or she is the victim of many conflicting signals and impulses. As Nobel laureate John Eccles has nicely phrased it, "Our brain is a democracy of ten thousand million nerve cells yet it provides us with a unified experience" (Eccles, 1965, p. 36).

How, then, does one square our rapidly emerging knowledge of the complexity and differentiation of the nervous system with a consideration of human intelligence? What does it mean, brainwise, to be smart? One line of research continues to examine the relationship of intelligence to gross measures of the brain. Physical anthropologist Harry Jerison, who has approached this question in the most sustained program of research, reports that, within the human population, the correlation between brain size (as measured, for example, by weight) and measured intelligence is low but positive (Jerison, 1982; see also Brody, 1992). A few authorities report a higher, though still moderate correlation (Willerman, Schultz, Rutledge, & Bigler, 1991). Interestingly, women have smaller brains than men, both in absolute terms and even when corrected for their overall smaller body size. Yet, women do not differ from men in measured intelligence; hence, the relation between brain size and intelligence remains enigmatic (Ankney, 1992).

Intelligence might well be more closely tied to the functioning of particular nervous centers than to overall brain size or shape. Some neuropsychologists have suggested that specific structures, such as the posterior parietal zones, where many forms of information from diverse cortical regions come together, may be particularly important for processes central in human intellect (Basso, DeRenzi, Faglioni, Scotti, & Spinnler, 1973; Luria, 1966; Zaidel, Zaidel, & Sperry, 1981). (Recall that Einstein's parietal lobe differed from parietal lobes observed in a control group.) Destruction of these strategically located areas causes diminished performance on intelligence tests, particularly those that require visual or spatial forms of problem solving.

Other neuropsychologists have suggested that the frontal lobes, which receive input from all regions of the brain, are the crucial centers of intellect. Injury to the frontal lobes can be cruelly damaging: individuals lose their sense of purpose and drive, and become, in a real sense, different kinds of persons (Damasio, 1994; Gardner, 1975; Hebb, 1949; Teuber, 1964). And yet, individuals can sustain massive damage to the frontal lobes and still score at a superior level in an intelligence test (Hebb, 1949). One reason is that intelligence tests place a high premium on "crystallized knowledge," information that has already been acquired—vocabulary, reasoning, and certain kinds of memory (Horn, 1985) (see Chapter 3). Intelligence tests generally place less of a premium on the ability to learn new things or to draw on one's learning when one must deal with a novel situation, and these aspects of "fluid knowledge" seem to be the functions for which an intact frontal lobe is especially crucial.

Such considerations have led some neuropsychologists, such as Marcel Kinsbourne (1993), to question the relevance of evidence about brain localization to a study of human intelligence. In their view, intelligence is a function not of the parietal lobes, the frontal lobes, or any other specific region. Rather, a person is smart to the extent that he or she has, altogether, a well-functioning neural machine. In this view, intellect is connected to a systemwide kind of fluency or flexibility, rather than to the superior or inferior functioning of any specific gear or widget in the neural machine. Performance can be undermined by the malfunctioning of a part that is important for the transport of information; one can disable any machine just by pulling out its plug. But to say that the critical mechanical function actually *inhered* in the plug is to commit an error of reasoning. Proper functioning reflects the smooth operation and reliable interaction of many parts.

New techniques, such as magnetic resonance imaging (MRI), have been developed for measuring the size and configuration of brain structures in the living human being. First reports indicate that individuals with known strengths in certain cognitive domains may well have brain regions that differ systematically in size and structure from those of individuals drawn from the same population who lack such talents. Thus, for example, highly verbal individuals may have somewhat larger linguistic zones in their left hemisphere than individuals who do not display appreciable linguistic skill; similar claims have been made about unusually large regions in the brains of artists and musicians (Scheibel, 1988). As of this writing, work in this tradition has not proceeded far enough to indicate how robust these findings are. But don't be surprised if you read in next Sunday's newspaper about additional work that relates specific brain structures to specific cognitive strengths.

The Brain as a Functioning Machine

While anatomists (and, more recently, neuroradiologists) have been peering at the physical brain, trying to figure out its structures and its wiring, many other scientists have been investigating its functioning over time. Ideally, such scientists would like to be able to peer directly, over time, at all parts of the brain while the individual is engaged in a cognitive activity—say, solving an algebra problem— and to compare the functioning of those parts of the brain at other times, when the individual is either involved in a contrasting activity (say, translating a passage from French to English), or is resting quietly (or sleeping).

The time when such total monitoring of the brain will prove possible is approaching; the rapid increase in sophistication of techniques that measure the functioning of the brain *in vivo* is staggering. One promising approach uses the technique of positron emission tomography (PET) scanning. This technique involves the ingestion of radioactive substances that figure in the body's physiological processing. By monitoring the blood supply and brain metabolism, PET furnishes *in vivo* measures of relative levels of activity in different regions of the brain. The operative assumption is that those parts of the brain focally involved in an activity will demand a greater supply of blood.

Preliminary PET scan studies have suggested a variety of intriguing phenomena. Individuals who score well in the Raven's Progressive Matrices (see Chapter 3) exhibit less cortical functioning after completion of that test (Haier, Nuechterlein, Hazlett, et al., 1988); similarly, subjects of high intellectual ability show greater decrease in glucose metabolism as they learn to master a task (Haier, Siegel, Tang, Abel, & Buchsbaum, 1992). These and other studies by Haier and colleagues suggest that individuals who are intellectually more able can more readily mobilize the appropriate neural centers and are soon able to succeed on tasks while using less neural power. Other studies have revealed different regional blood flow patterns in individuals with unusual skill in a particular area; thus, expert chess players and skilled musicians exhibit different patterns of blood circulation than do nonexperts who have been posed comparable sets of problems. These findings are consistent with those obtained from noninvasive techniques, such as dichotic listening. Once again, these clues announce an area of study that promises to flourish in the months and years ahead.

Until recently, however, scientists have had to use less precise techniques in order to monitor the brain. They have had to be satisfied with very partial sampling of its operation. And they have had to "triangulate" this sampling with two other indexes: first, the individual's performance on very simple kinds of behavioral measures; second, the individual's performance on standard measures of intellect.

One method favored by researchers has involved attaching a dozen or so electrical "leads" to the scalp and then measuring the functioning of the type and level of brain activity that occurs at these crucial spots. Electroencephalograms (EEGs) record alpha, beta, delta, and theta waves. The different waves refer to different characteristic periodicities or frequencies that are picked up by the electrodes and then amplified. Researchers of EEGs compare the patterns of spontaneous wave activity when the individual is at rest, to the patterns when the individual is aroused, attentive, and engaged in various kinds of effortful mental activity.

For several decades, researchers have been looking at the relationship between intelligence and specific EEG measures. It is therefore disappointing to report that there are still no firm conclusions in the area (Brody, 1992; Ceci, 1990). Some researchers, like Hendrickson and Hendrickson (1980), have consistently reported substantial correlations between IQ and EEG measures; indeed, in their view, the correlation is so substantial that EEG measures can be substituted for other measures of general intelligence. However, other researchers, whether using similar or different techniques, have not been able to replicate these findings. Even those who discern a definite relationship between brain waves and intelligence disagree about its meaning. One camp feels that EEGs directly measure "hard-wired" neural functioning; another favors the view that EEG taps information processing properties of the brain that grow out of experience.

Evoked-response potentials (ERPs) are also obtained by placing electrodes on the scalp. In this technique, the examiner focuses on the wave patterns of the brain in response to specific kinds of stimuli, such as an isolated sound, a sudden touch to the skin, or a flash of light. Researchers look at specific brain indexes, such as the response at a fixed number of milliseconds after the onset of the stimulus; they also probe more exotic waves such as the so-called P300 wave, which occurs when an event is unexpected, or when an expected event is not forthcoming. Other variations of these event-related techniques, such as readiness potentials, or contingent negative variations (CNVs), are also used to monitor the electrical activity of the brain under various conditions of stimulation.

One line of studies that makes use of this technology has looked at the average number of evoked potentials (AEP). Analyses of the length of AEP have shown a high correlation (about .8) with IQ test results: specifically, the length of the AEP wave pattern is longer for persons who score higher on IQ tests. One explanation offered is that, for persons with high IQs, EPs will form a similar pattern because information about the stimuli is transmitted through these persons' brains with little error or "noise." Hence, when averaged, these peaks and troughs remain distinct. For those with lower IQs, the length of the AEP is shorter because the individual EPs carry a lot of noise. When averaged in these individuals, the peaks and troughs of their waves tend to cancel each other out, making for a flatter average wave of shorter length (Anderson, 1992; Eysenck, 1986). (See Figure 5.3.)

In another set of evoked potentials (EP) studies, Schafer (1982) found dramatic differences between high- and low-intelligence subjects. Individuals with high IQs who listened to clicks that appeared at regular intervals were found to emit fewer EP responses than they did on the occasions when they listened to randomly presented clicks. Low-IQ subjects emitted disproportionately larger EPs to clicks that appeared at predictable intervals. Schafer interpreted this result as indicating that highly intelligent individuals can ignore highly predictable events, while still monitoring less predictable ones; less intelligent individuals have more difficulty distinguishing between the two classes of events.

Yet another biologically based approach examines the speed of information transmission in a brain nerve pathway; the measure is called nerve conduction velocity (NCV). In this case, the measure may be obtained in the peripheral nerve system (e.g., in the arm) rather than in the brain. Working with university students, Vernon and Mori (1989) obtained moderate correlations between the speed of nerve conduction and a measure of nonverbal intelligence (cf., Vernon & Mori, 1992). Probing the speed of nerve conduction in the visual system (retina to visual cortex), Reed and Jensen (1992) also discerned a moderate correlation between the speed of nerve conduction and measured intelligence.

We are faced with a situation that is not unprecedented in science but one that proves quite problematic for the nonspecialist. Over the course of the several

FIGURE 5.3
Evoked potential waveforms for six high-IQ and six low-IQ subjects (from Eysenck, 1986, p. 21). The length of the AEP is longer for those subjects with higher IQ test results.

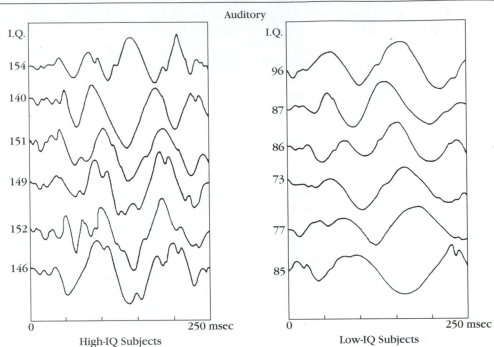

Auditory

High-IQ Subjects

Low-IQ Subjects

decades since methods for measuring brain waves were first discovered, there have been hundreds of studies that attempted to link various measures of brain activity to an array of measures of intelligence: simple response tasks, more complex forms of problem solving, or scores on tests of intelligence. Typically, there have been moderate correlations between the EEG, the ERP, the NCV, or some other rough measure of brain activity, on the one hand, and some generally accepted measure of intellectual competence (like an IQ score) on the other.

As noted, interpretation of the results of these studies has been a controversial matter. Recurrent brain-behavior correlates have encouraged some investigators to conclude that intelligence is a property of the nervous system and that these researchers are en route to figuring out just which property it is (Eysenck, 1986). Arthur Jensen (1993a, 1993c), for example, suggests that individuals with higher *g* (general intelligence) may have a nervous system that functions more rapidly or has less "noise" in it. He also proposes that *g* may involve a more capacious short-term memory, and that the key component of information processing capacity may be discernible in basic brain activity.

Critics point out that the correlations between electrophysiological measures and behavioral indexes have not been that impressive (.4 to .5, accounting for perhaps one quarter of the variation in scores); that there has been little consistency in results from one test or one laboratory to another; that the EEG and other such methods have been very gross and approximate and are affected by such features as skull thickness; and that issues of motivation, training, and context can affect performance even on such seemingly "pure," "basic," and "objective" measures. Stephen Ceci (1990), for example, indicates that individuals who do not customarily fare well in tests may become more nervous when they find themselves in the psychological laboratory, and that their different brain responses could reflect their anxiety rather than their customary modes of processing. Alternatively, those who are comfortable in testing situations, or those who are competitive in tasks, will perform at a higher level than anxious or apathetic individuals. Ceci's point is not that anxiety is necessarily the culprit; but rather that all kinds of intervening variables—ranging from test anxiety to motivation to temperament—rather than "sheer intelligence," might account for differing patterns of brain activity in laboratory studies.

Genetics: The Classical Issue

Whatever amount of controversy may obtain about the significance and the interpretation of studies of the anatomical structure and the *in vivo* functioning of the brain, it is dwarfed by the interest in, and controversy surrounding, studies of the genetics of intelligence. It is probably not an exaggeration to say that the relative influences of nature versus nurture constitute the most controversial issue in the behavioral sciences; and nowhere are the weapons more poised to be fired than with respect to the question of the extent to which measured intelligence is a product—wholly or in large measure—of genetic endowment (cf. Bouchard, 1993; Eysenck, 1973; Herrnstein, 1973; Herrnstein & Murray, 1994; Jensen, 1969, 1980; Lewontin, Rose, & Kamin, 1984; Sternberg & Grigerenko, in press).

At first blush, this issue would seem to be straightforward. In fact, Francis Galton suggested the basic methodology for investigating it more than a century ago: Study the extent to which closely and more distantly related individuals resemble each other in intelligence. As noted in Chapter 2, Galton argued that heredity accounted for the frequency of genius or "eminence" in particular families such as the Darwins and Huxleys. He recognized, however, that some others would argue that family environments might explain this phenomenon. To control for the effect of environment on behavior, Galton suggested studying the mental ability of twins who were raised in different households. He hypothesized that those who had inherited from their parents the capacity to be eminent would grow to be eminent adults even if they were adopted and reared by people outside their family (Galton, 1869).

Since the late 1970s, using sophisticated methods derived from Galton's basic ideas, the field of behavioral genetics has flourished. However, behavioral geneticists do not assume, as Galton did, that biology dictates intellect. Instead, most behavioral geneticists recognize that, though genetics influences intelligence and other behaviors, so does environment (Plomin, 1986, 1990).

Behavioral geneticists' methods allow them to partial out, or control for, the relative effects of heredity and environment (Bouchard & Propping, 1993; Loehlin, 1993). Researchers quantify the extent to which different relatives resemble each other genetically. For example, monozygotic (identical) twins share all their genes. In contrast, adopted siblings, or adoptive parents and children, share no genes. On average, ordinary siblings share half their genes. Such quantification helps behavioral geneticists to calculate heritability: the proportion of observed (or phenotypic) variance due to genetics.

Alongside quantifying the degree of genetic resemblance, behavioral geneticists use family, twin, and adoption research designs to see how relatives reared together or apart vary with respect to intelligence (and other characteristics). This procedure helps them to understand the extent of influence exerted by genetics and environment.

Some of the most clear-cut findings come from studying identical twins reared apart. Because such twins are genetically identical, any *differences* in their measured IQ are largely attributable to environment (and error of measurement; see Chapter 3). Another clear-cut way to see the relative influences of genes and environment is by looking at genetically unrelated individuals who are reared together, such as adopted siblings. Because genes are not shared among such siblings, *similarities* in measures of their intelligence may be explained largely in terms of environmental influences.

Using these and other techniques, a range of behavioral genetics research indicates genes have a very powerful influence on intelligence (Bouchard, 1991; Horn, 1983; Juel-Nielsen, 1965; Shields, 1962). For example, among identical twins reared apart, the correlation of IQ scores is about .72 (Bouchard & McGue, 1981; Bouchard, Lykken, McGue, Segal, & Tellegen, 1990; Plomin, 1990). Though they share little in the way of home environment (see Bouchard, 1983), such adopted twins nevertheless have strikingly similar IQs. To appreciate the influence of genetics on their scores, consider the correlations of other siblings (see Figure 5.4). Fraternal twins and ordinary siblings, raised in the same households, have far lower correlations (respectively, .60 and .47). Of all familial relationships, only identical twins reared together have more closely correlated scores (.86).

Studies of genetically unrelated adoptive siblings who are reared together also provide powerful evidence for the influence of genetics on intelligence. As children, the IQ correlation of such siblings is about .32. However, as these siblings mature, the correlation in their IQs diminishes (Scarr-Salapatek & Weinberg, 1983). In adulthood, such siblings resemble each other in intelligence no more than do any other genetically unrelated individuals. Similar environments do not ultimately yield similar IQs among this group. One conclusion from such findings is that, in the expression of cognitive abilities, genetic factors become more important with age (Plomin, 1990).

FIGURE 5.4

Average weighted correlations table of IQ scores for twins, siblings, and adopted siblings (after Bouchard and McGue, 1981, p. 1056).

	No. Pairs Studied	Weighted Averages
Twins		
Monozygotic (identical)		
Raised together	4,672	.86
Raised apart	65	.72
Dyzygotic (fraternal)		
Raised together	5,546	.60
Ordinary Siblings		
Raised together	26,473	.47
Raised apart	203	.24

In recent years, behavioral geneticists have found another, more subtle influence of heredity on intelligence. It now appears that heredity helps to shape the home environment. As Robert Plomin (1990) explains, a home with lots of books (a commonly used measure in assessing home environment) may reflect parental IQ: bright people tend to read more. In addition, parents respond to genetically influenced variables in their children, such as intelligence. So, the measurement of an environmental variable such as time spent reading to children may reflect,

Robert Plomin.

Thomas Bouchard.

in part, brighter children's genetically influenced interest in such activity (Plomin, 1990; see also Scarr, 1989; Scarr & McCartney, 1983). In short, environmental influences are not necessarily purely environmental; they may reflect genetic influences as well.

These results give little comfort to committed environmentalists. Conservatively speaking, nearly all experts place the heritability of intelligence at a minimum of 50%. That is, at least half of the variation in intelligence test scores within a population is attributable to the influence of the genetic pool—and many experts would place the figure closer to 60% or 70% (Bouchard, 1990; Horn, Loehlin, & Willerman, 1979; Plomin & Thompson, 1993).

It is worth noting, incidentally, that the same technology used for behavioral genetics can be applied to any measurable trait. Studies that measure intellectual traits such as spatial and verbal abilities indicate heritabilities in the .5 range; other intellectual capacities, like memory and speed of processing, have lower heritabilities (Plomin, 1994). Personality traits, and even such exotic features as political leanings and susceptibility to divorce, also turn out to be substantially heritable (Bouchard, 1990). These heritabilities emerge in most dramatic (and satirizable) form when identical twins separated at birth turn out to have precisely the same hairstyle, pet preference, sense of humor, and/or religious beliefs. For example, such twins have been found to have similar occupations, marry wives with similar names, and give their children and pets nearly identical names (Holden, 1980).

Behavioral genetics studies have revealed other interesting findings. In children as young as 7 years, specific intellectual factors have been found to have their own heritability, apart from the heritability of general intelligence (Cardon, Fulker, DeFries, & Plomin, 1992). Specific disorders, such as reading disabilities, have been linked to markers on specific chromosomes: number 14 and, possibly, number 6. Finally, though most behavioral geneticists believe that intelligence is a complex, polygenetic trait that entails a large number of genes, one report has suggested that individuals with very high psychometric intelligence may have an identifiable gene structure (Plomin, quoted in Kelner & Benditt, 1994; Plomin & Thompson, 1993).

The finding that psychometric intelligence is significantly heritable has the following implications. The most important thing that one should know about a person, if one wants to predict that person's psychometric intelligence on the basis of a single index, is the identity of both biological parents. The moment when the child is conceived proves crucial for the determination of how that individual will perform on intelligence tests years—even decades—hence. On the average, information about the identity of parents is more determinant than information about the individual's race, sex, ethnic group, or the quality of the home or school that person has experienced.

Think of the explanatory power of genetics in terms of monozygotic twins and adoptive siblings. If one wants to know how one monozygotic twin will perform on a test of intelligence, simply test the other one. Even if they have been separated at birth and their homes turn out to be quite different from one another,

Separated at birth, the Mallifert twins meet accidentally.
Drawing by Chas. Addams, © 1981 The New Yorker Magazine, Inc.

these twins' performance on intelligence tests is still likely to be quite similar—rarely differing by as much as one standard deviation (about ±15 points). By the same token, if one wants to know how an adopted child will do on a test of intelligence, test the child's biological parents or, if they are not known or not available, the child's biological siblings, if any. Except in rare circumstances, the prediction is more accurate (the correlation is much higher) than if one tests the other biologically unrelated children raised in the same household.

Even the most committed hereditarian will concede that there are limits to the contributions of biology. If a child is seriously deprived of nutrition or of cognitive or affective stimulation, his or her intelligence test score will go down. Being locked in a closet or being deprived of healthy foods is no way to raise one's IQ score. By the same token, if a child from modest intellectual background is afforded every educational advantage—a decade-long education with Aristotle on one end of a log and the student on the other—the child's intelligence score will go up (Scarr-Salapatek, 1975; Scarr-Salapatek & Weinberg, 1976; Watson, 1980;

Woodworth, 1941)—perhaps as much as 20 or 25 IQ points. After all, at least 30% and perhaps as much as 50% of the variation in intelligence is due to factors other than the identity of one's biological parents. And it is here that education, modeling, and training (or the lack of them!) can make a significant difference in the overall "life options" available to a child.

Committed environmentalists are not likely to declare these concessions on the part of hereditarians as sufficient (LeVine, 1991; Lewontin, Rose, & Kamin, 1984). They will instead criticize hereditarian claims at every point in their chain of argument. Critics point out, first of all, the many acknowledged limitations in the whole theory of intelligence and in the particular instruments that have so far been designed to test intelligence. They turn next to the assumptions involved in adoption studies. It is often claimed that adoption is a random process, but there is some reason to believe that monozygotic twins reared apart are often reared in families that are quite similar to one another, or even in families that are biologically related to the child (but see Bouchard, 1983). Moreover, children within the same household are often motivated to be different from one another. This important fact causes the intellectual profiles of siblings to differ. By the same token, children who look alike and who show similar behaviors, but who are reared in different households, may be treated in ways that are *more* similar, yielding similar intellectual profiles.

Critics point out, finally, that nearly all studies take place within a Western context. How much of the variation in intelligence would be seen as genetically based, had studies been carried out in dramatically different environments? What if one monozygotic twin were reared in a middle-class American town and the other were removed to a Chinese village or a South Seas island?

Such a line of reasoning has led a few critics to question all the inferences drawn from twin studies. Leon Kamin is perhaps the most vociferous critic of this entire line of research (Eysenck & Kamin, 1981). After carefully reviewing all of the major findings that examine the genetic basis of intelligence, he believes he has found flaws in all of them. These flaws range from the criteria used to determine eligibility for the study, to the precise test measures used, to the kinds of statistical analyses that have been performed, to a possible confound between the age at which twins are tested and their average IQ. Kamin concludes: "The same data from which [Sandra] Scarr concludes that IQ is substantially heritable can be used—since Scarr is willing to share her raw data—to show that IQ is not at all heritable. The data are not, after all, the product of clearly designed and well-controlled experimentation. They are necessarily correlational data collected in difficult and inevitably flawed field settings" (Kamin, 1981, p. 468).

Critics of the genetics approach to intelligence save their most harsh criticism for two often-voiced views. These views do not necessarily follow from a behavioral genetic approach but have sometimes been put forth by those sympathetic to a hereditarian perspective.

The first is the implication that the heritability of intelligence may explain the consistently poorer performance on intelligence tests of certain racial and ethnic groups (cf. Herrnstein & Murray, 1994). Critics point out that all of the assumptions of heredity theory apply only *within* a single population; there is no way to prove that differences between populations (say, White and Black, or Asians and Caucasians) are due to heredity rather than, say, to different life experiences or to different treatments at the hands of others. Indeed, many authorities argue that long-standing prejudicial attitudes toward minority groups make it impossible to draw *any* inferences from apparent racial differences in IQ scores. The reportedly poorer average performance of Black students can be readily explained by a combination of fewer life opportunities, prejudices, and lowered expectations on the part of teachers and others. To invoke genetic explanations is unnecessary and potentially harmful. A reverse explanation can be given for the higher scores of Asian students.

The second contentious implication is that intelligence is refractory to training. Even if much of the variation in intelligence, as usually measured and developed, appears to be the consequence of genetic factors, there is no reason why intelligence cannot be markedly changed and improved. After all, no one disputes that height is largely inherited, and yet entire populations have gained in stature because of improved diet and health practices. By the same token, apparent differences in intelligence ought to serve as a stimulus for improved education and training, and not as an excuse to lay down the books, close the schoolhouse, or abandon all special education and tutoring.

Arthur Jensen.

The coincidence of these two issues probably resulted in the unprecedented critical response to an article written by Arthur Jensen (1969), a respected but hitherto little-known professor of education at the University of California at Berkeley. In an article commissioned by the *Harvard Educational Review,* Jensen posed the question "How much can we boost IQ and scholastic achievement?" (see Chapter 3). Reviewing a great deal of evidence of the sort that we have just summarized, Jensen put forth his view that racial differences in intelligence were genuine, were due significantly to hereditary factors, and were not much susceptible to remediation or erasure. In that article and in other writings, Jensen even proposed one means (primarily, rote) for educating students of low intellectual potential, and a more active and challenging means for educating more promising students. As noted in Chapter 3, Jensen's

(1969) views drew little support from the rest of the scientific and educational community. He has directed most of his subsequent research energies to the investigation of the biological bases of *g* or general intelligence.

An entirely different way to think about group differences in IQ is through the notions of cumulative advantage and cumulative disadvantage. Suppose that one child, or one group, has a dozen positive experiences each day, from conception until the age of 5. Suppose another child, or another group, has a dozen negative experiences each day. These experiences can include nutrition, loving care, cognitive stimulation, physical exercise. By the age of 5, the first individual(s) have had over 25,000 positive experiences; the second individual(s) have had an equal number of negative experiences.

At age 5, both individuals take an intelligence test, and their scores differ by one standard deviation. One can hardly argue that the resulting difference is a product of biological destiny or an inborn IQ. It is far more parsimonious to assume that the children's 25,000 positive or negative experiences have produced divergent individuals. It is worth noting, in this context, that IQ scores are not reliable enough before the age of 5 to allow accurate predictions to be made about life chances.

As we saw in Chapter 3, the arguments continue between those who attribute individual or group differences to biological factors, and those who attribute them wholly or significantly to experiential factors. The brouhaha about Terman's claims in the 1920s (see Box 3.2, p. 87) have been echoed by responses to eugenicist claims during the Nazi era, Jensen's arguments in the 1960s, and Herrnstein and Murray's claims in the 1990s. It would be ahistorical to infer that we have heard the last of such struggles between two entrenched perspectives on the biological underpinning of intellectual achievements.

The controversy over the biological (or nonbiological) basis of intelligence is more than an ordinary scientific controversy; it has to do with *which* sciences will dominate in the future. If those in pursuit of a biological basis of intelligence (and of other traits of organisms) are largely successful in their efforts (Wilson, 1975), then the need for other disciplinary forms, such as psychology, sociology, or anthropology, is accordingly reduced. No wonder social scientists reach for their intellectual weapons whenever the prospect of biological determinism is raised (Degler, 1991; Wheeler, 1992).

Critics of the biological approach worry about another state of affairs as well. To the extent that biologically based findings gain currency among the public and among politicians, they will lead to a conclusion—incorrect but inviting—that there is no reason for society to intervene in other ways. One of the reasons for the instant and highly critical response to Jensen's (1969) article, and to more recent writings in the same tradition (Herrnstein & Murray, 1994), was the belief that such conclusions would lead to proposals to suspend, as useless, Head Start and similar early-intervention programs. (Such proposals have indeed been made.)

Even if most of the variation in intelligence turns out to be inherited, this fact is in itself no argument against early childhood interventions. Indeed, exactly the same data can be used as an argument for earlier and greater interventions that just might "even the playing field." Such calls for greater intervention, however, have rarely been made by scientists who attempt to document high heritabilities of psychometric intelligence.

Developmental Views

If intelligence has a significant hereditary component, then evidence of intellectual differences ought to be detectable early in life. Research early in the century, using "rough-and-ready" measures of intelligence, suggested little "continuity" between early and later measures of intelligence. But new technologies have permitted far more probing investigations of the mental life of young infants. Such studies indicate that, as early as the first months of life, one can distinguish infants from one another in terms of the speed with which they respond to new information, are able to remember it, and can adapt to it (Bornstein & Sigman, 1986; Fagan, 1990). Those infants who learn to recognize and to habituate more rapidly to sights and sounds turn out to have higher IQs upon entering school than those infants who respond more slowly or less consistently to these sensory stimuli.

The course of the development of intelligence may constitute a more complex biological story than is suggested by these findings. Human beings develop quite rapidly from the moment of conception and for at least 20 years post-birth; many facilitating and many disruptive events can occur over that period of time. Adoption of a developmental perspective may ultimately yield a more complex view of what intelligence is and of how it relates to "strictly" biological factors.

In a developmental view, both genetic and environmental factors are operating and interacting from the moment of conception. The fetus is not maturing in a vacuum; it is housed within the uterus of a woman who herself is undergoing diverse stressful and relaxing experiences, and whose hormones, blood supply, and other metabolic processes are contributing directly to the welfare of the unborn child. We now know that the fetus, at 5 or 6 months, can hear, can see, and can feel. Who would be so confident as to suggest that these prenatal perceptual experiences have no effect on the child's ultimate makeup and capacity to learn?

Once born, the child is subjected to a welter of experiences at the hands of the particular individuals with whom he or she comes into contact and the particular society in which he or she lives. Each of these experiences has its impact, and most will have implications for the mind as well as the body. Even if these influences do not manifest themselves automatically on psychometric intelligence, they certainly have impact on the child's life prospects. Moreover, the differences within particular industrialized societies may be relatively small; but once one considers the differences between, say, life in a Western urban center and life in a Stone Age hunting society or in an agrarian setting that has remained unchanged for thousands of years, the role played by environmental factors comes to be seen as considerable, if not determining (Berry, 1974; Berry & Irvine, 1986; Cole & Cole, 1989; Collier, 1994; LeVine, 1991; Rogoff, 1990).

It is equally important to realize that all of these environmental factors are not played out on a blank slate; rather, they exercise their impact on an infant who comes equipped with a certain nervous system and a certain temperament, both of which are heavily influenced by genetic factors. This realization has stimulated one of the less intuitive but very important ideas in the study of human development: the growing organism *selects* its own environment (Scarr & McCartney, 1983).

Let us consider two children from the same family. Both are female. Paulina has a very active temperament and responds rapidly and enthusiastically to new stimuli; Edith is much more phlegmatic and her responses are very inhibited and considered. Paulina and Edith spend the day at the same amusement park. Can one say that they have the same experience at that site?

Not at all. Paulina gravitates immediately to the roller coaster, the ferris wheel, and other stimulating rides; and when she goes on these rides, she becomes very excited and happy. Edith visits the booth where nature movies are shown, and peers endlessly at the map of the site, trying to figure out how to reach an area where she can sit by herself.

Consider, now, what happens if Edith is forced to go on the rides and if Paulina is compelled to visit the nature films and to study the map. On an objective basis, the girls have had the "same experiences," but, subjectively, their experiences may be as different as night and day (Kagan, 1994). Edith's time on the roller coaster proves an ordeal for her, and Paulina's session in the nature movie theater is a low point of Paulina's day.

As developmentalists now put it, youngsters "select" environments that are consistent with their own needs and interests; left to their own devices, Paulina and Edith "use" the amusement park in very different ways. Moreover, they experience objectively identical events and learn from them in ways that are compatible with their temperament and their cognitive strengths and styles. Even if both girls are compelled to look at the movies or to ride on the roller coaster, each girl's learnings and reactions are likely to be very different.

What is notable here is that the developmental view cannot give complete comfort to either the hereditarian or the environmentalist. The hereditarian must recognize that, even if genetic heritage is ordinarily very important, every individual still has a unique set of formative experiences. If these experiences are quite unusual, they are likely to exert dramatic effects on the adult personality. The environmentalist must recognize that every child comes equipped with certain givens and proclivities; whatever the child's experiences, they will be played out by virtue of what the child brings to those experiences and what the child is able to extract from them.

Environmental factors may play important roles at different points in development. As noted earlier in this chapter, recent research suggests that, with age, genetic factors are more likely to assert themselves. For example, monozygotic twins become more similar in intelligence in later life than they are in adolescence. In contrast, there are certain "critical" or "sensitive" periods, such as adolescence, when societal and cultural factors are relatively more influential (Plomin, 1994). But even if, in the long run, most individuals reveal their genetic heritage, this still gives much latitude to the environmentalist; for, to the extent that the "windows of opportunity" offered by development are maximally exploited, the older individual will be an individual quite different from the one who would have evolved, had nature been allowed simply to take its usual course.

We return now to what is known about the physical brain's development before and after birth. The general pattern of neural development is determined by our genome—our species membership. Much of brain development has occurred before birth; the young infant is already in some ways quite a mature organism: it is capable of detecting sounds and viewing objects in ways that are surprisingly adultlike. Even the establishment of brain dominance, once thought to occur over the first 5 years of life, seems to be established very early in infancy (Lewkowicz & Turkewitz, 1981; Molfese & Molfese, 1972). Except in cases of pathology, the brains of all human beings develop in quite similar ways: the myelinization (shielding) of nerve cells occurs rapidly in the first years of life; the development of association cortexes takes place during the same period as well; neural growth spurts occur prior to the time of major intellectual milestones (Thatcher, Walker, & Giudice, 1987); and the more gradual maturation of the frontal cortex happens during the first decade of life in the world.

Yet, it would be precipitous to conclude that, across individuals, there are no differences in brain development. Many studies conducted with animals over a period of years indicate that those animals reared in a rich environment end up having larger and better-connected cortical areas than those who are reared in impoverished milieus (Greenough, 1981; Greenough, Black, & Wallace, 1987; Rosenzweig, 1966). Studies of adult monkeys who have sustained injuries to the "hand region" of the cortex indicate that new areas of the cortex become available to serve some of the functions once under the control of injured areas. Functions can recover, even in adulthood! In the cortical regions of congenitally deaf human beings, areas that are devoted to auditory processing in hearing individuals end up being dedicated to the spared visual processing (Neville, 1991).

Most intriguingly, there is evidence to suggest that fetuses whose mothers undergo unusual stress may develop brains that are organized differently from those of normal infants. Surveying a number of reports, Geschwind and Galaburda (1987) propose that such early trauma may result in precocious growth in the infant's right hemisphere, leading ultimately to reading problems, on the one hand, and to compensatory spatial gifts on the other. The idea that there is a "pathology of superiority," with anomalous brain development leading to unexpected weaknesses and compensatory strengths, may help to illuminate the topography of the minds of individuals with unusual talents and deficits and even suggest possible modes of education.

None of these recent findings, in itself, reveals the extent to which individual brains may differ from one another structurally in a systematic way, let alone whether these differences point to accompanying intellectual strengths or weaknesses. The results are even more preliminary than those reported on electrophysiological concomitants of intellectual differences. Nonetheless, they suggest that all kinds of experiences, prenatal as well as postnatal, may affect the ultimate structure and functioning of the brain. We are likely to discover, over the next few decades of behavioral and brain research, the ways in which experiences make their biological marks.

Summary

As a way of recalling the principal points in this chapter, let us return to the case of Einstein. On the basis of the genetics material reviewed in this chapter, we might infer that he came from a family with high intellectual potential, if not achievement. (It is true that his parents' achievements were modest, but his uncle was a budding scientist.) We can also assume that, had more sophisticated measuring techniques been available, scientists might well have documented further differences in the structure and the functioning of his nervous system. His EEG, ERP, or NCV might have been noticeably different from that of others of his background, particularly when he was solving challenging problems; and perhaps the larger number of glial cells in his parietal lobe could be linked to Einstein's particular intellectual gifts.

The question of whether the differences in the adult Einstein would have been manifest in the young Einstein, however, cannot be answered in the absence of developmental evidence. It is as likely that small initial differences were fanned and consolidated by environmental factors, as it is likely that young Albert was fated from the first to be—or to become—Einstein. Perhaps Einstein selected particular environments precisely because they suited his temperamental and intellectual proclivities, and these in turn drove him toward a career as a creative scientist. It is worth mentioning that some behavioral geneticists believe that individuals like Einstein are genetic accidents whose rise could not be predicted even from complete knowledge of their family background (Lykken, McGue, Tellegen, & Bouchard, 1992).

At the time of this writing, the study of the biological bases of intelligence is in its earliest phases: this is why scholars can disagree almost totally about how to interpret findings. Some scholars feel that electrophysiological measures can already be substituted for standard tests of intelligence; others point to the inconsistency of results, the modest correlations, and the various personality or contextual factors that may affect responses on an apparently simple laboratory task, like reaction time to a flashing light. With the perfection of far more sensitive tools for measuring neural activity from birth, in all of its complexity, at least some of these puzzles are likely to be answered in the next quarter century. Moreover, as tools of genetic analysis themselves are enhanced, it appears likely that one may soon be able to point to quite precise gene loci as the cause of whatever factors may contribute to high psychometric intelligence.

As we shall see, some researchers think it is a mistake to spend time looking at the brains—or even the minds—of unusually gifted individuals. For them, Einstein is better explained in terms of the society in which he lived, the training he received from his parents and teachers, his contact and competition with brilliant peers, or the state of the domain of physics at the time when he began his researches. Einstein might have had exactly the same nervous system, but if he had been born on the Galapagos Islands rather than in Germany, if his father had been a hunter rather than a businessman who sold electrical devices, or if the physics of his time had required more mathematical and less spatial imagination, then Albert Einstein might not have died as a man whose name is synonymous with genius.

Social scientists and historians feel that students of unusual human accomplishment are looking at the wrong place, so long as they focus on the brain—or, for that matter, on the individual in isolation. From their vantage point, Einstein became who he was because of where and when he lived—because of Germany and Switzerland in 1900, and because of some conceptual problems that fellow scientists Jules-Henri Poincaré and Hendrick Lorentz had left unsolved—and not because of the size of his brain, its number of glial cells, or the ways in which information was transmitted from one cortical region to the other (Gardner, 1993a).

The study of intelligence must, at present, be broad enough to encompass these two seemingly different, but perhaps ultimately reconcilable, points of view. As more and more authorities agree, the question is not "biology versus culture" or "heredity versus environment," but how best to think about the interaction of the givens in each pair. As Robert Woodworth (1941) concluded in an influential early review of work in this area, "To ask whether heredity or environment is more important to life is like asking whether fuel or oxygen is more necessary for making a fire" (p. 1).

With our look at the biological bases of intelligence, we have completed our examination of the human individual as seen within the confines of his or her skin. For many—perhaps most—students of intelligence, an understanding of human biology and psychology is the most important basis of work in this field.

In recent years, however, insights into intelligence have come from a new and unexpected source: the kinds of cognitive and problem-solving abilities of which computers are capable. As we see in Chapter 6, though computers were originally designed to carry out rather mechanical tasks, they have developed to the point where they not only can tackle issues of a challenging nature but also can provide insights about how human beings use their own minds.

Suggested Readings

Bloom, F., & Lazerson, A. (1988). *Brain, mind, and behavior* (2nd ed.). New York: Freeman.

Damasio, A. (1994). *Descartes' error: Emotion, reason, and the human brain.* New York: Putnam.

Gardner, H. (1975). *The shattered mind: The person after brain damage.* New York: Knopf.

Gazzaniga, M. (1985). *The social brain.* New York: Basic Books.

Plomin, R. (1986). *Developmental genetics and psychology.* Hillsdale, NJ: Erlbaum.

Restak, R. M. (1988). *The mind.* New York: Bantam Books. Videocassette series also available through PBS, Washington, DC.

Springer, S. P., & Deutch, G. (1993). *Left brain, right brain* (4th ed.). San Francisco: Freeman. (Original work published in 1981)

Chapter 6

The Cognitive Perspective

Introduction

In November 1991, a contest, widely covered by the media, was held at Boston's Computer Museum (Dewdney, 1992). Ten human judges sat down at computer terminals to engage in dialogues on topics such as pets, Shakespeare, and whimsical conversation. Connected to each terminal, out of sight of the judges, was either another terminal with a human operator or an artificial intelligence (AI) computer program. The task for the judges was to spend 5 minutes conversing through each terminal and then determine which conversations were carried on with humans and which were with machines. As it turned out, the Shakespeare dialogue was carried on with a human Shakespeare buff. Nonetheless, she was identified by several judges to be a machine, in part because of her quick and accurate answers to questions about the Bard's works. The whimsical conversation, however, was carried on by a machine, running a program called PC Therapist. Some judges determined whimsical conversation's silicon nature through the program's grammatical errors, but 5 of the 10 judges were convinced that this conversation could have been carried on only by a human.

This contest was the first annual Loebner Prize competition, in which programs compete in a limited version of the Turing test. The Turing test, first proposed by the pioneering computer scientist Alan Turing in 1950, defines a baseline for machines to merit the description "intelligent." That baseline is met when machines are able to carry on a conversation as well as a human would. Turing referred to this task as "the imitation game." Turing's prediction with respect to the task was:

> . . . that in about fifty years' time it will be possible to programme computers, with a storage capacity of about 10^9 [one billion], to make them play the imitation

game so well that an average interrogator will not have more than 70 per cent chance of making the right identification after five minutes of questioning. (Turing, 1950/1963, p. 19)

In the 1991 contest, programming contestants were allowed to limit conversation to a particular topic. Turing's prediction that the judges would have no more than 70% chance of correctly identifying the human and computer participants was more than achieved in the contest, at least within some areas of conversation. At present, no computer can carry on a reasonable conversation in all areas. It remains to be seen whether Turing's subsequent prediction will come true, that at the end of the century "one will be able to speak of machines thinking without expecting to be contradicted" (Turing, 1950/1963, p. 19).

During the World War II era, there were targeted efforts to build machines that could solve complex problems such as tracking planes in flight or computing ballistic trajectories. Those efforts often required detailed descriptions of intelligent processes. Then-prevailing investigations in psychology were of little help in understanding intelligent problem solving: As discussed in Chapter 3, psychometric assessment supports a view of intelligence as a stable trait of individuals. The psychometric approach does not examine the problem-solving processes people use in answering test questions, let alone creating radar systems or atomic weapons. As discussed in Chapter 2, behaviorist psychology plumbed observable behaviors: stimuli and responses ("S–R"). It did not attempt to fathom the internal workings of the mind, which behaviorists tended to regard as "a black box."

Alongside the pressures for advanced war technology were other forces that began to pry open the black box. There was a growing discontent with S–R theory and its failure to offer insights into how people solved problems of consequence. There were indications from neuroscience that people did not just respond to incoming stimuli in the serial fashion proposed by behaviorists (Lashley, 1951). A number of psychologists were gathering evidence that behaviors were not evoked simply by stimuli; rather, people had mental maps or schemes that guided their thoughts and actions and allowed flexibility in the manner or order of their expressions (Lashley, 1951).

Gradually, researchers began focusing less on the products of intelligent behavior, such as test scores, and more on the processes that led to them. The convergence of these investigations with the rapid development of electronic computers spurred "the cognitive revolution." This revolution continues to shed light on how intelligent systems, both mechanical and biological, use and organize information, solve problems, and learn.

In this chapter, we trace the emergence of the cognitive revolution in work from diverse fields, including cognitive psychology, cybernetics, computer science, and artificial intelligence. We see how a new understanding of the nature of intelligence has emerged from the development of progressively more intelligent machines. As increasingly more sophisticated intellectual capabilities have been embodied in machines, there follows a continual redefinition of human intelligence. This constant scrutiny grows out of comparison of the capabilities of machines and humans. It also stems in part from the reluctance of many to acknowledge the possibility that a machine can be intelligent. As we examine the differences between human and machine intelligence, we will see why, at each stage along the way, researchers have concluded that their understanding of intelligence is not yet complete.

Emergence of the Cognitive Revolution

The Rise of Intelligent Machines

The desire to create intelligent objects is ancient. Several stories of intelligent machines can be found in Greek mythology. In Homer's *Iliad*, for instance, Hephaestus, the god of fire, describes his intelligent metal assistants:

> These are golden, and in appearance like living young women. There is intelligence in their hearts, and there is speech in them and strength, and from the immortal gods they have learned how to do things. (Lattimore, 1951, cited in McCorduck, 1979)

We refer to the ancient Greek accounts as myths, but, in Hellenic Egypt, devices that "spoke," gestured, and prophesied were actually constructed (McCorduck, 1979). Yet another example of the human desire to create intelligent objects was documented by the philosopher Descartes. Walking through the royal gardens of 17th-century France, Descartes saw human-shaped machines (automata) that moved and made noises when he stepped on the hidden hydraulic actuators (Jaynes, 1970, cited in Pratt, 1987).

Unlike clocks, or other types of complex machines of this era, the automata looked "real" and performed simple humanlike motions. Their appearance and actions made some observers wonder whether such a machine could be intelligent. Descartes came to the conclusion that no machine, and for that matter no material substance, was truly capable of thinking (see Chapter 2). Thought was not the realm of matter, but rather of God-given human souls.

The automata of the 17th century were limited to several simple motions; for instance, they apparently chased one another around a circular path. However, in the next century, Jacques de Vaucanson became an international celebrity for his sophisticated machines, including two human automata, a drummer and a flute player, exhibited at the Académie Royale des Sciences in 1738 (Hultén, 1968, p. 20). In the same century, Pierre Jacquet-Droz developed an automaton in the form of a young boy that could write. These apparently highly skilled machines profoundly impressed those who saw them. A French physician, Julien Offray de La Mettrie, was so impressed with Vaucanson's automata that he daringly contradicted Descartes and the Catholic church. He published a book entitled *Man a*

Machine, wherein he asserted that the action of the brain in the process of thought could be explained in as straightforward a manner as legs in the process of walking. Intelligence, by La Mettrie's argument, could well inhere in material substances, and he speculated that material substances might even be fashioned to make "a talking man" (La Mettrie, 1747/1982, p. 407).

As the Loebner Prize competition demonstrates, giving a machine the ability to talk and to carry on an intelligent conversation was then centuries away. By our contemporary standards, the automata of the 17th and 18th centuries executed interesting actions but performed no intellectual tasks, as Descartes would have anticipated. Their motions were limited to those prescribed by their clockwork gears. The gears were designed to produce the motions that would accompany intelligent thought, rather than the intelligent thought that might guide such motions.

Efforts to apply machines to intellectual problems began in earnest with the development of automatic calculators. Calculation has long been considered a human intellectual capability; even now, Webster's dictionary defines a *calculator* as a *person* who calculates (Webster's, 1994). But in early 19th-century England, Charles Babbage applied automatic machinery to the task of computing mathematical tables. In 1822, he constructed a working model of an automatic table calculator he called *The Difference Engine* (McCorduck, 1979).

As an outgrowth of this effort, Babbage envisioned an even grander computing device, *The Analytical Engine,* a steam-powered, mechanical programmable computer. Though it was never completed, the Analytical Engine would have been able to calculate, process statistics, and automatically guide its own actions based on the answers it was producing (Eames & Eames, 1990).[1] Babbage is noteworthy in the history of the science of intelligence because he was among the first to demonstrate that intellectual tasks, at least those of a mathematical and analytical nature, could be performed automatically by machines. Box 6.1 describes some of the implications for judging machine intelligence stirred by his work.

Just as the flute playing of Vaucanson's automata could alter the perception of what intelligence is, so did the creation of calculating machines. Until the invention of such machines, calculation was considered a uniquely human intellectual capability. Today, however, many would argue that calculation is a mechanical task. As computers develop increasingly sophisticated skills—skills that we now consider uniquely human intellectual capabilities—will these, too, be explained away in the future as having been mechanical in nature to begin with? There are two alternative views we may consider: (a) we can acknowledge that machines are becoming intelligent, or (b) we may decide that many, or perhaps even all, of our intellectual processes are ultimately mechanical in nature. These views may be reconciled if we can accept that something can be describable, and mechanically modeled, and yet still be considered intelligent.

---

[1] The Analytical Engine introduced many features that would appear in computers of the next century, including punched card data and program entry, internal memory for storage of intermediate results, and printed output.

Box 6.1
Judging Artificial Intelligence Versus Human Intelligence

Without common sense and natural language understanding, computers cannot be expected to perform well on standardized intelligence tests intended for humans (see Chapter 5). This does not mean that there is no means by which to gauge their intelligence or abilities. (A similar problem is faced in attempting to judge animal intelligence.) Since Babbage's time, numerous individuals have proposed means of judging machine intelligence. Most such proposals evaluate machine intelligence through at least implicit comparisons with human intelligence.

Lord Byron's daughter, Ada, the Countess Lovelace, collaborated with Babbage, and developed programs that could run on the Analytical Engine. Countess Lovelace was asked directly about the intelligence of Babbage's Analytical Engine. In part because she hoped to raise funds to build the machine, her response was: "that the actual existence of the machine and experience with its practical results would be the only way to answer questions about the machine's intelligence with any finality" (McCorduck, 1979, p. 28). Notably, though, she stated that "the Analytical Engine has no pretensions whatever to originate anything. It can do whatever we know how to order it to perform" (McCorduck, 1979, p. 27). Countess Lovelace had allowed the possibility that the machine might be described as intelligent, but she had set up, whether or not intentionally, the criterion of *originality* as a basis for machines to be called intelligent.

In February 1947, Turing gave a lecture to the London Mathematical Society. Having read Countess Lovelace's accounts, he criticized the viewpoint that computing machines can only carry out the processes that they are instructed to do (Turing, 1947/1986). He described a process by which a computer's instruction tables could be modified by the results of its own computations. Of this process, he said:

> It would be like a pupil who had learnt much from his master, but had added much more by his own work. When this happens I feel that one is obliged to regard the machine as showing intelligence. (Turing, 1947/1986, p. 123)

Turing acknowledged that this approach would not by itself achieve a sophisticated intelligence, but he pleaded for "fair play for the machines when testing their I.Q." (Turing, 1947/1986, p. 124). He reminded the audience that humans must undergo extensive training, so one should

Continued

Box 6.1 (Continued)

not expect a machine to develop its own knowledge without training. He evidently felt that good performance on an IQ test would require that one be socialized, presumably the process by which one acquires common sense: "the machine must be allowed to have contact with human beings in order that it may adapt itself to their standards" (p. 124). Turing proposed the game of chess for this purpose.

Turing's lecture to the London Mathematical Society was not made broadly available until 1986. Consequently, other statements of his about machine intelligence are more widely known. He is probably best known for the Turing Test, which remains the most widely accepted test to define a machine as intelligent.

It is important to consider these options as we examine the later efforts that extended computing far beyond the realm of mathematics. Expanding the range of computable subject matter was the focus of much of the work of Claude Shannon. As a graduate student at MIT in the 1930s, Shannon knew that systems of logic, as described by mathematicians and philosophers before him, may be reduced to true and false propositions. These propositions he realized, may in turn be fully represented and processed by the *on* and *off* states of systems of electrical switches, or relays. During the next 10 years, Shannon and his colleagues developed this line of thinking into a new discipline called *information theory*. Generalizing from logic to information, they proposed that all information, regardless of content, can be broken down into binary digits ("bits," or ones and zeros), and therefore could ultimately be represented and processed by machines. Information theory, together with the rise of electrical computers, helped lay the groundwork for the development of general-purpose digital computers, whose capacities continue to challenge and reshape notions of intellectual functioning.

Many brilliant minds came to the forefront during the computer-building efforts of the 1940s. These efforts were mainly focused on solving the immediate problems brought on by World War II. However, several of these pioneers, including John von Neumann and Alan Turing, also spent time thinking deeply about how to build intelligence into their machines. Such researchers undertook the prerequisite task of studying and describing intelligent behavior, a task necessary for specifying the circuits and computer programs that could emulate intelligent behavior.

One might imagine that psychologists would have been better equipped than scientists, engineers, and mathematicians, to study intelligent human behavior. Yet, as noted earlier, psychology at that time was dominated by behaviorism. Behaviorist doctrine held that behavior is guided by a system of stimuli and responses. To build a computer based on this premise, the computer would have to be built first with no conception of how the internal circuits should be constructed or should behave. Once constructed, rather than being programmed to carry out certain logical operations, its behavior would be modified by experiences, over time, to achieve the desired results.

At about the time when information theory and computers were flowering, psychology was beginning to move in sympathetic directions. In the late 1940s, an important voice from within the behaviorist ranks began to challenge traditional behaviorist assumptions. Psychologist Karl Lashley argued that stimulus and response could not account for complex behaviors like speech or playing a musical instrument. These complex tasks often require *simultaneous* actions and a *sequence* of motions that suggest advanced planning and mental representations or maps (Lashley, 1951). This formulation was contrary to the behaviorist supposition that actions take place strictly serially, with each action guided by feedback from the previous action. In an activity like language, noted Lashley, there simply isn't adequate time for feedback to guide each action. Further, evidence of advanced planning in language came from such errors as slips of the tongue, where words or parts of words might occur well in advance of their intended location (Lashley, 1951). Lashley proposed a new model of behavior in which a stimulus is still significant, but it acts on an "actively excited and organized" mind (Lashley, 1951, p. 112). In order to peek into the organization of the mind, Lashley recommended a study of language and syntax, noting that "Speech is the only window through which the physiologist can view the cerebral life" (Lashley, 1951, p. 113, quoting Fournier, *Essai de psychologie,* 1887).

Lashley's recommendation was soon pursued. Psychologists and others interested in understanding complex problem solving increasingly turned their attention from observable events, as behaviorism required, to the cognitive processes underlying behaviors. Linguist Noam Chomsky (1956, 1957) followed Lashley's lead in thinking about language and syntax. In 1956, he presented a paper in which he laid out a basis for language to be defined with the precision of mathematics (Miller, 1979). Chomsky described the rules that operate when we create sentences. Those rules are systematic and logical. Chomsky argued that the rules reflect the fundamental mental mechanisms underlying our ability to speak. His work not only provided insight into language processing within the brain, but also laid the groundwork for computers that would actually generate and/or understand language.

In the same year that Chomsky delivered his seminal paper, another key contribution to understanding cognitive processes was made by psychologist George Miller. In his essay, "The Magic Number Seven, Plus or Minus Two: Some Limits on Our Capacity for Processing Information," Miller suggested that there exist built-in limitations in human information-processing capabilities (Miller, 1956). Among these, he documented that short-term memory appeared to be capable of holding only about 7 pieces of information; that is, asked to remember a disparate group of elements, a person can remember only a small number of them, unless the person has a strategy to remember more. Miller's work did more than expose the limitations on human information-processing ability. Perhaps more importantly, he helped to uncover the means by which we can accomplish complex tasks *despite* these limits. For example, it is difficult for most people to remember a string of 12 random digits. We can overcome this difficulty, however, through strategies such as *chunking,* in which we might reorganize the 12 digits into 3 "chunks" of 4-digit numbers. Thus, the string 177620011945 might be memorized by breaking it into 3 familiar 4-digit dates.

Miller's work, plus that of other psychologists, probed the nature and structure of human information processing. Their efforts helped to form a theoretical basis for positing fundamental mechanisms underlying human information processing. Donald Broadbent, the first to apply *flow charting* to human information processing (Lachman, Lachman, & Butterfield, 1979), diagrammed his theory of the flow of information within the human brain, as illustrated in Figure 6.1.

The diagram shows how information may be detected through the human senses, and may enter short-term memory, which in turn is filtered with the aid of the "store of conditional probabilities of past events," or long-term memory. This process ultimately results in actions or thoughts. Though this is a simplistic diagram of the elements of human information processing, the resemblance to flow charts used in writing computer programs is significant. If a detailed diagram could be developed that adequately described human thought, might it serve as a blueprint for designing intelligent computers?

The insights gained through explorations of human information processing came nowhere close to explaining fully human thought, but they did help lay a groundwork for designing computer-based intelligence. In designing computers, for instance, it was found that long-term information storage, on punched cards or magnetic tape, was fairly inexpensive. Comparing elements from that memory,

FIGURE 6.1
An early flowchart of human information processing. From Broadbent (1958).

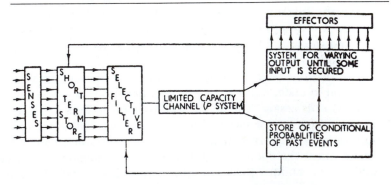

however, required that the information be loaded into expensive, instantly accessible short-term storage. Because cost prevented all memory from being of the fast, expensive type, there was clearly much to learn from the human information processing model: Humans seemed to store 7 (plus or minus 2) pieces of information in short-term memory, plus a virtually unlimited amount in long-term memory. What were the methods that allowed thinking under such limitations, and how could these methods be built into computer systems?

Modeling Intelligent Processes: Learning About Human Intelligence by Creating Intelligent Machines

Development of Artificial Intelligence

The year 1956 marked not only the publication of Chomsky's and Miller's seminal papers, but also the emergence of artificial intelligence (AI) programming. That summer, an important conference in the new field of AI was held at Dartmouth College in New Hampshire. Its charter encouraged researchers:

> . . . to proceed on the basis of the conjecture that every aspect of learning or any other feature of intelligence can in principle be so precisely described that a machine can be made to simulate it. (McCorduck, 1979, p. 93)

From this conference emerged the fathers of artificial intelligence, including John McCarthy, Marvin Minsky, Allen Newell, and Herbert Simon. These and other researchers came from around the country to discuss their efforts at developing intelligent programs. Programs to play chess and checkers were shown. Marvin Minsky discussed how programs could be developed to prove Euclidean theorems (see Box 6.2). Along a similar line, Newell and Simon demonstrated their program Logic Theorist (LT), which was already able to prove mathematical theorems (Gardner, 1985).

The Logic Theorist was designed to discover proofs for theorems in symbolic logic. It worked by maintaining, and selectively applying, a list of axioms and previously proved theorems to newly created logical expressions. The program would run through all of the operations it was capable of, applying such techniques as substitution of one kind of expression for another, and syllogistic-type reasoning (if "a implies b," and "b implies c," then "a implies c") (Gardner, 1985, p. 147). Further, it used some elementary strategies for breaking down problems into goals and subgoals.

Newell and Simon were quick to point out that LT did not operate by mere brute force. When LT was first employed on this task, it generated proofs for 38 of the first 52 theorems in Chapter 2 of Russell and Whitehead's symbolic logic treatise, *Principia Mathematica*. Most of these were completed in less than 5 minutes each, and the longest took less than 45 minutes. If LT had tried to find a solution

Marvin Minsky.

Herbert A. Simon.

by random or iterative (sequential) search through the *solution space* (the combination of all possible logical operations that could yield a solution), the proofs would have taken hundreds or even thousands of years to complete (Gardner, 1985). In LT, the size of the solution space (and consequently, the time required to generate a solution) was greatly reduced by applying a series of *heuristics,* or rules of thumb, like working backward from a desired solution, and breaking down large problems into smaller ones.

It is important to realize that LT was created to simulate human problem solving, not to generate proofs (Pratt, 1987; see Newell, Simon, & Shaw, 1958). To gain insight into human problem-solving processes, Newell and Simon used a technique known as *protocol analysis.* A protocol is a record of human subjects' verbalization of their thoughts as they solve problems. This method helped reveal what the subjects were thinking, what they were looking for, and why they were performing certain actions. Researchers hypothesized about the heuristics that were implicit in the subjects' protocols, and then encoded these heuristics into LT. Once LT was operational, the protocol studies were again analyzed in a side-by-side comparison with traces of the operations performed by LT. By studying the differences between the human and computer-based approaches to problem solving, Newell and Simon were able to refine the LT program further.

Newell and Simon's analyses of human and LT problem-solving processes led them to develop a new and larger-scale program, the General Problem Solver, or GPS (Pratt, 1987). They intended the General Problem Solver to be applicable to all manner of problems, as is evident in the name of the program. In its basic

Box 6.2
A Program by Marvin Minsky Solves a Euclidean Proof

Around the same time that Newell and Simon's LT program was applied to mathematical proofs from Russell and Whitehead's *Principia Mathematica,* Marvin Minsky was working on programs to solve Euclidean proofs. Minsky developed a program that produced a new solution to the well-known Euclidean proof that the two angles at the base of an isosceles triangle are equal to each other. Whereas Euclid's proof required construction of a straight line from the apex to the base, the computer-derived proof is far simpler and more elegant, requiring no construction (Michie, 1986). The proof is described below:

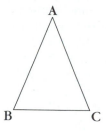

$$AB = AC \text{ (given)}$$
$$AC = AB \text{ (given)}$$
$$\angle BAC = \angle CAB$$
$$\therefore \triangle ABC = \triangle ACB$$
$$\therefore \angle ABC = \angle ACB \quad \text{Q.E.D.}$$

The technique used here may be called insightful, or even brilliant (Michie, 1986) and deserves a moment's consideration. Rather than drawing a line to the base to create two triangles to compare, this simply treats triangles ABC and ACB as separate entities for the purposes of the proof. If the triangle, and a copy of the triangle flipped over onto itself, are equivalent, so too must be their angles.

approach, GPS divided problems into goals and subgoals, and applied operations according to a set of rules, called *productions.* When an operation was performed, either a solution was reached, or the program was yet some distance, d, from a solution. The objective then was to minimize d. As Newell and Simon (1961) explain:

> These methods form a recursive system that generates a tree of subgoals in attempting to attain a given goal. For every new difficulty that is encountered a new subgoal is created to overcome this difficulty. GPS has a number of tests it applies to keep the expansion of this goal tree from proceeding in unprofitable directions. . . . [For example] GPS will not try a subgoal if it is harder than one of its supergoals. It will also not try a goal if it follows an easier goal. That is, GPS insists on working on the hard differences first and expects to find easier ones as it goes along. (p. 286)

The title of their paper, "GPS, A Program that Simulates Human Thought," reflected a feeling at the time that problem solving comprised much or all of human thought. Newell and Simon had some initial success with GPS, applying it to puzzles and playing chess (Campbell, 1989), but the program turned out to be far less universally applicable than they had hoped. Eventually, they would conclude that GPS's limitations existed not because of an inability to solve problems, but rather because of the inadequacy of *problem solving* as a characterization of human thought.

Yet, there was much to be learned by studying problem solving, which is clearly an important aspect of intelligence. John McCarthy, another AI pioneer, also contributed to understanding problem-solving processes. Soon after the Dartmouth conference, he proposed that a version of a well-known animal psychology experiment—the chimpanzee and banana problem—was an appropriate and challenging test of AI techniques. In this classic problem-solving test, a chimpanzee is locked in a room with a banana dangling from the ceiling. The chimp must figure out that, to reach the fruit, it must stack and then climb several boxes that have been placed in the room.

The computer version of this problem was first solved by the Artificial Intelligence Group at Stanford Research Institute (Michie, 1986). The SRI group recast the problem as the "robot and box" problem, in which a box rests on a platform out of reach of an armless robot with a video camera "eye." The solution, for which the robot was not preprogrammed, required the robot to push a ramp-shaped block to the platform and then roll itself up the ramp to get to the box. This seemingly trivial task took over a half-hour. To accomplish the task, many subproblems had to be set up and solved. We can gain some insight into the robot's thinking processes by studying its sequence of objectives and decisions, here translated into English from traces of the robot's decision tree:

> I must . . . discover where the ramp is. To do this, I must first see it. To do this, I must first go to the place where, if I looked in the right direction, I might see it. This sets up the subtask of computing the coordinates of a desirable vantage

point. . . . Next, I have the problem of getting to the vantage point. Can I go directly, or will I have to plan a journey around obstacles? Will I be required to travel through unknown territory to get there if I go by an optimal trajectory; and, if so, what weight should I give to avoiding this unknown territory? When I get there, I will have to turn myself, and tilt the television camera to an appropriate angle, then take a picture in. Will I see a ramp? The whole ramp? Nothing but the ramp? Do I need to make a correction for depth perception? (Coles, quoted in Michie, 1986, p. 120)

Machines were now clearly demonstrating the ability to solve problems. However, as noted earlier, critics of machine intelligence might argue that these problems were mechanical in nature to begin with. Or, they might acknowledge the presence of an intelligence, but qualify it as only an apelike intelligence. Perhaps out of a desire to answer the critics, many researchers sought to define and emulate human abilities that set human intelligence apart from other animals. They turned again to the problem of natural language.

Natural Language

Among AI researchers, there was a strong desire to create computers that would use natural language. The ability to communicate through natural language, as opposed to the computer languages used in GPS and other early programs, would give the appearance of greater intelligence. Additionally, language is integrally tied with human thought, so much so that Turing made conversation central to his test for intelligence. There were other reasons to develop natural language capabilities: it was presumed that giving verbal instructions to a computer would be easier than writing programs; further, researchers saw potential commercial applications for language capabilities, such as automatically translating between English and French or Japanese.

A number of programs developed in the early 1960s appeared to have the ability to carry on intelligent conversations. Characteristic of these was Joseph Weizenbaum's well-known program, ELIZA, which mimicked the conversational behavior of a Rogerian psychotherapist. In the ELIZA program, persons interacting with the program play the role of patients in nondirective psychotherapy. ELIZA's style was "to elicit feelings from, and then reflect them back to, her patient so that they can be recognized and acknowledged" (Boden, 1987, p. 106). This mode is seen in the following example, with ELIZA's contributions capitalized:

I am unhappy.
DO YOU THINK COMING HERE WILL HELP YOU NOT TO BE UNHAPPY
I need some help, that much seems certain.
WHAT WOULD IT MEAN TO YOU IF YOU GOT SOME HELP
Perhaps I could learn to get along with my mother.
TELL ME MORE ABOUT YOUR FAMILY
My mother takes care of me.

WHO ELSE IN YOUR FAMILY TAKES CARE OF YOU
My father.
YOUR FATHER
You are like my father in some ways.
WHAT RESEMBLANCE DO YOU SEE
You are not very aggressive but I don't think you want me to notice that.
WHAT MAKES YOU THINK I'M NOT VERY AGGRESSIVE
(Weizenbaum, 1976, pp. 3-4)

A first reading of these sentences suggests that the goal of creating an intelligent, speaking machine had been achieved. The appearance of intelligent conversation here is deceptive, however. The responses ELIZA gives are generated with a few simple rules, using a pattern-matching technique. When the user of the program types in "My sister is mean to me," the program searches for certain keywords. Finding the keyword "sister," the program selects from a list of preformed responses to "family" words, for instance "WHAT ELSE COMES TO MIND WHEN YOU THINK OF YOUR [sister]" or "TELL ME MORE ABOUT YOUR FAMILY." When ELIZA failed to find keywords in a sentence, a selection was made from a list of neutral responses such as "I SEE," or "THAT'S VERY INTERESTING" (McCorduck, 1979). Furthermore, ELIZA was unable to recognize nonsense, and consequently would respond to input like "My dkwoo is lwkdfj" with "GO ON" or "YOU SAY YOUR DKWOO IS LWKDFJ." In essence, ELIZA performed with language as the automata centuries earlier had performed with motion. ELIZA provided responses that were entirely predefined.

ELIZA lacked both any real understanding of English conversation, as well as content knowledge of any subject. Consequently, ELIZA was unable genuinely to answer even the simplest questions. This inability was masked by turning all questions around with a response like "WHY DO YOU ASK?" (Boden, 1987, p. 96). This tack proved maddening to anyone trying in earnest to carry on a conversation with ELIZA, as shown in the following exchange with a vice-president of a computer company who sat down to use a computer terminal, not knowing that it was connected to a computer running ELIZA:

Do you think that I can use the computer this morning?
WHY DO YOU ASK?
I might be able to make some additional telcomp sales.
WHY AREN'T YOU SURE?
My prospective customers have never seen a demonstration of the system.
DOES THIS MEAN VERY MUCH TO YOU?
Of course it does.
YOU SEEM VERY POSITIVE ABOUT THAT.
This is ridiculous.
WHAT DO YOU MEAN THIS IS RIDICULOUS?
Is there any reason why I can't use the computer now?
TELL ME MORE ABOUT YOUR PROSPECTIVE CUSTOMERS.
(Boden, 1987, p. 96)

As this example illustrates, ELIZA had no real ability to carry on an intelligent conversation. In interchanges that appeared otherwise, "the 'sense' and the continuity the person conversing with ELIZA [perceived were] supplied largely by the person himself" (Weizenbaum, 1976, p. 190).

Knowledge

Following ELIZA, a number of programs greatly improved the ability of computers to understand speech and respond appropriately (Firebaugh, 1988). However, few researchers worked solely on developing natural language techniques. The shortcomings of programs like ELIZA had shown that a genuine ability to answer questions requires basing the answers on *knowledge* about the actual conditions in the world, and not on just a grammatical analysis of the questions. Developing programs that would operate from knowledge bases soon became the primary focus of much of the research in AI.

Understanding even simple questions, in any reasonable sense of the word, is a huge and complex task. The complexity of the task can be narrowed, however, by severely limiting the topic of conversation. One of the early programs to achieve success in this manner was D. G. Bobrow's program STUDENT, which could respond to high school-level algebra problems posed in English—the type that might start, "A man is rowing upstream in a boat at 3 miles per hour." This was a convenient area for computer interpretation, because the algebraic interpretation (and solution) of the problem is not dependent on having any understanding of the definition of a man, a boat, a stream, or anything other than the mathematical relationship of the elements involved. The task required, however, that a real knowledge of algebraic relationships be embedded in the program. This competence was facilitated by already well-developed computer techniques for representing and computing algebraic problems.

Bobrow's program was quite successful in the domain he had chosen, but by itself, the ability to answer algebraic questions with numeric answers was not a very compelling model of robust intelligence. Bobrow's program could extract the answers implied by algebraic relationships of the problems, but nothing else. It was unable, for instance, to appreciate the nonsensical nature of a problem that began: "A rock was floating upstream at 75 miles per hour."

In contrast, Terry Winograd (1972) sought to create a program that could answer a far wider range of questions with nonmathematical solutions, and that had a sense of what was possible or impossible. To limit the scope of the task, however, it was necessary to create a very small "world." Winograd's world consists of several shapes (Figure 6.2) and a robot named SHRDLU to manipulate them.[2]

---

[2] Winograd chose the name SHRDLU as gibberish, an obscure reference to a proofreading error made when type was composed on Linotype machines (Boden, 1987). SHRDLU, as described by Winograd (1972), is not a physical robot, but rather a program that operates only on a computer screen, manipulating objects in a theoretical world. Its behavior was modeled on contemporary simple robots, having single manipulator arms and simple electronic eyes.

Figure 6.2
Winograd's "block world." Adapted from Winograd, 1972, p. 9.

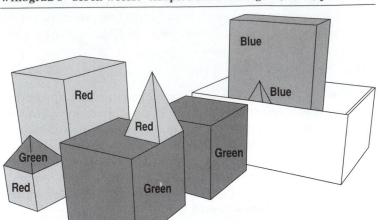

Winograd's approach was an exhaustive encoding of knowledge of this very small world, with a natural language interface that allowed users to change things in that world, and to interrogate SHRDLU about that world. Because SHRDLU had a robust knowledge about this world, it was able to give reasonable responses to questions, as is evident in the following exchange (SHRDLU's responses are capitalized):

what does the box contain?
THE BLUE PYRAMID AND THE BLUE BLOCK.
what is the pyramid supported by?
THE BOX.
how many blocks are not in the box?
FOUR OF THEM.
is at least one of them narrower than the one which I told you to pick up?
YES, THE RED CUBE.
is it supported?
YES, BY THE TABLE.
can the table pick up blocks?
NO.
can a pyramid be supported by a block?
YES.
can a pyramid support a pyramid?
I DON'T KNOW.
stack up two pyramids.
I CAN'T.
(Winograd, 1972, pp. 9–10)

Beyond simply recognizing questions about the relationships between objects, SHRDLU also recognized the semantic rules for word relationships. This knowledge allowed SHRDLU to recognize that a table picking up a block is nonsense, and, therefore, to assume the answer to be false (Winograd, 1972). In addition, SHRDLU could acknowledge that a block could support a pyramid without verifying it experimentally, but didn't know whether two pyramids could be stacked. When SHRDLU was instructed to stack two pyramids, it was able to recognize its inability to do so.

Terry Winograd's success with SHRDLU demonstrated the critical role of detailed background knowledge in intelligent behavior. The program took an important step toward genuine understanding, rather than merely mimicking understanding (Gardner, 1985). The program also arrived at a crucial time, as AI was coming under increasing attack by critics. Earlier, there were bold predictions, like Herbert Simon's assertion that "machines will be capable, within twenty years, of doing any work that a man can do" (Simon, 1965, p. 96). However, by the late 1960s, computers programs were clearly falling well short of human capabilities (Campbell, 1989; Glaser & Chi, 1988). At best, most AI programs, including Newell and Simon's GPS, could only work in a world of perfect information with well-defined problems (Campbell, 1989). This situation is uncharacteristic of most problems humans deal with in real life (see Chapter 9). Edward Feigenbaum, in a late 1960s talk at Pittsburgh's Carnegie Institute of Technology,[3] challenged the audience of researchers, which included Newell and Simon, to take on real problems: "Chess and logic are toy problems. If you solve them, you'll have solved toy problems. . . . Get out into the real world and solve real-world problems" (Feigenbaum, quoted in Gardner, 1985, p. 161).

Expert Systems

Partly in response to such gibes, and partly to ensure continued funding, research shifted dramatically away from projects like GPS, which were aimed at finding universal rules of thought, and toward systems that would "reason, make tentative recommendations, and advise on courses of action in such fields as medicine, chemistry, business, and engineering" (Campbell, 1989, p. 61). The success of programs such as SHRDLU suggested that knowledge bases would be the key to developing these new systems. To solve the hard problems, however, the systems would require the level of knowledge characteristic of human experts (see Chapter 9). Thus, these programs came to be known as *expert systems* or *knowledge-based systems*.

One of the first expert systems was Feigenbaum's own program, Heuristic DENDRAL. DENDRAL took its name from the Greek word for "tree," a reference to the need to search a tree of possibilities for a solution (Crevier, 1993). This program incorporated knowledge in the area of organic compounds into a program

---

[3] Now Carnegie-Mellon University.

used to identify the structure of unknown molecules given a spectroscopic analysis (Barr & Feigenbaum, 1982). This program, which began at Stanford in 1965, encoded knowledge as a set of rules that expert chemists used to solve mass spectrometry problems. The program proved useful in determining the structure of a number of organic molecules, helping to unlock the secrets of antibiotics, pheromones, and hormones. DENDRAL demonstrated that knowledge-augmented, heuristically driven programs could readily be applied to solving practical problems. The following 20 years brought a great deal of activity in expert systems applied to problems ranging from geological prospecting to medical diagnosis, with a number of legitimate accomplishments to their credit (see Box 6.3).

Box 6.3
Expert Systems For Medical Reasoning

Expert systems require coding expert knowledge into production (if–then) rules. V. L. Patel and G. J. Groen's (1986) study of seven human expert cardiologists is characteristic of the cognitive research necessary to code that information (Wagman, 1991). The doctors were asked to read a patient's case, which begins:

> This 27-year-old unemployed male was admitted to the emergency room with the complaint of shaking chills and fever of four days' duration. . . . He also complained of some shortness of breath when he tried to climb the two flights of stairs in his apartment. (Patel & Groen, 1986)

After reading the entire case, they were asked to write down as much of it as they could recall. Protocol analysis on the changes in this description relative to the original gave hints as to the doctors' structuring of the information, and the importance placed on individual details. The doctors then produced written protocols explaining the pathophysiological basis of the case, and their diagnosis:

> THE IMPORTANT POINTS ARE THE ACUTE ONSET OF CHILLS AND FEVER IN A YOUNG MALE WITH PUNCTURE WOUNDS IN THE LEFT ANTECUBITAL FOSSA INDICATING HIGH PROBABILITY OF DRUG ABUSE AND THEREFORE SUSCEPTIBLE TO ENDOCARDITIS. . . . THE SHORTNESS OF BREATH (SOB) ON EXERTION AND THE EARLY DIASTOLIC MURMUR PLUS WIDE PULSE PRESSURE SUPPORT AORTIC INSUFFICIENCY AND THUS AORTIC VALVE ENDOCARDITIS. (Patel & Groen, 1986)

Continued

Box 6.3 (Continued)

One cardiologist was asked to state the relevant canonical knowledge of endocarditis in the form of causal rules. This knowledge, readily available in textbooks, is a part of the knowledge base of expert cardiologists. A diagram based on Patel and Groen's (1986) work of the causal rules is shown below:

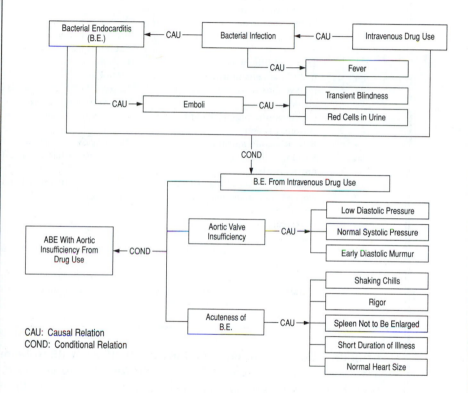

Protocol analysis was applied to the doctors' summaries to yield a set of if–then propositions, as shown in the table on page 180. The information is now in a form suitable for encoding in an expert system, wherein vast sets of such productions may be tested and applied to real-life problems.

In the Patel and Groen study, four of the cardiologists arrived at the correct diagnosis, and three were incorrect. The four subjects who arrived at the correct diagnosis made use of critical rules 2 (IF intravenous

Continued

Box 6.3 (Continued)

Production rules to yield an accurate diagnosis of acute bacterial endocarditis with aortic insufficiency from drug use (Patel & Groen, 1986).

Production Rule (#)	Antecedent (If)	Consequence (Then)
1.	Puncture wounds and young unemployed male	Intravenous drug use
2.	Intravenous drug use	Bacterial infection
3.	Bacterial infection and emboli	Bacterial endocarditis
4.	Fever	Bacterial infection
5.	Transient blindness	Emboli
6.	Red blood cells in urine	Emboli
7.	Intravenous drug use and bacterial endocarditis	Bacterial endocarditis from intravenous drug use
8.	Low diastolic pressure and normal systolic pressure	Aortic valve insufficiency
9.	Early diastolic murmur	Aortic valve insufficiency
10.	Shaking chills and bacterial endocarditis	Acuteness of bacterial endocarditis
11.	Rigor and bacterial endocarditis	Acuteness of bacterial endocarditis
12.	Normal spleen and bacterial endocarditis	Acuteness of bacterial endocarditis
13.	Short duration of illness and bacterial endocarditis	Acuteness of bacterial endocarditis
14.	Normal heart size and bacterial endocarditis	Acuteness of bacterial endocarditis
15.	Bacterial endocarditis from intravenous drug use, aortic valve insufficiency, and acuteness of bacterial endocarditis	Acute bacterial endocarditis with aortic insufficiency from drug use

drug use, THEN bacterial infection) and 9 (IF early diastolic murmur, THEN aortic insufficiency). None of the three who generated incorrect diagnoses applied these two rules (Patel & Groen, 1986). Further analysis of the protocols indicated that the correct diagnoses were uniformly the result of forward reasoning, wherein the consequent is generated from the antecedent (see Chapter 9). The subjects who generated the inaccurate diagnoses used irrelevant rules and backward chaining rules. The incorrect diagnoses also involved deviations from the forward reasoning approach, such as top-down reasoning, beginning with a general hypothesis and working backward looking for symptoms (Wagman, 1991).

Yet, problems arose in creating and operating expert systems. Collecting and coding the information often proved tedious and difficult. The systems had to be fed their knowledge base as a set of carefully coded rules. "Knowledge engineers," sent to interview experts and translate their rules into computer code, frequently found (as Feigenbaum did) that many of the "rules" the experts used were inexact. Further, the knowledge of a particular area was often incomplete.

An even more vexing problem concerns the fact that expert systems may provide expert responses, but only in a narrow discipline, or task domain. The result is sometimes called *brittleness:* a breakdown of the abilities of the programs when problems extend beyond their expertise. Expert systems are unable to recognize incongruities or to relate information to anything outside their narrow knowledge bases. Given a description of a rusty car, brittleness in a medical diagnosis system led it to conclude that the car was suffering from measles. Similarly, a car loan authorization system approved a loan from someone whose years on the job exceeded the applicant's reported age (Lenat, Guha, Pittman, Pratt, & Shepherd, 1990). As this example illustrates, the brittleness of expert systems may appear when simple data entry errors are made in the course of normal operation. However, such problems readily move from amusing to dangerous: A digitalis dosage system, for instance, noted nothing unusual when a patient's age and weight were entered in the wrong order, even though the records indicated that this "49-pound 102-year-old patient" was taken to the hospital by his mother (Lenat et al., 1990, pp. 32–33).

Most problems of this type are readily discovered by humans, through the aggregate of knowledge and abilities we call common sense. In ordinary human interactions, common sense is taken for granted. However, experiences with expert systems, like those described just above, showed that common sense is a very important component of intelligent behavior. How might computers learn common sense? To understand this, we must first turn to the issue of how computers might learn.

When a programmer or knowledge engineer collects a large quantity of information and enters it into a computer program, he or she is, in effect, learning or thinking for the computer. This type of knowledge transfer is not particularly applicable to human learning: we must build our own mental connections between bits of information. Others, notably parents and teachers, can help those connections to occur. However, these mentors cannot explicitly create them. Given the vast quantity of typically unarticulated information entailed in common sense, it would be ideal if a computer could acquire common sense the way humans do, by gradual learning on its own, through exposure to the world over time.

Neural Networks

The desire to build a machine that would learn as people do inspired the design of computing structures based on the structure of neurons. These programs or devices, called *neural networks*,[4] or neural nets, demonstrate a learning capability that more closely resembles human learning than does the programming of knowledge by knowledge engineers. Neural networks are able to learn from experience and can generalize; there is no need to program each explicit piece of information.

Neural network techniques were pioneered by Warren McCulloch and Walter Pitts in the 1940s (McCulloch & Pitts, 1943), but the explosion of interest among psychologists, computer scientists, and other cognitive scientists is a fairly recent phenomenon (Rumelhart, 1989). Neural networks, sometimes known as "connectionist models," typically run on standard digital computers, but they perform their computations in a parallel processing style: many simple tasks are performed at the same time (in parallel), rather than via the more conventional sequential processing of a list of instructions. This mode more closely resembles the operation of brains than of digital computer programs (Rumelhart, 1989). A simple neural network diagram is illustrated in Figure 6.3.

We may think of a neural network as being made of nodes, which are analogous to neurons, and the weighted connections among the nodes. The input units (nodes) receive binary digits that collectively represent information. According to information theory, as laid down by Claude Shannon, the binary digits may represent numbers, words, images, or any other type of information. The sequence 1001 at the top of Figure 6.3 might represent a portion of an image, for instance, where the digits indicate the presence or absence of light at individual points on the digitized image. Alternately, the 1001 might be a binary representation of the number 9, or could stand for the letter "i."

Each input unit is linked to the middle level, or "hidden units," with connections of various positive and negative strengths. The hidden units in turn transmit signals to the output units only if a threshold value is reached, shown in the circles representing the units. The output units in turn output a 1 if they achieve a certain threshold value, also indicated in the circles representing those units.

Instead of giving a neural network a program to execute, in the manner that computers had more conventionally been instructed, the neural net is "trained" for a desired outcome, with no specific instructions as to how to achieve the result. The most popular training technique, called *back propagation* (Rumelhart, 1989), is illustrated in Figure 6.3. The net is being trained to produce the output 0011 in response to the input 1001. It is currently producing 0111 instead of the desired 0011, so the connections producing the extra 1 (shown in heavy lines) need to be modified. The positive values would therefore be lowered slightly, while negative values would be increased in magnitude.

---

[4] The term neural network (or parallel distributed processing) currently applies primarily to computer programs, though they can be constructed of mechanical and/or electronic parts. The term is used as an analogy in describing functioning brains.

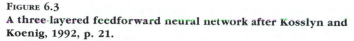

FIGURE 6.3
A three-layered feedforward neural network after Kosslyn and Koenig, 1992, p. 21.

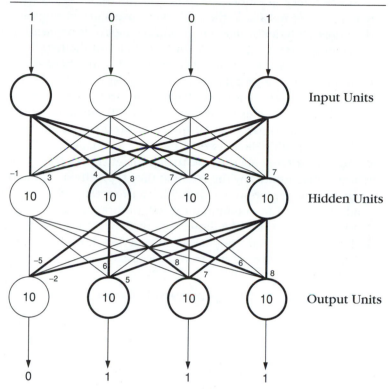

This process is repeated many times for every possible input ranging from 0000 to 1111. After completing this training, the net is able to convert reliably every possible input to the desired output without further modification. The example given in Figure 6.3 is trivial, but larger neural nets have been trained for such tasks as handwriting recognition, speech, diagnosing eye diseases, and playing backgammon (Rumelhart, 1989).

An outstanding feature of the connectionist approach is that the teaching techniques, like back propagation, are so simple that they may easily be automated. When the procedure is built into the neural network programs, they become self-programming. This is a blessing in most respects, because it relieves programmers of many hours of tedious work. In other respects, it is problematic. Self-programming makes it unclear how a network actually performs its tasks. In Germany, for instance, a neural network was recently trained to drive a car at 60 miles per hour on the Autobahn (Daviss, 1992), and performed well. Because of the automated teaching procedures, however, it is unclear what cues the net was using to guide its steering. If the net was steering the car along the road by maintaining a distance from a guardrail, for instance, it could conceivably steer off the road when it reached a section of road that had no guardrail. Beyond possible safety questions, there is also the unfortunate aspect that, after neural nets have learned a task, the rules they have learned cannot easily be conveyed to the human builder. Inside the networks, one finds no clean rules and no programming, only a set of weights attached to nodes of the nets.

Neural networks would have appealed to the behaviorists of years past (see Chapter 2). These programs achieve sophisticated behaviors through little more than a system of stimulus and response. However, there are limitations to the tasks they are able to learn and perform. For instance, the neural network approach would probably not be applicable to the task of designing a house. Present techniques enable the networks to learn only tasks that have a well defined outcome, after practicing the task thousands of times. The application of neural networks is also limited by the fact that they typically do not allow one to specify, or even determine, the method by which a program performs a task. These problems might be solved by combining the self-programming features of neural networks with rule structures, like those used in GPS. Ideally, such a machine would learn and use not only domain-specific information, but also common sense. These are the goals of an ongoing research project called Cyc.

Cyc and the Search for Computational Common Sense

As noted earlier, one of the most elusive areas of artificial intelligence is something that humans take for granted, namely, common sense. In 1984, a serious effort began to build a "common sense" knowledge base, in a project called Cyc (pronounced "psych"). Whereas expert systems performed reasonably in narrow domains with only hundreds or thousands of assertions or rules, Cyc is intended to work in a much wider range of situations. Cyc is to embody perhaps 100 million axioms, covering the enormous variety of things that most people in Western culture know but would rarely articulate (Lenat et al., 1990). As an example, knowledge about "buying" might include several hundred rules and meta-level rules (rules based on other rules), such as the following:

1. Adults typically carry 10–100 dollars (when dressed and away from their residence).
2. Payments of less than 10 dollars are usually made with cash.
3. Payments over 50 dollars are usually made via check or credit card.
4. Payments made through the mail are not generally made using cash.
5. Rule 4 overrides 2 and 3.
6. Candy bars cost approximately a dollar.
7. Candy costs approximately twice as much at movie theaters.

(Lenat et al., 1990, p. 43)

A wide range of knowledge of this type is necessary to understand even a simple sentence. To illustrate, for Cyc truly to understand that "Fred went to the movies and bought a candy bar," Cyc must have the common sense knowledge that Fred was not sleeping when he bought it, and probably didn't pay with a credit card. Further, if the sentence was "Fred is trying to raise 20 million dollars to buy Nestlé's Crunch," Cyc must grasp that the speaker is probably referring to a business deal rather than to a candy bar (Lenat et al., 1990, p. 43).

Rules and meta-rules can provide a great deal of information that may be applied to help interpret information. In human communication, however, the words themselves are often less important than the context. Therefore, understanding may be greatly enhanced by trying to fit sentences into likely scripts (Firebaugh, 1988; Schank, 1991). These scripts may describe the range of usual events one might encounter at a movie or restaurant, or in other situations, giving a basis for interpretation of new information or situations. If told, for instance, that "Fred went to the movies and bought a Zagnut," the script might suggest that buying candy is a frequent occurrence at movies, providing a basis for the supposition that Zagnut might be a brand name of a candy bar.

The breadth of knowledge being built into Cyc is also intended to allow it to generate its own new information by examining and analyzing the information it already has. Cyc is being programmed for analogical reasoning, a type humans often use. In such reasoning, solutions to new problems are ventured on the basis of their structural similarities to known problems. Along these lines, the developers set Cyc to roam over its knowledge base at night looking for symmetries and asymmetries in the hopes of turning up useful but hitherto unentered knowledge (Lenat et al., 1990), inviting a comparison to human dreaming.

In these first years of development, Cyc's information has been painstakingly entered into the computer by hand. However, the developers anticipate a transition point, after which the program will have a large enough knowledge base to read books on its own. This "grade promotion" should greatly accelerate the pace of Cyc's knowledge acquisition. The developers anticipate that knowledge-based, commonsense capabilities will soon be reliable, useful, and economical enough to become a standard feature on computers. Since von Neumann's early work in digital computers, it has become unthinkable to buy a computer that lacks the ability to store the programs it uses electronically and internally. We wouldn't want to open the case and change chips and wires around each time we wanted to run a different program. Similarly, the day may come when it becomes unthinkable to buy a machine lacking common sense.

Toward Unified Theories

Increasingly, AI systems are not based on a single technique or approach to building machine intelligence. These systems are typically hybrids combining the best problem solving, knowledge bases, and other techniques. One such hybrid system is Laird, Newell, and Rosenbloom's Soar, which, according to Newell, embodied a unified theory of cognition. Newell described such unified theories as accounting for the full breadth of human intellectual activity, including problem solving, decision making, memory, learning, language, motivation, emotion, imagination, and dreaming (Newell, 1990).

When expert systems emerged, much of the AI community shifted its attention from problem solving to expert knowledge. Newell acknowledged the limitations encountered by problem-solving systems such as GPS and the successes of knowledge-based systems that began with DENDRAL. Unlike many of his contemporaries, however, he didn't jump to the conclusion that a replacement of one with the other was the path to progress. Rather than abandon productions, Newell searched for a way to integrate a knowledge base and learning with production-based problem solving.

Soar was the product of this research. It kept the production-based design of GPS but also incorporated some new features. To introduce the key ideas of Soar, let us use an example from a well-known puzzle, the *Tower of Hanoi.* The subject in a Tower of Hanoi problem is shown an initial configuration of several discs and pegs and is asked to move the discs, one at a time, so that they realize another (target) configuration. A portion of the problem is depicted in Box 6.4, placed in its *problem space.* A problem space may be thought of as all of the possible steps in the solution of a problem, including solutions and dead-ends, along with the operations that may be applied to the problem.

When Soar gets to a point when it has no information about which of the possible courses of action it should take, and it doesn't know how to proceed, it is in a situation Newell calls an *impasse.* Soar solves impasses with a technique called *universal subgoaling:* Soar sets up a new subgoal of determining which of the available options is preferable, and solves the subgoal in a problem space just as it had the original problem. Then Soar puts all of its problem-solving ability to work on solving the subgoal (Newell, 1990). Universal subgoaling allows all problems and subproblems to be handled in a uniform manner (Laird, 1984).

For instance, in Box 6.4, Soar would reach an impasse if no information existed as to whether state S2, S3, or S4 is the best step toward reaching the desired state. Soar responds by creating the subgoal of selecting among these options, and in effect starts anew to solve this subgoal. Upon completion of the subtask, Soar returns to complete the previous task. Newell and Simon's early effort, LT, had also employed subgoaling, but in a far simpler form. LT employed a technique they called "detachment." LT would attempt to resolve a problem "b" by searching for an axiom or theorem of the form "a implies b." If one was found, "a" became the new subproblem. Proving "a" then provided the proof of "b" as well, since "a implies b" (Newell, Shaw, & Simon, 1963). Soar, in contrast, is in effect redirecting effort at its own decision-making process rather than merely looking at the problem, and may bring all of its problem-solving resources to bear, not merely substitution.

Soar also required a technique for incorporating learning. Existing learning models such as neural networks didn't fit neatly with the production system base. However, an alternate, and compatible, method based on chunking was discovered by Newell's student Paul Rosenbloom (Rosenbloom, 1983). Chunking, as

Box 6.4
Soar Problem Solving

Soar's problem-solving abilities can easily solve puzzles like *the Tower of Hanoi*, illustrated below. With practice, Soar's performance improves, since it has the ability to learn from its experience.

The figure illustrates a problem space for the task of rearranging three discs. The objective is to move the discs in some sequence, such that the discs in state S1 are rearranged to the order in state SN where the disks are stacked in order of size. A number of rules are provided by the knowledge base, such as "if there is no disc above the selected disc, then you can move it onto another peg." Given the set of rules, there are three possible operations from state S1: Operator 1 (O1) moves disc A from on top of disc B to the top of disc C, which results in state S2. O2 moves disc A onto the leftmost peg, and O3 moves disc C onto disc A. Each time an operator is applied, a new state results. Some combination of operators (not shown here) may be applied to states S2, S3, or S4 to reach the desired state SN.

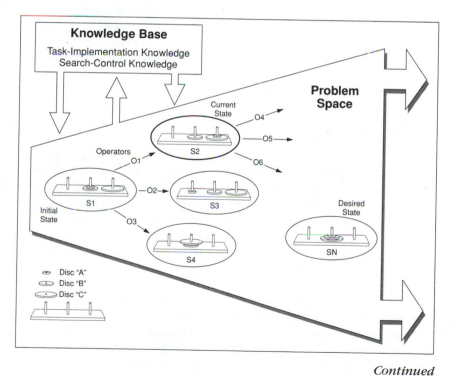

Continued

Box 6.4 (Continued)

To arrive at the desired state, Soar must apply a sequence of operators and move through a sequence of states. The first task it faces is choosing among the three operators that may be applied to the initial state. Soar looks to its knowledge base for information about which of these choices is preferable. If no such information exists, Soar tries each option. Soar then compares the results of these and stores the preferred option in the knowledge base for future use. After applying the preferred operator and reaching the next state (for example, S3), Soar can focus on the subgoal of moving from S3 by setting up a new problem space wherein S3 occupies the leftmost (initial state) position, occupied by S1 in the figure.

posited by Miller (1956), entails organizing information into chunks in order to circumvent humans' limitations of short-term memory (Chase & Simon, 1973; Simon, 1974; Simon & Gilmartin, 1973).

To examine Rosenbloom's approach to chunking, let's consider Soar's behavior when it reaches an impasse in the course of solving a problem. A sequence of steps in solving a problem is represented as a map in Figure 6.4. In Figure 6.4, the program encountered an impasse with respect to nodes A and B, because it had no basis for selecting among the possible operations. Soar applied the available operations to search for a solution. Some sequences of operations resulted in dead ends, marked with Xs. Eventually, Soar found some combinations of steps from states A, B, and C which yielded progress toward a solution, and produced states D and E.

Resolution of the impasse created an opportunity to apply chunking. All of the steps between the appearance and the resolution of the impasse (the entire shaded area) are no longer necessary. These steps become a single chunk. The chunk is represented by a new production, which states that *if* the starting condition ABC exists, *then* produce the results D and E. Thus, when the condition ABC is encountered again, all of the steps between the point of the impasse and its resolution are avoided by a single production. Consequently, there will be no impasse situation the next time around, and there will be no need to attempt solutions that will lead to dead ends.

The effect of chunking is that Soar learns from its problem-solving activities. Soar first faces a problem like a novice, in a slow, methodical, trial-and-error fashion. With experience, however, it soon provides the near-instantaneous solutions characteristic of an expert who has insight into the structure of the problems. A version of Soar called R1 was programmed with a portion of the knowledge base

FIGURE 6.4
A model of Soar behavior during chunking.

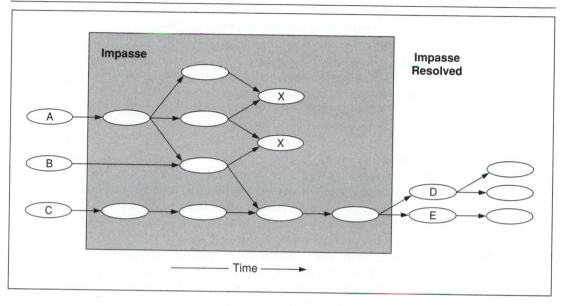

of a well-known and successful expert system that Digital Equipment Corporation used to configure its VAX minicomputers. Though it contained only a quarter of the knowledge base of the original, its accuracy was comparable with the original, suggesting that, to some extent, a good problem-solving capability may substitute for knowledge in that problem-solving domain. The improvement in efficiency due to chunking was profound: a problem that first took Soar 1,731 steps to solve was later solved in only 7 steps.

How the Cognitive Revolution Has Changed Our Conceptions of Human Intelligence

Analyzing Human Intelligence

As the preceding discussion of expert systems indicates, efforts to understand human intelligence proceeded in parallel with efforts to develop artificial intelligence. Some of the principal investigators in AI were equally motivated by their interests in understanding human intelligence. Allen Newell, for instance, stated:

> In Herbert [Simon]'s and my stuff is . . . always the concern for artificial intelligence . . . right there with the concern with cognitive psychology. Large parts of

the rest of the AI field believe that this is exactly the wrong way to look at it: you ought to know whether you're being a psychologist or an engineer. Herb and I have always taken the view that maximal confusion between those is the way to make progress (Newell, quoted in Crevier, 1993, p. 258).

Newell's bilateral interests are clearly evident in the progression of his and Simon's work. LT was the embodiment of a study of human problem solving, using protocol studies of human subjects to derive a set of problem-solving heuristics. GPS was introduced as a program that simulates human thought. Finally, Soar emerged as the centerpiece of Newell's Unified Theory of Cognition—his most comprehensive attempt to explain human intelligence and to demonstrate its functional equivalent embodied in AI systems.

The simultaneous exploration of human and machine intelligence has been synergistic in several ways. For instance, studies of human problem solving and expertise yielded many of the techniques now used in AI. An example of this is the incorporation of chunking into Soar. In turn, computer-based techniques have in some cases led researchers to search for biological equivalents. This happened in the late 1950s, when work on Pandemonium, an early computer vision program, suggested the use of feature-detectors (Selfridge, 1959, cited in Boden, 1989). In creatures such as frogs, these are specialized retinal cells that detect certain changes in the visual features, such as moving edges. Their existence was first suggested to neurophysiologists by Pandemonium; the neurophysiologists then searched for, and discovered, them in a frog's retina (Lettvin, Maturana, McCulloch, & Pitts, 1959, cited in Boden, 1989).

More importantly, however, the fact that theories of human cognition may be embodied in machines makes it possible to test the theories. LT served as a model to test heuristics as the basis for problem solving. Seeing the limitations of the program in action did more than suggest changes that led to GPS and Soar. It also revised our understanding of human problem-solving processes in the direction of incorporating knowledge and common sense.

As AI research develops models that can be applied to a broader range of problems, the programs may embody, and thereby test, more robust theories of human cognition. In cognitive neuropsychology research, the structure of the mind is being probed through techniques such as studying the effects of brain damage. Complex theories of human cognition are gradually emerging from the research. Like Broadbent's information processing model (Figure 6.1), these theories attempt to define functional components of thought rooted not in silicon, but in the "wetware" of the human brain. The models and their diagrams grow in complexity as our understanding of the human mind grows. An information processing diagram published by Kosslyn and Koenig (1992) demonstrates this growth. Whereas Broadbent's model was strictly serial, Kosslyn and Koenig's also uses parallel information processing; where Broadbent described 7 subsystems, Kosslyn and Koenig's includes nearly 50.

The validity of these models has been supported by studies of neurological disorders and, more recently, by PET (positron emission tomography) scans and MRI (magnetic resonance imaging) techniques (Kosslyn & Koenig, 1992) (see Chapter 5). These imaging techniques reveal that when subjects perform certain tasks, there is increased blood flow and oxygen usage in small regions of the brain that are theorized to support those functions. However, the human brain is not as neatly compartmentalized as the information processing diagrams. Activity may increase in one area, but other areas are simultaneously active as well. To test fully the adequacy of the theories in explaining human thought, detailed working models of brain activity over time will have to be developed. This will require what may be the next phase in AI: even more brainlike computers, enabled through the convergence of the neuropsychological attempts to describe human intelligence with the AI efforts to build mechanical intelligence.

Artificial Intelligence: The Case Against It

Traditional human intelligence tests, and most of the tests proposed for computers, deal with the evaluation of performed tasks but fail to examine the mental processes involved in performing the tasks. In the evaluation of machine intelligence, perhaps more so than with humans, it may be important to judge intelligence not only by outcome, but also by the underlying thought processes. Consider the conclusions one might come to by judging the intelligence of a radio, for instance, based solely on its behavior. One could easily conclude, based on its apparent ability to create fine music and sometimes thoughtful commentary, that it is an intelligent and creative device.

John Searle, a philosopher and vocal critic of AI, believes a variation on this problem pervades artificial intelligence. Searle (1984) claims that computers cannot be intelligent, because they manipulate symbols according to rules, but, unlike humans, they have no conception of what the symbols mean. Searle suggests that, as an analogy, one might imagine a Westerner being locked in a room with a basket of Chinese characters. Knowing no Chinese, the person is supplied with an English rule book describing how to manipulate the symbols, with rules like "Take a squiggle-squiggle sign out of basket number one and put it next to a squoggle-squoggle sign from basket number two" (Searle, 1984, p. 32). As Chinese characters representing questions are passed into the room, the Westerner uses the rules to pass characters out representing answers. Searle's contention is that, given a good enough rule book, this person might appear to a Chinese-speaking questioner to have a good understanding of Chinese, while in fact the person may understand nothing. Similarly, computers may be assumed to be intelligent merely because they give a correct response, though they may have no conception of the meaning of that response.

Based in part on this argument, Searle challenges the validity of the Turing test. He contends that it may easily be faked by any individual or machine supplied with a good enough set of rules for generating responses (Gardner, 1985). Searle finds many *weak* artificial intelligence claims acceptable, such as the possibility that computers may be useful as tools to study the mind. He argues against *strong* artificial intelligence claims, however, such as the claim that computers may ever achieve genuine understanding or have mental states, such as pain, desire, or happiness. This assertion is rooted in his claim that computers lack an understanding of meaning. Searle further holds that unless a machine is a molecule-for-molecule duplicate of a brain, lesser simulations of the structure of the brain "won't have simulated what matters about the brain, namely its causal properties, its ability to produce intentional states" (quoted in Gardner, 1985, p. 174).

Searle's Chinese room analogy is effective in illustrating the shortcomings of programs such as ELIZA, which processed speech by following a relatively simple set of rules. There is little basis, however, for Searle's assertions that programs may only work in this manner. Programs beginning with SHRDLU, and many others since then, demonstrate the ability of computer programs to do more than blindly follow rules. These programs demonstrate at least a rudimentary understanding of terms. They provide appropriate responses to requests without the benefit of preprogrammed responses. A program operating by simple rules might be instructed always to answer "Where is the red box?" with "The red box is on the table." This would not have worked in SHRDLU's world, however, where the relationships of objects could be changed. SHRDLU answered questions by extracting the requested information from an internally maintained model of its admittedly very small world. The task ahead, for Cyc, Soar, and the next generation of AI programs, is to enlarge the size of their worlds.

Will Artificial Intelligence Cause People to Stop Thinking?

A common plot in science fiction depicts a future in which technological advances like artificial intelligence render people unable to think on their own. Their brains subsequently atrophy, leading to the downfall of their societies (Wells, 1931/1956). Some readers of this book may recall that when the pocket calculator was introduced, many educators felt that if students used the devices, they would forget how to add. Similar fears have been voiced for millennia. One of the earliest is revealed by Socrates, in Plato's *Phaedrus* (Michie, 1986). His tale was even then ancient, telling of the Egyptian god Theuth, who invented calculation, geometry, and writing. In explaining his inventions to Thamus, king of Egypt, he said of writing that it "will make the Egyptians wiser and give them better memories." Thamus replied with concern that "this discovery of yours will create forgetfulness in the learners' souls, because they will not use their memories; they will trust to the external written characters and not remember of themselves" (Plato, 1928, p. 323).

Perhaps there is a legitimate point made here. Indeed, few individuals today are able to recite large works from memory. This ability was once expected of learned individuals, including those studying for the Chinese civil service exams described in Chapter 1. However, it is not so clear that memory has suffered with the invention of writing. We can speculate, for instance, that most individuals, when accompanied by the library of books they have read, can retrieve more information, and do so with greater accuracy, than persons limited to what they can memorize. The price for the improved quantity and accuracy of information storage, however, is dependence—the reliance on the external written characters of which Thamus warned. Just as memory may be enhanced by using writing, the possibility of enhanced human intelligence lies in its augmentation, rather than its replacement, by artificial intelligence. Similarly, the cost of that augmentation will be dependence.

Summary

A book on intelligence written 50 years ago would not have mentioned the computer, but any contemporary work would be delinquent if it did not cover machine as well as human intellect. In this chapter, we have met this responsibility, tracing the development of machines that model human cognitive abilities and perhaps intelligence. We have also explored how efforts to develop artificial intelligence have reshaped ideas of human intelligence.

The desire to build such machines dates back at least to ancient Greece. Though the interest had existed for many centuries, actually building such machines awaited two things: First, a detailed understanding of the intelligent processes; and second, the technical skill required to build machines capable of executing such complex processes. Understanding intelligent processes was facilitated by the rise of cognitive psychology over behaviorism. The ability to build machines capable of executing complex processes arose with the development of digital computers. Consequently, the prerequisite conditions simply didn't exist prior to 1956, considered the birth year of the cognitive revolution (Miller, 1979).

Since 1956, efforts in artificial intelligence have produced an ever more impressive list of accomplishments. Early work by Newell, Simon, and Minsky showed that computers could perform new, novel, and useful work in areas of intellectual pursuit once thought to be exclusively human. As each AI effort has been tested with real-life problems, perhaps as much has been learned from its limitations as from its abilities. The limitations of the general problem-solving approach stimulated the development of expert, knowledge-based systems. Ever more complex programs are emerging from the research laboratories, each an attempt at overcoming the limitations of its predecessors. The programs are demonstrating an increasing array of intellectual activity, moving from problem solving to natural language, expertise, learning, and common sense.

AI has long had its critics. The Cartesian view is that no machine, and for that matter, no material substance, can ever be intelligent. Contemporary critics have raised many valid points, and have helped to temper the sometimes inflated claims of the AI researchers. Nonetheless, it is indisputable that computers are today performing well in domains that were until recently thought to be the exclusive domain of human intellect. Progress in artificial intelligence continues at a fast pace. Researchers have been quick to announce that machines are becoming intelligent. Critics in Descartes' tradition have been equally quick to respond that the behavior of the machines does not indicate that they are intelligent, but rather that the increasingly long list of intellectual processes the machines can perform was mechanical in nature to begin with. The resolution of these two views is possible when we accept that creating a detailed description of an intelligent behavior, and perhaps mechanically modeling it, does not preclude our calling it intelligent. Indeed, as we shall show in the next chapter, contemporary theorists of intelligence have drawn on the approaches and findings of cognitive science as they put forth their own frameworks for understanding the mind.

Suggested Readings

Born, R. (1987). *Artificial intelligence: The case against.* London and Sydney: Croom Helm.

Crevier, D. (1993). *AI: The tumultuous history of the search for artificial intelligence.* New York: Basic Books.

Eames, C., & Eames, R. (1990). *A computer perspective: Background to the computer age* (2nd ed.). Cambridge, MA: Harvard University Press.

Gardner, H. (1985). *The mind's new science: A history of the cognitive revolution.* New York: Basic Books.

Kosslyn, S. M., & Koenig, O. (1992). *Wet mind: The new cognitive neuroscience.* New York: Free Press.

Posner, M. I. (Ed.). (1989). *Foundations of cognitive science.* Cambridge, MA: Bradford Books/MIT Press.

Chapter 7

Recent Perspectives

Skeptics might claim with some justification that what are purported to be theories of "intelligence" would better be called theories of laboratory-task or test cognition. If intelligence is indeed more than what is measured by IQ tests, then strong demonstrations of the validity of existing theories for real-world performance are needed.

—ROBERT J. STERNBERG (1985, P. 29)

Introduction

As we saw in the previous chapter, new technologies, such as the computer, can exert a profound influence on how we think about intellect. Indeed, some scholars, such as the Carnegie Mellon researchers mentioned in Chapters 4 and 6, have built their model of intelligence on the operations of the computer.

But there are other sources of information that have altered our conceptions of intelligence in recent decades. Among these are the findings about the functions of different parts of the brain, the studies of the use of mind in different cultures and contexts, and the interpretation and reinterpretation of new findings from the laboratory and from the field.

After a period of relative quiescence in the 1950s and 1960s, several scholars have recently put forth quite new formulations about intelligence. In each case, these formulations are in part a reaction to the standard psychometric approach introduced in the opening chapters of this book. But each formulation also draws on new sources of information and takes the study of intelligence in new directions, both theoretically and practically.

In this chapter, we explore four recent reconceptualizations of intelligence. Among other goals, each of the four seeks to explain the bases for individual differences in intelligence. As discussed in Chapter 3, the study of individual differences has been greatly influenced by the pioneering work of Binet and Spearman. Binet is credited with devising the first intelligence tests sensitive to age differences in children. Spearman studied and mathematically analyzed relationships among mental test scores. Techniques devised by Spearman were used by later factor theorists and psychometricians in devising their theories of intelligence (see Chapter 3).

More recently, a number of researchers and theorists (e.g., Eysenck, 1986; Jensen, 1980, 1991; Vernon, 1987) have used laboratory tasks to study intelligence. These researchers have examined the relationship between IQ and performance on choice reaction time tasks, inspection time tasks, and other measures (see Chapters 3 and 5).

The use of mental tests and laboratory tasks has provided many insights into human intelligence and individual differences. However, all the theories in this chapter[1] argue that psychometric tests and laboratory tasks cannot by themselves explain the variations in intelligence that exist outside the testing situation. Thus, to a greater or lesser extent, each of the new theories draws on research and methods from other disciplines—biology, neuropsychology, developmental psychology, anthropology, sociology, and education.

Though each of the reconceptualizations is based on a response to work in psychometrics and incorporates other perspectives, the theories are quite different from each other. We will illustrate these differences by looking at what each theorist posits, the evidence each has considered, and the methods each uses. As we'll see, two theorists, Anderson and Sternberg, continue to draw extensively on psychometric work or laboratory-based research (e.g., Anderson, 1992; Sternberg, 1985). Gardner's theory draws on traditional testing to a much more limited degree. Ceci's framework is aimed in large measure at undermining notions of intelligence based on psychometrics and decontextualized laboratory tasks.

Sternberg and, to an even greater extent, Ceci emphasize that elements *beyond the individual* are critical to individual intelligence. In explaining differences in intellectual performance, Ceci and a number of other investigators give substantial weight to diverse aspects of the wider context (hence, they are often called "contextualists"). Contextualists consider how intelligence is affected by schooling, by interaction with human and technological resources, by historical era, and by other aspects of the environment (e.g., Ceci, 1990; Cole & Scribner, 1974; Goodnow, 1990; Heath, 1983; Keating, 1984, 1990; Lave, 1988; Lave, Murtaugh, & de la Rocha, 1984; Perkins, 1995; Resnick, 1987, 1991; Rogoff, 1990; Salomon, 1993; Scribner & Cole, 1973; Vygotsky, 1978; Wertsch, 1991).

We begin this chapter by briefly critiquing notions of intelligence based on psychometrics and laboratory tasks. We then look at four recent reconceptualizations of intelligence that attempt to explain individual differences in intelligence, especially as found outside of testing situations. We conclude the chapter with

---

[1] Ceci regards his reconceptualization as a "framework." For the sake of convenience, we will also refer to it as a theory.

Ceci's framework, which, of the four reconceptualizations, places the greatest emphasis on context. This ordering helps to set the stage for the last two chapters of the book, which focus directly on intelligence in the context of school and in the context of the workplace.

A Brief Critique of Psychometric and Laboratory-Based Notions of Intelligence

Numerous books are devoted in whole or part to critiquing psychometrics and laboratory-based views of intelligence (e.g., Block & Dworkin, 1976; Ceci, 1990; Gould, 1981; Lewontin, Rose, & Kamin, 1984; Resnick, Levine, & Teasley, 1991; Sternberg & Wagner, 1986). We offer a brief summary of criticisms as an orientation to the four theories, each of which is in part a response to test and laboratory models of intelligence.

Limited Types of Problem Solving

One of the commonest criticisms of psychometric and laboratory-based notions of intelligence is that they emphasize a narrow band of human thinking (Ceci, 1990; Gardner, 1993b). As discussed in Chapters 2 and 3, much psychometric testing is linked to predicting children's performance in school. Therefore, it is not surprising that psychometric views of intelligence are sometimes said to focus on language and mathematics, or "academic intelligence," to the exclusion of other, important human problem-solving abilities (Ceci & Liker, 1986a; Fredericksen, 1986; Gardner, 1993b; Olson, 1986).

Similar criticisms are aimed at information processing research, which often analyzes how people solve traditional intelligence test items. For example, there have been studies based on how people solve items on the Raven's Progressive Matrices Test (e.g., Carpenter, Just, & Shell, 1990) and analogies (e.g., Holyoak, 1991; Sternberg, 1977). Other laboratory work, such as investigations of choice reaction time and inspection time (see Chapter 5), focus on even simpler kinds of tasks. Thus, as with psychometric approaches, critics assert that this research does not take into account "real-world" manifestations of intelligence (Ceci, 1990; Sternberg, 1985). For example, such research does not address how people organize a successful conference in Shanghai, how they invest their money in the stock market, or how they repair a broken motorcycle.

Atypical Contexts

Just as the range of problems often used in psychometric and laboratory approaches is criticized as being narrow, so is the *context* in which this problem solving occurs. As mentioned in Chapter 3, psychometric tests are typically

Laboratory tests of intelligence limit context and content.

administered by a psychologist to a subject in a one-on-one setting, or they are administered in a group setting, where many individuals are given tests to complete on their own, often as quickly as possible. In laboratory investigations of intelligence, people may be asked to sit alone at an electronic display or computer keyboard and respond as fast as possible to simple tasks as they are presented.

Critics argue that these formats are not "ecologically valid." They do not resemble the everyday settings in which people ordinarily think (Bronfenbrenner, 1979). Thus, according to some critics, inferences about intelligence or problem-solving abilities based on such situations may apply only to test or lab situations (Resnick, 1991; Resnick & Neches, 1984; Scribner, 1986).

In the context of their daily lives, people encounter problems that often are not clearly defined and ordered in the way tests present them (Csikszentmihalyi, 1988b; Fredericksen, 1986; Lave, Murtaugh, & de la Rocha, 1984; Newman, Griffin, & Cole, 1984; Scribner, 1986). Furthermore, people typically have some freedom to decide which questions they will take on, to skip questions that mean little to them, and to estimate their answers (Lave et al., 1984). They can also usually spend more than a few seconds to solve a problem. In addition, in daily life, conversations and interactions do not resemble those found in a test or task situation (Perret-Clermont, Perret, & Bell, 1991; Rogoff & Lave, 1984; Siegel, 1991). Beyond test settings, people often ask questions and get advice from others in thinking through problems. They can also make use of books and technological resources, including computers and a wide array of tools or instruments (Ceci, 1990; Olson, 1986; Pea, 1990; Resnick, 1987; Salomon, 1993; Vygotsky, 1978). As David Olson has argued:

> Almost any form of human cognition requires one to deal productively and imaginatively with some technology. To attempt to characterize intelligence independently of those technologies seems to be a fundamental error. (1986, p. 356)

Critics argue that intelligence is not a global ability applied in all settings. Rather, critics assert that intelligence is *situated* within particular contexts (e.g., Resnick, 1987; Resnick, Levine, & Teasley, 1991). Some critics further state that intelligence is not located solely within individuals' heads, but is instead *distributed*. To these critics, the ability to manage a complex task is a joint product of knowledge and resources contained within an individual, other people, elements of the setting, and various technological tools (Gardner, 1993a; Lave, 1988; Perkins, 1993; Salomon, 1993).

An example of problem solving in daily life.

To illustrate these critics' point, think of an individual stripped to the skin and isolated from everyone else. This person's intelligence, or ability to solve complex problems, is limited. However, add some books, paper, and pencils, and the ability increases. The person becomes even smarter with access to a computer and telephone (and clothes!). Thus, to these critics, understanding the nature of intelligence requires looking beyond the capacities of an isolated individual.

THE INFLUENCE OF VYGOTSKY

Many critics who maintain a situated or "contextualist" viewpoint trace their intellectual origins to the seminal work of the Soviet psychologist Lev Vygotsky (1896–1934). Vygotsky's research agenda was complex. Figuring prominently on it were efforts to describe and explain the *social origins* of higher mental functions, such as problem solving and concept formation (Kozulin, 1984; Vygotsky, 1978; Wertsch, 1979).

Vygotsky claimed that individuals' attainment of higher mental functions was rooted in the use of physical tools (e.g., sticks, oars, scalpels) and symbols (e.g., gesture, music, and, especially, language). He emphasized that both physical and symbolic tools are invented by the culture and that children are exposed to and come to master such tools during the process of socialization.

Lev Vygotsky.

Both tools and symbols enable people to mediate—to act on, and within—their environment. At the same time, tool and symbol use broadens and provides new possibilities for problem solving (Vygotsky, 1978). So, for example, a young child banging on a pot with a stick may later see the stick as useful for keeping siblings at bay or knocking a favorite puzzle off a shelf and into reach.

In addition, Vygotsky asserted that higher mental functions are integrally tied to social interaction. Two notions illustrate the importance of social interaction in Vygotsky's theory. First, Vygotsky argued: "All higher mental functions are internalized social relationships" (Vygotsky, 1979, p. 164). In essence, the sense or meanings individuals make for themselves, even when they are alone, have their origins in interactions with others. For example, Vygotsky wrote, parents and other adults bring meaning to the early gestures and words of children. A baby holding out a hand to reach an out-of-range object has no sense of the meaning the outstretched arm might convey to others. The baby is merely trying to reach something. However, when mother comes along, sees the baby's outstretched arm and the object, and then gives the child the object, the child comes to understand that an arm outstretched toward an object can convey meaning to others (Vygotsky, 1979).

A second illustration of the importance of social interaction in Vygotsky's theory is provided by his concept of the "zone of proximal development" ("ZPD"). Vygotsky's work in the area of educational assessment led him to realize that a standard intelligence test score does not reveal what a student is truly capable of doing when he or she is guided by others or collaborates with them. The ZPD is the zone between the level of problem solving an individual can do in isolation and the level of problem solving the individual can do in social situations involving other, somewhat more knowledgeable individuals. The ZPD is a useful concept not only when considering intellectual assessment; as we will see in Chapters 8 and 9, it is a powerful concept when considering how people learn in school and at work. Essentially, good learning situations are those that engage learners within their zone of proximal development—the edge of what they are capable of doing when interacting with more skillful others. As a student comes to master the problem or skill in question, external guidance or "scaffolding" can be reduced, or a much more challenging task, with its own appropriate new ZPD, can be posed instead.

Individuals develop problem-solving skills by interacting with others who are more knowledgeable. Here, a child learns to fit together nuts and bolts with guidance from her father.

Minimizing Knowledge, Practice, and Experience

Many psychometric tests call on people to solve problems without reference to their usual base of knowledge and experience. For example, the Raven's Progressive Matrices test does not require people to have knowledge in any particular discipline, and it presents visual problems of a type few people have seen before (Cooper & Regan, 1982; Jensen, 1980) (see Figure 3.10 for an example of Raven's matrices). Similarly, laboratory tasks, such as inspection time studies (see Chapter 3) seek to be "knowledge-free" (Anderson, 1992) and are not common, everyday experiences. It is true that controlling for variables such as knowledge and experience makes it possible to compare different individuals' performance on a given task. However, it is also true that the comparisons made on the basis of these performances do not reflect the wealth of experience people usually bring to bear in their thinking. Critics claim that theories based on tests and tasks do not truly represent human intelligence but only thinking as manifested in these sorts of tasks (Ceci, 1990; Cole & Scribner, 1974; Gardner, 1991a; Scribner, 1986).

In contrast to these approaches (and as we explore in Chapter 9), some researchers study learning and problem solving as they occur during the course of apprenticeships or on the job (Hamilton, 1990; Lave, 1990, 1991; Rogoff, 1990, 1991), or among experts (Boster, 1991; Ceci & Liker, 1986a, 1986b; Chi, Glaser, & Rees, 1982).

Downplaying Cognitive Development

This criticism is especially leveled at psychometric notions of intelligence. Sternberg (1990) has pointed out that psychometric theorists have generally given little attention to cognitive development, even though questions relating to development could well be tackled within the discipline of psychometrics. For example, does the number of factors change with development? Does the importance of particular factors change with development? Anderson (1992) notes the irony of this neglect:

> . . . although there are massive changes in intellectual competence through childhood and the whole practice of intelligence testing was based, originally, on this very phenomenon, there is virtually no developmental story to psychometric intelligence. (p. 29)

Psychometric notions of intelligence mask development in part because they tend to focus on IQ scores (Anderson, 1992). As discussed in Chapter 3, these generally remain stable over time, after the years of early childhood. Yet, normal individuals become more knowledgeable and capable as they develop.

Recent Theories of Intelligence

Recent reconceptualizations of intelligence try to explain some of the findings of psychometrics and information processing theories. At the same time, they attempt to address the weaknesses of these approaches, some of which we have just discussed. Despite these worthwhile aims, it is important to note that none of the recent reconceptualizations presented below has as much experimental or other supporting data as do the psychometric or information processing approaches with which it is taking issue. It is rather as if the work of Binet or Terman were being reviewed around 1920, instead of 75 years later. We offer these theories as new and provocative ideas. We consider each theory's aims, discuss its claims, review some of the methods and evidence given in support of those claims, and present the criticisms each has received.

Howard Gardner's Theory of Multiple Intelligences

Howard Gardner proposed his theory of multiple intelligences in 1983 as a direct challenge to the "classical view of intelligence" (Gardner, 1993b, p. 5). According to Gardner, the classical view holds that intelligence is a unitary capacity for logical

Howard Gardner.

reasoning of the sort exemplified by mathematicians, scientists, and logicians (Gardner, 1993b). In line with the classical view, abstract reasoning is most valued. This view of intelligence is in accord with that of Spearman (1904) and some later psychometricians. Spearman argued strongly for the role of general intelligence, or *g*. Spearman viewed *g* as an underlying mental energy that was drawn on in various degrees during all intellectual activity (see Chapter 3).

Gardner, a Harvard University psychologist, notes that the unitary view was challenged long before he proposed his theory. For example, L. L. Thurstone (1938) and other psychometricians asserted that human intellect encompasses several mental abilities (see Chapter 3). However, as we will discuss below, the evidence Gardner draws on to make this point is far more diverse than that used by psychometricians. In essence, Gardner's theory of multiple intelligences (or "MI") is not so much concerned with explaining and presenting patterns of scores on psychometric tests as with accounting for the variety of adult roles (or "endstates") that exist across cultures (Gardner, 1993b).

Parting from the unitary notion of intelligence, Gardner makes a strong claim for several relatively autonomous intelligences. He defines an intelligence as the "ability to solve problems or fashion products that are of consequence in a particular cultural setting or community" (Gardner, 1993c, p. 15). In his original presentation of the theory Gardner proposed seven such intelligences but noted that there may be more or fewer.[2] The key point is that there is not just one underlying mental capacity. Rather, a variety of intelligences, working in combination, are needed to explain how human beings take on such diverse roles as physicist, farmer, shaman, and dancer (Gardner, 1993b).

DIVERSE SOURCES OF EVIDENCE

Gardner's theory is based on a synthesis of evidence from diverse sources. Because other theorists included in this chapter also rely on a broader base of support than

---

[2] Indeed, in recent writings, he speculates about the existence of a new, eighth intelligence, called the "naturalist's intelligence"—the kind of skill at recognizing flora and fauna that one associates with biologists like Darwin (Gardner, 1995b).

is offered by psychometric findings, it is worth providing an overview of these sources via Gardner's work. However, it is important to note that, though the other theorists may use similar sources, they clearly do not all come to the same conclusions as Gardner does about them. (As an example, see the comparison of Ceci's findings from neuropsychology with Gardner's, later in this chapter.)

Gardner believes the strongest evidence for MI comes from studies of once-normal people who have become brain-damaged via stroke or trauma. In particular, he finds evidence for a discrete intelligence in the sparing or breakdown of a capacity following brain damage. For instance, some stroke patients may have unimpaired speech yet are unable to find their way around the hospital or their home; others may exhibit the opposite pattern of strengths and deficits. That these two abilities can be isolated from each other in this way helps Gardner to support the notion of separate intelligences governing language and spatial thinking.

Strong support also comes from the intellectual profiles of special populations, such as prodigies and *idiots savants* (now often simply called *savants*). Prodigies are individuals who demonstrate extreme accomplishments in chess, mathematics, music, or other disciplines at a young age, but who turn out to be unexceptional in other areas. *Savants* are individuals of low IQ, who nevertheless show some remarkable skills. For example, they may be able to draw with great accuracy, play the piano by ear, or quickly figure out whether March 15, 2018, will fall on a Wednesday. Among these special populations, certain capacities are operating in isolation from others. For instance, as we'll see in Anderson's theory below, *savants* may be able to calculate prime numbers but not interact with other human beings. The appearance of specific high-level abilities in people who are otherwise unexceptional, or even are classified as retarded, again indicates to Gardner that intelligences are separable abilities.

Gardner looks for evidence in information processing mechanisms as well. "One might go so far as to define a human intelligence as a neural mechanism or computation system which is genetically programmed to be activated or 'triggered' by certain kinds of internally or externally presented information" (Gardner, 1993b, p. 64). Thus, each of the proposed intelligences should have some core information processing operations, such as pitch discrimination in music, or syntactic ordering in language.

Gardner also uses experimental psychology and cognitive psychology to support his theory. For example, the results of studies in which people are asked to carry out two tasks simultaneously suggest that some abilities operate autonomously, while others do not (Brooks, 1968). Such research suggests that certain musical and linguistic information processing functions are carried out independently from each other, as are spatial and linguistic processing.

Psychometric findings are an additional basis of support for MI. Though Gardner has criticized psychometric assessment (Gardner, 1993b, 1993c), he believes that patterns of correlations, or the absence of high correlations, help to indicate the relative autonomy of some intelligences. For example, factor analyses generally support the idea of two big group factors, often labeled verbal and spatial (see Chapter 3).

Another source of evidence for an intelligence is a characteristic developmental trajectory leading from basic and universal manifestations to a possible expert endstate. To illustrate, spoken language develops rapidly and to great competence in all normal people. In contrast, all normal individuals can count small quantities, but, without years of formal schooling, few progress to higher mathematics.

Findings from evolutionary biology are yet another, more speculative, source of evidence for Gardner. He looks for origins of human intelligences in the intelligences of the species that predate humans. Thus, the existence of birdsong undergirds the notion of a separate human musical intelligence, and there are strong continuities in the spatial abilities of humans and other primates.

Unique among the theorists mentioned in this chapter, Gardner supports his theory by looking at symbol systems (see Figure 7.1). Among such systems are the notations used in mathematics, mapmaking, architecture, written language, music, dance, and football. Symbol systems are means by which cultures capture and transmit important information. Gardner (1993b) speculates that such "symbol systems may have evolved *just in those cases* where there exists a computational capacity ripe for harnessing by the culture"; thus, "a primary characteristic of human intelligence may well be its 'natural' gravitation toward embodiment in a symbolic system" (p. 66).

By analyzing and synthesizing these sources of evidence, Gardner makes a case for seven intelligences: linguistic intelligence, musical intelligence, logical–mathematical intelligence, spatial intelligence, bodily–kinesthetic intelligence, intrapersonal intelligence, and interpersonal intelligence. Descriptions of each are provided below, along with endstates that exemplify them. It is crucial to remember that Gardner regards the intelligences "only as potentially useful scientific constructs" (Gardner, 1983, p. 70). An intelligence is a term for organizing and describing human capabilities, rather than a reference to some commodity inside the head. An intelligence is not a "'thing,' but rather . . . a potential, the presence of which allows an individual access to forms of thinking appropriate to specific kinds of content" (Kornhaber & Gardner, 1991, p. 155).

1. *Linguistic intelligence* is likely the most thoroughly studied human competence. Evidence for this intelligence comes from developmental psychology, which reveals a universal, rapidly developing capacity for speech among normal individuals. Neuropsychology has documented cases of language breakdown and sparing in brain-damaged patients. Neurobiology also helps to point out core information processing mechanisms associated with this intelligence. These include mechanisms dedicated to phonology (speech sounds), syntax (grammar), semantics (meaning), and pragmatics (implications and uses of language in various settings). Linguistic intelligence is exemplified by poets, who are keenly attuned to the sound and rich meanings of the language they use. It is also a crucial asset for journalists, advertising copywriters, and lawyers.

2. *Musical intelligence* allows people to create, communicate, and understand meanings made out of sound. Unlike linguistic intelligence, which develops

FIGURE 7.1
Gardner asserts that symbol systems may have evolved to capture intellectual capacities valued by a culture.

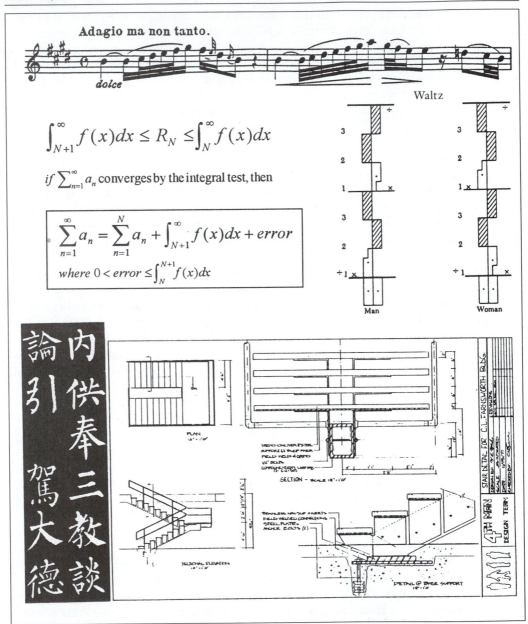

to a rather high degree across cultures without formal instruction, high-level mu-sical intelligence may require more intensive exposure; in the West, few people achieve great skill without years of training. Studies of prodigies and *savants* in-dicate this intelligence is autonomous from other capabilities: it may be mani-fested at a high level in someone whose other abilities are average or even impaired (Miller, 1989; Treffert, 1989). Neuropsychological and other brain stud-ies show that areas of the brain dedicated to processing music are distinct from those dedicated to processing language. Core information processing components include pitch, rhythm, and timbre (sound quality). Musical intelligence is clearly exhibited in composers, conductors, and instrumentalists, as well as acousticians and audio engineers.

3. *Logical–mathematical intelligence* involves using and appreciating ab-stract relations. Its development has been best documented by Piaget (see Chap-ter 4). In Piaget's work, abstract reasoning begins with exploring and ordering objects. It progresses to manipulating objects and appreciating actions that can be performed on objects, and then, to making propositions about real or possible actions and their interrelationships. Finally, it advances to the appreciation of re-lationships in the absence of action or objects—pure, abstract thought (Piaget, 1965; Piaget & Inhelder, 1969).

Although Piaget argued that this sequence was a universal phenomenon, many subsequent investigators have found that the development of abstract thought often depends on schooling (e.g., Ceci, 1990; Cole & Scribner, 1974), or from an alternative perspective, that it can be prompted at points earlier than Pi-aget imagined, by using materials more suitable to younger children (e.g., Bryant, 1974; Gelman & Gallistel, 1978; Siegel, 1991; see Chapter 4). One core operation of this intelligence is numbering—the capacity to assign a numeral corresponding to an object in a series of objects. Evidence for the relative autonomy of logical–mathematical intelligence comes from its appearance in isolation in some *savants,* who can perform mathematical feats in the absence of other abilities, and from the existence of mathematical prodigies. There are also neurological problems, such as developmental Gerstmann's syndrome, in which arithmetic learning, but little else, is impaired. Endstates that draw heavily on logical–mathematical intelligence in-clude mathematician, computer programmer, financial analyst, accountant, engi-neer, and scientist.

4. *Spatial intelligence* concerns the ability to perceive visual or spatial infor-mation, to transform and modify this information, and to recreate visual images even without reference to an original physical stimulus. This intelligence is needed to work through the problems illustrated in Figure 7.2. Spatial intelli-gence is not dependent on visual sensation. Blind people use it as well (Landau, Gleitman, & Spelke, 1981), for example, in constructing a mental image of their homes or figuring out routes to work. Core abilities of this intelligence include the capacity to construct images in three dimensions, and to move and rotate

FIGURE 7.2
**Gardner asserts that spatial intelligence is needed to determine whether the
second form in each of the pairs below is a rotation of the first.**

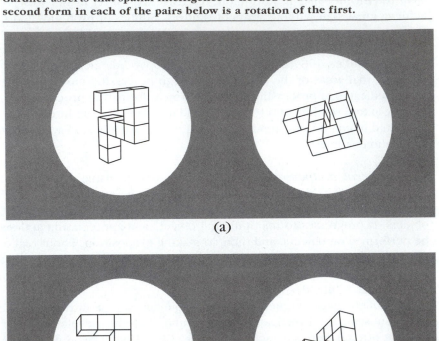

(a)

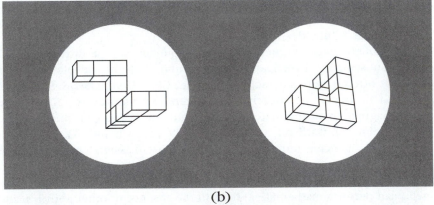

(b)

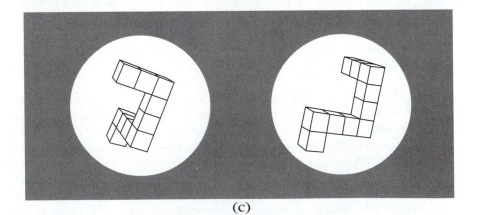

(c)

these representations. In most Westerners, the development of this intelligence, at least as applied within the visual arts, ceases in middle childhood unless support and education are provided (Davis, 1991; Lowenfeld & Brittain, 1982; Winner, 1982). However, this intelligence is also harnessed outside the visual arts, for example, among geographers, surgeons, and navigators.

Even though both logical–mathematical and spatial skills develop from the perception of objects, neurological research supports the autonomy of spatial intelligence. Spatial intelligence is "hardwired" into the brain. It requires intact functioning of the right parietal and temporal lobes, and connections between these and other regions of the brain. Support for a separate spatial intelligence comes again from literature on prodigies and *savants*. For example, spatial intelligence is found in isolation in the case of Nadia, an autistic girl who possessed great drawing skills. (See page 210 for an example of Nadia's work.) Prodigies in the visual arts, such as Picasso, and in chess also help Gardner make the case for the independence of this intelligence.

5. *Bodily-kinesthetic intelligence* may seem the most removed from traditional views of intelligence. Recall from the beginning of Chapter 1 that Terman regarded as "disturbed" anyone who thought that a person who could "handle tools skillfully, or play a good game of baseball" was as intelligent as someone "who can solve mathematical equations . . ." (Terman, 1921, p. 124). However, if one thinks of the meanings constructed by choreographers and conveyed by dancers, or of the tremendous skill of rock climbers suspended on the side of a cliff, then the case for this intelligence no longer seems quite so odd. As these examples indicate, bodily-kinesthetic intelligence involves the use of all or part of one's body to solve problems or fashion products. Core operations associated with this intelligence are control over fine and gross motor actions and the ability to manipulate external objects.

The biological underpinnings of this intelligence are complex. They include coordination among neural, muscular, and perceptual systems. The case for a bodily-kinesthetic intelligence is supported by *apraxias*—neurological syndromes typically related to left-hemisphere damage. People with apraxias are unable to perform sequences of movements despite the ability to understand a request to perform a sequence of movements and the physical capacity to execute each movement within that sequence. Gardner speculates that the development of bodily-kinesthetic intelligence advances from early reflexes such as sucking, to increasingly intentional activities, to the ability to mimic and create, using movement. Along with dancers and rock climbers, bodily-kinesthetic intelligence is exemplified by gymnasts and other athletes and by jugglers.

6. *Intrapersonal intelligence* depends on core processes that enable people to distinguish among their own feelings. Gardner sees this intelligence as developing from an ability to distinguish pleasure from pain and to act on that discrimination. At its highest level, discriminations among one's feelings, intentions,

This drawing is very detailed. Note the bridle, tunic, trumpet and hand, together with the inappropriate and disturbing face, and squirrel on the horse's side. Drawn at approximately 5 years 6 months.

Nadia's capacity for accurate drawing in the absence of other abilities serves as evidence for spatial intelligence in Gardner's theory of multiple intelligences.

and motivations yield a deep self-knowledge of the sort elders draw on when making a crucial decision or when advising others in their community. Novelists like Proust employ it in creating their introspective accounts (Gardner, 1993b). More recently, Gardner (1993c) has emphasized the role played by this intelligence in enabling individuals to build an accurate mental model of themselves and to draw on such a model to make good decisions about their lives. Thus, this intelligence may act as a "central intelligences agency," enabling individuals to know their own abilities and perceive how to best use them (Kornhaber & Gardner, 1991).

7. *Interpersonal intelligence* makes use of core capacities to recognize and make distinctions among *others'* feelings, beliefs, and intentions. Early in development, this intelligence is seen in the ability of young children to discriminate among the individuals in their environment and to discern others' moods. In its most developed forms, interpersonal intelligence manifests itself in the ability to understand, act on, and shape others' feelings and attitudes for good or otherwise. This intelligence enabled such varied actors as Mother Teresa, Mao Zedong, and Martin Luther King to carry out their work. This intelligence is broadly called on by therapists, parents, and dedicated teachers.

Functioning of the personal intelligences is linked to the frontal lobes of the brain. If this area is injured, an individual's motivation and responses to others may be impaired, even though the ability to perform on an IQ test is unaffected (Hebb, 1949). In day-to-day life, it may seem difficult to separate the two personal intelligences. Yet, some evidence for their autonomy, in the form of pathologies affecting each, can be seen in various disorders. For instance, interpersonal intelligence appears to be lacking among autistic youngsters, and there are psychopathological illnesses in which an individual may be keenly aware of others' feelings and motivations while unable to make sense of his or her own (Damasio, 1994; Gardner, 1993b; Goleman, 1989).

Having now sketched out each intelligence, it is important to emphasize that all endstates draw on *combinations* of several intelligences (Gardner, 1993b). For example, dancers need to rely on bodily–kinesthetic intelligence, but they must also possess musical intelligence to move expressively and in correct rhythm. They must make use of personal intelligences if they are to interpret characters and have audiences care about them. It may seem that mathematicians could rely solely on logical–mathematical intelligence. However, they must also draw on interpersonal intelligence in order to get their work published and to get along in a university faculty.

Gardner argues that all normal people are capable of drawing on all the intelligences, but individuals are distinguished by their particular "profile of intelligences." This profile features their own, unique combination of relatively stronger and weaker intelligences which they use to solve problems or fashion products (Walters & Gardner, 1985). These relative strengths and weaknesses help to account for individual differences.

IMPACT OF THE THEORY

Gardner developed his theory with the aim of broadening psychological notions of intelligence. However, so far, the major impact of his work has been in the field of education (Gardner, 1993c). Within a few years of the theory's publication in 1983, several schools were formed or reorganized around the notion of multiple intelligences. Though they use the theory in a variety of ways, they all attempt to help children develop and learn by drawing more broadly on the range of their intelligences (Kornhaber, 1994; Kornhaber & Krechevsky, 1995; Olson, 1988).

Gardner's work is also having some effect on schools' assessment of children's abilities. Gardner argues strongly for the development and adoption of "intelligence-fair" assessments (Kornhaber, Krechevsky, & Gardner, 1990, p. 192). These are assessments that allow children to demonstrate their abilities using intelligence-appropriate media and contexts, rather than relying exclusively on paper-and-pencil tests. For example, Gardner's colleagues have devised assessments of young children's abilities that are integrated into the regular classroom curriculum. Thus, children can practice their spatial skills by putting together gears and food grinders in the classroom. They can demonstrate interpersonal skills using a model of the classroom that contains miniatures of all their classmates. These activities, and the development of the intelligences needed for them, are regularly observed by their teachers and by researchers (Krechevsky, 1994; Krechevsky & Gardner, 1990a, 1990b; Malkus, Feldman, & Gardner, 1988). In Chapter 8, we explore further the relationship of intelligence and schooling.

Criticisms of the Theory of Multiple Intelligences

Gardner's theory has existed long enough to be criticized on both theoretical and applied, or educational, grounds. On the theoretical front, Scarr (1985) has criticized Gardner for constructing MI on the premise that psychology regards intelligence as a unitary ability reflected by IQ scores. Scarr claims that most psychologists do not maintain that IQ reflects the universe of human abilities. Instead, she asserts, psychologists understand that IQ tests assess only "a *sample* of intellectual performance" useful for academic and occupational purposes (Scarr, 1985, p. 96). She also argues that labeling diverse abilities, such as bodily–kinesthetic, social, and musical skills, as intelligence does not advance understanding of intelligence, personality, or areas of special ability like music or movement (Scarr, 1989). She and others (e.g., Herrnstein, personal communication, 1991) have asserted that such labeling muddies distinctions between intelligence and other human characteristics (Herrnstein & Murray, 1994).

Scarr (1985) argues that Gardner's claims for the various intelligences are motivated more by social than scientific considerations. She claims that calling diverse talents intelligences does not "solve the problem of social allocation" (Scarr, 1985, p. 99)—that society rewards good skills in some abilities (interpersonal, logical, and language) more than it rewards good skills in other abilities (music, bodily-kinesthetic). Gardner's counterargument to such criticisms is that the common practice of regarding only skills in language and logic as intelligence reflects the Western tradition and the influence of intelligence testing. In order to step away from the Western bias, he argues, it is reasonable to call the diverse faculties he has posited by the same term—calling them all "intelligences" or all "talents" (Gardner, 1993b, 1993c).

At least two criticisms have also been advanced against Gardner's assertion that the intelligences are autonomous. First, decades of psychometric research indicate that abilities are positively correlated; no traditionally measured intellectual capacity is wholly distinct from the others (Messick, 1992; Scarr, 1985). Gardner counters that positive correlations are obtained because psychometric measures detect not only aptitude within a given intelligence, but also skill in taking short-answer, paper-and-pencil tests, which are common to many psychometric measures. To understand whether the intelligences are autonomous, Gardner argues, one would need to use measures that are "intelligence-fair." Such measures would allow people to use the materials and media most relevant to the intelligence (e.g., for music, performing or composing; for interpersonal, negotiating with others). If such measures were available, it might then become possible to determine whether the intelligences were autonomous.

The second argument against autonomy of intelligences stems from the notion that the various intelligences must be harnessed together by an executive function that would coordinate the disparate intelligences' role in carrying out particular tasks (Messick, 1992). Gardner argues against such a hierarchical executive. Instead, he claims that the intrapersonal intelligence may serve this coordinating function. To one critic, this assertion still "smells a bit like g" (Sternberg, personal communication, 1994).

On the applied front, Gardner has been criticized for not offering a clear program for educators to use in implementing MI theory in schools (Levin, 1994). Indeed, *Frames of Mind* (Gardner, 1993b) contained only a few paragraphs to indicate how the theory might be used in the teaching of reading and computer programming. Thus, schools have used the theory in diverse ways, "some brilliant, some idiotic" (Gardner, 1994, p. 581). In his defense, Gardner notes that theories may be put into practice in different ways: some with direct guidance, and others—like those of John Dewey and Jean Piaget—by practitioners with little direct guidance from their originators. He speculates that MI has been adopted in the latter way because it allows educators

> to look more carefully at children, to examine their own assumptions about potential and achievement, to consider a variety of approaches to teaching, to try out alternative forms of assessment—in short, to begin the fundamental kind of self-transformation that is necessary if schooling is to improve significantly. (Gardner, 1994, p. 582)

In part to bolster such self-transformation, Gardner and his colleagues are now exploring how the theory is adopted and implemented in schools (Gardner, 1994; Kornhaber, 1994; Kornhaber & Krechevsky, 1995).

Mike Anderson's Theory of Intelligence and Cognitive Development

Mike Anderson, a psychologist who has worked in England and Australia, has put forth an ambitious theory that strives to accomplish several things:

SUPPORT THE NOTION OF GENERAL INTELLIGENCE

In marked contrast to Gardner, who sought to pluralize intelligence, one of Anderson's major goals is to "make plausible the psychological reality of general intelligence" (1992, p. 24). He argues that evidence for multiple intelligences or mental abilities, as put forward by Thurstone (1938) and other psychometricians, rests on statistical artifacts. He believes that Gardner's multiple intelligences are ill-defined: they are "sometimes a behavior, sometimes a cognitive process, and sometimes a structure in the brain" (Anderson, 1992, p. 67).

SYNTHESIZE FINDINGS FROM VARIOUS DISCIPLINES

Anderson attempts to bring together findings from various fields, especially cognitive development and psychometrics. According to Anderson (1992), the psychometric tradition tends to regard intelligence in terms of factorial *structure* (see Chapter 3, which presented several such structures). This view yields a somewhat static notion of intelligence (Anderson, 1992; Sternberg, 1985). In contrast, Anderson notes, cognitive developmentalists tend to regard intelligence as something that *evolves* through changes in the organization of knowledge and skills (see Chapter 4). Like Gardner, Anderson draws on neuropsychology and studies of special populations, such as brain-damaged patients and *savants.* In addition, he looks closely at laboratory studies of inspection time, reaction time, and averaged evoked potentials (Anderson, 1986; see Chapter 5).

Mike Anderson.

INCORPORATE HIGH- AND LOW-LEVEL VIEWS

Related to his multidisciplinary approach, Anderson seeks to encompass what he calls "low-level and high-level views" (Anderson, 1992, p. 2). Low-level views of intelligence are those built on basic physiological processes, of the sort that Eysenck and Jensen have explored (Anderson, 1992; see Chapters 3 and 5). High-level views are similar to what we have previously termed "higher-order skills," like judgment and reasoning, and the sort of skills Binet emphasized (see Chapters 2 and 3). Higher-order skills are associated with knowledge gained through experience and culture (Anderson, 1992).

According to Anderson, the low-level "neural-efficiency school" and the high-level "cognitive school" share the incorrect belief that both developmental changes and adult intelligence have a single underlying explanation (or "mechanism"). For the low-level theorists, physiological processes explain development and adult intelligence. For the high-level theorists, the knowledge base and strategies for using the knowledge base explain development and adult intelligence.

EXPLAIN FIVE FINDINGS IN INTELLIGENCE RESEARCH

Anderson argues that high- and low-level theories have continued to exist side-by-side because each type of theory explains particular aspects of intelligence. The low-level theories account for three "regularities" prominent in psychometric research:

1. "Cognitive abilities increase with development" (Anderson, 1992, p. 6). As noted in Chapter 3, psychometric work indicates that individuals' performance on a variety of psychometric tests, especially those associated with "fluid" intelligence, improve at least through the teenage years. Performance on tests associated with crystallized intelligence (abilities associated with school and cultural learning) often continue to improve at least into middle age (Anderson, 1992; Cattell, 1987; see Chapter 3).

2. "Individual differences are remarkably stable in development" (Anderson, 1992, p. 7). Psychometricians have found that the ranking of individuals' IQs relative to each other remains rather constant. Thus, Anderson says, "How well you are performing at five years old relative to other five-year-olds predicts quite well how well you will perform at 16 years old relative to other 16-year-olds" (p. 7).

3. "Cognitive abilities co-vary" (Anderson, 1992, p. 8). Scores on different psychometric tests and subtests vary together, a finding that Spearman (1904) described as the "positive manifold" (see Chapter 3). In other words, individuals who do well on one type of psychometric test tend to do well on a heterogeneous assortment of such tests. Anderson (like Spearman) argues that this covariation is due to general intelligence, or g.

High-level views coexist with low-level views because they account for two phenomena that form prominent "exceptions" to these regularities, completing the list of five findings.

4. "There are also specific cognitive abilities" (Anderson, 1992, p. 9). As Anderson notes, and as we saw in Chapter 3, several theorists have claimed that intelligence is not "one thing," such as general intelligence, or *g*. Rather, it is a collection of diverse abilities (e.g., Gardner, 1993b). In addition, a number of psychometricians have argued for group factors, along with *g* (e.g., Gustafsson, 1988; P. E. Vernon, 1950), or instead of *g* (e.g., Guilford, 1967; Horn & Cattell, 1966; Thurstone, 1938).

5. "There are cognitive mechanisms that are universal for human beings and which show no individual differences" (Anderson, 1992, p. 10). In contrast to many cognitive abilities (or "group factors"), such as musical aptitude or mathematical prowess, on which individuals clearly vary, there are certain cognitive functions that do not reveal a range of variation. These *universal* abilities include such things as interpreting the visual world in 3-D or understanding that other people have beliefs.

SPECIFY A MINIMUM COGNITIVE ARCHITECTURE

Anderson says his theory differs from low- and high-level views by positing that individual differences in intelligence and developmental changes in intellectual competence must each be explained by *different mechanisms.* His theory attempts to explain these different mechanisms and how they relate to each other (1992). Anderson's theory details what he calls a *minimum cognitive architecture*—the minimum arrangement of mechanisms underlying intelligence. Taken together, these mechanisms can explain the five phenomena outlined above.

The Basic Processing Mechanism. As mentioned, Anderson argues that *g* is a "psychological reality" (Anderson, 1992, p. 24) that pervades all domains and all cognitive activities. He finds evidence for *g* in correlations of general intelligence with "tasks that are relatively *knowledge-free,*" such as inspection time tasks, choice reaction time tasks, and average evoked potentials (see Chapters 3 and 5). Such correlations indicate to Anderson that *g* stems from "low-level cognitive processes that underlie intelligent thinking" (Anderson, 1992, p. 58). He groups these low-level processes together in what he terms "the basic processing mechanism."

Anderson asserts that individuals vary in psychometric tests of *g* because these basic processes vary in *speed* among individuals (Anderson, 1992, p. 58). According to Anderson, the basic processing mechanism implements thinking. Thinking then yields knowledge. All other things being equal, a slower basic processing mechanism would hinder acquisition of knowledge, and a fast processing mechanism would facilitate acquisition of knowledge. The relationship between the speed of the basic processing mechanism and knowledge is illustrated by Anderson as shown in Figure 7.3.

To Anderson, the basic processing mechanism underlies the stability of individual differences in intelligence: individuals born with a fast basic processing mechanism will acquire new knowledge more quickly than those with a slower mechanism, and will continue to do so. This leads to the rather stable ordering of individuals over time, when each is ranked by IQ scores.

Modules. The next piece of the cognitive architecture addresses one of the exceptions to the regularities: There are universal cognitive mechanisms that show no individual differences (Anderson, 1992). Anderson points out that some knowledge is universal, despite individual differences in measured intelligence; other knowledge is correlated with psychometric tests. As an example, Anderson notes that people with Down syndrome may not be able to add 2 plus 2, yet they can recognize that others hold beliefs and may act on those beliefs. "It must be the case that the mechanism responsible for computing 2 plus 2 . . . cannot be the mechanism responsible for computing that 'because person A believes X, then it follows that A will exhibit behaviour Y'" (Anderson, 1992, p. 10). Anderson asserts that

FIGURE 7.3
In Anderson's (1992) theory, the ***basic processing mechanism*** encompasses low-level cognitive processes which implement thinking. The greater the speed of the basic processing mechanism, the more knowledge an individual acquires.

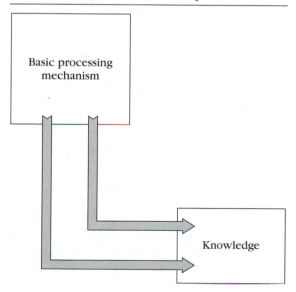

the basic processing mechanism can help explain why individuals will show variation in measured intelligence or *g,* but that a different kind of mechanism must account for universal abilities.

According to Anderson, the mechanisms that provide us with such universal capacities are "modules" (see Fodor, 1983). Modules each function independently, performing complex computations of evolutionary significance. They show no relationship to measured individual differences because they are not affected by the basic processing mechanism. Unlike the basic processing mechanism, which varies from slow to fast, modules reveal little variation: they either work or they don't.

Anderson finds evidence for modules in neuropsychology. He notes that some brain-damaged patients may lose particular complex skills—for example, the ability to recognize faces—while not losing measured IQ. This finding indicates to him that a damaged module is coexisting with an unimpaired basic processing mechanism. Some *savants* may show an opposite pattern: functioning modules, but a slow basic processing mechanism. (The case of D. H., discussed in Box 7.1 below, is an example.) Figure 7.4 illustrates several proposed modules and their relationship to the basic processing mechanism and to knowledge.

Anderson uses the notion of modules to help explain another of the regularities: the increase of cognitive abilities with development. He asserts that this increase is due to the maturation of new modules during development. These new modules underlie what are often considered universal and rather sudden qualitative changes, such as Piagetian stages (see Chapter 4). Anderson claims that modules, though virtually automatic and therefore not really a form of thinking, may have a "generalized effect on thought" (Anderson, 1992, p. 118). For example, the maturation of a module devoted to language might give access to thinking that involves linguistic propositions. This emergence would allow for a sweeping, stage-like change.

Specific Processors.   Anderson then takes on another of the exceptions to the psychometric regularities: specific cognitive abilities (Anderson, 1992). He uses evidence from psychometrics, neuropsychology, and behavioral genetics to argue for two "specific abilities." As noted earlier, many psychometric theories posit two big group factors, namely verbal and spatial abilities. Neuropsychological studies of the brain indicate that the left hemisphere tends to govern propositional functions, like language and mathematics, and the right hemisphere tends to govern visual and spatial functions. Behavioral genetics reveals that each of several genetic disorders exhibits particular patterns of deficits in spatial and verbal abilities.

Based on such evidence, Anderson posits that there are at least two "distinct abilities." One of these abilities deals with propositional thought—the sort of thought associated with language and mathematical expression. The other ability likely concerns visual and spatial functioning. To carry out tasks associated with such abilities, Anderson proposes another kind of mechanism, *specific processors*.

Box 7.1
Understanding Perplexing Phenomena

Having laid out his theoretical cognitive architecture, Anderson illustrates how the theory can be used to understand perplexing phenomena in the study of intelligence. He does this by exploring patterns of strengths and deficits found among *savants*. He claims that such patterns are due to brain damage that has spared a module, a specific processor, or the basic processing mechanism.

One case involves a 21-year-old man known as M.A. As an infant and young child, M.A. suffered convulsions. He did not communicate with others and, at age 3, was diagnosed as autistic. As an adult, he still cannot talk, but he can copy numbers and letters "very poorly." He achieves very low scores on most psychometric tests. However, on the Raven's Progressive Matrices, his performance is consistent with an IQ of 128. Even more notable, M.A. has an extraordinary ability to detect prime numbers. On various tasks involving detecting prime numbers and factoring large numbers, he is more accurate than a scientist who also holds a mathematics degree and quicker than a university technician who graduated from an engineering program and who is quite knowledgeable in mathematics (Anderson, 1992).

One of the intriguing aspects of such comparisons is that, though quicker and more accurate, M.A.'s pattern of responses resembles those of the two normal men. For example, both M.A. and the technician need longer periods of time to detect a prime number than to detect a nonprime. Also, for each individual, harder nonprime numbers, those divisible by 13, 17, or 19, take longer than those divisible by 2, 3, 5, 7, and 11. Both M.A. and the research scientist would often mistake the same nonprime numbers for a prime number. That M.A.'s pattern of responses resembles those of normal people suggests that he solves these math problems using mental processes similar to those of normal people. He was not merely recalling a memorized list of prime numbers.

Psychometric and laboratory tests provide additional information concerning M.A.'s patterns of strengths and deficits. He performs better than average on an inspection time test and on Raven's. However, he cannot solve psychometric tests that require an understanding of the "real world"; for example, he cannot indicate that a ladder does not belong in a set of illustrations that depict objects on which one sits. Nevertheless, he can select the incorrect symbol from a set of shapes or abstract symbols.

Continued

Box 7.1 (Continued)

These test results, along with analyses of responses with the two controls, indicate to Anderson that M.A. has an intact basic processing mechanism, which allows him to "think" at least about abstract symbols. It may be that he cannot solve problems involving real-world objects, such as ladders and chairs, in part because of "extensive damage to his linguistic modules" (Anderson, 1992, p. 186). This could hinder acquisition of much everyday knowledge and communication. Anderson speculates that M.A.'s problem entails other "vital mechanisms" beyond linguistic modules, and that M.A. generally cannot apply his basic processing mechanism to problems requiring "semantic properties of the real world" (p. 187).

The case of D.H. is in many ways opposite to M.A.'s. D.H., a young woman, cannot read, write, count, or give a reliable ordering of the days of the week. Nevertheless, in everyday situations, she uses a large vocabulary and complex syntax, and she employs unusually good conversational skills—an autistic strength that has been called "cocktail party syndrome" (Hadenius, Hagberg, Hyttnes-Beusch, & Sjogren, 1962, cited in Anderson, 1992, p. 174).

Testing revealed other strengths and deficits: D.H. can distinguish correct from incorrect usages of "prepositions, singular/plural agreement, tense markers, passives, and relative clauses." Nevertheless, her verbal IQ was 57 and her nonverbal test performance was "unscorable" (Anderson, 1992, p. 174). Thus, it appears that D.H. is capable of manipulating language without understanding much of the meaning conveyed by language. (This is akin to the skill of the ELIZA program, mentioned in Chapter 6.)

To Anderson, D.H.'s lack of everyday understanding and meanings is consistent with a slow basic processing mechanism. This hypothesis is shored up by results from an inspection time task. Unlike M.A.'s performance, D.H.'s on this task was extremely slow. A slow basic processing mechanism would give inadequate support for the specific processors through which everyday knowledge is acquired. Instead linguistic modules are allowing D.H. to use grammar and vocabulary in the absence of their meaning.

FIGURE 7.4
Anderson (1992) depicts several proposed *modules* in the upper right side of this diagram and shows how these provide knowledge without being affected by the speed of the basic processing mechanism (p. 74).

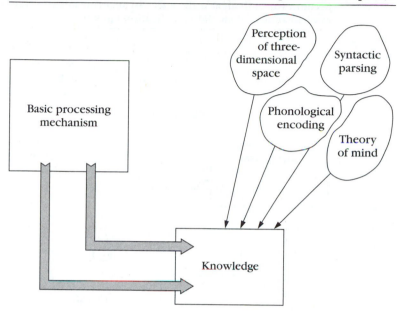

Anderson says that, unlike modules, which have very particular and important functions to which they are "dedicated," each of the specific processors handles much broader classes of problems or knowledge. Also, in contrast to modules, specific processors are constrained by the basic processing mechanism. Variation in the processors depends in part on the strength of the processor as well as on the speed of the basic processing mechanism.

That the speed of the basic processing mechanism constrains specific processors helps Anderson explain another of the three "regularities": the covariance of abilities. With a "low-speed" basic processing mechanism or low general intelligence, only limited acquisition of knowledge and skills is possible. However, with a high-speed basic processing mechanism, the capacities of the specific processors themselves can be better realized and put to a variety of tasks. In other words, high-IQ people can do many things that draw on their powerful specific processors. They exhibit high scores on various tests and can demonstrate varied areas of accomplishment in the real world. Similarly, low-IQ people do not develop powerful specific processors because theirs are constrained by a slow basic processing mechanism. Therefore, they show covariation of low scores on various psychometric tests and generally do not demonstrate high-level, varied abilities. The relationship of the specific processors to the rest of the cognitive architecture Anderson has laid out is illustrated in Figure 7.5.

Figure 7.5
Anderson (1992) posits at least 2 *specific processors* (SP1 and SP2) responsible for propositional and spatial processing. Because these are constrained by the basic processing mechanism, they may help account for individual differences in specific abilities like language, mathematics, and spatial visualization (p. 97).

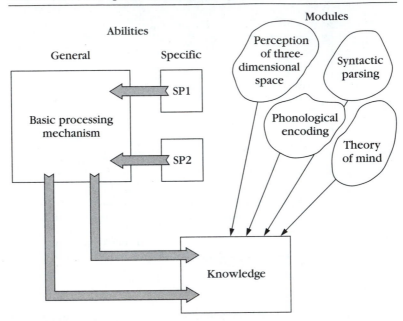

Two Different Routes to Knowledge.   Completing Anderson's minimal cognitive architecture are two different "routes" to knowledge (see Figure 7.6):

- Route 1 relies on the use of specific processors, fueled by the basic processing mechanism, to acquire knowledge. These, plus the different experiences people have access to, yield the variation in knowledge that individuals display. In Anderson's theory, this route constitutes "thinking" (Anderson, 1992).

- Route 2 involves the use of modules to obtain knowledge. Module-generated knowledge, such as seeing the world in 3-D, is part of our evolutionary inheritance. Knowledge obtained through this route does not involve thought: such knowledge comes to us automatically and directly, provided the modules are working.

Anderson notes that the term "intelligence" does not map onto any one piece of his theorized cognitive architecture. In his theory, *individual differences* in

FIGURE 7.6
Anderson (1992) proposes 2 routes to knowledge. Route 1 entails the specific processors plus experiences individuals encounter and yields the variation in individuals' knowledge. Route 1 knowledge acquisition entails thinking. Route 2 knowledge is acquired through modules and does not entail thought (p. 107).

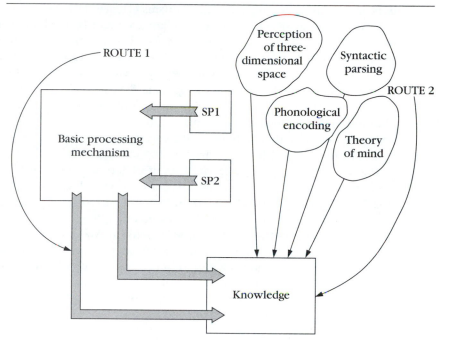

intelligence (the realm of psychometrics) amount to "individual differences in *knowledge*" (Anderson, 1992, p. 108), reflecting largely the differences in the speed of the basic processing mechanism and the functioning of specific processors. The *development of intelligence* (the realm of cognitive development) is due largely to the appearance of new modules, which may affect thought and allow "new *modes of representation*" to be accessed. Thus, for Anderson, "the processes underlying individual differences in intelligence and the processes underlying the development of intelligence are quite different" (Anderson, 1992, p. 141). The cases described in Box 7.1 offer relevant examples.

Critique of Anderson's Theory

Anderson's theory is so recent that it has not yet undergone much debate in scientific and psychological literature. One criticism that has emerged is that certain aspects of the theory lack much evidence (Deary, 1992). For example, though Anderson claims that modules show no individual differences, certain ones, like syntactic parsing, might. More empirical data need to be presented and argued to support such a claim.

Other claims appear to be argued in a tautological fashion. To illustrate, the specific processors and modules are proposed because some individuals demonstrate particular cognitive deficits. Yet, later, Anderson explains that the disorders are due to these impaired mechanisms (Deary, 1992).

The idea that sweeping stagelike changes might be explained as simple maturations of new modules is also problematic. If maturation were responsible, then all normal people would achieve stages such as the formal operations described by Piaget (see Chapter 4). Instead, we know that schooling and other aspects of culture affect such development (e.g., Cole & Scribner, 1974).

Despite these criticisms, Anderson's theory is a concise framework for explaining several consistent findings in the study of intelligence: that cognitive abilities increase, that individual differences remain stable with development, that abilities covary (though, Gardner (1993b) and Ceci (below) claim this is due to the similarity of psychometric tests of different abilities); that there are specific cognitive abilities; and that there are universal abilities. As we can see in Box 7.1, his theory also helps account for some puzzling findings in the real-world behaviors of special populations and normal people.

In contrast to all the others in this chapter, Anderson's theory focuses on a single level of explanation—the computational or information processing level and the mechanisms underlying these. Anderson acknowledges that biological and cultural explanations are important, but he argues that they are at other levels of description. His goal, unlike the others', is to have an elegant theory that explains a particular level rather than "a unified theory of all the manifestations of what is termed 'intelligence'" (Anderson, 1992, p. 210).

Robert Sternberg's Triarchic Theory of Human Intelligence

Robert Sternberg, a professor of psychology at Yale University, has been described by Mike Anderson as "the most influential and prolific of current theorists" of intelligence (Anderson, 1992, p. 33). Yet, Sternberg's approach to a theory of intelligence contrasts sharply with Anderson's (Anderson, 1992). Sternberg claims that many theories of intelligence are not incorrect but instead are incomplete (Sternberg, 1985). Thus, while Anderson's is a concise, cognitively oriented theory, Sternberg's triarchic theory strives to be all-encompassing.

As its name implies, Sternberg's theory is comprised of three interrelated parts or "subtheories":

1. The *componential subtheory* addresses the internal, elementary information processes underlying intelligent thought. "What goes on inside a person's head when he thinks intelligently?" (Sternberg, 1988, p. 57).

2. The *experiential subtheory* deals with both the external and internal aspects of intelligence. This subtheory considers intelligence in light of an

individual's experience with particular tasks. It asks: "How does experience affect a person's intelligence, and how does his intelligence affect the kinds of experiences he has?" (Sternberg, 1988, p. 57).

3. The *contextual subtheory* considers individual intelligence in relation to the culture and environment of the external world. Through this subtheory, Sternberg seeks to understand how a person's interactions in the world "affect his intelligence and how does his intelligence affect the world in which he lives?" (Sternberg, 1988, p. 57).

THE COMPONENTIAL SUBTHEORY

The componential subtheory is the most highly elaborated of the three subtheories, because it is based on Sternberg's extensive research in information processing. The subtheory considers the various types of *components* individuals use in problem solving. Sternberg posits three broad kinds of components and enumerates several functions in each of the three categories:

1. *Metacomponents* can be thought of as playing a supervisory or "white collar" role in problem solving (Sternberg, 1988). These are used to plan, control, monitor, and evaluate processing during problem solving.

2. *Performance components* are the "blue collar" processes (Sternberg, 1988). They carry out problem-solving strategies specified by metacomponents.

3. *Knowledge-acquisition components,* which Sternberg calls "the students of mental self-management" (1988, p. 170), selectively encode, combine, and compare information during the course of problem solving and thereby enable new learning to occur (Sternberg, 1985).

Sternberg gives an example to show both how various components work and how extensively the three types of components are intertwined. In writing a paper, metacomponents are in play when a person decides on a topic, organizes the paper, monitors the writing,

Robert Sternberg.

and evaluates the final work. Knowledge-acquisition components enable the writer to carry out research work for the paper. Performance components are brought to bear in the writing of the paper, perhaps, for example, in searching for—and fetching from memory—apt words and phrases. Figure 7.7 illustrates the relationship among these three types of components.

Methods.   Much of the componential subtheory is based on Sternberg's research into how people solve analogies and other problem types often used in intelligence tests. For example, Sternberg and his colleagues have broken down the task of solving analogies into numerous subtasks, using a method called *precueing*. In precueing, subjects are presented with part of the analogy. This allows them to process that part prior to solving the analogy as a whole. In essence, data drawn from precueing methodology enables Sternberg to subtract out and analyze a particular problem-solving process—or component—from the process of solving the analogy as a whole.

One of Sternberg's sample analogies will serve as a concrete example:

"Four score and seven years ago" is to Lincoln as "I'm not a crook" is to (a. Nixon, b. Capone). (Sternberg, 1985, p. 350)

FIGURE 7.7
The relationships among Sternberg's metacomponents, performance components, and knowledge-acquisition components. Metacomponents activate the other two kinds of components, which in turn provide feedback to the metacomponents (1988, p. 60).

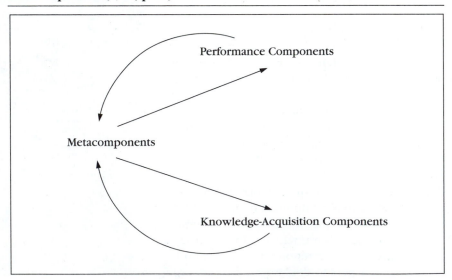

One form of precueing initially presents to a subject the first term of the analogy: "Four score and seven years ago." A subject who has processed the first term can press a button, see the remainder of the analogy, and then solve it. Another form of precueing could initially present the first two terms, "Four score and seven years ago": Lincoln. When these terms have been processed, the subject can hit a button, get the remaining terms, and then indicate the solution.

By applying various permutations of precueing to the types of problems often found on IQ tests, Sternberg has found that individuals with higher IQs solve problems more quickly than other individuals. However, overall problem-solving speed masks important differences in the information processing of higher-and lower-IQ subjects. High scorers spend more time "encoding the terms of a problem" and "less time operating on these encodings" (Sternberg, 1985, p. 104). In other words, they spend more of their time grasping the nature of the analogy's terms than on moving from this grasp to the solution of the analogy. Sternberg also has found that those who score highest spend relatively more of their time working on "global planning," which concerns understanding the nature of the problem to be solved. For example, high scorers spend more time in figuring out whether the problem demands analogical reasoning, a search for antonyms, or retrieval of a definition. They spend less time on "local planning," the strategy needed for solving an individual problem (Sternberg, 1985). In short, when solving analogies, high scorers seem to devote more time to "white collar" processes than to "blue collar" ones.

Sternberg's work in this area also gives greater meaning to the role of speed in intelligence. According to Sternberg, speed of processing is correlated with IQ scores, as others have noted (e.g., Anderson, 1992; Jensen, 1980). However, "What is critical is not speed per se but rather . . . knowing when and being able to function rapidly or slowly according to task or situational demands" (Sternberg, 1985, p. 301).

EXPERIENTIAL SUBTHEORY

Although much of Sternberg's early efforts were devoted to componential analyses of the sort just described, he found that the workings of internal and largely low-level components were not sufficient to explain intelligence. The experiential subtheory was developed to address an aspect of intelligence that was missing from the componential theory: the role of experience in intelligent performance.

As Sternberg sees it, a given problem does not draw on intelligent use of mental components to the same degree for different people. For example, to a kindergartener, reading the word "zero" is likely a novel experience requiring a great deal of effort to sound out and understand. However, an adult who is literate in English probably reads and understands the word automatically. Because a particular task may be more or less new to one person or within one culture, the degree to which a problem requires intelligence will vary from person to person and from culture to culture (Sternberg, 1985).

Sternberg states that experience with a task or problem falls on a continuum from totally novel to completely automated. Flowing from this notion, the experiential subtheory posits that intelligence is partly a function of two abilities: the ability to work through novel tasks and situations; and the ability to automate information processing. The two interact: the more one is able to automate information processing, the more mental resources can be devoted to processing novelty (Sternberg, 1985).

According to Sternberg, the most important implication of the experiential subtheory concerns selection of tasks for measuring intelligence (Sternberg, 1985). Tasks that are completely novel or completely automated won't reveal much about a person's intelligence. Why? If a task is utterly novel, a person has no frame of reference for handling the problem. It doesn't tap any problem-solving abilities (Sternberg, 1988). Similarly, if it is completely automated, a task won't reveal much about a person's intelligence, because such tasks bypass problem solving. Therefore, the best tasks to use in measuring intelligence are those that are relatively novel or are in the process of becoming automated (Sternberg, 1985).

Sternberg believes the experiential subtheory also helps explain why measures of speed on some simple tasks, such as reaction time measures, are correlated with IQ (see Chapter 3): these tasks largely measure automatization skills. Similarly, tests like Raven's Progressive Matrices or other tests of "fluid intelligence" (see Chapter 3) also measure intelligence, because they address the ability to solve more novel kinds of problems.

Methods.   Sternberg has used various methods for exploring the experiential subtheory. For example, he and his colleagues have given IQ tests, inductive and deductive reasoning tests, and 12 novel, "insight" problems to a group of 30 adults. These problems required selective encoding, selective combination, or both, or were "trick" problems merely requiring careful reading (e.g., "A farmer has 17 sheep. All but 9 broke through a hole in the fence and wandered away. How many were left?" [Sternberg, 1985, p. 81]).

Using this and other methods, Sternberg and his colleagues have found that the ability to solve insight problems correlates rather highly (r = .66–.77) with IQ (Sternberg, 1985, 1988). Not surprisingly, solving insight problems correlates more highly (.63) with tests of inductive reasoning ("which requires an individual to go beyond the information given"), than with tests of deductive reasoning (.34) ("which merely requires him to analyze the given information and draw the proper conclusion") (Sternberg, 1988, p. 174).

Once again, Sternberg looks at the relationship of speed to problem solving. In this case, he found that high scorers on insight tests spend more time working on the problems than do those who score less well. He believes that high scorers spend more time because they are engaged and motivated to solve the problem. In contrast, low scorers too often choose an obvious but incorrect answer, or they lose interest in the problem (Sternberg, 1988).

CONTEXTUAL SUBTHEORY

The contextual subtheory strives to go beyond "the internal world of the individual" (Sternberg, 1985, p. 44), the primary focus of the componential subtheory and also of traditional psychometric notions. This subtheory is concerned with the cognitive activity needed to fit into environmental contexts (Sternberg, 1985).

Three kinds of mental processes are central to the contextual subtheory: (a) adaptation, (b) selection, and (c) shaping of real-world environments. The three are somewhat hierarchically ordered. Thus, according to Sternberg, an individual first looks for ways to adapt, or fit into, the environment (Sternberg, 1985). If adaptation to the environment is not possible, then the person will try to select a different environment or alternatively, may try to shape the environment in order to achieve a better fit.

Sternberg gives an example from the realm of marriage. If a spouse is unhappy in the marriage, adaptation to the current circumstances may no longer be feasible. The spouse may then *select* a different environment by getting out of the marriage, or may attempt to *shape* the current unhappy relationship into something better (Sternberg, 1985).

Methods. A major focus of Sternberg's work on the contextual subtheory involves exploring individuals' tacit knowledge. Tacit knowledge consists of information that is "picked up" in the real world but is rarely explicitly taught or articulated (Polanyi, 1958; Senge, 1990; Sternberg, 1985). In the real world, these bits of information amount to the "ins and outs" or "practical knowledge" one needs to fit into the workplace or other everyday contexts (Sternberg, 1985, 1988; Sternberg & Wagner, 1986).

To study practical intelligence, Sternberg has sent questionnaires to individuals who are at different career points within different occupational groups. For example, he has sent questionnaires to graduate students and faculty members in the field of psychology, and to business executives from Fortune 500 and non-Fortune 500 companies as well as MBA students from top- and lesser-rated business schools.

The questionnaires sought to ascertain respondents' "knowledge and understanding of the hidden agenda" of their field (Sternberg, 1985, p. 270). Respondents were asked to rate the importance of particular behaviors for achieving a particular goal. (See Box 7.2 for sample items from tacit knowledge questionnaires.)

These investigations revealed a positive correlation between scores on the questionnaires and measures of professional success. For example, psychology faculty members who scored higher on the questionnaire of tacit knowledge tended to have more publications that year, attend more conferences, and be working in more prestigious departments. Business executives' scores on the questionnaire were positively correlated with status of the company, salary, and years of schooling. Such results led Sternberg to conclude that tacit knowledge,

Box 7.2
Sample Items From Tacit Knowledge Questionnaires

Psychology

1. It is your second year as an assistant professor in a prestigious psychology department. This past year you published two unrelated empirical articles in established journals. You don't, however, believe there is yet a research area that can be identified as your own. You believe yourself to be about as productive as others. The feedback about your first year of teaching has been generally good. You have yet to serve on a university committee. There is one graduate student who has chosen to work with you. You have no external source of funding, nor have you applied for funding.

   Your goals are to become one of the top people in your field and to get tenure in your department. The following is a list of things you are considering doing in the next two months. You obviously cannot do them all. Rate the importance of each by its priority as a means of reaching your goals.
   a. Improve the quality of your teaching.
   b. Write a grant proposal.
   c. Begin long-term research that may lead to a major theoretical article.
   d. Serve on a committee studying university-community relations.
   e. Begin several related short-term research projects, each of which may lead to an empirical article.
   f. Write a paper for presentation to an upcoming American Psychological Association convention.
   g. Ask for comments from senior members of the department on future papers.

2. Rate the importance of the following in deciding to which journal to submit an article for possible publication:
   a. Reputation of the journal in your field of expertise.
   b. Number of years the journal has been in existence.
   c. Publication lag of the journal.
   d. Rejection rate of the journal.
   e. Overall circulation of the journal.
   f. Appropriateness of the journal for content of your paper.

3. An undergraduate student has asked for your advice in deciding to which graduate programs in psychology to apply. Consider the following dimensions for rating the overall quality of a graduate program in psychology and rate their importance:

Continued

Box 7.2 (Continued)

a. Breadth of the program.
b. Prestige of the faculty.
c. Quality of the undergraduate student population.
d. Job placements of recent graduates of the program.
e. Number of required courses.
f. Current grants and research projects underway.

Business

1. It is your second year as a midlevel manager in a company in the communications industry. You head a department of about 30 people. The evaluation of your first year on the job has been generally favorable. Performance ratings for your department are at least as good as they were before you took over, and perhaps even a little better. You have two assistants. One is quite capable. The other just seems to go through the motions but to be of little real help.

   You believe that although you are well liked, there is little that would distinguish you in the eyes of your superiors from the nine other managers at a comparable level in the company.

   Your goal is rapid promotion to the top of the company. The following is a list of things you are considering doing in the next two months. You obviously cannot do them all. Rate the importance of each by its priority as a means of reaching your goal.
   a. Find a way to get rid of the "dead wood," e.g., the less helpful assistant and three or four others.
   b. Become more involved in local public service organizations.
   c. Find ways to make sure your superiors are aware of your important accomplishments.
   d. As a means of being noticed, propose a solution to a problem outside the scope of your immediate department that you would be willing to take charge of.
   e. When making decisions, give a great deal of weight to the way your superior likes things to be done.
   f. Accept a friend's invitation to join the exclusive country club that many higher-level executives belong to.
   g. Ask for comments from superiors about important decisions you need to make.
   h. Adjust your work habits to increase your productivity.

Continued

Box 7.2 (Continued)

2. Rate the following strategies of working according to how important you believe them to be for doing well at the day-to-day work of a business manager:
   a. Always have a variety of projects in progress—many "irons in the fire."
   b. Do not force yourself to do tasks you don't feel like doing.
   c. Use a daily list of goals arranged according to your priorities.
   d. Don't try to do everything well—many tasks are trivial.
   e. Delegate tasks to competent others whenever possible.
   f. Carefully consider the optimal strategy before beginning a task.
3. You have just been promoted to head an important department in the company. The previous head had been transferred to an equivalent position in a less important department. Your understanding of the reason for the move is that the performance of the department as a whole was mediocre. There were not any glaring deficiencies, just a perception of the department as so-so rather than as very good. Your charge was to shape up the department. Results are expected quickly. Rate the following pieces of advice colleagues have given you by their importance to succeeding in your new position:
   a. Always delegate to the most junior person who can be trusted with the task.
   b. Make people feel completely responsible for their work.
   c. Be intolerant of your own mistakes and of the mistakes of others.
   d. Be careful to avoid the company's "sacred cows."
   e. Do not try to do too much too soon.
   f. Promote open communication.

though not traditionally measured in test batteries, is an important factor for success in real-world contexts (Sternberg, 1985, 1993).

Critique of the Theory

Perhaps the greatest strength of the triarchic theory is that it brings together diverse aspects of intelligence. The componential subtheory considers low-level explanations. It examines the basic mental mechanisms or processing components underlying intelligence. The experiential subtheory considers the role of experience in intelligence. It looks at intelligent performances in light of a continuum of experience, from novelty to automatization. The contextual subtheory is meant to address high-level views of intelligence, those that deal with judgment and adaptation in the "real world." It is aimed at explaining how internal, mental mechanisms are used by individuals to make "an intelligent fit" with the external world (Sternberg, 1990, p. 268). In addition, Sternberg has tried to study empirically the various processes that he has posited. Thus, unlike Gardner's and Anderson's theories, Sternberg's is not primarily an organization of the work of other researchers.

Yet, the comprehensiveness of the triarchic theory may also be a weakness. The theory encompasses so many disparate pieces that some critics claim it is not coherent (Richardson, 1986). For example, in contrast to Gardner's theory, there are no clear criteria to explain why particular pieces of the theory are included. In contrast to Gardner's and Anderson's theories, Sternberg's many and varied elements do not provide an elegant means for understanding the behaviors of either gifted or intellectually impaired individuals.

Another criticism of Sternberg's theory is that it largely ignores the biological aspects of intelligence. The various components and processes Sternberg discusses are not linked to brain functioning. They therefore seem to be convenient verbal labels rather than actual mental processes. As Sternberg acknowledged (1985, 1986b), no theory of intelligence can be all-encompassing. Yet, in an age of neuroscientific advances, the absence of biology is a notable gap in a theory that strives to be comprehensive.

It is also worth noting that while Sternberg's contextual subtheory finds correlations between "practical intelligence" and real-world performance, it does not reveal how problem solving takes place within, and is affected by, everyday contexts. For the most part, Sternberg has focused on analyzing data gathered with traditional psychological tools: test questions. However, Sternberg has become increasingly interested in how people function in real-world settings (e.g., Sternberg & Wagner, 1986). In fact, he and Gardner have undertaken collaborative research to explore practical intelligence as it plays out in schoolchildren (Gardner, Krechevsky, Sternberg, & Okagaki, 1994; Krechevsky & Gardner, 1990b; Sternberg, Okagaki, & Jackson, 1990). However, the investigation of such behavior is an area explored in greater depth by a varied group of researchers (e.g., Ceci, 1990; Cole & Scribner, 1974; Lave, 1988; Rogoff, 1990). We will consider next one such researcher, Stephen Ceci.

Stephen Ceci's Bioecological Treatise on Intellectual Development

Stephen Ceci, a psychologist based at Cornell University in Ithaca, New York, acknowledges that his framework grows from Sternberg's triarchic theory (Ceci, 1990). Ceci, like Sternberg, addresses information processing components, experience, and context. However, in his effort to explain individual differences in intelligence, he places a much greater emphasis on *context* and its impact on

Stephen Ceci.

complex problem solving. Furthermore, while both Anderson and Sternberg emphasize mental mechanisms over knowledge in their theories, Ceci argues that knowledge plays a key role in understanding individual differences. He believes that basic, low-level mental processing does not just enable the acquisition of knowledge, but that such processing is affected by knowledge and experience (Ceci, 1990). Finally, like Gardner, Ceci argues against the notion of a single, underlying *g,* (general intelligence), and he claims that there are *multiple cognitive potentials* and that these have a biological basis.

Multiple cognitive potentials, context, and knowledge are interoven in Ceci's bioecological framework (Ceci, 1990). Though we will discuss them individually, strains of all three should be evident throughout. However, before turning to the three aspects of the bioecological framework, several related concepts that are central to understanding Ceci's theory are worth our attention:

- *Cognitive processes* are hypothetical mental mechanisms, such as encoding and memory retrieval, used to gather and interpret information. These are similar to Sternberg's components. Ceci argues that individual intelligence is constrained both by these biological processes and by "the nature of one's knowledge" (Ceci, 1990, p. 15).

- *Knowledge* is the "information, rules, beliefs, attitudes, etc." that are acquired by cognitive processes. "Knowledge is organized into structures in long-term memory that vary in their degree of elaborateness and interrelatedness" (Ceci, 1990, p. 15). The more elaborated and interrelated, the more usable and powerful the knowledge. Knowledge and cognitive processes are intertwined: the more organized one's knowledge, the more efficient one's cognitive processes can be. The more efficient one's processes, the more organized and elaborated the knowledge base can become.

- A *domain* is defined by Ceci as an organized region of declarative knowledge (1990). One can think of statistics, gardening, or architecture as domains of knowledge. Domains act as a context for bits of knowledge. For instance, retrieving knowledge about "columns" would vary, depending on whether the knowledge was relevant to architecture or statistics or military history. The same bit of knowledge can be part of many different domains. According to Ceci, the ability to function well in some domains and not others is based partly on knowledge and its organization into structures within a domain.

- *Cognitive complexity* is the extent to which one's cognitive processes can "operate on one's knowledge structures in a complex, efficient, and flexible manner" (1990, p. 15). It is reasonable to view cognitive complexity as the ability to think well in a particular domain. In Ceci's theory, cognitive complexity reveals much more about one's intellectual ability than does an IQ score.

- *IQ* is a score on a test intended to measure general intelligence. However, much like Gardner (1993b; Walters & Gardner, 1985), Ceci believes an IQ score really reflects only "one underlying type of intelligence" (Ceci & Liker, 1986a, p. 135). This type of intelligence is related to academic learning:

  > . . . schooling is seen as an environment that induces specific knowledge and modes of cognizing that are relevant for performance on tests of academic intelligence (e.g., paper-and-pencil tasks, IQ tests, achievement tests) but is not necessary for successful performance on tasks that do not depend on academic learning. (Ceci & Liker, 1986a, p. 135)

According to Ceci, IQ doesn't reflect other, nonacademic abilities, even though such abilities can require a great deal of cognitive complexity and abstract thought (Ceci & Liker, 1986a, 1986b).

THE ROLE OF MULTIPLE COGNITIVE POTENTIALS

In contrast to many in the psychometric tradition, Ceci claims there is no one underlying form of mental "energy" responsible for intelligence. He asserts instead that there are multiple abilities, intelligences, or "cognitive potentials." Each potential enables relationships to be discovered, thoughts to be monitored, and knowledge to be acquired within a domain (Ceci, 1990; Ceci & Liker, 1986a).

According to Ceci, intelligences are biologically based and they constrain mental processes, such as the ability to encode and retrieve information. However, Ceci argues that these biological potentials are inextricably linked to the environmental challenges and opportunities in which they develop. In other words, and in contrast to the approaches taken by behavioral geneticists (see Chapter 5), Ceci asserts it is not possible to analyze the environmental contributions separately from the biological contributions to intellectual functioning. The two are in "a state of constant symbiosis" (Ceci, Ramey, & Ramey, 1990).

Ceci's method for establishing multiple cognitive potentials entails two sets of arguments. One undermines general intelligence (*g*), and the other bolsters multiple cognitive potentials.

***Undermining* g.**   To make the point that IQ detects only the type of intelligence associated with schooling, and to underscore the symbiosis of cognitive potentials with the environment, Ceci (1990) draws on some 30 research studies. These enable him to assert that if one has little opportunity to attend school or if one drops out of school, the academic type of intelligence associated with IQ scores will not develop as highly as if one attended school. Therefore, this lack of development does not reflect primarily biology, as some psychologists have asserted (Jensen 1969, 1980; Terman, 1916).

For example, Ceci reports on studies, done in the 1920s and 1930s in England and the United States, of children who had little or no access to schooling. In England, investigators found that in families of gypsies and canal boat pilots, who spent most of their time traveling, the children's IQs had an inverse relation to their age. Children of kindergarten age had IQs of about 90, while adolescent children averaged IQs of about 60.

> The most reasonable explanation seems to be this: the younger children appear to be about "normal" in intelligence, because success in the tests of the earlier years does not depend upon the opportunity for mental stimulus and exercise such as is offered by school. . . . (Freeman, 1934, as reported in Ceci, 1990, p. 74)

Similar conclusions were reached in a 1932 study of communities in the Blue Ridge Mountains area of the United States (Sherman & Key, 1932, reported in Ceci, 1990). Researchers found that children who were raised in the most remote community (where schools were generally closed and adults were illiterate) had lower IQs than children raised in less remote communities. As in the British study, IQs were found to be about average for young children, but adolescents scored as retarded. Lack of access to schooling and related opportunities was again cited to explain this decrease in scores with age (Sherman & Key, 1932; Tyler, 1965; both cited in Ceci, 1990).

Bolstering Multiple Cognitive Potentials.   Like Gardner, Ceci relies on various forms of evidence to support the notion of multiple cognitive potentials. This evidence includes psychometric literature, neuropsychology, and cognitive studies and experiments. Unlike Gardner, Ceci believes neuropsychology provides only weak evidence for multiple cognitive potentials. In fact, he claims such evidence can be used either to support or undermine the case for multiple potentials (Ceci, 1990, p. 104).

Recall from Chapter 5 (and the discussion of Gardner's theory, above) that damage to a specific area of the brain or to connections between areas may impair particular functions. For instance, damage to Wernicke's area in the left temporal lobe can result in speech production that sounds nonsensical, and an inability to comprehend speech. Such localized brain damage could be used, as Gardner has, to support the notion of separable cognitive potentials (Ceci, 1990). But what if localized function only represented a necessary but not sufficient condition for a specific ability (Ceci, 1990)? In other words, some general intelligence might still be needed for producing and comprehending sensible speech, but damage to Wernicke's region might mask the role of the general factor. In such a case, the general factor's role can no longer be expressed without the functioning of the specific region. Thus, it is hard to know from breakdowns in specific regions whether some general, neurologically based factor—perhaps akin to Anderson's central processing mechanism—also underlies intelligence.

For Ceci, stronger evidence for multiple cognitive potentials comes from psychometrics. (Gardner draws on this area much less to support his theory.) For example, factor analyses of psychometric tests indicate that there are "specific mental abilities," such as linguistic and spatial abilities, that help explain individual differences. (The specific mental abilities Ceci refers to are often called "group factors." These are discussed in Chapter 3.)

Ceci also draws on a range of cognitive studies to support the notion of multiple cognitive potentials. Some cognitive studies, such as the handicappers study (described below in the section on the role of knowledge), indicate that individuals are capable of highly complex thought in some domains and not in others. Ceci argues that such findings bolster the notion that different domains are supported by different cognitive potentials. Other cognitive studies involving anthropological investigations have revealed that individuals in other cultures who score poorly on mental tests may nevertheless demonstrate great competence in some domains. Chapter 1 provides such an example: the case of Puluwat navigators (Gladwin, 1970). These navigators could not achieve an impressive result on an IQ test. Yet, without maps or compasses, they successfully sail the open ocean among scores of Pacific islands.

In Ceci's framework, the development and expression of multiple cognitive potentials are intertwined with the context of problem solving and with the environment. The studies mentioned in this section, which touch on issues such as access to schooling and the variety of skills demonstrated by those in other cultures, underscore this relationship. The role of context in Ceci's framework is highlighted in the following section.

THE ROLE OF CONTEXT

Ceci argues that context is vital to the demonstration of underlying cognitive abilities. Context is a broadly encompassing term in his bioecological framework. It includes domains of knowledge, as well as working materials, motivation, personality, schooling, and even the historical era in which one lives. Its range encompasses the mental, social, and physical contexts of problem solving, each of which can influence cognition (Ceci & Roazzi, 1994). As noted earlier, many other researchers have investigated the relationship of various aspects of context to intelligence. By focusing on Ceci's treatise, we seek to convey the flavor of contextual research.

Ceci's method for asserting the importance of context is varied. Among other things, it includes logical arguments that undermine previous studies. For example, he has noted that a famous longitudinal study of high-IQ children conducted by Lewis Terman (Terman & Oden, 1959) was too quick to assert that high IQ led to high achievement. Ceci and others assert that variables such as social class and job opportunities also influence achievement. For example, these researchers have found that nearly all of the Terman study youngsters (known as "Termites") who came from upper-income families went on to be the most successful adults; in contrast, few of the most successful adults came from poor families. In addition, the Termites who became adults during the Great Depression turned out to be less successful than those who came of age later, when there were more job opportunities. To Ceci, ". . . the bottom line . . . is that the ecological niche one occupies, including individual and historical development, is a far more potent determinant of one's professional and economic success than is IQ" (Ceci, 1990, p. 62).

Along with his critiques of previous studies, Ceci has conducted his own studies to demonstrate how context affects intellectual performance. For Ceci, and other contextualist researchers, context is not just a "package" surrounding a problem; it is part of the problem itself (Ceci, Ramey, & Ramey, 1990). This view is in marked contrast to traditional psychometric ideas, such as Spearman's "indifference of the indicator" (Spearman, 1923). To Spearman, the test items that were used to indicate a capacity for abstract thinking were not terribly important. In his scheme, *g* pervaded all problem solving; therefore, various types of problems could serve as means to demonstrate one's intelligence.

Ceci shows the importance of context for demonstrating intellectual abilities in studies involving *problem isomorphs.* These are problems that are structurally identical—they call on the same underlying problem-solving processes—but use different materials to pose the problem.

Ceci and his colleagues have constructed rather elaborate problem isomorphs. In one problem, children are seated in front of a computer screen and asked to observe the motion of colored, geometric shapes. Based on their observations, the children are then asked to predict where on the screen the shapes will terminate. They indicate the termination point by using a joystick to place a cross on the screen. Basic rules were used to drive the movements of different shapes: squares went up, circles went down, and triangles remained horizontal. Dark objects moved right, light objects moved left. Large objects moved diagonally upward from the lower left. Small objects moved diagonally downward from the upper right. The accuracy of the children's predictions was only 22% after 750 trials.

In the isomorph to this task, the same rules were used to drive a video game. However, the context for the problem solving was changed. The geometric shapes were replaced by a butterfly, a bumblebee, and a bird. In addition, the children were told to move the joystick to "capture the prey" with "a butterfly net" rather than mark the screen with a cross. After 750 trials, the children's accuracy rate was about 90% (Ceci, 1990) (see Figure 7.8).

Through this and other examples, Ceci illustrates that a particular individual or population may appear to lack mental abilities, such as the ability to abstract rules. However, given a more interesting and motivating context, the same individual or population can demonstrate high-level performance.

Context is one means by which Ceci disputes findings of a positive manifold in test scores. In Chapter 3, and from the discussion of Anderson's theory above, we saw that the positive manifold refers to positive correlations among test scores for various intelligence tests. Thus, a person tends to score poorly, average, or well across different intelligence tests. Some psychologists argue that the positive manifold is driven by one's level of general intelligence. (Anderson would fit into this group. His basic processing mechanism is an umbrella for simple processes underlying *g*.) However, Ceci, like Gardner, claims the positive manifold is due to the narrow range of questions, materials, and contexts called for in intelligence tests. To him, all these tests basically require similar kinds of academically oriented intelligence (Ceci, 1990). If various tests share a similar format and ask for a limited range of problem solving, as do many paper-and-pencil intelligence tests, then it is no surprise that the tests correlate with each other, creating a positive manifold. As we will see in the next section, Ceci argues that those who do not

FIGURE 7.8
Ceci's investigations of problem solving using problem isomorphs help him to establish the importance of context for demonstrating intellectual ability. The lower line of this graph illustrates youngsters' performance in a rule-driven laboratory task. The upper line illustrates youngsters' performance using the same rules but in a video game context (1990, p. 39).

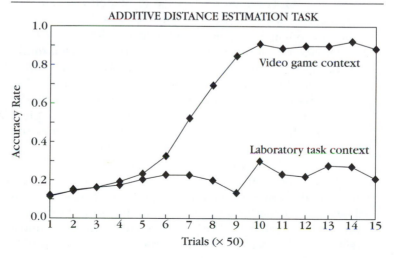

score well on IQ tests and have not done well in school may demonstrate sophisticated thinking using knowledge bases and tasks that schools do not emphasize.

THE ROLE OF KNOWLEDGE

As we saw in Chapter 2, the psychometric tradition has often linked intelligence to a global capacity for abstract thinking that can detect underlying relationships regardless of the subject matter. To some extent, Sternberg's metacomponents reflect this tradition: one's metacomponents can be applied to any sort of information. In contrast, Ceci (1990) has argued that the ability to think complexly is almost always tied to a rich base of knowledge gained in context or "on the job" (Ceci & Liker, 1986a). Intelligent people are not endowed with some greater power for abstract reasoning; rather, they have sufficient knowledge in a domain to let them think in a complex way (Ceci, 1990).

In this regard, Ceci's work is linked to a host of research on expertise (see Chapter 9). Some of this research suggests that talent or intelligence is not adequate to explain high-level, complex performances. Rather, by working in a domain over a significant period of time, one's knowledge base grows and becomes better organized. This effort, over time, allows for intelligent performances (Chi, Glaser, & Rees, 1982; Ericsson & Smith, 1991b, Hayes, 1985; Keating, 1990). Gardner (1993c) has suggested that certain families—those who have many books, read widely, write, and discuss their work—promote academic expertise. Children from these families bring a great deal of relevant experience to school and test situations, and are far more likely to become good students.

To illustrate the role of knowledge and its importance over a presumed global capacity for abstract thinking, Ceci and his colleagues have studied individuals who are exceptionally successful racetrack handicappers. The subjects were 30 middle-aged or older men who were "ardent horse-racing fans" (Ceci & Liker, 1986a, p. 124). Fourteen of these were "experts"—individuals who, on average, could successfully pick the first-, second-, and third-place horses ("trifectas") 53% of the time (chance selection of a trifecta is .00025%) (Ceci & Liker, 1986a).

The method for uncovering the experts' approach to picking horses was not straightforward. Simply asking them to explain what they did revealed little: the subjects found it hard to articulate their handicapping techniques. Therefore, the investigators constructed hypothetical races, which provided information about variables that are important to handicapping (for example, track length, horse's past record, horse's sire and dam) (see Figure 7.9). They then documented what the experts did as they picked horses for 50 hypothetical races.

Ceci and Liker (1986a, 1986b) found that the experts had very complex models for selecting winning horses. On average, the experts considered 6 variables. These variables were weighted differently and considered interactively. In statistical language, "experts appeared to assess the unique variance associated with each level of a given variable, then proceeded to qualify this contribution through its interactions with other variables and groups of variables" (1986a, pp. 130–131).

FIGURE 7.9

Ceci argues that expert handicappers are supported not by IQ, but by knowledge about how to use esoteric information like this from the *Racing Form*.

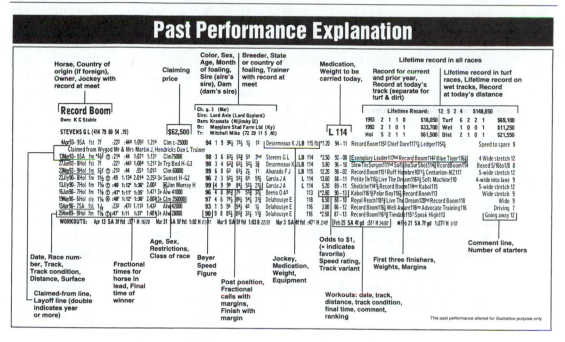

In this study, Ceci found no correlation between the handicappers' IQ and their handicapping performance (r = −.07) (Ceci & Liker, 1986a). This finding helps him to argue that knowledge, rather than IQ, is the key to abstract thinking. If intelligence is a general capacity for abstract thinking, then those with higher IQs should do better at handicapping than those with lower IQs. However, this did not prove to be the case.

The handicappers study helps Ceci to argue that "real-world" performances—the kind Sternberg emphasized in this chapter's opening quote—cannot be explained largely by IQ or by some biological precursors to IQ, such as *g*. In Ceci's framework, real-world success draws not only on multiple cognitive potentials, but on an interaction of these potentials with rich and elaborated knowledge bases, of the sort the handicappers possessed. Along with multiple cognitive potentials and knowledge, intelligence requires contexts that afford resources, meaning, and motivation. The children in the video-game isomorph showed a power for abstract reasoning that a nonmotivating problem did not elicit. Given such contexts and knowledge bases, people are more likely to demonstrate intellectual resources that elude the nets of formal intelligence testing.

Critique of Ceci's Theory

Like Anderson's theory, relatively little criticism of Ceci's bioecological framework has appeared in the scholarly literature. Not surprisingly, the sharpest critique of Ceci's work so far surrounds his finding that there was no correlation between expert handicappers' IQ and success in the complex task of handicapping horse races. Such a claim contradicts a long line of psychometric research demonstrating positive correlations between IQ and intellectual performance. For example, as noted in Chapter 3, IQ has been found to correlate with school performance and occupational status.

Much criticism focuses on Ceci's methods. For example, Detterman and Spry (1988) have argued that failure to find a correlation between IQ and handicapping stems from Ceci and Liker's sample selection. Like the Wissler study discussed in Chapter 3, Ceci and Liker's sample suffers from a restricted range: there is not enough distribution in handicapping ability among experts to find a correlation with IQ. In their reply to this criticism, Ceci and Liker (1988) argue that they were not trying to determine the relationship between intelligence and handicapping ability in the general population. They were trying to understand the relationship that exists between intelligence and handicapping among expert handicappers. Thus, to them, their sample is a reasonable one.

Even if sampling problems mar their statistical analysis of the relationship of handicapping skill and IQ, Ceci and Liker (1988) argue that their analysis of data gained from 50 hypothetical races handicapped by all 30 men shores up their basic claim. From these races, Ceci and Liker were able to determine the extent to which each subject relied on interactive reasoning involving up to 7 variables. They found that higher-level interactive reasoning was correlated more with the 14 experts than with the 16 nonexperts. Yet, such reasoning was not correlated with IQ. In other words, whether they had lower or higher IQs, the experts still engaged in this complex reasoning.

Detterman and Spry (1988) justifiably argue with Ceci's methods, and evidence continues to support *g* (e.g., Carroll, 1993; Jensen, 1993; Scarr, 1989). Yet, a growing body of research also supports the basic claim of Ceci and other contextualists: context, in such forms as knowledge, experience, resources, and social setting, is important to intellectual performance.

Summary

In this chapter, we have focused on recent reconceptualizations of intelligence. We have considered, in some depth, the work of four theorists and researchers: Gardner, Anderson, Sternberg, and Ceci. Though each attempts to explain individual differences, the researchers' goals, methods, and ideas about the nature of intelligence vary. Gardner seeks to explain the wide variety of adult roles or endstates found across cultures. He argues that a single underlying general intelligence is inadequate to explain this diversity. Thus, he has pluralized intelligence, arguing for at least 7 relatively autonomous intelligences, which people use in different combinations. To Gardner, an intelligence is an ability to solve problems or fashion products that are of consequence in one or more cultural settings. In recent years, Gardner has adapted his view: intelligence is not only plural; it is related to the context in which one works, and it is distributed among various resources beyond the individual (Gardner, 1993c).

Anderson's theory arose as an effort to explain various, somewhat contradictory findings in the study of intelligence. Anderson has stated that a theory of intelligence needs to account for five of these: the increase of cognitive abilities with development; the stability of individual differences throughout development; the covariation of cognitive abilities; the existence of specific abilities; and the existence of universal abilities that show no variation among individuals. To explain these findings, Anderson joins data from the fields of cognitive development and the study of individual differences. To Anderson, individual differences and development have until now offered isolated explanations of intelligence. From the two, and other disciplines, he has constructed an elegant cognitive architecture.

Sternberg has defined intelligence in various ways,[3] but, in line with his goal of explaining real-world performances, the following definition is most relevant: Intelligence "is purposive adaptation to and selection and shaping of real-world environments relevant to one's life" (Sternberg, 1988, p. 72). Sternberg's triarchic theory stems from the notion that earlier theories are not wrong, but are merely incomplete (Sternberg, 1985). The theory consists of three interrelated subtheories, each a big portion of the intelligence pie. The componential subtheory looks at the internal information processing mechanisms that individuals apply to problem solving. Sternberg posits an experiential subtheory, because intelligence must be considered in light of an individual's experience with a task or situation. A task can range from utterly novel to completely automated. Finally, by considering implicit theories of intelligence, the contextual subtheory begins to explore the relationship of the external environment to individuals' intelligence.

Ceci's framework builds on the triarchic theory's effort at exploring internal processing mechanisms, experience, and context. However, it examines the role of context in more depth. In Ceci's scheme, context incorporates such things as the domain of knowledge in which one thinks, institutions such as schooling, and the historical era in which one lives. Two other foci are intertwined with context

---

[3] For example, he has said intelligence is "mental self-government" (Sternberg, 1986, p. 141), "mental self-management" (1988, p. 72), or "the mental capability of emitting contextually appropriate behavior at those regions in the experiential continuum that involve response to novelty or automatization of information processing as a function of metacomponents, performance components, and knowledge-acquisition components" (Sternberg, 1985, p. 12).

in Ceci's scheme. Ceci argues that intelligence also rests on multiple cognitive potentials, rather than on a single general capacity for abstract problem solving (*g*). Furthermore, knowledge is crucial to intelligence. To Ceci, the existence of highly elaborated and organized bases of knowledge, rather than a general capacity for abstract problem solving, enables a person to carry out complex intellectual activities. In Ceci's scheme, cognitive complexity—the ability to use one's knowledge bases flexibly and efficiently—is much more a marker of intelligence in real life than is an IQ score.

Despite their differences, the theories above have some commonalities. Whether or not they explicitly state it, all take into consideration what Anderson calls "low-level and high-level views" of intelligence (Anderson, 1992, p. 2). All the theories attend in some measure to low-level, biological bases for intelligence. The low-level view is seen in Gardner's core components. It is evident in Anderson's consideration of findings from inspection time studies and in his construction of modules and the basic processing mechanism. We see it in Ceci's concern with cognitive processes. Sternberg's componential subtheory is an effort to explore and test such basic mental mechanisms.

Each theorist also addresses high-level issues such as knowledge, judgment, and adaptation to the environment. We see this in the importance Gardner places on adult endstates and in his consideration of cross-cultural research. Anderson deals with the high level in his discussion of knowledge acquisition through thinking (Route 1). Sternberg's contextual subtheory is an effort to understand how individuals adapt to, shape, or select environments. The impact of context on problem solving and the role of knowledge in intelligent behavior are central in Ceci's framework.

In addition, all the theorists have gone beyond building theories based primarily on intelligence tests and factor analysis. Along with the study of individual differences and factor analysis, they have considered a wide variety of disciplines within psychology: cognitive psychology, developmental psychology, and, with the exception of Sternberg, neuropsychology. They have also considered data outside psychology. For example, in developing his theory, Gardner has considered evolutionary biology and anthropology. Ceci has drawn on findings from sociology and education. To a greater or lesser degree, each of the theories has incorporated multiple perspectives. In this way, they have drawn on the appreciable progress in biological and psychological sciences since Binet and Spearman did their pioneering work at the turn of the century.

It is not an accident that three of the four new theorists of intelligence place a heavy focus on the contexts in which individuals operate. Even as our biological understanding has increased in recent years, an appreciation of the importance of contextual factors—familial, cultural, societal—is one of the most important trends in the social sciences in several decades. As this book moves toward conclusion, it is therefore appropriate to consider the manifestation of intelligence in the two most important institutions in our contemporary world: the school and the workplace.

Suggested Readings

Anderson, M. (1992). *Intelligence and development: A cognitive theory.* Oxford: Blackwell.

Ceci, S. (1990). *On intelligence . . . more or less: A bioecological treatise.* Englewood Cliffs, NJ: Prentice-Hall.

Gardner, H. (1993). *Frames of mind: The theory of multiple intelligences.* New York: Basic Books.

Gardner, H. (1993). *Multiple intelligences: The theory in practice.* New York: Basic Books.

Sternberg, R. J. (1985). *Beyond IQ: A triarchic theory of human intelligence.* Cambridge: Cambridge University Press.

Sternberg, R. J. (1988). *The triarchic mind: A new theory of human intelligence.* New York: Viking.

Chapter 8

From the Perspective of School

Introduction

The Defining Characteristics of a School

In traditional West African society, boys and girls move during middle child-hood to a separate locus in their community—one that has been termed a "bush school" (Caine, 1959; Watkins, 1943). There, under the training of a high-status "master," they learn how to perform arts, crafts, and other skills important for survival and for the cultural life of the community. As a means of stimulating personal courage and of building up a sense of group identity, particular attention is sometimes given to the past history of the society. Often, challenges are posed in an effort to ferret out individual attributes and talents: there are, for example, mock battles and skirmishes to ascertain the war-making abilities of the boys. As a culminating event, adolescents are subjected to trials in an initiation rite; those who do not exhibit sufficient toughness or ingenuity are sometimes allowed to die.

For as long as there have been family units, it has been the task of the adults to train the children. Such training is the best way to ensure that these future adults will be able to carry out the assignments of the society and become absorbed into the adult community. In preliterate settings, much of this training has been implicit: young children have "hung around" adults, watched them perform their given tasks, and gradually been drawn into these activities at a pace that they can handle. Anthropologist Mary Catherine Bateson (1994) describes the pattern:

A San (Bushman) father takes his son out on the veldt with a spear to learn to track wild animals, just as an American father takes his son to the park to learn to hit a baseball. A village mother in Iran may give a warning or a demonstration before a daughter is allowed to use a loom or a sewing machine, wool or butter, knives or fire. Often what is taught would not be learned if it were not embedded in a relationship. (p. 204)

As the tasks of the society became more demanding and skills increasingly involved technology, such casual learning no longer sufficed, and more formal kinds of educational institutions gradually evolved.

Bush schools are one such phenomenon. Specific times and places are allocated for instruction, and a rough match is sought between an individual's talents and the kinds of skills in which he or she is trained. Formal apprenticeships, introduced in our opening chapter, represent another effort to provide training. In the typical apprenticeship relationship, a boy spends much of his time in the company of a recognized master. Often a contract is drawn up, and the apprentice (or his family) owes money or services to the master for a specified period of time. The novice begins by observing the master at work. As soon as possible, he is drawn in at his level of skill to active participation in the domain of the apprenticeship, be it carving, weaving, or playing an instrument. A regular progression of learning, often in the company of other learners, culminates in the creation of a "master work." At that point, the young master is free to return to the larger community, and, indeed, is empowered to take on his own students (Bowen, 1972).

Though each clearly performs educational functions, neither the bush school nor the traditional apprenticeship resembles our contemporary prototype of a school. The defining characteristic of today's school is the transmission of skill in specific kinds of literacies—reading, writing, computation, and the mastery of other similar systems. Large numbers of students are put through their paces, in more or less simultaneous fashion, and, by the conclusion of the process, all are expected to read, write, and compute competently.

Having acquired the basic literacies, youngsters proceed to study specific subject matter. In the Middle Ages, youngsters studied subjects like logic, rhetoric, music, geometry, and astronomy. In modern times, students are more likely to study algebra, chemistry, world history, and the literature of their region of the world. Some proportion of these students—by now in late adolescence—proceed to higher education, where they may either study liberal arts (itself a medieval term), or "major" in specific subjects, like African history, biochemistry, or even cognitive psychology.

In this chapter, we focus on schools—those institutions that have evolved over the millenia in most societies, to prepare youngsters to assume valued positions in the adult world. Given the thrust of this book, we focus specifically on the relationship between schooling and intelligence. There is no necessary relation between school, however institutionalized, and intelligence, however defined. Yet, in practice, the operation of schools within societies provides a window on how those societies think about the realm of the intellect.

With reference to the schools in various societies, one can raise three primary questions:

1. What does the school see as its central educational mission?
2. On what bases are students selected for a school?
3. How do schools deal with students who apparently differ in their aptitudes and their achievements?

We have already seen that bush schools are institutions that address all the children in the community; that they transmit the fundamental skills for economic and spiritual survival; and that they make relatively few concessions to differences among youngsters—all are expected to master "the curriculum," and those who do not are at severe risk. Keep the three questions above in mind as we consider the variety of schools that have evolved so far, and the ones that might emerge in the future.

The Evolution of Schools and Their Students

With roots in craft training, apprenticeships, and informal instruction at the feet of parents or other relatives, schools evolved gradually in different areas of the world. Their flourishing has been promoted universally by two factors. On the one hand, the successful functioning of the society requires individuals with specific skills of literacy, particularly skills related to commerce. If a society is to flourish, to trade with others, to build up its resources, to be in a position to wage war skillfully and to draw up favorable agreements of peace, it is necessary to have individuals who can read and write well, who can carry out computations about goods and money, who can apply principles consistently, and, if necessary, create and enforce written codes as well. Schools carry out the task of giving youngsters the tools to live in a notation-rich society.

Accompanying this functional or practical facet of schooling has been an equally powerful desire to create certain kinds of individuals—people who exhibit specific values and behaviors. In addition to traditional scholastic goals, schools have been designed to produce the kind of citizen that is desired by the society. Initially, much of this impulse was religious. Schools were administered by clerics; their aim was to produce individuals who would embody a spiritual dimension and who could themselves one day provide religious leadership. Indeed, for centuries, university professors had to be members of the clergy. More broadly, other kinds of leadership, especially in the political, military, and economic realms, were supposed to be fostered in the schools.

The functions of literacy and citizenship can be separated, but they are by no means necessarily at odds with one another. Traditional religious schools—the Jewish *cheder,* the Islamic Koranic schools, the Christian cathedral schools—have managed to pursue both ends in tandem. They place stock on the mastery—perhaps even the memorization—of large segments of the religious texts that are central to the practice of their religion. At the same time, the teachers exhibit the code of behaviors and practices that they expect their students to master and, ultimately, to model directly to the next generation of youngsters growing up in their community (cf. Fischer, 1980; LeVine, 1978; Wagner, 1980).

With the rise, in the past few centuries, of vast new domains of scholarship, schools have taken on a new function (Connell, 1980; Henry, 1960; Oakeshott, 1975). The creation of new knowledge—either for its own sake, or, more typically, because such creation is deemed necessary for the welfare of the nation—is seen as a novel and yet important function of the educational system. At the very least, every student should receive a taste of what it is like to execute mathematical proofs, perform an historical analysis, conduct a biological experiment, and critique a work of literature. A certain percentage

In the Jewish cheder *pictured here, as well as in other traditional religious schools, youngsters are taught both literacy skills and values.*

of students should pursue this line of study with sufficient energy and persistence to be able to join the professoriate themselves one day. In that capacity, much like religious leaders of an earlier time, they can themselves contribute to the society's accumulated wisdom and ultimately disseminate their findings and conclusions to *their* students. To the arts and crafts cultivated in the bush school, one can now add the arts and sciences pursued in the colleges and universities of the world.

But who should be the students in these schools? Only recently—indeed, only in the past century—have societies advanced the notion that *every* individual in the community should be educated. In the past, it was simply assumed that schools were for only a circumscribed proportion of the population: most probably boys rather than girls; the elite rather than the masses; representatives of the majority population rather than minorities or lower-status groups; certain ethnic or racial groups rather than others—in general, those with high political, religious, or economic status. The remaining members of the society were expected to pick up these skills on their own—as some individuals (even slaves) were able to do—or to remain uneducated, illiterate, ignorant, suited only to serve (or, in rare instances, to rebel against) the educated (Cremin, 1982).

Education has been seen as a precious resource, one that could not be lavished on everyone. Often, in the past, education was made available on the basis of *ascriptive status: who* you were determined how much education you were entitled to. However, even when it has served as the chief criterion of access to education, ascriptive status has rarely been the only criterion. Most societies, and most schools, have believed that not all youngsters are *scholastically equal.* And so, efforts have been undertaken for many years to provide education to those who could most readily benefit from it, and to those who were most likely to put it to a use that society values. In the terminology of sociology, education has also been apportioned on the basis of *achieved (or meritocratic) status—*what you can accomplish when given an opportunity to learn (Klitgaard, 1985) (see Chapter 1).

School and Intelligence

Once a society decides to open up education to those outside a preselected population, the question arises: Who is entitled to such an education? Here, the institution of schooling intersects directly with the topic of this book—the nature of human intelligence.

Decisions about access to education turn on a society's conceptions about the strengths and attributes of individuals living within that society. In some traditional societies, there may be no separate conceptualization about intellect. Youngsters are considered to be good or bad, and the gloss of "good" is likely to be applied to those who behave well, who listen attentively, and/or who do what they are told (LeVine & White, 1986) (see Chapter 1). Once a separate realm of scholastic or intellectual skill has been delineated, there remains the question of which talents within that realm are valued. For instance, some cultures might value individuals who are quick and flexible; others might prefer youngsters who are calm, reflective, and measured in their responses.

One way to apportion educational opportunities, then, is to allocate them, *at the outset,* to individuals who are most likely to be able to profit from them. If a conception of the "good student" centers on civility, the most civil youngsters will be permitted to attend school, and the less civil ones will be either expelled rapidly or denied entrance altogether. If, on the other hand, the promising student is one who is quick-witted or one who is pensive, then decisions about access will be made on that basis.

Until very recently, these decisions were made subjectively and intuitively. However, it is possible to allocate opportunities on the basis of performance on some kind of a *measure of potential.* If one believes that intelligent students are most likely to benefit from school, one can devise a *test of intelligence.* Those students who do well on the test are given the opportunity to attend schools, enroll in schools with special resources, or be placed in programs for "the gifted." Those judged as less intelligent are denied such opportunities or placed on a lower track. It is worth recalling that Binet's initial commission to create a test was occasioned by a desire on the part of French authorities to identify students who were likely to have learning problems, presumably so that these students could receive additional resources (see Chapters 2 and 5).

Another approach to education looks at performance or *achievement.* According to this perspective, a large number of students are given access to the early years of the educational system. Performance in the system becomes the principal means of ascertaining who should be permitted to remain in the system, and who should be consigned to the less-highly-educated quarters of the society. This judgment can be made by evaluations of the students' performances on a day-to-day basis. However, in many if not most cases, schools have preferred to administer *specific tests of achievement* in order to determine who is educationally most fit. As discussed in Chapter 1, these tests range from the ancient Chinese civil service examination system to the examinations of the American College Entrance Examination Board.

In modern European countries, there have been similar hurdles. On the Continent, students take a baccalaureate or Abitur or "Bacc" examination at the conclusion of secondary school; and important life opportunities, including the chance to attend university, hang on the results of such tests. In England, students have taken the 0 level and A level tests, which serve as ways of controlling access to the more highly regarded secondary schools and universities. Despite growing talk of national goals and standards, no formal equivalent yet exists in the United

Students taking a computerized version of the Scholastic Assessment Test (SAT).

States. The tests of the College Entrance Examination Board, and especially the Scholastic Assessment Test (formerly named the Scholastic Aptitude Test), serve as unofficial surrogate gatekeepers to the more precious educational opportunities in the United States—such as admission to selective "Ivy League" or "Big Ten" colleges.

In principle, these achievement tests and examinations are supposed to be democratic or meritocratic. That is, students from any walk of life should be able to take, and do well on, these measures of accomplishment. And, indeed, both in the United States and abroad, there are always heartwarming examples of individuals from modest backgrounds who "ace" these instruments and thus make the "leap" from the masses to the intellectual elite. In practice, however, one's own background and the kind of schooling one has received turn out to be important factors in determining just how well a student will do in the formal examination system. If one knows the socioeconomic status of a student, and the kind of school to which he or she has gone, one can predict the likelihood that the student will be able to perform well on gateway examinations (Crouse & Trusheim, 1988; Jencks et al., 1972; Owen, 1985).

The Modern Secular School

It seems curious that members of our species should, during the early years of life, spend so much of their time in school. Caricaturing a wee bit, one can say that human beings evolved over the millenia to roam wide savannahs, to scavenge for food, to hunt animals, to stick together in bands under the leadership of a dominant figure, to rear families, and, from time to time, to wage war. And yet, completely ignoring this background, we now place a great premium on amassing 20–50 students together in a classroom for 6–8 hours a day over many years, disallowing most kinds of physical activity or contact, discouraging socializing, and saving rewards for those who can pore over books or papers, make small squiggles on lined pieces of paper, repeat back what has been told to them, and on occasional "high-stake" tests, provide precise forms of information on demand.

If the institution of school is to be characterized by one or two descriptive terms, the best ones are probably *decontextualized* and *notational*. Individuals who thrive in school are those who are able to think about actions, events, and phenomena even when these entities are not accessible to perception and direct contact—that is, they think well in the absence of the usual contextual cues. Such scholastically oriented persons can shift readily from a consideration of the causes of the First World War, to a probing of the reasons why spheres with varying masses fall in the way and at the rate that they do, to a consideration of the meaning of such apparently meaningless concepts as zero, infinity, or negative numbers (Bruner, Olver, & Greenfield, 1966). Whether some individuals are born with a greater proclivity to think decontextually, or whether these individuals have been "scaffolded" so they no longer need contextualized support, is not known (see Chapter 7).

By the same token, those individuals who thrive in school are those who can deal not just with phenomena or ideas in themselves, but with the notations that human beings have created in order to *symbolize* those entities in economical and readily deciphered form. It is not enough to be able to think about zero in the abstract; one needs to be able to carry out computations that use zeros. It is not enough to drop spheres from varying heights; one needs to be able to develop and use equations about mass and acceleration. And it is not enough to be able to debate about the First World War; one needs to be able to read crucial texts, analyze them, and compose one's own thoughts in literate language (Goodman, 1976; Goody, 1977; Olson, 1977, 1994).

It would be too much to claim that school is an *unnatural* habitat. Many individuals do perfectly well in the environment of school and some—including many readers of this book—thrive in it, perhaps more so than they would elsewhere, and better than they might perform on the savannah or on the battlefield. The world over, youngsters begin school at the time that they do because it has been observed that the average 7-year-old—but not the average 3-year-old—is ready to master alphabetic and numerical symbols; and that the 10-year-old, but not the 5-year-old, is ready to talk about entities that cannot be easily seen, heard, or felt (White, 1965) (see Chapter 4).

Schools have, over the centuries, been orchestrated so that they foreground notational activities in a decontextualized setting. Think of work sheets, where one chooses one of four responses or where one fills in a missing item; think of problem exercises, where one is posed a puzzle and expected to solve it that evening or over the weekend; think of classroom recitation where one is expected to locate information obtained from reading or from lecture and present it back in something like its original form; think of regular and of high-stake examinations where, with the clock ticking, one is expected to access information gathered over a fairly long period of time and re-present it, if possible, in a form that is both accurate and reflective of a measure of thought and a dollop of originality.

It is by no means self-evident why these activities are carried out in the form just described. Perhaps the activities serve a variety of purposes. Some are designed so that the individual will be able to read and write effectively in the adult civil society; some are designed so that the individual will be able to pursue academic disciplines at a high level of sophistication; some are designed to institute habits of regularity and discipline in the future citizenry; some are designed to separate those with greater scholastic talents from those who might be better off enlisting in a "hands-on" apprenticeship or attending a vocational institution. But some of the activities may be carried out in this manner for the reason that was given in China, a decade ago, when a visitor criticized a lesson that was completely rote learning. After 10 minutes of desultory discussion, an exasperated teacher turned to the visitor and said, "We have been doing it this way for so long that we *know* it is right" (Gardner, 1989). We should consider the possibility that some school practices are carried out because of habit, rather than because they are necessarily the best way to instruct youngsters today.

Who Does Well in School?

Given the importance of school in society today, and its undoubted continuing significance in the world of tomorrow, the issue of who does well in school, and why, is of considerable importance.

One answer, which may beg the question, is to state that individuals who are intelligent do well in school. This answer has less merit than meets the eye because our definitions—and our operationalizations—of intelligence have been based in significant measure on what individuals are expected to do in school. If, for example, school is the site par excellence for notational work in a decontextualized setting, and if tests of intelligence require the manipulation of symbols in a decontextualized setting, then it is scarcely surprising when individuals who score well on an intelligence test do well in school, or vice versa. If intelligence tests had been designed by entrepreneurs (rather than by scholars), they would yield individuals who would succeed at the marketplace, and not necessarily individuals who would shine in the classroom (Gardner, Krechevsky, Sternberg, & Okagaki, 1994; Sternberg & Wagner, 1986).

Yet, there is by no means an absolute correlation between IQ scores and school performance. Indeed, most studies yield a correlation of about .5. This finding means that most of the variability in school is *not* a simple product of psychometric intelligence, though school performance seems to correlate more highly with measured intelligence than with any other single identifiable factor (Snow & Yalow, 1982). This state of affairs gives rise to the interesting phenomena of over- and underachievement. If a student does better in school than the IQ score would have predicted, the student is said to be an overachiever; that is, the student has done better than he or she is supposed to do (which does sound like a contradiction in terms!). If, on the other hand, the student does not do as well in school as the measured intelligence results predicted, then he or she is said to be an underachiever.

This last characterization may be important, if it reveals some factor that is blocking the student's performance in school—for example, a difficulty in relating to figures of authority. It may also be insidious, however. Consider the cases where high-IQ students are given access to precious resources—such as special schools or programs for gifted students—even though they have not in other ways demonstrated that they deserve, or could benefit from, such enrichment.

Intelligence, however measured and documented, is one predictor of success in school, but other factors are worth equal consideration. Recently, much attention has been directed at the performance in school of Asian children, particularly those living in Japan, China, Korea, Taiwan, and Singapore. In comparison with youngsters in American schools, in cities like Minneapolis and Chicago, these Asian students do not merely do well; their performance in areas like mathematics is so outstanding that there is scarcely an overlap between the best American students and the average Asian students (Stevenson & Stigler, 1992).

A few iconoclastic scholars have speculated that Asian students may have more intelligent brains (Rushton, 1995). But most experts agree that the superior performance of Asians has little if anything to do with biology and much to do with attitudes and values. Indeed, American students do about as well as Asians only as kindergarteners; differences in performance begin to emerge in first grade and fan out thereafter. Moreover, American IQs are comparable to those of Asian students. However, as heirs to the Confucian tradition, Asian families value study, discipline, and hard work. Asian youngsters are expected to study hard, every day, to apply themselves, to succeed in school for the honor of their family and their larger cultural group. Parents are active participants in this process on a daily—or nightly—basis. There are clear positive rewards for high performance and clear sanctions for poor performance. The results are: a far higher mean performance in this population, and a hint of smaller differences—less variation—between the best and worst performing students in a cohort (Gardner, 1989; Stevenson & Stigler, 1992).

Given the ultimately superior performance of Asian students on nearly every measure of academic achievement, it is tempting to conclude that academics are stressed above all else in these countries, even at the expense of fun, physical well-being, and a rounded life. Careful studies of classrooms in Japan, China, and Taiwan show that this is not the case (Lewis, 1994; Stevenson & Stigler, 1992; Tobin, Wu, & Davidson, 1989). Indeed, much of the time in the early school years is devoted to developing a feeling of comfort in school, helping students to work and play cooperatively with one another, and forming children who are patient, attentive, able to control their emotions, ready and eager to apply themselves and to learn, and willing to take responsibility not only for their own behavior but also for that of their classmates. Personal and social growth are emphasized *more* than pure academics. If anything, it is middle-class American parents who

The high performance of students in schools in Asia is supported by social values, such as hard work and study, and by greater amounts of time spent in academic work.

emerge as more "up tight" about academic achievements (Elkind, 1987). Cultural myths notwithstanding, there is no evidence that these Asian students are more anxious than their American counterparts (Crystal, Chen, Fuligni et al., 1994).

When children complete the earlier years of school, there is more of an emphasis on academics throughout the Asian world. Students in Japan, for example, spend about two-thirds of the year in school (American students spend only half the year), and classes in the Asian countries typically run for 8 hours a day during the week and a half-day on Saturday. In American classrooms, over half of the time is spent on something other than academic work, while 74% of the time in Japanese classrooms and 90% of the time in Chinese classrooms is spent working directly on academic material.

An emphasis on the quantitative aspects should not obscure more important differences in the quality of classroom life. Especially in Japan, children spend a great deal of class time solving difficult problems together. Rather than being overtly competitive, students root for one another to succeed; and there is little tracking. Teachers are accorded up to half of the time each day to prepare their classes. The goals of lessons are stated explicitly, and the tactics used by teachers are well worked out and much practiced. Parents are vitally interested in classroom work and make the child's homework the central activity of each evening. In contrast, American parents are often ignorant of what their children are doing in school; echo their youngsters' complaints if there is more than an hour's worth of homework on a given night; and, while decrying the schools in other towns, nearly always declare that their own children's schools are just fine (Stevenson & Stigler, 1992). Recalling claims uttered in the fictitious town of Lake Wobegone, American parents also declare that their children are doing well and are all "above average." Against this background, it is difficult to bring about the changes that would heighten the performances of American schoolchildren.

After describing Asian schools so sympathetically, we need to stress two points. First, the schools of these nations are by no means identical to one another. For example, there is much more of an emphasis on academics in Chinese kindergartens than elsewhere in Asia, and Japan features a set of parallel *juku* schools that help students to bone up for the highly competitive examination system. Second, the high quality of Asian precollegiate education is not matched by equal excellence at the university level. Indeed, throughout most of the world, American colleges and universities are held in esteem. It has been quipped that youngsters are best served if they attend elementary school in Japan, secondary school in Germany, and college in the United States.

Within the United States (and other countries), quite sizable differences have been observed in the scholastic performances of different racial and ethnic groups (Ogbu, 1978). A few individuals have sought biological explanations for these differences, but most researchers are inclined to stress sociocultural forces (such as lingering racism) and attitudinal and motivational factors. Students from families or from ethnic/racial groups that place a high premium on education, that encourage hard work and study on a regular basis, and that model this kind of seriousness themselves, are far more likely to succeed academically than students from families that are dysfunctional, that lack these scholarly values, or that do not know how to pursue these values in an effective manner.

Within certain groups in America, high scholastic performance may be injurious to one's mental health. The groundbreaking work of John Ogbu (1991) has called attention to the fact that, among African American students, it is often considered to be disloyal—even to be "White-y" or "Uncle Tom"—if one hits the books and does well in schoolwork. In response to these social pressures, students—particularly males—either slough off or learn to hide their successes. Ogbu attributes much of the difference in academic performance among racial and ethnic groups to the issue of whether their ancestors were voluntary immigrants—like Europeans in search of religious freedom—or involuntary immigrants—like Africans brought to the Americas as slaves. This singular explanation is controversial. Nonetheless, clear attitudinal variations with respect to education seem an important contributor to the observed differences in academic achievement among groups within societies, and to the differences observed in international comparisons, of the sort carried out by Stevenson and Stigler, and their colleagues (1994).

Another possible clue to differences in school performances can be found in students' own theories about their minds and the tasks of school. Work by Carol

John Ogbu.

Carol Dweck.

Dweck and her associates has documented a distinction between two conceptualizations of intelligence (Dweck & Elliot, 1983). Some youngsters are *entity* theorists: like selected psychometricians, they believe that individuals are born with a certain amount of intelligence, which is not susceptible to appreciable change. School is simply an institution that reveals one's native intelligence; if the amount of intelligence is modest, one is doomed to failure (Brand, 1993).

In contrast, other youngsters are *incremental* theorists; like some socially oriented psychologists, they are less concerned about their inborn intellect and believe instead that one makes oneself smart by working hard and by constantly improving one's knowledge base and mental skills. Even if the incremental perspective is only partially accurate, it constitutes a much more productive attitude toward school. An incremental attitude holds out the possibility that one can improve one's performance through hard work and the strategic use of human and other resources. The foregoing discussion of Asian society highlights the Confucian belief—somewhat like a Puritan precept—that hard work is what counts. Indeed, interviews document that Asian parents are more likely to attribute poor mathematical grades to a lack of effort, while American parents tend to attribute similarly low performance to being "dumb in math" (Stevenson & Stigler, 1992).

Two other, related factors that may contribute to success in school are worth mentioning. One involves the expectations of parents and teachers. Succinctly put, if one's elders have high expectations and expect one to do well, one is more likely to do well. The most dramatic demonstration of this phenomenon occurs in the well-known Pygmalion studies. Here, teachers were told that certain students were of higher intelligence than others, even though, in fact, the measured intelligence was the same for the two groups. Not only did the teachers treat the two groups of youngsters differently, but those in the group that were (misleadingly) labeled as smart actually outperformed those who had not been so labeled (Rosenthal & Jacobsen, 1968).

More generally, within a given society, those schools that place a very high premium on intellectual performance, and those instructors who believe that their students can succeed, are far more likely to produce students who graduate and who perform well in comparison to their peers (Edmonds, 1986; Rutter, Maughan, Mortimore, Ouston, & Smith, 1979).

The second factor has to do with the reasons why students work in school. There is now increasing evidence that extrinsic motivation is a risky business; when students are given grounds for believing that one works only to gain extrinsic rewards, they are likely to cease working once such rewards have been withdrawn. Conversely, to the extent that students find work to be intrinsically rewarding and enjoy doing it, they are likely to continue to work even in the absence of such regular public reinforcement (Amabile, 1983; Csikszentmihalyi, 1990; Dweck & Elliot 1983; Kohn, 1993) (see Chapter 9).

These findings should not be pushed too far; especially in the early years of school, there is a place for reward, and even seasoned professionals may have a hard time continuing to work, in the absence of at least an occasional acknowledgment or evidence of appreciation. Nonetheless, sustained mastery is a time-consuming and demanding process. Unless the individual gains personal satisfaction that is not integrally tied to some regular public recognition, he or she is unlikely to persevere.

Schools of Tomorrow: New Demands, New Opportunities

Thus far in our discussion, we have accepted schools pretty much as given, and our reasons for success and failure pertain to the schools of today, in this country and abroad.

Recently, however, throughout the world, educators (and the societies that they represent) have been calling for schools that are different in two senses. First, there is a call for more *democracy,* for greater equity. Schools need to succeed not just with an elite, not just with a minority, but with all youngsters—or at least with a healthy majority. Beyond democratic niceties, such universal success is necessary for the survival of society. Unless the full talents of a nation are mobilized, that nation will not fare well in the struggle with other societies where education is more truly universal (Kearns & Doyle, 1988).

The second difference concerns *depth*. It is now recognized that, though schools have done a reasonable job in conveying content to students and having the students memorize and subsequently regurgitate that content, schools the world over have not produced a population that thinks well and deeply. Usually, these gaps are spoken of as the need for inculcating *critical and creative thinking* and for designing an education that yields *understanding* (Gardner, 1991b; Perkins, 1992, 1995; Resnick, 1987b; Sizer, 1992).

An individual who understands is one who can apply knowledge, skills, concepts, and the like in new situations in which that form of learning (knowledge, skills, or whatever) proves appropriate. Unless a student can apply his or her knowledge appropriately, we can have no confidence in that student's understanding; one may be dealing simply with memorization or rote learning. Knowing when one does *not* understand is also important: many students apply knowledge or skills in an inappropriate way.

Researchers have documented a lack of understanding among even the best students in the best schools. In fact, wherever one looks in the curriculum, the signs of nonunderstanding, misunderstanding, or *misconceptions* are blatant. In the sciences, students who score well on tests in biology or physics fail to use their knowledge when they are asked to explain phenomena in daily life; in fact, they tend to answer in the same way that "unschooled" 5-year-olds do. For instance, they claim that a just-flipped coin is being propelled by a force obtained from the thumb that has expelled it—even though, in terms of physics, the only force operating on the coin following its release is gravity (Caramazza, McCloskey, & Green, 1981; Carey, 1985; DiSessa, 1982; Gardner, 1991b; Gentner & Stevens, 1983; Hatano & Inagaki, 1987).

In the area of mathematics, the alternative to understanding is the *memorization of formulas or algorithms*. Rather than understanding the meanings of formulas and thus knowing when they are, or are not, applicable, students simply commit the formulas to memory and employ those formulas whenever their usage happens to be triggered by a key word or sign. So long as the appropriate triggering circumstances are known, students appear to understand (cf. Searle's (1984) Chinese room example in Chapter 6). But when the eliciting circumstances are not familiar, students do not know which formulas—if any—can help them deal with the mathematical dilemma in question.

Finally, in the area of the humanities and the arts, students fall victim to *scripts* and *stereotypes*. When young, they develop notions of how the world works—for example, that it is divided into good and bad people, that the good people "look like me" and the bad people don't, that there is a struggle between the goods and the bads, and that, with luck, the goods will prevail (Nelson, 1986). We have dubbed this view the "Star Wars Script." Even when students have learned that events in the world typically have complex causes, they tend to revert to this simplistic way of thinking when questioned about a new crisis on the world political scene and, equally, when puzzling out a problem that arises in their own daily lives.

Indeed, stereotypical perspectives endure even with reference to the topic of this book. Presumably, a reader of this book will have appreciated the authors' points that intelligence is a complex construct, and that many factors can account for an individual's performances within and outside school. And yet, as the memory of this course or this book fades, many students will revert to the simple idea with which they (and we) began: that intelligence is a single thing, inborn, not subject to change, casting a determinist shadow on one's future life course. As authors, we know about this tendency because we sometimes catch ourselves falling prey to it!

Will the schools of tomorrow be able to achieve these new and ambitious twin goals of educating all individuals, and achieving a high degree of sophistication in the process? It is far too early to say. Many educational reformers are engaged in redrawing the maps of classrooms—in changing the "CIA" of Curriculum, Instruction, and Assessment (Fiske, 1991; Gardner, 1993c; Mitchell, 1992; Perkins, 1992, 1995; Perkins & Blythe, 1994; Perrone, 1994; Sizer, 1992). They are calling for:

- Curricula that attempt to cover fewer topics but delve into materials in greater detail; curricula centered on *essential questions* and *generative ideas.*

- Instruction that takes into account individual learning styles and strengths; that makes strategic use of technology and media; that involves teachers' modeling of sophisticated forms of discussion and analysis.

- An approach to assessment that goes well beyond standardized tests with multiple-choice, machine-scored answers. In this new dispensation, assessment is to be *authentic,* probing the kinds of performances that individuals actually must carry out in the world, rather than featuring tests that purport to be "proxies" for these performances. Rather than being saved for the end of the term, or left to outsiders, assessment is to be *ongoing,* to take place regularly as a seamless part of the curriculum. Moreover, assessment is to involve not only outsiders and teachers, but peers and, most importantly, the students themselves. As an example of authentic assessment, students are asked to discover patterns in data that they have generated in their own projects, rather than being required to select, from a set of multiple choices, the principle that appears to govern the form of someone else's data.

New Kinds of Schools, New Views of Intelligence

Discussion of possible future schools may be intriguing, but readers may well have begun to wonder how such discussion pertains to issues of intelligence. The answer is: Our current conceptions of intelligence and our views of the connections between intelligence and school have rested for many years on the assumption of a certain kind of school, one we have here labeled the *modern secular school.* As described above, that school is a very specific kind of milieu—one in which notational mastery, learning of disciplinary content, and ability to deal with materials outside of their customary context are at a premium.

If schools were to become different kinds of institutions, and if they had to serve their clientele in different kinds of ways, this altered state of affairs could have enormous implications for how we think about human beings and about their intellects. To begin, if schools need to educate all individuals to a high level, then considerations of presumed differences in endowment and potential become unimportant. One instead proceeds on the assumption that all can so achieve, and one does what is necessary to bring about that ambitious and laudable accomplishment.

There is an important decision point here. In a "uniform school," the assumption is made that all individuals basically can learn in the same way and can ultimately reach the same high level of performance. Asian methods, including out-of-school approaches like the Suzuki technique of instrumental musical training, have proceeded on that basis. But one may operate as well on the assumption of "individually configured" education. Recognizing or stipulating that individuals have different strengths, learn in different kinds of ways, and may even demonstrate their understanding by varied means, one instead tries to configure those forms of education that are most likely to succeed with various types of learners.

Thus far, in education history, most school systems—for reasons of ideology or of efficiency—have opted for the uniform solution. But nowadays, armed with a more nuanced knowledge of individual differences, and with far more curricular and technological options, many educators are interested in exploring the second alternative. Indeed, this perspective provides the impulse behind schooling based on the theory of multiple intelligences (Gardner, 1993c) (see Chapter 7).

Whether one pursues individual-centered or uniform education, teaching and learning will need to be reconfigured, if the aims of school are to encompass *understanding* and *critical and creative thinking.* At present, both in the United States and abroad, many efforts are afoot to create this new kind of education, to ground education more firmly on what we know about human conceptions and misconceptions. The learner, as well as the teacher, must be much more actively involved in deciding what to learn, how it is to be learned, and whether learning in fact is taking place. There needs to be more attention to meta-cognitive activity, with students themselves reflecting on what they have learned (and not learned) and how they approach their learning. Because teachers must themselves exhibit and embody these forms of thinking and understanding, new forms of teacher education and staff development are indicated.

At present, it is an open question whether the schools of tomorrow will tease out fresh definitions of intelligence, which may also come to be documented by old or new forms of assessment. Some see intelligence as a capacity so flexible and basic that it will come out, independent of the kind of scholastic environment in which it finds itself. However, it is at least as likely that every form of human performance draws on somewhat different kinds of competences. To the extent that schools become different kinds of places, they will not only draw on new forms of competence but will also develop new forms of competence. Each of these will need to be demonstrated in new ways, and the results may be quite altered views of intelligence or intelligences.

In this context, a new view of intelligence, recently been put forth by David Perkins (1995), is noteworthy. Perkins

David Perkins.

acknowledges the importance of neural intelligence—the computational power in the brain—and of experiential intelligence—the practical knowledge that one acquires by having rich and sustained experiences in particular domains (see Chapter 7). But he focuses his attention on a form of intelligence that has not been much considered; he terms it changeable, learnable, or reflective intelligence (see also Gardner et al., 1994).

Educational institutions can make a decisive difference in the training of learnable intelligence. Teachers can create a culture of thoughtfulness, where individuals regularly reflect on what they are learning; they can help students to consider the resources that they have at their disposal and how best to deploy them; they can teach students general strategies (e.g., how to consider alternative positions in an argument, how to organize one's time, how to benefit from feedback on homework); and they can show them how to use these strategies in carrying out work in specific disciplines.

Perkins proposes the creation of a "metacurriculum": a curriculum centered on *reflection* that helps students to think about their own thinking, and about thinking in general. Perhaps, in the end, a better understanding of intelligence in general, and of one's own intelligences in particular, will help all individuals to make optimal uses of their minds.

Summary

When cognitive and experimental psychologists first brought their bags of tricks to the bush, they discovered a discouraging state of affairs. On nearly every test and task devised by experimentalists, the indigenous people performed poorly. Whether asked to define words, group objects, tell stories, remember facts, or explain the physical world, subjects did not do well and tended to resemble much younger individuals in the West (Luria, 1976; Scribner & Cole, 1973, 1981).

At first, this set of findings led to quite useful explorations of the nature of schools and literacy. Investigators like Jack Goody, Michael Cole, Jerome Bruner, Patricia Greenfield, and others, indicated that schools develop important habits of mind: the ability to think logically, to classify consistently, to define with precision, and to understand the world in a scientific rather than a magical way. By implication, individuals in uneducated societies were like our young Western children: animistic, functional, simplistic, in need of a good dosage of schooling (Werner, 1948).

In the intervening decades, two things happened. First, as already noted, some of the limitations of our own Western schools became more manifest. And then, during the same period, researchers returned to traditional cultures but began to carry out investigations in different ways. For one thing, they used materials that were familiar rather than unfamiliar. For another, they modeled the kinds of behaviors that they were looking for. Finally, they focused their attention on the processes themselves—the basic operation of classification, memory, logic, and the like—rather than on the manifestations of these operations on Western, Piaget-style materials (Cole & Cole, 1989) (see Chapter 1).

The results were dramatic. Instead of appearing stupid and childlike, the subjects began to seem very much like modern Westerners. They could indeed remember, classify, tell stories, be analytical and logical (Kagan & Klein, 1973). It was only necessary that they understand what was expected of them, witness some instances of how to do it, and have the opportunity to work with materials that were not exotic for them. Indeed, according to one often-cited anecdote, once the desired form of classification had been modeled by an experimenter, a reflective subject answered: "Oh, that's easy—you want me to do it the way that a stupid person would do it" (See Luria, 1976).

The upshot of this work was not to indicate that there are no differences between schooled and unschooled societies; there are indeed distinctions, and the habits of mind instilled by decades spent within a schoolroom are real and lasting (Ceci, 1990; Olson, 1994). Indeed, one's scores on intelligence tests correlates quite highly with the number of years in school (Ceci, 1990); and the average reported intelligence in industrialized (and schooled) nations has gone up about 15 points in one generation (Flynn, 1987). However, the reported differences between schooled and unschooled individuals are often less profound and of a form other than was suggested by the first transplantations of psychological laboratories to the bush a few decades ago.

In the end, this cross-cultural line of work has led to an intriguing conclusion: it is not that schools are truly decontextualized. Indeed, almost by definition, no place is decontextualized; rather, each place has its own contextual characteristics. To paraphrase Abraham Lincoln, "Schools are the kinds of contexts that are liked by individuals who like those kinds of contexts." In the modern West, we have developed to a high degree a certain kind of school, and our conceptions and measures of intelligence are closely—even brilliantly—keyed to that particular institution.

Looking back at the kinds of schools reviewed in this chapter, we can discern the following picture. Traditional, religiously oriented schools were intent on producing individuals who exhibited a certain kind of character; they were highly restricted in admission, and they favored students who could behave in a prescribed way and could master literacies.

Modern secular schools have been much freer in initial access; moreover, they have tended to minimize the training of character. However, they have cherished a certain kind of academic intelligence and have denied access to higher institutions if students cannot master this form of achievement. Secular schools differ in the extent to which they expect, and provide support for, the majority of students to succeed academically. Asian schools, in particular, are quite different from schools in the United States; the Asian schools expect a high level of commitment from all students, and typically end up with a population that achieves at a higher level.

In countries all over the world, the role of schooling in the future is being debated. There is growing agreement that schooling needs to succeed for all students, and that a higher standard of critical thinking, creative thinking, and understanding needs to be achieved. It remains to be seen whether, when schools are dramatically reconfigured, as they may well be in the next century, our views of intelligence undergo a parallel kind of reformulation.

Suggested Readings

Cole, M., & Scribner, S. (1974). *Culture and thought: A psychological introduction.* New York: Wiley.

Comer, J. P. (1980). *School power: Implications of an intervention project.* New York: Free Press.

Damon, W. (1994). *Greater expectations.* New York: Free Press.

Gardner, H. (1991). *The unschooled mind.* New York: Basic Books.

Gardner, H. (1993). *Multiple intelligences: The theory in practice.* New York: Basic Books.

Perkins, D. (1995). *Outsmarting IQ: The emerging science of learnable intelligence.* New York: Free Press.

Sizer, T. R. (1992). *Horace's school: Redesigning the American high school.* Boston: Houghton Mifflin.

Stevenson, H. W., & Stigler, J. (1992). *The learning gap: Why our schools are failing and what we can learn from Japanese and Chinese education.* New York: Simon & Schuster.

Chapter 9

From the Perspective of the Workplace

Introduction

Defining intelligence defies consensus. Yet, acknowledging intelligent behavior when we encounter it is commonplace. For example, readers of this book, as well as most other schooled people, would regard a renowned composer, a professor of political science, and an inventor of new computer chips as intelligent. Many, perhaps most, might also consider a concert pianist, an architect, or a coach of a professional football team to be intelligent. Yet, these are very different activities; they require different kinds of training, and they yield different kinds of products.

An insight into this eclecticism comes from psychologist David Olson, who asserts that "intelligence is . . . skill in a cultural medium" (Olson, 1974, p. 61). That is, intelligence is a matter of how well people perform within a domain of knowledge valued by a culture. If we can accept Olson's idea, then a chapter on work, which intrinsically involves exercising skill in domains of knowledge, makes a great deal of sense. It complements our investigation of intelligence in the schools and it extends our consideration of intelligence in cultural contexts. It also raises a number of questions, around which this chapter is organized: How do people develop work-related intelligence? What makes for expert-level skill? How have changes in the nature of work affected intellectual demands? How can work organizations foster or impede intelligence? How have intelligence tests been applied in the workplace?

The Development of Work-Related Skills

To get a sense of how skills in a cultural medium develop, we take two perspectives. The first, a now-familiar one, considers skill development via apprenticeship.

This draws on findings from anthropology and cross-cultural psychology. The second perspective looks at skill development through psychological studies of expertise.

Apprenticeship

In Chapters 1 and 8, we discussed selection for training and for mastery in an apprenticeship system. But how do individuals' skills develop via apprenticeships? In these situations, young people develop skills by being "peripheral participants" (Lave, 1991, p. 64). The description in Chapter 1 of young Puluwat children gives the flavor of peripheral participation. Puluwat boys become able sailors by observing their elders while sailing, participating in sea voyages, and getting largely informal instruction and evaluation.

Informal apprenticeship also plays a key role in skill acquisition among young girls in traditional cultures. For example, Mayan women apprentice as midwives. Just as boys traditionally apprentice with their fathers or other close relatives, a Mayan girl may become a midwife by learning from her mother or grandmother. Girls in such families gather much knowledge about remedies and techniques just by growing up among midwives and observing pre- and postnatal care (Jordan, 1989, cited in Lave, 1991). After having a child of her own, a young Mayan woman is eligible to help another midwife deliver babies. Should the informal apprentice make a decision to become a midwife herself, she will observe more carefully. Then, gradually, she takes over more and more of the midwife's work until she herself becomes expert at the task.

As these examples illustrate, apprentices develop skills by being drawn into increasingly more challenging activities associated with work that is valued in their community. First, they have opportunities to observe people skilled in the work at hand. They soon take part in doing work related to that practice. By doing work in their zone of proximal development (see Chapter 7), and through regular informal feedback from others, they eventually master the use of tools and techniques associated with more advanced areas of the domain.

In industrialized societies, young children generally do not participate in apprenticeships to gain work-related skills. Instead, they attend school. In part, they do so because, unlike traditional societies, it cannot be assumed that the work of knowledgeable elders will still exist by the time young children have reached adulthood, and also because schools specifically seek to build literacy skills (see Chapter 8). These skills are critical for grasping the rapidly developing knowledge base of a technological society (Kornhaber, Krechevsky, & Gardner, 1990).

Although young children in industrialized societies rarely undertake work-related apprenticeships, adolescents and adults still do. Such apprenticeships are a well-developed feature of vocational education in many European countries. For example, in Germany, apprenticeship has been considered a key component of education. Apprenticeships for German high school students are available in both blue-collar and white-collar workplaces. Most older students spend more time in their apprenticeship than in their school (Hamilton, 1990). Their academic studies are often linked to the apprenticeship, reinforcing and supporting the acquisition of work skills (Hamilton, 1990). For example, German students who apprentice in automotive systems learn to repair faulty engines in the shop, and they study principles of automotive engineering in school. The success of apprenticeships in Germany and elsewhere has led to calls for more apprenticeship learning in the United States.

In industrialized societies, trade unions may also promote apprenticeships for those outside of school. To illustrate, in order to be licensed as an electrician in the United States, the International Brotherhood of Electrical Workers requires an apprenticeship of about four years. During this time, an apprentice electrician does supervised work alongside a licensed practitioner in order to advance his or her skill.

Apprenticeships are not limited to traditional cultures and skilled trades: medical internships in hospitals are a kind of apprenticeship. First-year interns observe more experienced doctors and assist with small tasks. Over the course of their internship, they are given increasingly more challenging tasks. The same is true for graduates of architecture schools. In order to be licensed, they must first serve an apprenticeship with a registered architect. Graduate students, who work closely with professors, take part in a similar apprenticeship. Perhaps they first take a small role in ongoing research, learning research techniques and making contributions to papers for publication. They may then design research and become coauthors of papers. Through their classes and scaffolded participation in research, they move along a path from novice to highly skilled expert.

The Novice–Expert Continuum

An examination of apprenticeship offers one route into understanding how people become skilled in their work. Yet another way of studying skill development in domains valued by a culture stems from investigations into an area far removed from apprenticeship: artificial intelligence. As noted in Chapter 6, since the introduction of computers, it was evident that these machines could carry out certain functions, such as calculation, more swiftly and efficiently than people. Because of this capacity, there was a widespread belief, among those working in artificial intelligence, that other complex problems could also be tackled by computers.

However, toward the end of the 1960s, it became evident that computers were not surpassing their human competitors (Glaser & Chi, 1988). The first artificial intelligence programs were designed to use general problem-solving rules, or heuristics, to "search" through a "problem space" for an answer (Holyoak, 1991) (see Chapter 6). Heuristics might suggest problem-solving tactics such as dividing large problems into smaller ones. This tactic can be applied to problems in many different areas.

In contrast to early artificial intelligence programs, human experts, such as medical doctors or Puluwat navigators, possess much more than general rules about how to reach a solution. They have a great deal of detailed and organized knowledge about the area in which they work, and this knowledge makes human experts' problem solving qualitatively different from that of the most powerful heuristically driven computers. To program computers to be expert, it became important to understand the nature of human experts' knowledge-driven thinking and how this thinking develops (see Chapter 6).

METHODS OF STUDYING EXPERTISE:
LESSONS FROM CHESS MASTERS

Expertise is an area that can be studied from various vantage points (see Chi, Glaser, & Farr, 1988). For example, the acquisition of expertise may be investigated by studying the lives of various people widely considered to be experts. Experiences of such people are then compared to those of others whose work is less distinguished in the domain (e.g., Hayes, 1985; Sloboda, 1991).

More frequently, understanding of the acquisition of expertise is derived from research that focuses on *problem-solving processes.* This is often done by giving experts and novices a common set of domain-related tasks to solve (e.g., Chase & Simon, 1973; Chi, Feltovich, & Glaser, 1981; Chi, Glaser, & Rees, 1982; Ericsson & Polson, 1988; Lesgold, Rubinson, Feltovich et al., 1988; Scardamalia & Bereiter, 1991). Analysis of how thinking differs between the two groups provides clues to how skills may change over time. The goal of these and other methods of studying expertise is ". . . to understand and account for what distinguishes outstanding individuals in a domain from less outstanding individuals . . ." (Ericsson & Smith, 1991a, p. 2).

Although somewhat removed from what most people consider work, the domain of chess has yielded many key initial insights into expertise in various areas. Chess has been widely studied because it offers an agreed-on rating system for players. Therefore, experts are clearly identifiable. It also provides a system of game notation, which helps investigators present problems and results (Charness, 1991).

Early research on chess expertise found little difference in the heuristic rules or in the amount of search used by expert and novice chess players (deGroot, 1966). However, these studies did find differences in the experts' perceptual skills and memory (Chase & Simon, 1973; deGroot, 1966). For example, in one task, chess masters and less skilled players were shown positions from a game in progress. After 5 seconds, the view of this initial board was obscured, and the subjects were asked to reconstruct the positions of the pieces they had just seen. The chess masters were much better than less-skilled players at reconstructing the chess positions. Yet, better memory alone could not explain the experts' performance: when shown chess pieces randomly positioned on a board (i.e., not arranged as they would be during a game) chess masters performed at about the same level as lesser players (Chase & Simon, 1973; deGroot, 1966).

What differed, according to Chase and Simon (1973), was the organization of the experts' memory for chess positions. Both experts and novices were limited

Chess experts.

to a very few "chunks" or clusters of information (in this case, positions of pieces) which they could store in short-term memory (see Chapter 6). However, Chase and Simon asserted that the experts' chunks consisted of larger perceptual units. Novices might have only one piece in their chunk. In contrast, experts stored familiar patterns of pieces, or groups of patterns, as a single chunk.

Chase and Simon's investigations led them to claim that:

> chess skill depends in large part upon a vast, organized long-term memory of specific information about chessboard patterns. Only chess-related tasks that tap this organization (such as the 5-second recall task) are sensitive to chess skill. Although there clearly must be a set of specific aptitudes (e.g., aptitudes for handling spatial relations) that together comprise a talent for chess, individual differences in such aptitudes are largely overshadowed by immense individual differences in chess experience. Hence, the overriding factor in chess skill is practice. The organization of the master's elaborate repertoire of information takes thousands of hours to build up, and the same is true of any skilled task (e.g., football, music). That is why *practice* is the major independent variable in the acquisition of skill. (Simon, 1979, p. 426; italics in original)

Some General Characteristics of Expertise

Along with the importance of practice to the acquisition of expertise, findings from studies of chess provide several other widely recognized characteristics of expert performance in diverse fields. For example, experts, with their large and well-organized memory for domain information, are more accurate than novices in carrying out tasks in their area of expertise. Thus, as noted above, after briefly viewing a game in progress, chess masters made fewer errors in efforts to duplicate the game pieces on a test board. Experts' stored patterns of information allow them to operate with a greater degree of automaticity. This is why chess experts needed less time than novices to replace a similar number of board pieces following each glance at a target board (Chase & Simon, 1973). Research also indicates that experts' skill is largely confined to tasks in the domain. Therefore, the experts were not better at reconstructing random arrangements of pieces, since this task is outside of the domain of chess playing.

Additional studies, especially in the area of physics, have helped to flesh out characteristics of experts' problem-solving processes. Michelene Chi and her colleagues (Chi, Feltovich, & Glaser, 1981; Chi, Glaser, & Rees, 1982) have asked physics students and physicists to categorize physics problems. They have found that the students sorted problems according to "surface structures"—for instance, whether the problem involved an inclined plane, spring, or pulley. In contrast, experienced physicists sorted problems according to the problems' underlying principles, or "deep structures" (Anzai, 1991; Chi, Glaser, & Rees, 1982, p. 42). For example, experts' categorizing would be based on whether the problem's solution required one or the other of Newton's laws (Anzai, 1991; Chi, Glaser, & Rees, 1982), not whether the problem mentioned an inclined plane or pulley.

Michelene Chi.

In addition, Chi found that physicists and students solved problems using different processes. The experts often used what is called "forward reasoning." They worked from given information to new facts and on to the problem solution. In contrast, students used more "backward reasoning." They had a hypothesis or goal driving their problem solving, and they sought data to "satisfy" the goal or subgoals (Anzai, 1991; Chi, Glaser, & Rees, 1982).

Furthermore, like the General Problem Solver mentioned in Chapter 6, novices do not possess vast domain knowledge. Therefore, they tend to use heuristic or "weak" approaches. In contrast, experts more often drew on "strong" or knowledge-rich approaches: they used bits of given information to infer new information and achieve solutions (Patel & Groen, 1991). Weak methods are not necessarily poor or unsophisticated methods (Patel & Groen, 1991); rather, they are general methods that are especially useful when one is problem solving in the absence of specific knowledge. Even experts may call on weak methods when trying to explain anomalies or loose ends (Patel & Groen, 1991) or when they lack experience with a particular kind of problem (Anzai, 1991).

Finally, experts are better at representing problems with diagrams and mental models (Anzai, 1991; Schank, 1982). For example, chess masters can play blindfolded while average players have considerable difficulty performing this feat (Simon, 1979). Masters make use of mental representations of the game to carry on their strategies even when a board is not in view (Ericsson & Smith, 1991a).

Advances in Understanding Experts' Problem-Solving Processes and the Acquisition of Expertise

Investigations into chess and physics have yielded many of the widely accepted characteristics of expertise mentioned above, but subsequent studies are leading to a more textured view. Part of this richer texture comes from looking across a number of different fields to see whether findings from chess and physics also apply to medical diagnosis, social policy analysis, computer programming, sports, writing, and other kinds of work (e.g., Ericsson & Smith, 1991b; Chi, Glaser, & Farr, 1988). In addition, different methods are being used: comparisons of experts' and novices' problem solving in physics, by necessity, often used problems that were already familiar to the experts (Scardamalia & Bereiter, 1991). In more recent research, experts have been given problems that were genuinely challenging to them. For example, doctors at various levels of training may be asked to come up with a diagnosis in a complex case (e.g., Lesgold et al., 1988; Patel & Groen, 1991). (See Box 6.3, pages 178–180 for an example.)

One of the most important findings from all these investigations is that when experts in various domains are faced with new and challenging problems, they do not rely on a single type of reasoning. Rather, their thinking is varied and flexible; they move between forward and backward reasoning, strong and weak methods, and other strategies as needed in the course of working through problems (Dörner & Schölkopf, 1991; Groen & Patel, 1988; Holyoak, 1991; Patel & Groen, 1991).

This newer research has also shed light on some of the conundra associated with skill acquisition. For example, if expertise in chess, football, or music is associated with practice, why do some people who engage in these activities for the same number of years exceed others? Or, as Ericsson and Smith (1991a, p. 27) put it, "From everyday experience, anyone can cite countless examples of individuals whose performance never appears to improve in spite of more than 10 years of daily activity at a task."

Statistical estimates support this common observation. Statistics reveal that the relationship between experience and job success is modest. Only about 20% (a correlation of about .45) of the variance in success is explained by experience (Streufert & Swezey, 1986). Psychometrically oriented researchers might explain differences in acquisition of expertise among similarly experienced people in terms of general intelligence or specific abilities. However, measures of these abilities are better at explaining differences *between* occupational groups rather than high levels of achievement *within* them (Ericsson & Smith, 1991a). It is estimated that intelligence tests explain, at best, about 20% (a correlation of about .45) of the variance in job success (Streufert & Swezey, 1986). More typically, the correlations between intelligence tests and performance average only .20 to .25 (Jensen, 1980; Wagner & Sternberg, 1986). This statistic means that, on average, such tests predict only between 4% and 6% of the variance in job performance.

Thus, neither years of experience nor psychometric measures reveal very much about why some people in a domain gain expert-level skills while others do not. What else might help explain differences in within-field achievement?

One insight comes from distinguishing *experience* from *practice* (Ericsson & Smith, 1991a). The former basically entails "time on task." The latter involves *efforts to enhance one's ability over time* typically with training (Ericsson & Smith, 1991a) and through encountering varied and new problems (Hatano & Inagaki, 1986). For example, time on task might account for the reasonable proficiency of amateur violin players. However, professional violinists need to spend considerable effort thinking about and mentally rehearsing their performances. In addition, they must receive and apply feedback on technique and musical interpretation from others. Practice also entails developing knowledge about the effects of different kinds of weather conditions and the acoustics of particular concert halls on the sound of their instruments. Such knowledge enables them to adapt their playing during the course of a performance (see Hatano & Inagaki, 1986).

Another possible explanation for differences in the acquisition of expertise over time is that expertise draws on certain individual propensities. Perhaps the most important of these is *a propensity to reflect* on one's own efforts (Cattell, 1963, in Ericsson & Smith, 1991a).

What does reflection entail? Often, it involves a slowing down of one's problem-solving processes (Argyris, 1982), either during or after encountering a challenging situation (Schön, 1983). During this time, active questioning or "interrogation" of one's knowledge base, models, and theories occurs (Perkins, Allen, & Hafner, 1983; Schön, 1983). Donald Schön, who has written extensively on reflection among professionals in various fields, has described reflection among architects as "a conversation with the materials of a situation" (Schön, 1983, p. 78). This description is apt for other domains as well. For example, researchers have found that expert writers and skilled readers extend their expertise in a "dialectical process" (Scardamalia & Bereiter, 1991). The same is true for physicists when they confront problems that are genuinely challenging to them rather than problems from student textbooks (Scardamalia & Bereiter, 1991).

Such reflection enables individuals to modify their current understanding and actually improve what they do.

A third possibility is that experience and practice can be differentiated not only by individual activities, such as training and reflection, but also by certain kinds of social settings. Conditions for practice include getting useful feedback on one's efforts from others (Argyris, 1982; Argyris & Schön, 1978; Senge, 1990). They also include opportunities to explore new and varied kinds of problems (Hatano & Inagaki, 1986; Reich, 1991; Sloboda, 1991). An atmosphere in which some errors are tolerated is also important. Settings in which there is great pressure to produce only correct answers may inhibit exploration (Hatano & Inagaki, 1986).

In summary, *experience* may yield competence at routine kinds of problems, which many people achieve. Such competence is very useful in a stable environment (Hatano & Inagaki, 1986). However, the acquisition of expertise requires *practice.* This involves self-monitoring, reflection, exploration, and feedback from others. Practice fosters high-level mastery over complex and novel problems (Hatano & Inagaki, 1986; Holyoak, 1991; Schön, 1983). The high-level skills associated with expertise are growing increasingly important in rapidly changing industrial economies (Reich, 1991). Thus, it is vital to understand the conditions that foster the development of such skills.

As we will see in the following section, opportunities for people to develop their work skills depend in part on the settings of their jobs. Some settings strip away skills or allow only routine performances; others promote the development of high-level skills.

Work Organizations

The Changing Intellectual Demands of the Workplace

The study of expertise helps shed light on various aspects of high-level skill in diverse domains, but it does not provide much insight into one of the key aspects surrounding skill development: for most people, the opportunity to develop skill in one's work goes on within organizations. Thus, in industrialized societies, opportunities for development occur in such places as offices, industrial plants, schools, stores, hospitals, police departments, research labs, and restaurants. The common theme among these diverse settings is that they, and other organizations, are designed to coordinate many individuals' actions, including their interactions, plans, and products (Argyris, 1982; Streufert & Swezey, 1986). As we'll discuss below, *how organizations coordinate individuals' actions* has an impact on the range and level of intellectual skills that individuals develop.

From Craft to Specialization

In an apprenticeship or craft shop setting, most individuals gradually gain an understanding of the whole range of processes needed to do or make something that is valued in their culture. The coordination model for such settings might be seen as "familial." (Indeed, as discussed in Chapter 1, apprenticeships evolved from, and sometimes maintained, certain kinds of family relationships.) Younger, less experienced people are "brought up": they are expected to acquire the range and level of skills possessed by mature, adult practitioners. They are gradually given more complex tasks that facilitate their skill development.

In contrast to an apprenticeship setting, most large organizations cannot train the majority of their employees "from the bottom up" in the whole range of skills entailed in the organization's work. Rather, there is a "*division of cognitive labor*" (Hutchins, 1991, p. 284). People, or groups of people, are expected to have, or to develop, primarily those skills needed to carry out the functions associated with their jobs.

In large organizations, neither the chief executive nor any other individual has the complete set of skills needed to do the work of the organization as a whole. Thus, unlike a traditional Puluwat navigator, a modern U.S. Navy captain cannot take a vessel on a solo voyage around widely scattered Pacific Islands. In fact, just to leave the harbor in San Diego, the captain needs a great deal of assistance from crew members who have specialized skills:

> On the deck two people take visual sightings on predetermined landmarks, using special telescopic devices mounted on gyrocompasses that yield exact readings of direction. They call out their readings to two other individuals, who relay them by telephone to a specialist on the bridge. This individual records the bearings in a book and repeats them aloud for confirmation. Next to the recorder, another individual uses specialized tools to plot the ship's position on a navigational chart and to project where the ship will be at the next fix and beyond. These projections of position are used to decide what landmarks should be sighted next by those on deck and when a course correction will be required. The entire cycle is repeated every one to three minutes (Resnick, 1987a, p. 13).

The complex organization needed to run a warship helps illustrate a conundrum concerning intelligence: psychologists and laypeople have typically thought of intelligence as a property of individuals. However, if we regard intelligence as an ability to handle real-world problems rather than mental test problems (e.g., Neisser, 1976; Scribner, 1984; Sternberg, 1988), then ascribing intelligence to individuals becomes a bit tricky. We see that no one on the warship "has the intelligence" to sail away from the harbor and out to sea. Instead, various people are needed to accomplish this task. In addition, these people are dependent on tools, such as telephones and gyroscopes, and symbolic media, such as charts (Pea, 1990). Rather than being a property of a particular individual, the intelligence for this task is said by some researchers to be "socially shared" among individuals (Resnick, 1987a; Resnick, Levine, & Teasley, 1991), or "distributed" among people, tools, and symbolic media (Hutchins, 1991; Pea, 1990). This way of thinking is much closer to the ideas of Vygotsky (see Chapter 7) than to those of Spearman, Terman, Binet, or Piaget (see Chapters 1, 2, and 4).

FIGURE 9.1

Bureaucratic hierarchies can be represented in the form of organizational charts like this one. People at different levels within a bureaucratic hierarchy often require different skills. For people at the base of the hierarchy developing new skills for mobility upward in the organization may be hampered by a lack of interaction with those higher up who possess such skills. For example, the assistant garage manager of this large hotel will rarely, if ever, see or acquire the skills of the general manager. From G. W. Lattin, *The Lodging and Food Service Industry*. East Lansing, MI: Educational Institute of the American Hotel Association, 1989.

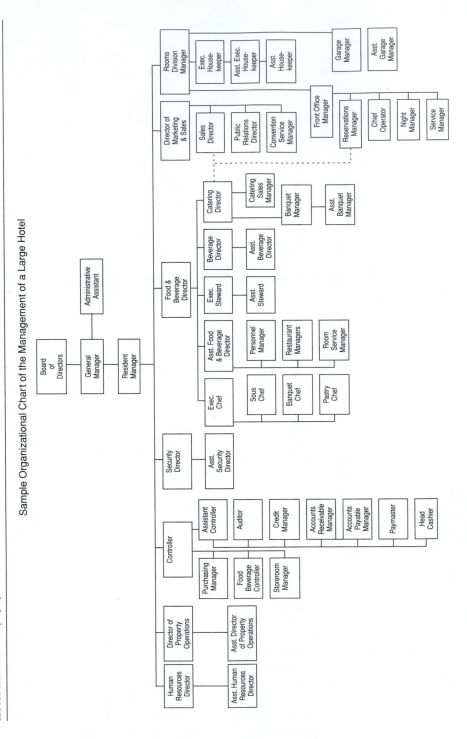

Sample Organizational Chart of the Management of a Large Hotel

As on a warship, the coordination of people in many complex organizations takes the form of a bureaucratic hierarchy (see Figure 9.1). Unlike the hierarchy of a family, a bureaucratic hierarchy is ideally determined not just ascriptively, by age, gender, or other birth-related attributes, but by merit (see Chapter 1). A bureaucratic hierarchy has an impact on development of skills. This may be especially true for those at the base of a hierarchy. In contrast to a familial apprenticeship or craft shop, individuals at the base of a hierarchy may never see practitioners carrying out many of the more complex tasks involved in the organization's work. Thus, for example, shipping clerks in Silicon Valley spend little if any time around the scientists who develop computer chips or the financial officers who keep the company afloat. Those at the base of the hierarchy are not expected to need the knowledge and skills of those at its apex, and there is little chance for them to gain such skills as peripheral participants.

The Rationalization of Labor via Scientific Management

The widespread shift from craft-based knowledge to industrial specialization began hundreds of years ago with changes in land laws, textile production, technology, and guild requirements (Braudel, 1982; Scott, 1914). However, in modern times, a spur to even greater specialization of tasks and skills came from the work of an American engineer named Frederick W. Taylor.

In the late 19th century, Taylor found that most factories were not nearly as productive as they might be. He believed this state of affairs was largely due to two problems: first, management did not know how much time different tasks should take, and second, industrial workers were using a variety of methods to carry out the same task. For instance, individual workers used whatever speeds they thought best for turning different kinds of metals on a lathe. Taylor found optimal speeds could be determined by rigorous study. He noted, though, that none of the workmen on their own appeared to have discovered and used these speeds (Taylor, 1911).

Frederick Taylor.

To improve productivity, and thereby secure the greatest prosperity for workers and employers, Taylor espoused *scientific management.* In theory, scientific management encompassed 4 principles designed to make organizational processes as rational and efficient as possible:

1. One best method could be established for performing any task, and this method should be established by scientific means. To do this, complex tasks had to be broken down into discrete elements. Then an efficiency expert, aided by a stopwatch, would figure out which physical maneuvers and tools workers should adopt in order to accomplish each element with as little effort and time as necessary.

2. Managers should "train, teach, and develop the workman" (Taylor, 1911, p. 36). Workers were to be trained to carry out elements of the task, according to the best method.

3. Managers should "heartily cooperate with the men" to make sure that the work is done according to the most efficient means, rather than by rule-of-thumb methods (Taylor, 1911, p. 36). Taylor argued that managers could, over a period of a few years, demonstrate that the best method required less physical effort, saved workers' jobs, and increased their pay.

4. Managers and workers should have "an almost equal division of the work and the responsibility" (Taylor, 1911, p. 37). Though this sounds egalitarian, the intended division was quite skewed. According to this principle, managers should assume the work of planning, analyzing tasks, and conducting training, instead of leaving those responsibilities—*and* the actual execution of the plans—to the workers. Ideally, workers were to receive, on each workday, written instructions from managers not only about "what is to be done but how it is to be done and the exact time for doing it" (Taylor, 1911, p. 39).

Taylor acknowledged that his approach might appear to reduce people to "automatons" (Taylor, 1911, p. 126). However, he argued against such a characterization:

. . . it should be remembered that the training of the surgeon has been almost identical in type with the teaching and training which is given to the workman under scientific management. The surgeon, all through his early years, is under the closest supervision of more experienced men, who show him in the minutest way how each element of his work is best done. They provide him with the finest implements, each one of which has been the subject of special study and development, and then insist upon his using each of these implements in the very best way. All of this teaching, however, in no way narrows him. On the contrary he is quickly given the very best knowledge of his predecessors; and . . . he is able to use his own originality and ingenuity to make *real additions to the world's knowledge, instead of reinventing things which are old.* (Taylor, 1911, p. 126; italics in original)

Yet, a critical analysis reveals that the surgeon-in-training is not an apt analogy for worker development in Taylor's model. Unlike the worker, the young surgeon is an apprentice who is ultimately expected to assume the expert's role. In contrast, the worker under scientific management occupies a low position in a steep hierarchy. Such a worker is not expected to assume a managerial job and is not provided opportunities to develop the skills that the managers/teachers possess. Workers merely accept tasks others have designed.

In practice, scientific management came to be dominated by the search for one best, most efficient method. Once the best way was discovered, workers were trained to carry out one or very few tasks in a uniform, repetitive fashion. With little opportunity for experimentation or exploration, and few encounters with nonroutine tasks, workers had little chance to develop expert skills.

Thus, despite Taylor's rhetoric, the development of workers' abilities was often stifled by practitioners of scientific management. Taylor himself actually granted workers little credit for their capacity to make thoughtful contributions to the organization's work. For example, when a mechanic who worked for Taylor attempted to participate in problem-solving discussions, Taylor told him he was "not supposed to think, there are other people paid for thinking around here" (quoted in Callahan, 1962, p. 28).

Although scientific management had a harsh impact on skill development, its promise to increase productivity, efficiency, and prosperity made it popular both in the United States and abroad. It influenced the practices of workers and managers not only in industry but in education, the military, and many other fields (Butler, 1989; Callahan, 1962). As we discuss below, its impact on intellectual demands at various organizational levels was marked.

Deskilling Workers While Increasing Intellectual Work of Managers

Scientific management, alongside modern industrial technology, helped to strip away skills and thinking requirements from many nonmanagerial workers (Callahan, 1962; Zuboff, 1988). Much of what was eliminated comprised a tacit knowledge base. This knowledge was generally learned via experience—by doing—rather than through explicit teaching (Wagner & Sternberg, 1986). Tacit knowledge is typically recalled and applied in context, often summoned "by feel," rather than being articulated and ordered in a rational way (see Chapter 7). As the following quote indicates, not only those who do physical labor but skilled practitioners in almost any field possess relevant tacit knowledge:

Although the expert diagnostician, taxonomist and cotton-classer can indicate their clues and formulate their maxims, they know many more things than they can tell, knowing them only in practice . . . and not explicitly. . . . (Polanyi, 1958, p. 88)

Once laborers' activities were analyzed and measured under Taylor's principles, what had been their tacit knowledge became explicit. After this occurred, the bases of their skill could be incorporated by management into labor-saving processes and machines, leaving many workers to carry out a narrow range of standardized procedures that others had designed. These procedures were simplified, sometimes to an excruciating degree. An auto worker employed by General Motors around 1970 exemplifies the trend toward simplification in this description of his job:

There's a lot of variety in the paint shop. . . . You clip on the color hose, bleed out the old color, and squirt. Clip, bleed, squirt, think; clip, bleed, squirt, yawn; clip, bleed, squirt, scratch your nose. Only now the . . . [new managers] have taken away the time to scratch your nose. (Garson, 1979a, p. 212)

Blue collar workers were not the only ones affected by scientific management and technological advances. An increasing proportion of clerical workers had

Factories that operate according to principles of scientific management allowed few opportunities for workers to develop their abilities.

little chance to develop high-level skills. Prior to scientific management and the invention of office machines, many clerks needed to be adept in foreign languages, informed about business principles, and polished in interpersonal skills. Most clerks and secretaries were men, and some were not much different from junior executives. Like apprentices, they had opportunities to observe more complex tasks. Thus, they might gain skills needed for promotion within the hierarchy.

However, after the introduction of new technologies, the ranks of clerical workers grew, and offices were staffed mostly by lower-paid women whose jobs came to resemble factory work. Many clerical tasks were concrete and repetitive (Zuboff, 1988). They demanded little skill or knowledge, and they provided scant opportunity for learning by observation or through encounters with varied and challenging tasks. As this former office worker explains:

> I worked for a while at the Fair Plan Insurance Company, where hundreds of women sat typing up and breaking down sextuplicate insurance forms. My job was in endorsements: *First, third, and fourth copies staple together/Place the pink sheet in the back of the yellow/If the endorsement shows a new mortgagee/Stamp the fifth copy "certificate needed. . . ."* (Garson, 1979b, p. 225; italics in original)

The role of managers changed as well. In contrast to industrial and clerical workers, an increasing proportion of managers' time was spent planning and coordinating tasks. This increase occurred for two reasons. First, as noted above, managers under Taylorism were to plan and orchestrate the work of all those directly involved in production. Second, with office machines and a growing supply of secretaries, managers were able to transfer the more routine elements of their own job to clerical employees.

Unlike most other workers, executives continued to rely on and develop tacit knowledge. They were called on to handle diverse problems involving the use of human and technological resources. They were also charged with devising improvements that would lead to greater efficiency and financial returns. Varied challenges and opportunities to learn help foster crucial intellectual skills, such as the ability to abstract principles and patterns, to make inferences from principles and patterns learned in past problems and apply them to new problems, and to reason logically (Reich, 1991; Schön, 1983; Zuboff, 1988).

For the better part of the 20th century, this centralization of intellectual skill stood fast in most industrial and business organizations. The isolation of intellectual work among managers was supported by scientific management. Taylor argued that "one type of man is needed to plan ahead and an entirely different type to execute the work" (Taylor, 1911, p. 38). The argument was supported by beliefs, among both managers and workers, that intellectual tasks should be shouldered by the generally better-educated white collar workers (Zuboff, 1988). Perhaps most importantly, the system lasted because it had material benefits: the efficiency resulting from the standardization Taylor had advocated helped to reduce consumer prices and create a better standard of living (Hunt, 1995). Were it not for major changes in technology and the world economy, the economic benefits of Taylor's system might have quelled attempts to devise alternatives.

Information Technology and the Possibilities for Intellectual Reskilling

Just as the rise of industrial machines and scientific management created shifts in intellectual demands on workers, so should the successful utilization of computers (Zuboff, 1988). Industrialization and scientific management mechanized and automated work. Automation removed much of the skill base of nonmanagerial workers, and demanded instead a large workforce capable of following management's instructions.

However, computerization not only automates, it "informates" (Zuboff, 1988, p. 10). It provides streams of potentially shareable information related to the ongoing work. In computerized organizations, workers may need to attend not only to preplanned directives from above. Increasingly, they may need to use, and confer over, computer information generated in real time. To use this technology well, workers must be able to respond flexibly and manipulate symbolic media using intellectual skills, instead of relying on rote—and often physical—procedures required in noncomputerized workplaces.

The shift from physical skills to intellectual skills has been studied by Shoshana Zuboff, a sociologist who teaches at the Harvard Business School. Zuboff (1988) carried out some of her research in two paper pulp plants. Making paper from pulp is an inexact process and is thus hard to automate fully. It involves variables associated with temperature, wood, water, chemicals, and equipment. In the past, workers at pulp plants controlled the process by tacit knowledge of physical cues, such as the smell and feel of the pulp, and a hands-on knowledge of the machinery. However, once the plants were computerized, the locus of action changed from the plant floor to an air-conditioned control room filled with computer screens and keyboards. Workers could no longer tell, simply by looking, whether the pulp was too dry or was spilling over the top of a vat. They could no longer know whether the pulping process was going well simply by squeezing a fistful of pulp. Instead, they had to look at a screen of computer data and figure out from that what was happening in the production process (Zuboff, 1988). Voicing an idea reminiscent of Piaget's concept of mental operations (see Chapter 4), one oldtimer noted that, with computerization, "Your past physical mobility must be translated into a mental thought process" (Zuboff, 1988, p. 71). Or, as another said of a computerized plant:

> . . . if something is going wrong, you don't go down and fix it. Instead, you stay up here and think about the sequence, and you think about how you want to affect the sequence. You get it done through your thinking. . . . It all occurs in your mind now. (Zuboff, 1988, p. 75)

In essence, computerization creates an electronic environment or medium for acting on or observing events in an organization (Zuboff, 1988). To act skillfully within this new medium—to act intelligently, in Olson's framework—the pulp plant workers could no longer rely on physical cues and personal activities in context. (In fact, some of the workers felt their jobs had disappeared into a two-dimensional space.) Instead, they needed to draw on such intellectual skills as abstraction, inference, and procedural reasoning based on symbolic data (Zuboff, 1988). These skills help make clear the connection between symbols and the reality they represent. They enable people to use symbolic information—instead of, or alongside, physical cues—to act, to monitor events, and to learn.

Shoshana Zuboff.

According to Zuboff, the ability of workers to develop these intellectual skills depends in part on individual competence. Drawing on Gardner's theory of multiple intelligences (see Chapter 7), Zuboff speculates that people dealing with computer media may need to draw more on logical–mathematical intelligence rather than on the bodily–kinesthetic intelligence vital to working with machinery. However, individual competence, while necessary, is not sufficient for the development of intellectual skills such as abstraction, inference, and procedural reasoning (Zuboff, 1988). In addition, organizations must create opportunities—scaffolding—for individuals to use these skills (Zuboff, 1988). Because such opportunities are limited to managers in Taylor's model of task coordination, it's worthwhile to consider how other organizational systems *do* promote these skills more broadly.

Fostering Intelligence Within Organizations

Various investigators point to a number of intertwined organizational features that affect individuals' learning and development at work. Among these are the availability and use of information within organizations, the degree of tolerance for experimentation, and the use of hierarchical structures to centralize thinking tasks among managers. By comparing the organizational practices at the pulp plants Zuboff observed with those of Japanese companies, it is possible to get a sense of how organizations may promote intellectual skill development.

Zuboff, among others, believes that information technologies may be problematic for organizations because such technologies blur the historical roles of managers as thinkers, and workers as laborers (Zuboff, 1988). For example, in the pulp plants, workers no longer had to wear work clothes and regularly tend heavy machinery. Instead, they spent most of their time sitting on comfortable chairs within an air-conditioned room. Like managers, they dealt with symbols from computers, and conferred with each other in interpreting and analyzing computer data (Zuboff, 1988).

These new responsibilities among workers were experienced by the managers at the pulp plant, and managers elsewhere, as a threat to their authority (Zuboff, 1988). Thus, following the logic of Taylorism, managers often used the technology to increase their control over work processes and to undermine the workers' growing intellectual skills. For instance, at one plant, the computers were programmed to report at more frequent intervals on operators' activities. This procedure made it impossible for the workers to figure out and address some problems before the computers "told on them." Thus, the workers were effectively discouraged from using or developing intellectual skills. In response, they withdrew their active problem-solving efforts at the plant. In contrast, the night shift at the plant had many more opportunities to exercise intellectual skills. Because managers were not so pervasive at night, the workers had more "freedom to play, experiment and enter into dialogue" (Zuboff, 1988, p. 306). As a result, they became more skilled than the day shift in using the new technology (Zuboff, 1988).

Lessons From Japan

Whereas a history of Taylorism may undermine workers' efforts to develop skills, alternatives to Taylor's system help Japanese workers to increase their skills. The Japanese style of management originated with the rebuilding of Japanese industry following World War II. At that time, the Japanese were struggling to produce goods that might compete in the world market. Consultants to Japanese industry, most notably the American engineer, W. Edwards Deming, helped to introduce a means of production commonly known as quality control (QC), or sometimes total quality control (TQC) (Deming, 1982; Ozeki & Asaka, 1990). In some ways, QC is a direct reaction to the pitfalls of scientific management. However, like scientific management, it has been applied not only in factories, but in a wide range of organizations.

QC as used by Japanese companies is a continual, organization-wide effort to ensure quality in the products and services that customers need. Although the system involves many features, most notably for our purposes, it emphasizes training and retraining of workers on the job, the use of data by workers and management, and workers' "right to pride of workmanship" (Deming, 1982, p. 12). On top of Deming's system, the Japanese have also developed the quality control circle (QCC), an alternative organizational structure aimed at continual learning in the workplace and enhancing the quality of output (Ozeki & Asaka, 1990).

EDUCATION AND TRAINING

Unlike the system of coordination advocated by Taylor, Japanese industry does not leave thinking to the managers and task execution to the workers. Furthermore, there does not appear to exist some unspoken assumption that ordinary workers are unable to master the science of their own jobs. Instead, "The Japanese model relies very heavily upon the information-processing capacity of the worker and this makes the body of employees a viable and indispensable element of the firm" (Aoki, 1990, p. 268). A quality control handbook written for Japanese foremen notes that it is necessary to "move away from the premodern management style that emphasized efficiency exclusively" and instead recognize the "unlimited potential" of "human capabilities" (Ozeki & Asaka, 1990, p. 84).

In line with this sentiment, in Japan there is a genuine effort to provide each worker with lifetime training. Such a commitment makes sense in a country that traditionally offered workers lifetime employment. In the United States, where workers frequently change jobs, such a commitment is viewed as less cost-effective for employers (Ozeki & Asaka, 1990).

USE OF DATA

One of the main areas of education involves training workers, as well as managers, to use the statistical methods that lie at the heart of Deming's quality control approach. Widespread generation and analysis of statistical data is accomplished not only by managers but among workers and foremen as well. Training is widespread: "Statistical symbols and methods . . . [have become] in Japan a second language for everybody, including hourly workers" (Deming, 1982, p. 105).

Basically, these data, displayed using diverse kinds of diagrams and charts, are a means of depicting variation (see Figure 9.2). The goal is to detect variation in production; locate its origin in human, material, or machine inputs; and correct the source of the variation. The correction might involve training workers, correcting the training program the workers originally received, making sure the workers' eyesight is unimpaired, ensuring the tools they use are in good order, or altering the production process (Deming, 1982). Elimination of variation makes quality and costs predictable. It also provides a clear and controlled basis against which to assess the outcome of any planned experimentation or effort at improvement.

Given their training in quality control methods, teams of Japanese workers can carry out improvement efforts and evaluate their impact. In comparison to Taylor's methods, the quality control approach widely used in Japan encourages workers to take responsibility for inventing improvements and helps train them to do so.

ALTERNATIVES TO STEEP HIERARCHICAL STRUCTURES

Training in statistical methods helps Japanese workers to analyze their own efforts and improve them. In addition, the structure of Japanese organizations supports workers' attempts to improve production and their own knowledge base. In fact, one of the ways in which Japanese foremen's management skills are measured is by "the number of improvements suggested per individual" working under that foreman (Ozeki & Asaka, 1990, p. 16).

FIGURE 9.2

Japanese automotive workers are trained in the collection and use of data to ensure quality in their products. This defect location sheet is but one of many tools a worker might use. Such intellectual tasks contrast sharply with the tasks described by the paint shop worker in an American automotive factory c. 1970 (p. 280), which was organized according to Taylor's principles of scientific management.

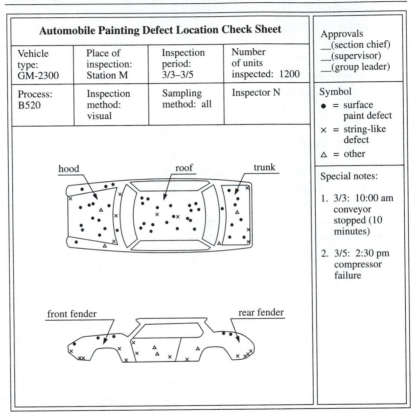

Automobile Painting Defect Location Check Sheet				Approvals __(section chief) __(supervisor) __(group leader)
Vehicle type: GM-2300	Place of inspection: Station M	Inspection period: 3/3–3/5	Number of units inspected: 1200	Symbol ● = surface paint defect × = string-like defect △ = other
Process: B520	Inspection method: visual	Sampling method: all	Inspector N	

Approvals
__(section chief)
__(supervisor)
__(group leader)

Symbol
● = surface paint defect
× = string-like defect
△ = other

Special notes:

1. 3/3: 10:00 am conveyor stopped (10 minutes)

2. 3/5: 2:30 pm compressor failure

As mentioned earlier, Japanese industry and businesses are frequently organized around quality control circles (QCCs)—small groups of employees who meet regularly to provide for their "mutual education" (Ozeki & Asaka, 1990, p. 85). In workplaces where such circles exist, everyone belongs to a circle, because "Everyone has something to contribute" (Ozeki & Asaka, 1990, p. 85).

Mutual education in QCCs occurs in the course of tackling quality-related problems. New groups begin by addressing a fairly manageable problem under the direction of the foreman. But over a period of time, groups gradually take on increasingly complex issues under a rotating leadership.

Within QCCs, there are explicit efforts to surface and articulate individuals' tacit knowledge, allowing those involved to gain skills more readily (Ozeki &

Asaka, 1990). For example, each QCC meets regularly to work on the problem it is addressing. After working through the issue, group members prepare a brief report summarizing what they have learned and the new methods they have uncovered to enhance quality. QCCs may also attend and present their findings at QC conferences outside of their firms. Ideally, all members of the group attend, prepare, and present their findings to other QC conferees. Like reflective practitioners examining their own effort, members of a QCC preparing for a conference come "to understand its [the circle's] successes and setbacks and move into higher levels of improvement activities" (Ozeki & Asaka, 1990, p. 94).

With the introduction of quality control circles, the Japanese have eliminated steep hierarchies in the operational side of their organizations (Aoki, 1990). Steep hierarchies may fragment many workers' jobs into narrow splinters. For example, the American system typically has a vast array of job titles and prescribed responsibilities for each (see Figure 9.1). In contrast, Japanese organizations have few job descriptions: people are expected to be able to assume varied roles (Aoki, 1990). Thus, rather than handling a tiny slice of the overall work, day after day (e.g., "clip, bleed, and squirt"), teams of Japanese workers are responsible for a group of related tasks. They are rotated through these tasks frequently—as often as "every few hours" (Aoki, p. 275). This procedure enables Japanese workers to learn new skills and keeps them engaged in their work. Because workers are responsible for groups of tasks and have opportunities to learn new ones, Japanese firms are better able to adapt to changes, such as absenteeism or new consumer demands.

There is hierarchical organization in Japanese industrial plants, but it primarily concerns strategic decision making, such as investments in equipment or in research (Aoki, 1990). At the operational level, which concerns such matters as responding to changing markets and production demands, the organization is "semihorizontal" (Aoki, 1990, p. 273). Unlike hierarchies prescribed by Taylor, all information related to production is not gathered at the top, digested, and then translated into workers' tasks. Instead, after some preliminary central planning, information about market demands is fed directly to the production level. Because workers and foremen have training and are adaptable, they have a fair amount of autonomy in deciding how to address the incoming production demands. They are also responsible for notifying other units in the organization about what needs to be done further up the pipeline to ensure that production quality and quantity are met (Aoki, 1990).

As Zuboff (1988, 1995) argued, organizational features are crucial to the development of workers' skills. It is true that conditions that show regard for workers' ability to learn, encourage their use and analysis of data, provide ongoing training, and reduce hierarchy have helped to make the Japanese workforce as capable as it is.

Our contrasting examples of scientific management and the Japanese approach should reveal that assumptions about work, made by organizational consultants and the society as a whole, actually shape what workers can do and how

U.S. car manufacturers have learned many lessons about worker training and development from their Japanese counterparts. Here an American Saturn car worker gathers information for quality control.

intelligent they appear. If it is assumed that workers are capable only of following orders designed by others, they are provided few opportunities to learn and take on complex tasks. On the other hand, if it is assumed that workers can think and learn, organizational opportunities are provided to help the workers develop their abilities and carry out more complex tasks. And, lo and behold, the workers appear to be far more intelligent!

Yet, scholars of the workplace caution that even such features are not sufficient. The Japanese system is built on a labor force whose initial levels of technical knowledge, problem-solving skills, and team approaches are already strong (Aoki, 1990; Deming, 1982). In the United States, those workers who are most likely to have responsibilities for using and analyzing data are generally highly educated, white collar "symbol analysts" (Reich, 1991). They, too, have long years of training in problem solving involving symbolic media, prior to beginning their work lives. Only then are they provided with intensive learning on the job, where, like many ordinary Japanese workers, they gain "new insights and approaches relevant to even more complex problems, and so on, as learning builds on itself" (Reich, 1991, p. 235).

Thus, whether a large proportion of workers in America and other countries will acquire the kinds of intellectual skills Zuboff believes are necessary depends not only on individual capabilities and organizational features of the workplace. It rests as well on educational experiences that begin long before people ever start their jobs (Reich, 1991).

Intelligence Testing and Job Selection

In industrialized countries, the growing reliance on information technology, plus the globalization of the economy, will make intellectual skills vital to work that pays reasonable wages (Herrnstein & Murray, 1994; Reich, 1991; Zuboff, 1988). Abstraction, inference, logical reasoning based on symbols, and the ability to think about systems and their interrelationships are among the skills frequently mentioned (Reich, 1991; Senge, 1990; Zuboff, 1988). Similar mental abilities—dealing with abstractions and establishing relations and correlates—were markers of intelligence to early psychometricians, such as Spearman and Terman (see Chapters 1 and 3). If we can accept, at least for the moment, that intelligence tests measure such abilities, then it would seem increasingly sensible to select workers on the basis of such tests. Yet, as is the case in education (see Chapters 3 and 8), the use of intelligence tests in employment has yielded many questions and controversies.

In this section, we first consider one of the controversies. This case study sets the stage for discussing some of the technical and social issues involved in employment testing.

Employment Testing and Equal Opportunity in the United States

Debates in the United States over reliance on intelligence (or similar) tests in employment mirror arguments voiced by Chinese authorities during periodic reforms of their civil service examination system (see Chapter 1):

- Do the tests measure what is needed for the job?

- Should the tests select people based on a strict meritocracy determined by test scores, or is it fairer to provide greater job access to groups of people who would often be excluded when tests alone are considered?

Differing positions on this second point represent poles in an ongoing issue sometimes known as the excellence v. equality debate, or the individual v. group rights controversy. This debate manifests itself both in employment and in admission to competitive academic programs (Bastian, Fruchter, Gittell, Greer, & Haskins, 1985; Gardner, 1961; Gifford, 1989; Klitgaard, 1985).

In the United States, the opening of the excellence–equality debate in employment testing occurred with the passage of the Civil Rights Act of 1964. Among other things, Title VII of this Act made it illegal for employers to hire, fire, segregate, or classify people in order to limit their job opportunities on the basis of "race, color, religion, sex, or national origin."

At the same time that Title VII called for equalizing opportunities, it endorsed meritocratic hiring. It explicitly allowed "for an employer to give and to act upon the results of any professionally developed ability test provided that such test . . .

is not designed, intended or used to discriminate because of race, color, religion, sex or national origin" (Title VII, Section 703(h)).

Shortly after this legislation passed, a group of Black employees of the Duke Power Company, in North Carolina, brought a legal action against their employer for violating the Civil Rights Act of 1964. The case, *Griggs et al. v. Duke Power Company,* was decided by the U.S. Supreme Court in 1971 (401 U.S. 424).

The decision noted that the power company had discriminated on the basis of race, prior to the passage of the Civil Rights Act. In the past, it assigned all Black employees to its Labor Department, the lowest of five departments at the plant. After the Act became effective in 1965, this practice was abandoned. However, within a few months, several new policies were instituted. Most notably for our purposes, the power company said that placement into the four higher depart-ments would depend on satisfactory scores on two standardized tests. One of these was a general intelligence test (the Wonderlic Personnel Test). The other was a test of mechanical comprehension (the Bennett Mechanical Comprehen-sion Test). A satisfactory score was one that approximated the median score achieved by high school graduates. This standard is actually more demanding than the high school degree: the median performance means that roughly half of those with the degree would be below the cutoff point (Griggs et al. v. Duke Power Co., 401 U.S. 424, footnote 3).

The Supreme Court said that, even though the test requirements were applied equally to Whites and Blacks, and the employer appeared to act without *intent* to discriminate, the *impact* of the company's policy was discriminatory. The Court reasoned that more Blacks than Whites did not meet the test standard because of the inferior education provided Blacks in North Carolina, rather than because they lacked the intelligence to perform the job.

The Court further noted that neither of the tests "was directed or intended to measure the ability to learn to perform a particular job or category of jobs." They were adopted "without meaningful study of their relationship to job-performance ability." This lack of a relationship between test performance and job perform-ance was illustrated by the fact that employees hired before 1955 were not re-quired to have a high school diploma. Thus, it was not reasonable to assume that such employees would have achieved the median test score of high school gradu-ates. Nevertheless, such employees performed satisfactorily and were promoted before the testing policy began.

The Use of Intelligence Tests in Employment: Validity Generalization and Score Conversion

The Court's decision in *Griggs* made clear that tests used in employment would have to demonstrate that they measured job-related abilities. Proving this relation-ship requires validity studies. Such studies are supposed to show that scores on a given test bear a relationship to relevant criteria, such as job training or perform-ance. Validity studies can be time-consuming and costly. Performance criteria have to be developed for the different jobs, adequately large samples of workers for different jobs have to be located, the workers must be tested, and then statistical studies must be carried out to determine the relationship of their test scores to the job performance criteria.

Because of the time and cost involved, many private employers abandoned ability and intelligence testing in hiring following the *Griggs* decision (Sharf, 1988). Instead, many of them relied on levels of educational attainment—basically, the number of years of schooling. There were some good reasons for doing so, besides avoidance of legal battles. Some research (e.g., Jencks, 1972) has indicated that people with similar amounts of schooling who enter similar occupations achieve at similar levels (as measured by income). That is, despite differences in measured mental abilities or grades received, if two individuals manage to get the same amount of schooling, they generally achieve at similar levels (Jencks, 1972). One possible explanation for this is that not only measured cognitive abilities, but social and other nonmeasured skills are important to job success. Thus, if an individual who performs less well on traditional measures can still manage to get through school, the individual may have what it takes to do well within an organization.

Though the Court's decision put a damper on private employers' use of mental tests, the U.S. Government was unaffected. It had been exempted from the provisions of Title VII. Therefore, it continued using intelligence and other aptitude tests on a widespread basis in the military and in the U.S. Employment Service (USES). The latter is a governmental agency that has hundreds of local offices. USES assists in making job placements for both public- and private-sector jobs.

Beginning in 1947, USES administered the General Aptitude Test Battery (GATB) to job seekers in order to assist its staff members in providing vocational counseling and making job placements. The test consists of 12 timed subtests that encompass numerical, verbal, and spatial problems, as well as tests of manual and finger dexterity. Between the late 1940s and the early 1980s, the test had been subjected to some 750 validity studies. These revealed relationships between GATB test results and performance (usually measured by supervisor ratings) in about 500 different kinds of jobs (Hartigan & Wigdor, 1989).

This large number of studies made it possible to carry out a validity generalization study of the GATB in the early 1980s. Validity generalization is a type of meta-analysis. It uses statistical techniques to combine and analyze the results from many validation studies in order to extrapolate from them the validity of a test for jobs that have not been examined (Hartigan & Wigdor, 1989). The results of this investigation indicated that the GATB had a mean validity of .5 for 12,000 kinds of jobs. This correlation meant the test seemed to predict job performance reasonably well for virtually every kind of job in the American economy (Hunter & Schmidt, 1983; Schmidt & Hunter, 1981). (But see Levin, 1989, for a critique of the methods used to reach this conclusion.)

This finding sparked a renewed interest in general intelligence, or *g* (Hartigan & Wigdor, 1989). If a test could be generalizable to so many different types of jobs, it must measure some basic attribute that can be applied in many kinds of tasks. This basic attribute was thought of as *g*. It now appeared that tests that measured *g* could meet the conditions established by *Griggs*—namely, that an employment test must prove relevant for job performance. Thus, it was once again possible to argue that intelligence tests should be used to evaluate potential employees.

Validity generalization results encouraged some researchers and policy makers to assert that not only should intelligence tests be used, but they should be used in a strictly meritocratic fashion. Arguments for meritocratic hiring based on tests were advanced not only on the ground of fairness, but also on the ground of national interest. Some investigators have claimed that hiring entry-level applicants with the best scores would result in higher national productivity and a stronger economy (Gottfredson, 1986, 1988; Hunter & Hunter, 1984; Hunter & Schmidt, 1983; Schmidt, 1988; Schmidt & Hunter, 1981; Sharf, 1988).

However, some of these same investigators acknowledge that this strictly meritocratic use of intelligence and ability tests could have drastic social consequences (e.g., Hunter & Hunter, 1984; Schmidt, 1988). As discussed in Chapter 3, African Americans, on average, score one standard deviation lower on such tests than do Whites. On average, Hispanics and Native Americans also score lower than Whites. If the GATB or other mental tests were used in a strictly meritocratic way, then many minority job seekers would not be referred for employment by USES (Hartigan & Wigdor, 1989).

To avoid the dilemma of excluding many minority job seekers and to promote equal employment opportunity, USES did not actually refer people on a strictly meritocratic basis. Instead, it converted test scores to percentile scores within three categories: Black, Hispanic, and "other." Thus, to take a theoretical example, a White applicant with a score of 90, a Hispanic applicant with a score of 85, and a Black applicant with a score of 80 might each be in the 90th percentile within their respective groups. In this way, the highest ranking people within each of these groups would be referred before lower-ranking people within each group.

Yet, this approach generated controversy (Kilborn, 1991). In the 1980s and continuing into the 1990s, many efforts formerly viewed as fostering equal opportunity for members of minority groups frequently came under attack for reverse discrimination. (That is, they were criticized for selecting minority job seekers over putatively more qualified White job seekers.) The USES score conversion was similarly attacked by the Department of Justice in 1986 (Delahunty, 1988). The Departments of Labor and Justice agreed to limit the GATB referral system, and the National Academy of Sciences convened a group of experts to study this collision between meritocracy and equal opportunity (Hartigan & Wigdor, 1989).

Among other issues, the experts found that the earlier validity generalization of the GATB overestimated the relationship between the test score and job performance. USES claimed a mean .5 validity. The experts found the test averaged only .25 validity with performance ratings. Furthermore, in a subgroup of 78 validity studies that included relatively large sample sizes (50 or more minority and nonminority workers), and were thus likely to give truer estimates, the correlations varied by race. The correlation between test results and supervisor ratings for Blacks was .12; for nonminorities it was .19. (The committee pointed out that measures of job performance might be biased. Most of these performance criteria were supervisor ratings, and most of the supervisors were White.)

The low correlations between test results and job performance criteria indicate that selection based on GATB scores often yields "false negatives." That is, it erroneously excludes people who would be qualified to do the job. Given the lower correlation for Blacks, more errors in selection befall that group. This finding led the investigating committee to recommend the use of score conversions "so that able minority workers have approximately the same chances of referral as able majority workers" (Hartigan & Wigdor, 1989, p. 7).

In general, the committee supported the continued use of the GATB (Hartigan & Wigdor, 1989). For a time, however, it appeared that the test would be abandoned altogether.[1] Its continued use was bolstered by problems associated with selection in the absence of tests (Hawk, personal communication, 1993).

It is important to realize that even though the GATB and all tests are imperfect, scrapping the test would create other selection problems. No other method of selection has proven to be any less biased than testing. For example, interview results are notoriously biased in favor of the beautiful and against "the aesthetically challenged" (Hawk, personal communication, 1993). Rather than abandoning the GATB, efforts were undertaken to modify it along lines proposed by the committee. Among other things, modifications are aimed at improving test reporting to make clear how the GATB test scores are derived.

What Intelligence Tests Tell Us About Individuals in the Workplace

Going beyond social controversy and technical issues, what information relevant to the workplace do intelligence tests yield? A question that would have sprung to the mind of the first intelligence tester, Francis Galton, is: Do the tests predict "eminence"? (See Chapter 3.) Scholarship on this subject provides mixed results (e.g., see Gifford, 1989; Jencks, 1977; Jensen, 1980).

As noted in Chapter 3, intelligence tests do correlate fairly highly (.50–.70) with occupational status (Cronbach, 1990; Gottfredson, 1986; Jensen, 1980). In other words, high scores help to predict whether one will become a doctor, lawyer, or scientist (Gottfredson, 1986; Jensen, 1980). However, tests are not very good at predicting how well one performs in one's job—whether one becomes truly eminent in the field. As we noted earlier in this chapter, on average correlations between test scores and job performance are in the range of .20 to .25.

It is worth noting that correlations between test scores and job performance vary by job type. Correlations for people who work in sales, or with machinery (Jensen, 1980), are typically quite low (in the range of .0–.19). There are even negative correlations between test scores and job performance for work that requires primarily simple repetition (Jensen, 1980). (This may indicate that high intelligence is something of a handicap in a repetitive job.) In contrast, the correlations

---

[1] Federal Register Notice, July 24, 1990, p. 30162; *New York Times,* January 14, 1991, p. 1.

between test scores and performance are highest for managers and professionals. For such workers, the correlations may be as high as .47.

That intelligence tests predict the performance of professionals better than those doing other kinds of work is not surprising. Intelligence tests are sometimes said to measure "academic intelligence" (Neisser, 1976). If one's job more closely resembles and draws on academic work, then the correlation between tests and such work ought to be higher. For similar reasons, intelligence tests also correlate more strongly with success in job training programs (in which there is typically some academic component), than with actual job performance (Jensen, 1980).

One thing that intelligence tests usually cannot reveal is how well those who are rejected based on their test scores might have fared (Hunt, 1995). In ordinary circumstances, there is no opportunity to assess the training or job performance of those who are not selected on the basis of test scores. However, a chance to study such a phenomenon arose not long ago in the U.S. military.

The U.S. military uses the Armed Services Vocational Aptitude Battery (ASVAB) to screen and categorize tens of thousands of recruits each year. The test seeks to measure aptitudes for an array of technical and vocational areas. In addition, four subtests of the ASVAB, known as the Armed Forces Qualifications Tests, serve as a measure of general intelligence and training potential.

Because of an error in the norming of the ASVAB, over 200,000 men, whose scores should have disqualified them, were mistakenly admitted into the military between 1976 and 1980 (Gifford, 1989). Again because of the norming error, many of the men were assigned to more demanding training programs than their scores would have ordinarily permitted. Despite test scores indicating that many of these enlistees would not succeed, the "on-the-job 'failure rate'" for this group of men was only slightly higher than for recruits with acceptable test scores (Gifford, 1989, p. 23). Nevertheless, there were indications that their functioning was not as high as those who would have been placed in the job if ASVAB had been correctly normed. For example, promotions among this group were slower, and they had more frequent, minor disciplinary problems (Hunt, personal communication, 1993). Still, they managed to do jobs that would have ordinarily been deemed beyond their ability level.

Probes into the reasons for this outcome underscore the complex nature of success in work (Gifford, 1989). As we noted, measured intelligence does correlate at least somewhat with performance in most jobs (.20–.25). However, numerous other factors play an important role as well. These we turn to next.

Beyond Intelligence in Employment

The committee that investigated the GATB noted ". . . there are many characteristics of importance to actual job performance that tests do not assess, and others that tests do not assess very well" (Hartigan & Wigdor, 1989, p. 4). If intelligence tests can explain at most about 22% of the variance in job success, what other features of individuals and of job settings may help to explain the rest?

Practical Intelligence

According to Sternberg, intelligence tests seek to detect and measure *g* using "well-defined" problems. Such problems are typified by standardized test questions: they have only a single answer, and one basic method for solving them. They require little information beyond what is presented in the problem, are not closely linked to everyday experience, and are generally not intrinsically interesting (Sternberg & Wagner, 1993).

In the real world, however, one rarely confronts problems that are so well defined. Rather, one must grapple with ill-defined, practical problems. Such problems are not clearly presented but must be identified and structured. For example, one may only know that paper pulp is spilling over the top of a vat. The reason for this spill may be too much water, a clogged pipe, or something else entirely. Practical problems may have many workable solutions (e.g., stop the flow of water, drain off the incoming water, unplug the clogged pipe). As this example illustrates, practical problems are related to, or "embedded," in everyday, purposeful events, and they require personal interest and involvement (Scribner, 1986; Sternberg & Wagner, 1993).

Sternberg and others argue that one needs practical intelligence to cope with such problems (Sternberg, 1988; Sternberg & Wagner, 1993; Wagner & Sternberg, 1986). Unlike *g*, which some researchers (e.g., Anderson, 1992; Eysenck, 1986; Jensen, 1991), ascribe to innate characteristics of the nervous system, practical intelligence is based on often tacit knowledge of oneself, others, tools, and various cultural domains.

The distinction between practical intelligence and *g* may be best illustrated by the words used to describe people strong and weak in these dimensions. Sternberg notes that those strong in *g* are called "experts" or "intelligent." Those weak in this area are called "stupid." In contrast, those strong in practical intelligence are called "shrewd." People lacking practical intelligence are called "naive" or "foolish" (Sternberg & Wagner, 1993, p. 2).

In essence, practical intelligence amounts to possessing and applying commonsense understandings to the problems we find in work and the everyday world. As the anthropologist Clifford Geertz (1983) has noted:

> this . . . has less to do with intellect, narrowly defined, than we generally imagine. As Saul Bellow, thinking of certain sorts of government advisors and certain sorts of radical writers, has remarked, the world is full of high-IQ morons. (p. 76)

Working Styles

A number of researchers have identified characteristics that are related to an individual's ability to realize his or her potential in the work world. These characteristics might be termed "working styles." They influence the way people apply their intelligence on the job.

For example, Sternberg (1988) notes that some people tend to persevere too long at a task. There are times when a problem is not tractable to one's abilities or methods, and it's best to let it go. Attention can then be turned to other areas in which it may be possible to achieve success. On the opposite end of the spectrum, many people don't persevere long enough. As we saw when we examined expertise, it takes many years of practice in a domain to achieve success (Hayes, 1985; Posner, 1988). Similarly, success at work may be related to the tenure of a working group. Deming (1982) has argued that it may take 10 to 15 years for a group of employees to know and maximize the strengths of the group's members. In the United States, such tenure is far rarer than it is in Japan.

Another working-style issue concerns productivity. Success in one's career is related to sheer output (Simonton, 1984, 1988). The more one produces, the more likely one will produce noteworthy products. Thus, compared with those who prefer mostly to ruminate, those with a "product orientation" (Sternberg, 1988, p. 299) have an edge on achieving success in their work.

A final item in the working-style category is a sense of dedication. Researchers have found that a person's dedication, sense of responsibility, and dependability, as measured by standardized instruments, have a substantial correlation with job performance (Schmidt & Hunter, 1992).

Motivation

Several investigators, including some who have argued that intelligence is the best predictor of job performance (e.g., Jensen, 1993; Schmidt & Hunter, 1992), make a strong case for the role of motivation in job success (McClelland, 1993; Sternberg, 1985). As Sternberg (1985) has put it, a lack of motivation

> is the most serious problem in an employment situation. If I have an employee who lacks certain abilities, I can usually find some kind of work for him to do. But if the person lacks motivation, then there is nothing he will get done in the way I want or in the time span that I am willing to allocate to a given task. (p. 297)

Motivation to do a good job may have been one of the keys to the success of the low-scoring military recruits (Gifford, 1989). Some were learning skills that would help them survive in life-threatening situations; they (and other recruits) may have seen the military as the way to secure educational and job opportunities that were hard to come by in civilian life.

Motivation is often divided into two distinct forms (Amabile, 1983; Csikszentmihalyi, 1988a, 1988b; Sternberg, 1988). *Extrinsic* motivation involves a desire for external rewards. Most of us work at least in part because we are extrinsically motivated by money. Fame, awards, and recognition by one's peers are other forms of extrinsic motivation. Researchers have found that extrinsic motivation may hinder one's long-term development of skill. If extrinsic rewards are the predominant reason for trying to meet challenging circumstances, once the extrinsic rewards cease, effort often decreases. Similarly, the introduction of extrinsic rewards has been found to hamper creativity (Amabile, 1983).

Intrinsic motivation is in play when a person pursues some task or work because it is interesting and "rewarding in and of itself" (Csikszentmihalyi, 1988a, p. 7). Intrinsic motivation is the stuff of legend in the arts: Emily Dickinson's prolific poetry writing in the absence of publications; van Gogh's pursuit of painting in the absence of sales. Yet it is also found in a wide range of work—for example, among farmers in traditional communities (Delle Fave & Massimini, 1988) and managers of big urban enterprises (LeFebre, 1988).

According to Csikszentmihalyi, tasks that are instrinsically motivating share certain structural and emotional characteristics (Csikszentmihalyi, 1988a, 1988b, 1990). On the structural front, intrinsically motivating work demands a level of challenge that is in balance with a person's current skills (Csikszentmihalyi, 1988c). When this balance occurs, a person gains pleasure from the work and tends to keep at it. Csikszentmihalyi describes this as a state of "flow." In contrast, if a task is too easy for a person's abilities, he or she becomes bored. The opposite situation—work that demands skills far beyond what one possesses—creates anxiety (Csikszentmihalyi, 1988a, 1988b, 1990).

An intrinsically motivating pursuit creates a dynamic conducive to the development of skill. Because a person enjoys the activity, he or she becomes engaged in it and continues at it over time. As a result, the person's skills increase. However, with increased skills, the same task may become boring. To maintain proper "flow" and avoid boredom, more demanding challenges must be sought to meet the higher level of skill (Csikszentmihalyi, 1988a, 1988c, 1990).

The flow model suggests that the kind of repetitive work fostered under Taylorism creates boredom and impedes skill development. (In contrast, the Japanese worker moves to increasing challenges via QCCs and rotates among challenges on the production floor.) Ultimately, greater productivity may depend less on standardizing tasks, and more on creating intrinsically motivating situations so that workers become more skilled. Workers' zone of proximal development (see Chapter 7) needs to be found and exploited continually.

Collaboration

The ability to collaborate with others is vital in many work settings. For example, one hypothesis concerning the success of many of the low-scoring recruits mentioned above is that most work in the military is done in small groups. The ASVAB test only measured individual performance (Gifford, 1989) and thus may not predict performance that occurs in collaboration.

Similarly, arguments that test-based hiring would markedly enhance the national economy (e.g., Gottfredson, 1986; 1988; Hunter & Schmidt, 1983) are regarded as simplistic by some critics. As one writer put it, ". . . the sum of individual efforts may not add up to the whole of productive outcomes . . . (Levin,

1988, p. 400). Productivity and the quality of output often depend on how well people work together within an organization (Argyris, 1982; Levin, 1988).

When people's collaborative skills are supported and they are given more intrinsically motivating tasks, their ability to be productive can increase. This point is illustrated in the case of a General Motors (GM) auto plant in Fremont, California. The plant was closed in the early 1980s because of poor productivity and quality. However, not long after, it reopened as a joint venture between GM and Toyota. The joint venture rehired 80% of the former GM employees, but organized them into small problem-solving teams. Under this system, productivity increased by 50%, rising to levels reached in auto plants in Japan. Absenteeism plunged from 25% to about 4%. In addition, the quality of the cars also got high marks from consumers and professionals. Given that most of the old workers were rehired, these changes occurred with a workforce whose average IQ was likely little different from that of the previously unproductive plant (Levin, 1988; Reich, 1991). What differed was the context in which the workers carried out their tasks.

Summary

In this final chapter, we have looked at intelligence as it relates to various aspects of work. We first linked intelligence to the notion of "skill in a cultural medium" (Olson, 1974, p. 61). Then we considered how work skills develop in apprenticeship situations, where instruction is largely informal and skill is acquired primarily in the course of observing and participating in work that is valued by the surrounding community. We next explored how high-level skill develops among experts and how their thought processes differ from those of novices. Essential to expertise is a large and well-organized base of knowledge in a particular discipline. This knowledge is acquired through years of practice, during which individuals actively work to enhance their skills. Recent research in the area of expertise indicates that experts are flexible thinkers who apply different problem-solving strategies, depending on the task and their degree of experience with it.

Because people rarely carry out their work alone, we considered skill in the context of work organizations. We focused on how the level of skill demanded of various workers has changed over time, with the implementation of new technologies in the workplace. As craft production gave way to industrial production and scientific management, many workers lost skill and were left to do repetitive tasks requiring little thought. However, with computer technology and an increasingly global economy, it is expected that intellectual abilities, such as the capacity for abstraction, inference, and procedural reasoning, will be increasingly needed for work that is intellectually and financially rewarding (Reich, 1991; Zuboff, 1988).

The issue of intelligence testing of workers seems especially pertinent in light of the growing need for intellectual skills on the job. However, as we saw in the case of the U.S. Employment Service, such tests present both social and technical dilemmas. On the technical front, the validity of one such test, the GATB, for a variety of jobs does not appear to be high enough to predict with reasonable certainty which applicants will perform the job best and which will do so adequately. On the social front, even if a test's validity were high (as initially claimed for the GATB), strictly meritocratic use of tests for hiring purposes will exclude many minority applicants. Yet, a failure to use the GATB in a strictly meritocratic fashion has led to charges of reverse discrimination. The use of intelligence tests in the workplace, as in the educational realm, is likely to remain fraught with controversy.

Some have argued that, though intelligence matters in job performance, other characteristics, such as motivation and an ability to collaborate, are also crucial in the work world. Yet, emphasis on variables associated with individuals, such as intelligence, motivation or dependability, cannot alone explain job success. Social factors associated with the work environment clearly matter: people must have opportunities to use and develop their abilities at work. But even such opportunities may not be enough. The development of abilities needed within the increasingly complex work world may extend beyond workplace opportunities and spread ever deeper into the social sphere. As Robert Reich (1991) has noted, the possibility for widespread attainment of the intellectual skills needed in our technological age may "rest heavily on education and training, as well as nutrition and health care sufficient to allow such learning to occur" (Reich, 1991, p. 249).

Concluding Note

We have traveled a long distance in this book, from sensory measures of intelligence and the structure of the brain, on the one hand, to the way in which students learn in school and adults perform at the workplace, on the other. In a way, this lengthy scholarly journey is inevitable, because intelligence is a complex and multifaceted topic. It cannot be understood unless one draws on different disciplines and takes into account a variety of perspectives.

Intelligence is an important scientific construct, but its great interest among the general public comes from the consensus that intellect—however defined—matters tremendously for the individual and for society. It is well to remember, in this context, that practical considerations have never been far from the minds of individuals who study and measure intelligence. Binet was motivated by the desire to identify schoolchildren who might need help; Yerkes and the other World War I Army psychologists wanted to identify soldiers who could carry out leadership roles; as we have seen, society also turns to test-makers for insights about whom to admit to college or to assign to a given position in the workplace. We have shown that none of these initiatives is devoid of controversy, and we can safely predict that, as the study of intelligence continues, the aura of controversy will continue as well. We hope that the information provided in this book, alongside any intrinsic interest it might have, will help readers to think in a more sophisticated way about these topics of great moment and to participate more thoughtfully in decisions that affect us all.

Suggested Readings

Ericsson, K. A., & Smith, J. (Eds.). (1991). *Toward a general theory of expertise: Prospects and limits.* Cambridge: Cambridge University Press.

Gifford, B. R. (1989). *Test policy and the politics of opportunity allocation: The workplace and the law.* Boston: Kluwer.

Schön, D. (1983). *The reflective practitioner: How professionals think in action.* New York: Basic Books.

Sternberg, R. J., & Wagner, R. K. (Eds.). (1986). *Practical intelligence: Nature and origins of competence in the everyday world.* Cambridge: Cambridge University Press.

Zuboff, S. (1988). *In the age of the smart machine: The future of work and power.* New York: Basic Books.

References

Allen, C. (1992, January 13). Gray matter, black-and-white controversy. *Insight,* 2–10, 32–36.

Amabile, T. M. (1983). *The social psychology of creativity.* New York: Springer-Verlag.

American Educational Research Association, American Psychological Association, & National Council on Measurement in Education. (1985). *Standards for educational and psychological testing.* Washington, DC: American Psychological Association.

Anderson, M. (1986). Inspection time and IQ in young children. *Personality and Individual Differences, 7,* 677–686.

Anderson, M. (1992). *Intelligence and development: A cognitive theory.* Oxford, England: Blackwell.

Angier, R. P., MacPhail, A. H., Rogers, D. C., Stone, C. L., & Brigham, C. C. (1926). The scholastic aptitude test of the college entrance examination board. In College Entrance Examination Board (Ed.), *The work of the college entrance examination board 1901–1926.* Boston: Ginn and Company.

Ankney, C. D. (1992). Sex differences in relative brain size: The mismeasure of women, too? *Intelligence, 16,* 329–336.

Anzai, Y. (1991). Learning and use of representations for physics expertise. In K. A. Ericsson & J. Smith (Eds.), *Toward a general theory of expertise: Prospects and limits* (pp. 64–92). Cambridge: Cambridge University Press.

Aoki, M. (1990). A new paradigm of work organization and co-ordination? Lessons from Japanese experience. In S. A. Marglin & J. B. Schor (Eds.), *The golden age of capitalism* (pp. 267–293). Oxford: Clarendon Press.

Argyris, C. (1982). *Reasoning, learning, and action: Individual and organizational.* San Francisco: Jossey-Bass.

Argyris, C., & Schön, D. A. (1978). *Organizational learning: A theory of action perspective.* Reading, MA: Addison-Wesley.

Ariès, P. (1962). *Centuries of childhood.* London: Jonathan Cape.

Aristotle. (1963). *Posterior analytics.* In R. Bambrough (Ed.). *The philosophy of Aristotle.* New York: New American Library.

Arlin, P. K. (1984). Adolescent and adult thought: A structural interpretation. In M. L. Commons, F. A. Richards, & C. Armon (Eds.), *Beyond formal operations: Late adolescent and adult cognitive development.* New York: Praeger.

Arlin, P. K. (1989). Problem solving and problem finding in young artists and young scientists. In M. L. Commons, J. D. Sinnott, F. A. Richards, & C. Armon (Eds.), *Adult development: Vol. 1. Comparisons and applications of developmental models.* New York: Praeger.

Baillargeon, R. (1987). Object permanence in 3.5 and 4.5 month old infants. *Developmental Psychology, 23,* 655–664.

Barr, A., & Feigenbaum, E.A. (1982). *The handbook of artificial intelligence* (Vol. 1-3). Stanford, CA: Hueristech Press/William Kaufman.

Basso, A., DeRenzi, E., Faglioni, P., Scotti, G., & Spinnler, H. (1973). Neuropsychological evidence for the existence of cerebral areas critical to the performance of intelligence tasks. *Brain, 96* (Part IV), 715-728.

Bastian, A., Fruchter, N., Gittell, M., Greer, C., & Haskins, K. (1985). *Choosing equality.* Philadelphia: Temple University Press.

Bateson, M. C. (1994). *Peripheral visions: Learning along the way.* New York: HarperCollins.

Berry, J. W. (1974). Radical cultural relativism and the concept of intelligence. In J. W. Berry & P. R. Dasen (Eds.), *Culture and cognition: Readings in cross-cultural psychology* (pp. 225-259). London: Methuen.

Berry, J. W. (1984). Toward a universal psychology of cognitive competence. *International Journal of Psychology, 19,* 335-361.

Berry, J. W. (1986). Cognitive values and cognitive competence among the bricoleurs. In J. W. Berry, S. H. Irvine, & E. B. Hunt (Eds.), *Indigenous cognition: Functioning in cultural context.* Dordrecht, Netherlands: Nijhoff.

Berry, J. W., & Irvine, S. W. (1986). Bricolage: Savages do it daily. In R. J. Sternberg & R. K. Wagner (Eds.), *Practical intelligence: Nature and origins of competence in the everyday world* (pp. 271-306). New York: Cambridge University Press.

Binet, A., & Simon, T. (1973). *The development of intelligence in children* (*The Binet-Simon Scale*) (Elizabeth S. Kite, Trans.). New York: The Arno Press. (Original work published 1916)

Block, N. J., & Dworkin, G. (Eds.). (1976). *The IQ controversy: Critical readings.* New York: Pantheon Books.

Bobrow, D. G. (1994). Artificial intelligence in perspective. Cambridge, MA: MIT Press/Bradford Books.

Boden, M. A. (1987). *Artificial intelligence and natural man* (2nd ed.). New York: Basic Books.

Boden, M. A. (1989). *Artificial intelligence in psychology: Interdisciplinary essays.* Cambridge, MA: MIT Press.

Boring, E. (1950). *A history of experimental psychology.* New York: Appleton-Century-Crofts.

Borke, H. (1975). Piaget's mountains revisited: Changes in the egocentric landscape. *Developmental Psychology, 11,* 240-243.

Born, R. (1987). *Artificial intelligence: The case against.* London: Croom Helm.

Bornstein, M., & Sigman, M. (1986). Continuity in mental development from infancy. *Child Development, 57*(2), 251-274.

Boster, M. (1991). The information economy model applied to biological similarity judgment. In L. B. Resnick, J. M. Levine, & S. D. Teasley (Eds.), *Perspectives on socially shared cognition.* Washington, DC: American Psychological Association.

Bouchard, T. J. (1983). Do environmental similarities explain the similarity in intelligence of identical twins reared apart? *Intelligence, 7,* 175-184.

Bouchard, T. J. (1991, February). *Identical twins reared apart: What they reveal about human intelligence.* Paper presented at the American Association for the Advancement of Science, Washington, DC.

Bouchard, T. J., Lykken, D., McGue, M., Segal, N., & Tellegen, A. (1990). Sources of human psychological difference: The Minnesota study of twins reared apart. *Science, 250,* 223-228.

Bouchard, T. J., & McGue, M. (1981). Familial studies of intelligence: A review. *Science, 212,* 1055–1059.

Bouchard, T. J., & Propping, P. (1993). *Twins as a tool of behavioral genetics: Report of the Dahlem Workshop on what are the mechanisms mediating the genetic and environmental determinants of behavior?* Chichester, England: Wiley.

Bowen, J. (1972). *A history of Western education* (Vol. 1). London: Methuen.

Brainerd, C. J. (1978). The stage question in cognitive-developmental theory. *The Behavioral and Brain Sciences, 2,* 172–213.

Brand, C. R. (1993). Cognitive abilities: Current theoretical issues. In T. Bouchard & P. Propping (Eds.), *Twins as a tool of behavioral genetics* (pp. 17–32). Chichester, England: Wiley.

Brigham, C. (1923). *A study of American intelligence.* Princeton, NJ: Princeton University Press.

Broadbent, D. E. (1958). *Perception and communication.* Elmsford, NY: Pergamon.

Brody, N. (1992). *Intelligence.* San Diego: Academic Press.

Bronfenbrenner, U. (1979). *The ecology of human development: Experiments by nature and design.* Cambridge, MA: Harvard University Press.

Brooks, L. R. (1968). Spatial and verbal components of the act of recall. *Canadian Journal of Psychology, 22,* 349–350.

Bruner, J. S., Olver, R. R., & Greenfield, P. M. (1966). *Studies in cognitive growth.* New York: Wiley.

Bryant, P. (1974). *Perception and understanding in young children.* New York: Basic Books.

Burt, C. (1947). *Mental and scholastic tests.* (2nd ed.). London: Staples.

Burtt, E. A. (Ed.). (1939). *The English philosophers from Bacon to Mill.* New York: Modern Library.

Butler, J. S. (1989). Test scores and evaluation: The military as data. In B. R. Gifford (Ed.), *Test policy and the politics of opportunity allocation: The workplace and the law* (pp. 265–291). Boston: Kluwer Academic Publishers.

Caine, A. F. (1959). *A study and comparison of the West African "bush" school and the southern Sotha circumcision school.* Master of Arts Thesis, Northwestern University, Evanston, IL.

Callahan, R. E. (1962). *Education and the cult of efficiency.* Chicago: University of Chicago Press.

Campbell, J. (1989). *The improbable machine: What the upheavals in artificial intelligence research reveal about how the mind really works.* New York: Simon & Schuster.

Capon, N., & Kuhn, D. (1979). Logical reasoning in the supermarket: Adult females' use of proportional reasoning strategies in an everyday context. *Developmental Psychology, 15,* 450–452.

Capron, C., & Duyme, M. (1989). Assessment of effects of socioeconomic status on IQ in a full cross-fostering study. *Nature, 340,* 552–553.

Caramazza, A., McCloskey, M., & Green, B. (1981). Naive beliefs in "sophisticated" subjects: Misconceptions about trajectories of objects. *Cognition, 9*(2), 117–123.

Cardon, L. R., Fulker, D., DeFries, J. C., & Plomin, R. (1992). Multivariate genetic analysis of specific cognitive abilities in the Colorado Adoption Project at age 7. *Intelligence, 16,* 383–400.

Carey, S. (1985). *Conceptual change in childhood.* Cambridge, MA: MIT Press.

Carey, S. (1991). Knowledge acquisition: Enrichment or conceptual change? In S. Carey & R. Gelman (Eds.), *The epigenesis of mind: Essays on biology and cognition.* Hillsdale, NJ: Erlbaum.

Carey, S., & Spelke, E. (1994). Domain-specific knowledge and conceptual change. In L. Hirshfield & S. Gelman (Ed.), *Mapping the mind* (pp. 169–200). New York: Cambridge University Press.

Carpenter, P. A., Just, M. A., & Shell, P. (1990). What one intelligence test measures: A theoretical account of the processing in the Raven Progressive Matrices Test. *Psychological Review, 97,* 404–431.

Carroll, J. (1993). *Human cognitive abilities: A survey of factor-analytic studies.* New York: Cambridge University Press.

Case, R. (1985). *Intellectual development: Birth to adulthood.* Orlando: Academic Press.

Case, R. (1992). *The mind's staircase.* Hillsdale, NJ: Erlbaum.

Case, R., & Griffin, S. (1990). Child cognitive development: The role of central conceptual structures in the development of scientific and social thought. *Developmental Psychology, 26,* 193–230.

Cattell, R. B. (1963). The personality and motivation of the researcher from measurements of contemporaries and from bibliography. In C. W. Taylor & F. Barron (Eds.), *Scientific creativity: Its recognition and development* (pp. 119–131). New York: Wiley.

Cattell, R. B. (1987). *Intelligence: Its structure, growth and action.* Amsterdam, The Netherlands: Elsevier.

Ceci, S. J. (1990). *On intelligence . . . more or less: A bio-ecological treatise on intellectual development.* Englewood Cliffs, NJ: Prentice Hall.

Ceci, S. J., & Liker, J. K. (1986a). Academic and non-academic intelligence: An experimental separation. In R. J. Sternberg & R. K. Wagner (Eds.), *Practical intelligence: Origins of competence in the everyday world.* New York: Cambridge University Press.

Ceci, S. J., & Liker, J. K. (1986b). A day at the races: A study of IQ, expertise, and cognitive complexity. *Journal of Experimental Psychology: General, 115,* 255–266.

Ceci, S. J., & Liker, J. K. (1988). Stalking the IQ-expertise relation: When the critics go fishing. *Journal of Experimental Psychology: General, 117,* 96–100.

Ceci, S. J., Ramey, S. L., & Ramey, C. T. (1990). Framing intellectual assessment in terms of a person-process-context model. *Educational Psychologist, 25*(3/4), 269–291.

Ceci, S. J., & Roazzi, A. (1994). The effect of context on cognition: Postcards from Brazil. In R. J. Sternberg & R. K. Wagner (Eds.), *Mind in context: Interactionist perspectives on human intelligence* (pp. 74–101). Cambridge, MA: Cambridge University Press.

Changeux, J. P. (1985). *Neuronal man.* (Laurence Carey, Trans.) New York: Pantheon Books.

Chapman, M. (1988). *Constructive evolution: Origins and development of Piaget's thought.* Cambridge: Cambridge University Press.

Charness, N. (1991). Expertise in chess: The balance between knowledge and search. In K. A. Ericsson & J. Smith (Eds.), *Toward a general theory of expertise: Prospects and limits* (pp. 39–63). Cambridge: Cambridge University Press.

Chase, W. G., & Simon, H. A. (1973). Perception in chess. *Cognitive Psychology, 4,* 55–81.

Chi, M. T. H., Feltovich, P., & Glaser, R. (1981). Categorization and representation of physics problems by experts and novices. *Cognitive Science, 5,* 121–152.

Chi, M. T. H., Glaser, R., & Farr, M. J. (Eds.). (1988). *The nature of expertise.* Hillsdale, NJ: Erlbaum.

Chi, M. T. H., Glaser, R., & Rees, E. (1982). Expertise in problem solving. In R. J. Sternberg (Ed.), *Advances in the psychology of human intelligence* (Vol. 1, pp. 7–75). Hillsdale, NJ: Erlbaum.

Chomsky, N. (1956, September 12). *Three models of language.* Paper presented at the Symposium on Information Theory. Massachusetts Institute of Technology, Cambridge, Massachusetts.

Chomsky, N. (1957). *Syntactic structures.* The Hague: Mouton.

Chomsky, N. (1980). *Rules and representations.* New York: Columbia University Press.

Clarke, A. M., & Clarke, A. D. B. (1976). *Early experience: Myth and evidence.* New York: Free Press.

Cleverley, J. (1985). *The schooling of China.* Sydney: Allen & Unwin.

Cole, M., & Cole, S. (1989). *The development of children.* New York: Freeman.

Cole, M., & Means, B. (1981). *Comparative studies of how people think: An introduction.* Cambridge, MA: Harvard University Press.

Cole, M., & Scribner, S. (1974). *Culture and thought: A psychological introduction.* New York: Wiley.

Collier, G. (1994). *Social origins of mental ability.* New York: Wiley.

Commons, M. L., Armon, C., Richards, F. A., Schrader, D. E., Farrell, E. W., Tappan, M. B., & Bauer, N. F. (1989). A multidomain study of adult development. In M. L. Commons, J. D. Sinnot, F. A. Richards, & D. Armon (Eds.), *Adult development: Vol. 1. Comparisons and applications of developmental models.* New York: Praeger.

Connell, W. F. (1980). *A history of education in the twentieth century world.* New York: Teachers College Press.

Cooper, L. A., & Regan, D. T. (1982). Attention, perception, and intelligence. In R. J. Sternberg (Ed.), *Handbook of human intelligence* (pp. 123–169). Cambridge: Cambridge University Press.

Cremin, L. (1982). *American education: The national experience (1783–1876).* New York: Harper & Row.

Crevier, D. (1993). *AI: The tumultuous history of the search for artificial intelligence.* New York: Basic Books.

Cronbach, L. J. (1969). Heredity, environment, and educational policy. *Harvard Educational Review, 39*(2), 338–347.

Cronbach, L. J. (1975). Five decades of public controversy over mental testing. *American Psychologist, 30*(1), 1–14.

Cronbach, L. J. (1989). Construct validation after thirty years. In R. L. Linn (Ed.), *Intelligence: Measurement, theory, and public policy.* Urbana and Chicago: University of Illinois Press.

Cronbach, L. J. (1990). *Essentials of psychological testing.* New York: Harper & Row.

Crouse, J., & Trusheim, D. (1988). The case against the SAT. *The Public Interest, 93,* 97–112.

Crystal, D., Chen, C., Fuligni, A., Stevenson, H., Hsu, C., Ko, H., Kitamura, S., & Kimura, S. (1994). Psychological maladjustment and academic achievement: A cross-cultural study of Japanese, Chinese, and American high school students. *Child Development, 65*(3), 738–753.

Csikszentmihalyi, M. (1988a). Introduction. In M. Csikszentmihalyi & I.S. Csikszentmihalyi (Eds.), *Optimal experience: Psychological studies of flow in consciousness* (pp. 3–14). Cambridge: Cambridge University Press.

Csikszentmihalyi, M. (1988b). Motivation and creativity: Towards a synthesis of structural and energistic approaches. *New ideas in psychology, 6*(2), 159-176.

Csikszentmihalyi, M. (1988c). The flow experience and its significance for human psychology. In M. Csikszentmihalyi & I. S. Csikszentmihalyi (Eds.), *Optimal experience: Psychological studies of flow in consciousness* (pp. 15-35). Cambridge: Cambridge University Press.

Csikszentmihalyi, M. (1990). *Flow: The psychology of optimal experience.* New York: Harper & Row.

Curtis, S. (1977). *Genie: A psycholinguistic study of modern-day "wild child".* New York: Academic Press.

Damasio, A. (1994). *Descartes' error: Emotion, reason, and the human brain.* New York: Putnam.

Damon, W. (1994). *Greater expectations.* New York: Free Press.

Darwin, C. (1964). *On the origin of species.* Cambridge: Harvard University Press. (Original work published 1859)

Darwin, C. (1871). *The descent of man and selection in relation to sex.* New York: Appleton.

Davis, J. (1991). *Artistry lost: U-shaped development in graphic symbolization.* Unpublished doctoral dissertation, Harvard University Graduate School of Education, Cambridge, MA.

Daviss, B. (1992). Robocar: Lean, mean, self-driving machines go cruising the streets of America. *Discover, 13*(7), 68-74.

Dawson, G., & Fischer, K. W. (Eds.). (1994). *Human behavior and the developing brain.* New York: Garland Press.

Deary, I. (1992). Multiple minds. *Science, 259,* 28.

Degler, C. (1991). *In search of human nature.* New York: Oxford University Press.

deGroot, A. D. (1966). Perception and memory versus thought: Some old ideas and recent findings. In B. K. Kleinmuntz (Ed.), *Problem solving* (pp. 19-50). New York: Wiley.

Delahunty, R. J. (1988). Perspectives on within-group scoring. *Journal of Vocational Behavior, 33,* 463-477.

Delle Fave, A., & Massimini, F. (1988). Modernization and the changing contexts of flow in work and leisure. In M. Csikszentmihalyi & I. S. Csikszentmihalyi (Eds.), *Optimal experience: Psychological studies of flow in consciousness* (pp. 193-213). Cambridge: Cambridge University Press.

Demetriou, A. (1990). Structural and developmental relations between formal and postformal capacities: Towards a comprehensive theory of adolescent and adult cognitive development. In M. L. Commons, C. Armon, L. Kohlberg, F. A. Richards, T. A. Grotzer, & J. D. Sinnott (Eds.), *Adult development: Vol 2. Models and methods in the study of adolescent and adult thought.* New York: Praeger.

Deming, W. E. (1982). *Quality, productivity, and competitive position.* Cambridge, MA: MIT Center for Advanced Engineering Study.

Denny, J. P. (1988). Contextualization and differentiation in cross-cultural cognition. In J. W. Berry, S. H. Irvine, & E. B. Hunt (Eds.), *Indigenous cognition: Functioning in cultural context.* Dordrecht, Netherlands: Nijhoff.

DeRenzi, E., Faglioni, P., Savoiardo, M., & Vignolo, L. A. (1966). The influence of aphasia and of the hemispheric side of the cerebral lesion on abstract thinking. *Cortex, 11*(4), 399-420.

Descartes, R. (1969). Discourse on the method of rightly conducting one's reason and seeking truth in the sciences. In M. D. Wilson (Ed.), *The essential Descartes.* New York: New American Library. (Original work published in 1637)

Detterman, D. K., & Spry, K. M. (1988). Is it smart to play the horses? Comment on a day at the races: A study of IQ, expertise, and cognitive complexity (Ceci & Liker, 1986). *Journal of Experimental Psychology: General, 117*(1), 91–95.

Dewdney, (1992). Turing test. *Scientific American, 266(1),* 30.

Diamond, A. (1991). Frontal lobe involvement in cognitive changes during the first year of life. In K. R. Gibson & A. C. Peterson (Eds.), *Brain maturation and cognitive development: Comparative and cross-cultural perspectives* (pp. 127–180). New York: Aldine de Gruyter.

DiSessa, A. (1982). Unlearning Aristotelian physics: A study of knowledge-based learning. *Cognitive Science, 6*(1), 37–75.

Donald, M. (1991). *Origins of the modern mind: Three stages in the evolution of culture and cognition.* Cambridge, MA: Harvard University Press.

Donaldson, M. (1978). *Children's minds.* New York: Norton.

Donchin, E., Karis, D., Bashore, T., Coles, M., & Gratton, G. (1986). Cognitive psychophysiology and human information processing. In M. G. H. Coles, E. Donchin, & S. W. Porges (Eds.), *Psychophysiology: Systems, processes, and applications* (pp. 244–267). New York: Guilford.

Dörner, D., & Schölkopf, J. (1991). Controlling complex systems: Or, expertise as "grandmother's know-how". In K. A. Ericsson & J. Smith (Eds.), *Toward a general theory of expertise: Prospects and limits* (pp. 218–239). Cambridge: Cambridge University Press.

Dweck, C., & Elliott, E. S. (1983). Achievement motivation. In P. H. Mussen (Ed.), *Handbook of child psychology* (Vol. 4). New York: Wiley.

Eames, C., & Eames, R. (1990). *A computer perspective: Background to the computer age* (2nd ed.). Cambridge, MA: Harvard University Press.

Eccles, J. (1965). *The brain and the unity of conscious experience.* Cambridge: Cambridge University Press.

Edmonds, R. (1986). Characteristics of effective schools. In U. Neisser (Eds.), *The school achievement of minority children: New perspectives.* Hillsdale, NJ: Erlbaum.

Elkind, D. (1987). *Miseducation: Preschoolers at risk.* New York: Knopf.

Ericsson, K. A., & Polson, P. G. (1988). A cognitive analysis of exceptional memory for restaurant orders. In M. T. H. Chi, R. Glaser, & M. Farr (Eds.), *The nature of expertise* (pp. 23–70). Hillsdale, NJ: Erlbaum.

Ericsson, K. A., & Smith, J. (1991a). Prospects and limits of the empirical study of expertise: An introduction. In K. A. Anderson & J. Smith (Eds.), *Toward a general theory of expertise: Prospects and limits* (pp. 1–38). Cambridge: Cambridge University Press.

Ericsson, K. A., & Smith, J. (Eds.). (1991b). *Toward a general theory of expertise: Prospects and limits.* Cambridge: Cambridge University Press.

Eysenck, H. J. (1973). *The inequality of man.* London: Temple Smith.

Eysenck, H. J. (1986). The theory of intelligence and the psychophysiology of cognition. In R. J. Sternberg (Ed.), *Advances in the psychology of human intelligence* (Vol. 3, pp. 1–34). Hillsdale, NJ: Erlbaum.

Eysenck, H. J., & Kamin, L. (1981). *The intelligence controversy: H. J. Eysenck versus Leon Kamin.* New York: Wiley.

Fagan, J. F. (1990, December). The paired-comparison paradigm and infant intelligence. *Annals of the New York Academy of Sciences, 608,* 337-364.

Fancher, R. E. (1985). *The intelligence men: Makers of the IQ controversy.* New York: Norton.

Farrand, D. (1926). A brief history of the college entrance examination board. In College Entrance Examination Board (Ed.), *The work of the college entrance examination board 1901-1926.* Boston: Ginn and Company.

Federal Register, Volume 55, July 24, 1990, p. 30162.

Feldman, D. H. (1986). *Nature's gambit: Child prodigies and the development of human potential.* New York: Basic Books.

Feldman, D. H. (1994). *Beyond universals in cognitive development* (2nd ed.). Norwood, NJ: Ablex. (Original work published 1980)

Firebaugh, M. (1988). *Artificial intelligence.* Boston: Boyd and Fraser.

Fischer, K. W. (1980). A theory of cognitive development: The control and construction of herarchies of skills. *Psychological Review, 87*(6), 477-531.

Fischer, K. W., Bullock, D., Rosenberg, E., & Raya, P. (in press). The dynamics of competence: How context contributes directly to skill. In R. H. Wozniak & K. W. Fischer (Eds.), *Development in context: Acting and thinking in specific environments.* Hillsdale, NJ: Erlbaum.

Fischer, K. W., & Pipp, S. L. (1984a). Development of the structures of unconscious thought. In K. Bowers & D. Meighenbaum (Eds.), *The unconscious reconsidered* (pp. 88-148). New York: Wiley.

Fischer, K. W., & Pipp, S. L. (1984b). Processes of cognitive development: Optimal level and skill aquisition. In R. J. Sternberg (Ed.), *Mechanisms of cognitive development* (pp. 45-80). New York: Freeman.

Fischer, K. W., Pipp, S. L., & Bullock, D. (1984). Detecting developmental discontinuities: Methods and measurement. In R. N. Emde & R. J. Harmon (Eds.), *Continuities and discontinuities in development* (pp. 95-121). New York: Plenum.

Fischer, K. W., & Rose, S. P. (1994). Dynamic development of coordination of components in brain and behavior. In G. Dawson & K. Fischer (Eds.), *Human behavior and the developing brain* (pp. 3-66). New York: Guilford.

Fischer, M. J. (1980). *Iran: From religious dispute to revolution.* Cambridge, MA: Harvard University Press.

Fiske, E. (1991). *Smart schools, smart kids.* New York: Simon & Schuster.

Flynn, J. R. (1987). Massive IQ gains in fourteen nations: What IQ tests really measure. *Psychological Bulletin, 101,* 171-191.

Flynn, J. R. (1991). *Asian Americans: Achievement beyond IQ.* Hillsdale, NJ: Erlbaum.

Fodor, J. A. (1975). *The language of thought.* New York: Crowell.

Fodor, J. A. (1983). *The modularity of mind.* Cambridge, MA: MIT Press.

Fraser, S. (Ed.). (1995). *The bell curve wars: Race, intelligence, and the future of America.* New York: Basic Books.

Fredericksen, J., & Collins, A. (1989). A systems theory of educational testing. *Educational Researcher, 18*(9), 27-32.

Fredericksen, N. (1986). Toward a broader conception of human intelligence. In R. J. Sternberg & R. K. Wagner (Eds.), *Practical intelligence: Nature and origins of competence in the everyday world* (pp. 84-116). New York: Cambridge University Press.

Freeman, F. S. (1934). *Individual differences.* New York: Henry Holt & Co.

Fulker, D. W., DeFries, J. C., & Plomin, R. (1988). Genetic influences on general mental ability increases between infancy and middle childhood. *Nature 336,* 767-769.

Galton, F. (1869). *Hereditary genius: An inquiry into its laws and consequences.* London: Julian Friedmann Publishers.

Galton, F. (1883). *Inquiries into human faculty and its development.* New York: Dutton.

Galton, F. (1892). *Hereditary genius: An inquiry into its laws and consequences* (2nd ed.). London: Watts and Co. (Original work published 1869)

Galton, F. (1961). Co-relations and their measurement, chiefly from anthropometric data. Reprinted in J. J. Jenkins & D. G. Patterson (Eds.), *Studies in Individual Differences: The search for intelligence* (pp. 17-26). New York: Appleton-Century-Crofts. (Original work published 1888)

Gardner, H. (1975). *The shattered mind: The person after brain damage.* New York: Knopf.

Gardner, H. (1979). Developmental psychology after Piaget: An approach in terms of symbolization. *Human Development, 22,* 73-88.

Gardner, H. (1981). *The quest for mind: Piaget, Lévi-Strauss, and the structuralist movement.* Chicago: University of Chicago Press. (Original work published 1973)

Gardner, H. (1985). *The mind's new science.* New York: Basic Books.

Gardner, H. (1989). *To open minds: Chinese clues to the dilemma of contemporary education.* New York: Basic Books.

Gardner, H. (1991a). Assessment in context. In B. R. Gifford & M. C. O'Connor (Eds.), *Changing assessments: Alternative views of aptitude, achievement, and instruction.* Boston: Kluwer.

Gardner, H. (1991b). *The unschooled mind: How children think and how schools should teach.* New York: Basic Books.

Gardner, H. (1993a). *Creating minds: An anatomy of creativity as seen through the lives of Freud, Einstein, Picasso, Stravinsky, Eliot, Graham, and Gandhi.* New York: Basic Books.

Gardner, H. (1993b). *Frames of mind: The theory of multiple intelligences.* New York: Basic Books. (Original work published 1983)

Gardner, H. (1993c). *Multiple intelligences: The theory in practice.* New York: Basic Books.

Gardner, H. (1994). Intelligences in theory and practice: A response to Elliot W. Eisner, Robert J. Sternberg, & Henry M. Levin. *Teacher's College Record, 95*(4), 576-583.

Gardner, H. (1995a). Green ideas sleeping furiously. *The New York Review of Books, 42*(5), 32-39.

Gardner, H. (1995b). Reflections on multiple intelligences: Myths and messages. *Phi Delta Kappan, 77*(2).

Gardner, H., & Dudai, Y. (1985). Biology and giftedness. *Items, 39,* 1-6.

Gardner, H., & Hatch, T. (1989). Multiple intelligences go to school. *Educational Researcher, 18,* 4-10.

Gardner, H., Krechevsky, M., Sternberg, R. J., & Okagaki, L. (1994). Intelligence in context: Enhancing students' practical intelligences for school. In K. McGilly (Ed.), *Classroom lessons: Integrating cognitive theory and classroom practice* (pp. 105-127). Cambridge: MIT Press, Bradford Books.

Gardner, H., & Wolf, D. (1983). Waves and streams of symbolization: Notes on the development of symbolic capacities in young children. In D. R. Rogers & J. A. Slobada (Eds.), *The acquisition of symbolic skills.* London: Plenum.

Gardner, J. (1961). *Excellence: Can we be equal and excellent too?* New York: Harper.

Garson, B. (1979a). Luddites in Lordstown. In R. Kantor & B. Stein (Eds.), *Life in organizations: Workplaces as people experience them* (pp. 211-217). New York: Basic Books.

Garson, B. (1979b). Some lousy offices to work in, and one good one. In R. Kantor & B. Stein (Eds.), *Life in organizations: Workplaces as people experience them* (pp. 225-239). New York: Basic Books.

Gazzaniga, M. (1985). *The social brain.* New York: Basic Books.

Geertz, C. (1983). *Local knowledge.* New York: Basic Books.

Gelman, R. (1972). Logical capacity of very young children: Number invariance rules. *Child Development, 43,* 75-90.

Gelman, R. (1991). Epigenetic foundations of knowledge structures: Initial and transcendent constructions. In S. Carey & R. Gelman (Eds.), *The epigenesis of mind: Essays on biology and cognition.* Hillsdale, NJ: Erlbaum.

Gelman, R., & Gallistel, C. R. (1978). *The child's understanding of number.* Cambridge, MA: Harvard University Press.

Gentner, D., & Stevens, A. L. (1983). *Mental models.* Hillsdale, NJ: Erlbaum.

George, F. (1983). *The Wechsler enterprise: An assessment of the development, structure, and use of the Wechsler tests of intelligence.* Oxford: Pergamon.

Geschwind, N. (1974). *Selected papers.* Dordrecht/Boston: Reidel.

Geschwind, N., & Galaburda, A. (1987). *Cerebral lateralization.* Cambridge: Harvard University Press.

Getzels, J. W., & Csikszentmihalyi, M. (1976). *The creative vision: A longitudinal study of problem finding in art.* New York: Wiley.

Giarratano, J., & Riley, G. (1989). *Expert systems: Principles and programming.* Boston: PWS-Kent Publishing.

Gifford, B. R. (1989). The allocation of opportunities and the politics of testing: A policy analytic perspective. In B. R. Gifford (Ed.), *Test policy and the politics of opportunity allocation: The workplace and the law* (pp. 3-32). Boston: Kluwer.

Ginsburg, H., & Opper, S. (1988). *Piaget's theory of intellectual development* (2nd ed.). Englewood Cliffs, NJ: Prentice-Hall.

Gladwin, T. (1970). *East is a big bird: Navigation and logic on Puluwat Atoll.* Cambridge, MA: Harvard University Press.

Glaser, R., & Chi, M. T. H. (1988). Overview. In M. T. H. Chi, R. Glaser, & M. Farr (Eds.), *The nature of expertise* (pp. 311-342). Hillsdale, NJ: Erlbaum.

Goddard, H. (1912). *The Kallikak family: A study in the heredity of feeble-mindedness.* New York: Macmillan.

Goleman, D. (1989, April 22). Subtle but intriguing differences found in the brain anatomy of men and women. *New York Times,* p. C1.

Goodman, N. (1976). *Languages of art: An approach to a theory of symbols.* Indianapolis: Hackett.

Goodnow, J. (1990). The socialization of cognition: What's involved? In J. W. Stigler, R. A. Shweder, & G. Herdt (Eds.), *Cultural psychology: Essays on comparative human development* (pp. 259-286). Cambridge: Cambridge University Press.

Goody, J. (1977). *Domestication of the savage mind.* Cambridge: Cambridge University Press.

Gottfredson, L. (1986). Societal consequences of the *g* factor in employment. *Journal of Vocational Behavior, 29*(3), 379-410.

Gottfredson, L. S. (1988). Reconsidering fairness: A matter of social and ethical priorities. *Journal of Vocational Behavior, 33*(3), 293–319.

Gould, S. J. (1981). *The mismeasure of man.* New York: Norton.

Gould, S. J. (1995). Curveball. In S. Fraser (Ed.), *The bell curve wars* (pp. 11–22). New York: Basic Books.

Greenough, W. T. (1981, April). Enriched environments and brain anatomy. The results and the assumptions. Symposium presented at the Society for Research in Child Development, Boston.

Greenough, W. T., Black, J. E., & Wallace, C. S. (1987). Experience and brain development. *Child Development, 58,* 539–559.

Grinder, R. E. (Ed.). (1975). *Studies in adolescence: A book of readings in adolescent development* (3rd Ed.). New York: Macmillan.

Groen, G. J., & Patel, V. L. (1988). The relationship between comprehension and reasoning in medical expertise. In M. T. H. Chi, R. Glaser, & M. Farr (Eds.), *The nature of expertise* (pp. 287–310). Hillsdale, NJ: Erlbaum.

Gruber, H. E. (1984). The emergence of a sense of purpose: A cognitive case study of young Darwin. In M. L. Commons, J. D. Sinnot, F. A. Richards, & D. Armon (Eds.), *Adult development: Vol. 1. Comparisons and applications of developmental models.* New York: Praeger.

Guilford, J. P. (1967). *The nature of human intelligence.* New York: McGraw-Hill.

Gustafsson, J. -E. (1984). A unifying model for the structure of intellectual abilities. *Intelligence, 8,* 179–203.

Gustafsson, J. -E. (1988). Hierarchical models of individual differences in cognitive abilities. In R. J. Sternberg (Ed.), *Advances in the psychology of human intelligence* (Vol. 4, pp. 35–71). Hillsdale, NJ: Erlbaum.

Hadenius, A. M., Hagberg, B., Hyttnas-Bensch, K., & Sjogren, I. (1962). The natural prognosis of infantile hydroencephalis. *Acta Paediatrica, 51,* 117–118.

Haeberlin, R. (1916). The theoretical foundations of Wundt's folk-psychology. *Psychological Review, 23,* 279–302.

Haier, R. J., Nuechterlein, K. H., Hazlett, E., Wu, J. C., Paek, J., Browning, H. L., & Buchsbaum, M. S. (1988). Cortical glucose metabolic rate correlates of abstract reasoning and attention studied with positron emission tomography. *Intelligence, 12,* 199–217.

Haier, R. J., Siegel, B., Tang, C., Abel, L., & Buchsbaum, M. S. (1992). Intelligence and changes in regional cerebral glucose metabolic rate following learning. *Intelligence, 116,* 415–426.

Hamilton, S. (1990). *Apprenticeship for adulthood: Preparing youth for the future.* New York: Free Press.

Harrington, D. M., Block, J. H., & Block, J. (1978). Intolerance of ambiguity in preschool children: Psychometric considerations, behavioral manifestations, and parental correlates. *Developmental Psychology, 14*(3), 242–256.

Hartigan, J. A., & Wigdor, A. K. (Eds.). (1989). *Fairness in employment testing: Validity generalization, minority issues, and the General Aptitude Test Battery.* Washington, DC: National Academy Press.

Hatano, G., & Inagaki, K. (1986). Two courses of expertise. In H. Stevenson, H. Azuma, & K. Hakuta (Eds.), *Child development and education in Japan* (pp. 262–272). San Francisco: Freeman.

Hatano, G., & Inagaki, K. (1987). Young children's spontaneous personification as analogy. *Child Development, 58*(4), 1013–1020.

Hatano, G., & Inagaki, K. (1991). Sharing cognition through collective comprehension activity. In L. B. Resnick, J. M. Levine, & S. D. Teasley (Eds.), *Perspectives in socially shared cognition* (pp. 331–348). Washington, DC: American Psychological Association.

Hatano, G., Miyake, K., & Tajima, N. (1980). Mother behavior in an unstructured situation and child's acquisition of number conservation. *Child Development, 51,* 379–385.

Hayes, J. R. (1985). Three problems in teaching general skills. In S. F. Chipman, J. W. Segal, & R. Glaser (Eds.), *Thinking and learning skills: Vol. 2: Research and open questions.* Hillsdale, NJ: Erlbaum.

Hearnshaw, L. S. (1979). *Cyril Burt, psychologist.* Ithaca, NY: Cornell University Press.

Heath, S. B. (1983). *Ways with words: Language, life, and work in communities and classrooms.* Cambridge: Cambridge University Press.

Hebb, D. O. (1949). *The organization of behavior: A neuropsychological theory.* New York: Wiley. London: Chapman and Hall, Limited.

Hebb, D. W., & Penfield, W. (1940). Human behavior after extensive bilateral removals from the frontal lobes. *Archives of Neurology and Psychiatry, 44,* 421–438.

Hendrickson, D. E., & Hendrickson, A. E. (1980). The biological basis of individual differences in intelligence. *Personality and Individual Differences, 1,* 3–33.

Henry, J. (1960). A cross-cultural outline of education. *Current Anthropology, 1*(4), 267–305.

Herrnstein, R. J. (1973). *I.Q. in the meritocracy.* Boston: Little, Brown.

Herrnstein, R. J., & Murray, C. (1994). *The bell curve: Intelligence and class structure in American life.* New York: Free Press.

Hess, R. D. (1970). Social class and ethnic influences upon socialization. In P. H. Mussen (Ed.), *Carmichael's manual of child psychology* (3rd ed., Vol. 2, pp. 457–557). New York: Wiley.

Hess, R. D., & Shipman, V. C. (1965). Early experience and the socialization of cognitive modes in children. *Child Development, 36,* 869–886.

Hilgard, E. (1987). *Psychology in America: A historical survey.* San Diego: Harcourt Brace Jovanovich.

Hirschfield, L., & Gelman, S. (Eds.). (1994). *Mapping the mind.* New York: Cambridge University Press.

Hobbes, T. (1969). Objections and replies (selections). In M. D. Wilson, (Ed.), *The essential Descartes.* New York: New American Library.

Hodgkinson, N. (1989). Electrodes lift the life on IQ tests. *London Observer.*

Hofstadter, R. (1955). *Social Darwinism in American thought.* Boston: Beacon Press. (Original work published 1944)

Holden, C. (1980). Identical twins reared apart. *Science, 207,* 1323–1328.

Holyoak, K. J. (1991). Symbolic connectionism: Toward third-generation theories of expertise. In K. A. Ericsson & J. Smith (Eds.), *Toward a general theory of expertise: Prospects and limits* (pp. 301–335). Cambridge: Cambridge University Press.

Horn, J. M. (1983). The Texas adoption project: Adopted children and their intellectual resemblance to biological and adoptive parents. *Child Development, 54,* 268–275.

Horn, J. (1985). Remodeling old models of intelligence. In B. B. Wolman (Ed.), *Handbook of intelligence.* New York: Wiley.

Horn, J. (1989). Models of intelligence. In R. L. Linn (Ed.), *Intelligence: Measurement, theory, and public policy.* Urbana and Chicago: University of Illinois Press.

Horn, J., & Cattell, R. B. (1966). Refinement and test of the theory of fluid and crystallized general intelligences. *Journal of educational psychology, 57*(5), 253–270.

Horn, J. M., Loehlin, J. L, & Willerman, L. (1979). Intellectual resemblance among adoptive and biological relatives: The Texas Adoption Project. *Behavior Genetics, 9,* 177–207.

Hubel, D. (1979). The brain. *Scientific American, 241,* 44–53.

Hubel, D., & Wiesel, T. (1962). Receptive fields, binocular interaction, and functional architecture in the cat's visual cortex. *Journal of Physiology, 160,* 106–154.

Hubel, D., & Wiesel, T. (1979). Brain mechanisms of vision. *Scientific American, 241,* 150–162.

Hultén, K. G. Pontus. (1968). *The machine.* New York: The Museum of Modern Art.

Humphreys, L. (1971). *Theory of intelligence.* In R. Cancro (Ed.), *Intelligence: Genetic and environmental influences.* New York and London: Grune & Stratton.

Hunt, E. (1987). Science, technology, and intelligence. In R. R. Ronning, J. A. Glover, J. C. Conoley, & J. C. Witt (Eds.), *The influence of cognitive psychology on testing* (pp. 11–40). Hillsdale, NJ: Erlbaum.

Hunt, E. (1995). *Will we be smart enough? A cognitive analysis of the coming workforce.* New York: Russell Sage Foundation.

Hunt, J. McV. (1969). Has compensatory education failed? *Harvard Educational Review, 39*(2), 278–300.

Hunter, J. E., & Hunter, R. F. (1984). Validity and utility of alternative predictors of job performance. *Psychological Bulletin, 96*(1), 72–98.

Hunter, J. E., & Schmidt, F. L. (1983). Quantifying the effects of psychological interventions on employee job performance and work-force productivity. *American Psychologist, 38,* 473–478.

Hutchins, E. (1991). The social organization of distributed cognition. In L. B. Resnick, J. M. Levine, & S. D. Teasley (Eds.), *Perspectives in socially shared cognition* (pp. 283–307). Washington, DC: American Psychological Association.

Inhelder, B., & Piaget, J. (1958). *The growth of logical thinking from childhood to adolescence: An essay on the construction of formal operational structures.* (A. Parsons & S. Milgram, Trans.). New York: Basic Books. (Original work published 1955)

Ischisada, M. (1974). The civil service examination: China's examination hell. *Chinese Education, 7*(3), 1–74.

Jacoby, R., & Glauberman, N. (Eds.). (1995). *The bell curve debate: History, documents, opinions.* New York: Times Books.

Jencks, C. (1977). *Who gets ahead? The determinants of economic success in America.* New York: Basic Books.

Jencks, C., Smith, M., Acland, H., Bane, M. J., Cohen, D., Gintis, H., Heyns, B., & Michelson, S. (1972). *Inequality.* New York: Basic Books.

Jenkins, J. J., & Patterson, D. G. (Eds.). (1961). *Studies in individual differences: The search for intelligence.* New York: Appleton-Century-Crofts.

Jensen, A. (1969). How much can we boost IQ and scholastic achievement? *Harvard Educational Review, 39*(1), 1–123.

Jensen, A. (1980). *Bias in mental testing.* New York: Free Press.

Jensen, A. (1987). Psychometric *g* as a focus of concerted research effort. *Intelligence, 11,* 193–198.

Jensen, A. (1991, February 17). *General mental ability: From psychometrics to biology.* Paper presented at the Annual Meeting of the American Association for the Advancement of Science, Washington, DC.

Jensen, A. R. (1993a). Spearman's *g:* Links between psychometrics and biology. *Brain Mechanisms, 701,* 103–129.

Jensen, A. R. (1993b). Test validity: *g* versus "tacit knowledge." *Current Directions in Psychological Science, 2*(1), 9–10.

Jensen, A. R. (1993c). Why is reaction time correlated with psychometric *g? Current Directions in Psychological Science, 2*(2) 53–56.

Jerison, H. (1982). The evolution of biological intelligence. In R. J. Sternberg (Ed.), *The handbook of intelligence* (pp. 723–791). New York: Cambridge University Press.

Jordan, B. (1989). Cosmopolitical obstetrics: Some insights from the training of traditional midwives. *Social Science and Medicine, 28*(9), 925–944.

Joynson, R. B. (1989). *The Burt affair.* London: Routledge.

Juel-Nielsen, N. (1965). Individual and environment: A psychiatric and psychological investigation of monozygous twins raised apart. *Acta Psychiatrica et Neurologica Scandinavica,* (Suppl. 183).

Kagan, J. (1969). Inadequate evidence and illogical conclusions. *Harvard Educational Review, 39*(2), 274–277.

Kagan, J. (1994). *Galen's prophecy.* New York: Basic Books.

Kagan, J., & Klein, R. (1973). Cross-cultural perspectives on early development. *American Psychologist, 28,* 947–961.

Kamin, L. (1974). *The science and politics of IQ.* Potomac, MD: Erlbaum.

Kamin, L. (1981). Commentary. In S. Scarr (Ed.), *IQ: Race, social class, and individual differences. New studies of old issues* (pp. 467–482). Hillsdale, NJ: Erlbaum.

Kant, I. (1958). *Critique of pure reason.* (N. Kemp Smith, Trans.) New York: Random House. (Original work published 1781)

Karmiloff-Smith, A. (1986). From meta-processes to conscious access: Evidence from children's metalinguistic and repair data. *Cognition, 23*(2), 95–147.

Karmiloff-Smith, A. (1991). Beyond modularity: Innate constraints and developmental change. In S. Carey & R. Gelman (Eds.), *The epigenesis of mind: Essays on biology and cognition.* Hillsdale, NJ: Erlbaum.

Karmiloff-Smith, A. (1992). *Beyond modularity: A developmental perspective on cognitive science.* Cambridge, MA: MIT Press.

Kearns, D., & Doyle, D. (1988). *Winning the brain race: A bold plan to make our schools competitive.* San Francisco, CA: ICS Press.

Keating, D. (1984). The emperor's new clothes: The "new look" in intelligence research. In R.J. Sternberg (Ed.), *Advances in the psychology of human intelligence* (Vol. 2, pp. 1–35). Hillsdale, NJ: Erlbaum.

Keating, D. (1990). Charting pathways to the development of expertise. *Educational Psychologist, 25*(3/4), 243–267.

Keil, F. C. (1981). Constraints on knowledge and cognitive development. *Psychological Review, 8*(3), 197–227.

Keil, F. C. (1989). *Concepts, kinds, and cognitive development.* Cambridge, MA: MIT Press.

Keil, F. C. (1991). The emergence of theoretical beliefs as constraints on concepts. In S. Carey & R. Gelman (Eds.), *The epigenesis of mind: Essays on biology and cognition.* Hillsdale, NJ: Erlbaum.

Kelner, K., & Benditt, J. (1994). Genes and behavior. *Science, 264,* 1685–1697.

Kevles, D. J. (1968). Testing the army's intelligence: Psychologists and the military in World War I. *Journal of American History, 55*(3), 565–581.

Kevles, D. J. (1985). *In the name of eugenics: Genetics and the uses of human heredity.* Berkeley and Los Angeles: University of California Press.

Kilborn, P. T. (1991). "Race Norming": Tests become a fiery issue. The controversy over different scoring procedures for minorities in aptitude tests used by state employment agencies. *The New York Times, 140,*(4), p. E3.

Kimura, D. (1973). The asymmetry of the human brain. *Scientific American, 228,* 70–80.

Kinsbourne, M. (1993). In T. J. Bouchard & P. Propping (1993). *Twins as a tool of behavioral genetics: Report of the Dalehm Workshop on what are the mechanisms mediating the genetic and environmental determinants of behavior?* Chichester, England: Wiley.

Klahr, D. (1984). Transition processes in quantitative development. In R. J. Sternberg (Ed.), *Mechanisms of cognitive development.* New York: Freeman.

Klahr, D., & Wallace, J. G. (1976). *Cognitive development: An information processing view.* Hillsdale, NJ: Erlbaum.

Kline, P. (1991). *Intelligence: The psychometric view.* London: Routledge.

Klitgaard, R. (1985). *Choosing elites.* New York: Basic Books.

Kohn, A. (1993). *Punished by rewards: The trouble with gold stars, incentive plans, A's, praise and other bribes.* Boston: Houghton Mifflin.

Korey, K. (1984). Preface. In R. Jastrow (Ed.), *The essential Darwin.* Boston: Little, Brown.

Kornhaber, M. (1994). *The theory of multiple intelligences: Why and how schools use it.* Cambridge, MA: Harvard Graduate School of Education.

Kornhaber, M., & Gardner, H. (1991). Critical thinking across multiple intelligences. In S. Maclure & P. Davies (Eds.), *Learning to think: Thinking to learn.* Oxford: Pergamon.

Kornhaber, M., & Krechevsky, M. (1995). Expanding definitions of teaching and learning: Notes from the MI underground. In P. Cookson & B. Schneider (Eds.), *Transforming schools.* New York: Garland Press.

Kornhaber, M., Krechevsky, M., & Gardner, H. (1990). Engaging intelligence. *Educational psychologist, 25*(3/4), 177–199.

Kosslyn, S. M., & Koenig, O. (1992). *Wet mind: The new cognitive neuroscience.* New York: Free Press.

Kozulin, A. (1984). *Psychology in Utopia: Toward a social history of Soviet psychology.* Cambridge, MA: MIT Press.

Krechevsky, M. (1994). *Project spectrum: Preschool assessment handbook.* Cambridge, MA: President and Fellows of Harvard College.

Krechevsky, M., & Gardner, H. (1990a). The emergence and nurturance of multiple intelligences. In M. J. A. Howe (Ed.), *Encouraging the development of exceptional abilities and talents* (pp. 221–244). Leicester, England: British Psychological Society.

Krechevsky, M., & Gardner, H. (1990b). Approaching school intelligently: An infusion approach. In D. Kuhn (Ed.), *Developmental perspectives on teaching and learning thinking skills. Series of contributions to human development* (Vol. 21, pp. 79–94). Basel: Karger.

La Mettrie, J. O. de. (1982). *Man a machine.* In M. J. Adler (Ed.), *The great ideas today, 1982.* Chicago: Encyclopedia Britannica. (Original work published in 1747)

Labouvie-Vief, G. (1990). Modes of knowledge and the organization of development. In M. L. Commons, C. Armon, L. Kohlberg, F. A. Richards, T. A. Grotzer, & J. D. Sinnott (Eds.), *Adult development: Vol. 2. Models and methods in the study of adolescent and adult thought.* New York: Praeger.

Lachman, R., Lachman, J., & Butterfield, E. (1979). *Cognitive psychology and information processing: An introduction.* Hillsdale, NJ: Erlbaum.

Laird, J. E. (1984). *Universal subgoaling.* Unpublished doctoral dissertation, Computer Science Department, Carnegie-Mellon University, Pittsburgh, PA.

Landau, B., Gleitman, H., & Spelke, E. (1981). Spatial knowledge and geometric representation in a child blind from birth. *Science, 213,* 1275–1278.

Lashley, K. (1950). In search of the engram. *Symposia of the Society for Experimental Biology,* 454–482.

Lashley, K. (1951). The problem of serial order in behavior. In L. A. Jeffress (Ed.), *Cerebral mechanisms in behavior: The Hixon symposium.* New York: Wiley.

Lave, J. (1988). *Cognition in practice: Mind, mathematics, and culture in everyday life.* New York: Cambridge University Press.

Lave, J. (1990). The culture of acquisition and the practice of understanding. In J. W. Stigler, R. A. Shweder, & G. Herdt (Eds.), *Cultural psychology. Essay on comparative human development.* Cambridge: Cambridge University Press.

Lave, J. (1991). Situating learning in communities of practice. In L. B. Resnick, J. M. Levine, & S. D. Teasley (Eds.), *Perspectives in socially shared cognition* (pp. 63–82). Washington, DC: American Psychological Association.

Lave, J., Murtaugh, M., & de la Rocha, O. (1984). The dialectic of arithmetic in grocery shopping. In B. Rogoff & J. Lave (Eds.), *Everyday cognition: Its development in social context* (pp. 67–94). Cambridge, MA: Harvard University Press.

Lee, T. H. C. (1985). *Government education and examinations in Sung China, 960–1278.* Hong Kong: Chinese University Press and New York: St. Martin's Press.

LeFebre, J. (1988). Flow and the quality of experience during work and leisure. In M. Csikszentmihalyi & I. S. Csikszentmihalyi (Eds.), *Optimal experience: Psychological studies of flow in consciousness* (pp. 307–318). Cambridge: Cambridge University Press.

Lenat, D. B., Guha, R. V., Pittman, K., Pratt, D., & Shepherd, M. (1990). CYC: Toward programs with common sense. *Communications of the Association for Computing Machinery, 33*(8), 30–49.

Lenneberg, E. H. (1967). *Biological foundations of language.* New York: Wiley.

Lesgold, A., Rubinson, H., Feltovich, P., Glaser, R., Klopfer, D., & Wang, Y. (1988). Expertise in a complex skill: Diagnosing x-ray pictures. In M. T. H. Chi, R. Glaser, & M. Farr (Eds.), *The nature of expertise* (pp. 311–342). Hillsdale, NJ: Erlbaum.

Leslie, A. M. (1988). The necessity of illusion: Perception and thought in infancy. In L. Weiskrantz (Ed.), *Thought without language* (pp. 168–182). Oxford: Oxford University Press.

Levin, H. M. (1988). Issues of agreement and contention in employment testing. *Journal of Vocational Behavior, 33,* 398–403.

Levin, H. M. (1989). Ability testing for job selection: Are the economic claims justified? In B. R. Gifford (Ed.), *Test policy and the politics of opportunity allocation: The workplace and the law* (pp. 211–232). Boston: Kluwer.

Levin, H. M. (1994). Multiple intelligence theory and everyday practices. *Teachers College Record, 95*(4), 571–575.

LeVine, R. A. (1978). Western schools in non-western societies: Psychosocial impact and cultural responses. *Teachers College Record, 79*(4), 49–55.

LeVine, R. (1991). Social and cultural influences on child development. Paper delivered at the 100th anniversary of the teaching of education at Harvard. *Harvard Graduate School of Education Alumni Bulletin, 36*(1), 12–13.

LeVine, R., & White, M. (1986). *Human conditions: The cultural basis of educational development.* New York and London: Routledge & Kegan Paul.

Lewis, C. (1994). *Educating hearts and minds: Reflections on Japanese preschool and elementary education.* New York: Cambridge University Press.

Lewkowicz, D., & Turkewitz, G. (1981, April). Hemispheric specialization in processing auditory information during infancy. Paper presented at the Society for Research in Child Development, Boston.

Lewontin, R. C., Rose, S., & Kamin, L. (1984). *Not in our genes: Biology, ideology, and human nature.* New York: Pantheon Books.

Lippmann, W. (1976). Readings from the Lippmann-Terman debate. In N.J. Block & G. Dworkin (Eds.), *The IQ controversy: Critical readings.* New York: Pantheon Books. (Original work published in 1922–1923)

Locke, J. (1939). An essay concerning human understanding. In E. A. Burtt (Ed.), *The English philosophers from Bacon to Mill.* New York: Modern Library. (Original work published 1690)

Loehlin, J. (1993). In T. J. Bouchard & P. Propping (Eds.), *Twins as a tool of behavioral genetics: Report of the Dalehm Workshop on what are the mechanisms mediating the genetic and environmental determinants of behavior?* Chichester, England: Wiley.

Longstreth, L. E. (1986). The real and the unreal: A reply to Jensen & Vernon. *Intelligence, 10,* 181–191.

Lowenfeld, V., & Brittain, W. L. (1982). *Creative and mental growth.* New York: Macmillan.

Luria, A. R. (1966). *The higher cortical functions in man.* New York: Basic Books.

Luria, A. R. (1976). *Cognitive development.* Cambridge, MA: Harvard University Press.

Lykken, D. T., McGue, M., Tellegen, A., & Bouchard, T. (1992). Emergenesis: Genetic traits that may not run in families. *American Psychologist, 47,* 1565–1577.

Lytton, H. (1977). Do parents create, or respond to, differences in twins? *Developmental Psychology, 13*(5), 456–459.

MacFarquhar, R. (1985). Deng Xiaoping's reform program in the perspective of Chinese history. *American Academy of Arts and Sciences Bulletin, 40,* 20–38.

Malkus, U., Feldman, D. H., & Gardner, H. (1988). Dimensions of mind in early childhood. In A. Pelligrini (Ed.), *The psychological bases of early education.* Chichester, England: Wiley.

Mandler, J. (1988). How to build a baby: On the development of an accessible representational system. *Cognitive Development, 3,* 113–136.

Manni, J. L., Winikur, D. W., & Keller, M. R. (1984). *Intelligence, mental retardation, and the culturally different child: A practitioner's guide.* Springfield, IL: Thomas.

Mayr, E. (1964). Introduction. In C. Darwin, *On the origin of species.* Cambridge, MA: Harvard University Press.

Mayr, E. (1982). *The growth of biological thought.* Cambridge, MA: Harvard University Press.

McClelland, D. C. (1993). Intelligence is not the best predictor of job performance. *Current Directions in Psychological Science, 2*(1), 5–6.

McCorduck, P. (1979). *Machines who think.* San Francisco: Freeman.

McCulloch, W., & Pitts, W. (1943). A logical calculus of the ideas immanent in nervous activity. *Bulletin of Mathematical Biophysics, 5,* 115–133.

McDonald, R. P. (1985). *Factor analysis and related methods.* Hillsdale, NJ: Erlbaum.

McGarrigle, J., Grieve, R., & Hughes, M. (1978). Interpreting inclusion: A contribution to the study of children's cognitive and linguistic development. *Journal of Experimental Child Psychology, 26,* 528–550.

McGarry, P. A., Stelmack, R. M., & Campbell, K. B. (1992). Intelligence, reaction time, and event-related potentials. *Intelligence, 16,* 289-313.

Merzernich, M., Nelson, R., Stryker, M., Cynader, A., Schoppman, A., & Zook, J. M. (1984). Somatosensory cortical map changes following digit amputation in adult monkeys. *Journal of Comparative Neurology, 224,* 591-605.

Messick, S. (1989). Validity. In R. L. Linn (Ed.), *Educational measurement* (3rd ed., pp. 13-103). New York: American Council on Education and Macmillan.

Messick, S. (1992). Multiple intelligences or multilevel intelligence? Selective emphasis on distinctive properties of hierarchy: On Gardner's *Frames of Mind* and Sternberg's *Beyond IQ* in the context of theory and research on the structure of human abilities. *Journal of Psychological Inquiry, 1*(3), 305-384.

Michie, D. (1986). *On machine intelligence* (2nd ed.). Chichester, England: Ellis Horwood Limited.

Miller, G. A. (1956). The magical number seven, plus or minus two: Some limits on our capacity for processing information. *Psychological Review, 63,* 81-97.

Miller, G. A. (1979, June 1). *A very personal history.* Talk given to the Cognitive Science Workshop, Massachusetts Institute of Technology, Cambridge, MA.

Miller, L. K. (1989). *Musical savants: Exceptional skill in the mentally retarded.* Hillsdale, NJ: Erlbaum.

Milner, B. (1967). Brain mechanisms suggested by studies of temporal lobes. In F. L. Darley (Ed.), *Brain mechanisms underlying speech and language.* New York: Grune & Stratton.

Minsky, M. (1985). *The society of mind.* New York: Touchstone Books.

Mitchell, R. (1992). *Testing for learning.* New York: Free Press.

Molfese, D., & Molfese, V. J. (1972). Hemisphere and stimulus differences as reflected in the cortical responses of newborn infants to speech stimuli. *Developmental Psychology, 15,* 505-511.

Murdoch, J. (1988). Cree cognition in natural and educational contexts. In J. W. Berry, S. H. Irvine, & E. B. Hunt (Eds.), *Indigenous cognition: Functioning in cultural context.* Dordrecht, Netherlands: Nijhoff.

Murray, D. J. (1983). *A history of western psychology.* Englewood Cliffs, NJ: Prentice-Hall.

Neill, D. M., & Medina, N. J. (1989). Standardized testing: Harmful to educational health. *Phi Delta Kappan, 70*(9), 688-697.

Neisser, U. (1976). General, academic, and artificial intelligence. In L. B. Resnick (Ed.), *The nature of intelligence* (pp. 135-144). Hillsdale, NJ: Erlbaum.

Nelson, K. (1973). Structure and strategy in learning to talk. *Monographs of the Society for Research in Child Development, 38* (1-2), (Serial No. 149).

Nelson, K. (1986). *Event knowledge: Structure and function in development.* Hillsdale, NJ: Erlbaum.

Nettlebeck, T. (1987). Inspection time and intelligence. In P. A. Vernon (Ed.), *Speed of information processing and intelligence.* Norwood, NJ: Ablex.

Neville, H. (1991). Neurobiology of cognitive and language processing. Effects of early experience. In K. R. Gibson & A. C. Petersen (Eds.), *Brain maturation and cognitive development: Comparative and cross-cultural perspectives* (pp. 355-380). Hawthorne, NY: Aldine de Gruyter.

Newell, A. (1990). *Unified theories of cognition.* Cambridge, MA: Harvard University Press.

Newell, A., Shaw, J. C., & Simon, H. A. (1958). Elements of a theory of human problem solving. *Psychological Review, 65,* 151–166.

Newell, A., Shaw, J. C., & Simon, H. A. (1963). Chess-playing programs and the problem of complexity. In E. A. Feigenbaum & J. Feldman (Eds.), *Computers and thought* (pp. 39–70). New York: McGraw-Hill.

Newell, A., & Simon, H. A. (1961). GPS, a program that simulates human thought, in E. A. Feigenbaum & J. Feldman (Eds.), *Computers and thought* (pp. 279–293). New York: McGraw-Hill.

Newell, A., & Simon, H. A. (1972). *Human problem-solving.* Englewood Cliffs, NJ: Prentice-Hall.

Newman, D., Griffin, P., & Cole, M. (1984). Social constraints in laboratory and classroom tasks. In B. Rogoff & J. Lave (Eds.), *Everyday cognition: Its development in social context.* Cambridge, MA: Harvard University Press.

Newman, H. H., Freeman, F. N., & Holzinger, K. J. (1937). *Twins: A study of heredity and environment.* Chicago: University of Chicago Press.

Oakes, J. (1985). *Keeping track: How schools structure inequality.* New Haven, CT: Yale University Press.

Oakeshott, M. (1975). Education: The engagement and its frustration. In R. F. Deardon, P. Hirst, & R. S. Peters (Eds.), *Education and the development of reason, Part I.* New York: Routledge and Kegan Paul.

Ogbu, J. (1978). *Minority education and caste: The American perspective in cross-cultural perspective.* New York: Academic Press.

Ogbu, J. (1991). Minority status and literacy in comparative perspective. In S. Graubard (Ed.), *Literacy: An overview by 14 experts* (pp. 141–168). New York: Hill and Wang.

Olson, D. (1970). *Cognitive development: The child's acquisition of diagonality.* New York: Academic Press.

Olson, D. (1974). *Media and symbols.* Chicago: University of Chicago Press.

Olson, D. (1977). From utterance to text: The bias of language in speech and writing. *Harvard Educational Review, 47,* 257–282.

Olson, D. (1986). Intelligence and literacy: The relationship between intelligence and the technologies of representation and communication. In R. J. Sternberg & R. K. Wagner (Eds.), *Practical intelligence: Nature and origins of competence in the everyday world* (pp. 338–360). New York: Cambridge University Press.

Olson, D. (1994). *The world on paper.* New York: Cambridge University Press.

Olson, L. (1988). Children flourish here: Eight teachers and a theory changed a school world. *Education Week, 7*(18), 1, 18–20.

Owen, D. (1985). *None of the above: Behind the myth of scholastic aptitude.* Boston: Houghton Mifflin.

Ozeki, K., & Asaka, T. (1990). *Handbook of quality tools: The Japanese approach.* Cambridge, MA: Productivity Press.

Patel, V. L., & Groen, G. J. (1986). Knowledge based solution strategies in medical reasoning. *Cognitive Science, 10,* 91–116.

Patel, V. L., & Groen, G. J. (1991). The general and specific nature of medical expertise: A critical look. In K. A. Ericsson & J. Smith (Eds.), *Toward a general theory of expertise: Prospects and limits* (pp. 93–125). Cambridge: Cambridge University Press.

Pea, R. D. (1990, April). Distributed intelligence and education. Paper presented at the annual meeting of the American Educational Research Association, Boston, MA.

Perkins, D. N. (1992). *Smart schools.* New York: Free Press.

Perkins, D. N. (1993). Person plus. In G. Salomon (Ed.), *Distributed cognitions: Psychological and educational considerations.* Cambridge: Cambridge University Press.

Perkins, D. N. (1995). *Outsmarting IQ: The emerging science of learnable intelligence.* New York: Free Press.

Perkins, D. N., Allen, R., & Hafner, J. (1983). Difficulties in everyday reasoning. In W. Maxwell (Ed.), *Thinking: The expanding frontier.* Philadelphia: The Franklin Institute.

Perkins, D. N., & Blythe, T. (1994). Putting understanding up front. *Educational Leadership, 51*(5), 4-7.

Perret-Clermont, A. -N., Perret, J. -F., & Bell, N. (1991). The social construction of meaning and cognitive activity in elementary school children. In L. Resnick, J. M. Levine, & S. D. Teasley (Eds.), *Perspectives on socially shared cognition* (pp. 41-62). Washington, DC: American Psychological Association.

Perrone, V. (1994). How to engage students in learning. In *Educational Leadership, 51*(5), 11-13.

Piaget, J. (1929). *The child's conception of the world.* New York: Harcourt Brace.

Piaget, J. (1952a). *The child's conception of number.* London: Routledge & Kegan Paul. (Abridged translation of Piaget and Szeminska, 1941/1964)

Piaget, J. (1952b). *The origins of intelligence in children.* Madison, CT: International Universities Press.

Piaget, J. (1952c). Autobiography. In E. G. Boring (Ed.), *A history of psychology in autobiography* (Vol. 4, pp. 237-256). New York: Russel.

Piaget, J. (1965). *The child's conception of number.* New York: Norton.

Piaget, J. (1974). *Biology and knowledge.* Chicago: University of Chicago Press. (Original work published 1967)

Piaget, J. (1977). The role of action in the development of thinking. In W. F. Overton & M. J. Gallagher (Eds.), *Knowledge and development. Vol. 1: Advances in research and theory.* New York: Plenum.

Piaget, J. (1983). Piaget's theory. In P. Mussen (Ed.), *Handbook of child psychology* (Vol. 1). New York: Wiley.

Piaget, J., & Inhelder, B. (1967). *The child's conception of space.* New York: Norton.

Piaget, J., & Inhelder, B. (1969). *The psychology of the child.* New York: Basic Books.

Piattelli-Palmarini, M. (Ed.). (1980). *Language and learning: The debate between Jean Piaget and Noam Chomsky.* Cambridge, MA: Harvard University Press.

Pinker, S. (1994). *The language instinct.* New York: Morrow.

Plato. (1928). Phaedrus. In Irwin Edman (Ed.), *The works of Plato* (Jowett translation). New York: Modern Library.

Plato. (1949). Timaeus. B. Jowett (Trans.), New York: The Liberal Arts Press.

Plato. (1956a). The Apology. In R. H. D. Rouse (Trans.), *Great dialogues of Plato.* New York: New American Library.

Plato. (1956b). Meno (Menon). In R. H. D. Rouse (Trans.), *Great dialogues of Plato.* New York: New American Library.

Plato. (1956c). The Republic. In R. H. D. Rouse (Trans.), *Great dialogues of Plato.* New York: New American Library.

Plomin, R. (1986). *Developmental genetics and psychology.* Hillsdale, NJ: Erlbaum.

Plomin, R. (1988). The nature and nurture of cognitive abilities. In R. J. Sternberg (Ed.), *Advances in the psychology of human intelligence* (Vol. 4, pp. 1-33). Hillsdale, NJ: Erlbaum.

Plomin, R. (1990). *Nature and nurture: An introduction to human behavioral genetics.* Pacific Grove, CA: Brooks/Cole Publishing.

Plomin, R. (1994). *Genetics and experience: The interplay between nature and nurture.* Thousand Oaks, CA: Sage.

Plomin, R., & DeFries, J. C. (1983). The Colorado adoption project. *Child Development, 54,* 276–289.

Plomin, R., DeFries, J. C., & Loehlin, J. C. (1977). Genotype-environment interaction and correlation in the analysis of human behavior. *Psychological Bulletin, 84*(2), 309–322.

Plomin, R., & Neisderhiser, J. (1991). Quantitative genetics, molecular genetics and intelligence. *Intelligence, 15,* 369–387.

Plomin, R., Owen, M., & McGuffin, P. (1994). The genetic basis of complex human behaviors. *Science, 264,* 1733–1739.

Plomin, R., & Thompson, L. (1993, January). *Genetics and high cognitive ability.* Paper presented at CIBA Conference, London.

Polanyi, M. (1958). *Personal knowledge: Towards a post-critical philosophy.* Chicago: University of Chicago Press.

Posner, M. (1988). What is it to be an expert? In M. T. H. Chi, R. Glaser, & M. J. Farr (Eds.), *The nature of expertise* (pp. xxix–xxxvi). Hillsdale, NJ: Erlbaum.

Posner, M. I. (Ed.). (1989). *Foundations of cognitive science.* Cambridge, MA: Bradford Books/MIT Press.

Pratt, V. (1987). *Thinking machines: The evolution of artificial intelligence.* Oxford: Basil Blackwell.

Raven, J. (1938). *Progressive matrices.* London: Lewis.

Reed, T. W., & Jensen, A. R. (1992). Conduction velocity in a brain nerve pathway of normal adults correlates with intelligence level. *Intelligence, 16,* 259–272.

Reich, R. B. (1991). *The work of nations: Preparing ourselves for 21st-century capitalism.* New York: Knopf.

Reschley, D. J. (1981). Psychological testing in educational classification and placement. *American Psychologist, 36*(10), 1094–1102.

Resnick, L. (1987a). Learning in school and out. *Educational Researcher, 16*(9), 13–20.

Resnick, L. (1987b). *Education and learning to think.* Washington: National Academy Press.

Resnick, L. (1991). Shared cognition: Thinking as social practice. In L. Resnick, J. M. Levine, & S. D. Teasley (Eds.), *Perspectives on socially shared cognition* (pp. 1–20). Washington, DC: American Psychological Association.

Resnick, L. B., Levine, J. M., & Teasley, S. D. (Eds.). (1991). *Perspectives on socially shared cognition.* Washington, DC: American Psychological Association.

Resnick, L., & Neches, R. (1984). Factors affecting individual differences in learning ability. In R. J. Sternberg (Ed.), *Advances in the psychology of human intelligence* (Vol. 2, pp. 275–323). Hillsdale, NJ: Erlbaum.

Richards, J. A., & Commons, M. L. (1984). Systematic, metasystematic, and cross-paradigmatic reasoning: A case for stages of reasoning beyond formal operations. In M. L. Commons, F. A. Richards, & C. Armon (Eds.), *Beyond formal operations: Late adolescent and adult cognitive development.* New York: Praeger.

Richardson, K. (1986). Theory? Or tools for social selection? *Behavioral and Brain Sciences, 9*(3), 579–581.

Rogoff, B. (1990). *Apprenticeship in thinking: Cognitive development in social context.* New York and Oxford: Oxford University Press.

Rogoff, B. (1991). Social interaction as apprenticeship in thinking: Guided participation in spatial planning. In L. B. Resnick, J. M. Levine, & S. D. Teasley, (Eds.), *Perspectives on socially shared cognition.* Washington, DC: American Psychological Association.

Rogoff, B., & Gardner, W. (1984). Adult guidance of cognitive development. *Everyday Cognition: Its development in social context.* In B. Rogoff & J. Lave, (Eds.). Cambridge, MA: Harvard University Press.

Romanes, G. (1883). *Animal intelligence.* New York: Appleton. (Original work published 1882)

Rorabaugh, B. (1986). *The craft apprentice: From Franklin to the machine age in America.* New York: Oxford University Press.

Rosenbloom, P. S. (1983). *The chunking of goal hierarchies: A model of practice and stimulus-response compatibility.* Unpublished doctorial dissertation, Computer Science Department, Carnegie-Mellon University, Pittsburgh, PA.

Rosenthal, R., & Jacobsen, L. (1968). *Pygmalion in the classroom: Teacher expectation and pupils' intellectual development.* New York: Holt, Rinehart & Winston.

Rosenzweig, M. (1966). Environmental complexity, cerebral change, and behavior. *American Psychologist, 21,* 321–332.

Rudy, W., & Brubacher, J. S. (1976). *Higher education in transition: A history of American colleges and universities.* (3rd ed.). New York: Harper & Row.

Rumelhart, D. E. (1989). The architecture of mind: A connectionist approach. In M. I. Posner (Ed.), *Foundations of cognitive science* (pp. 133–159). Cambridge, MA: Bradford Books/MIT Press.

Rushton, J. P. (1988). Race differences in behavior: A review and evolutionary analysis. *Personality and Individual Differences, 9*(6), 1021–1031.

Rushton, J. P. (1995). *Race, evolution, and behavior: A life history perspective.* New Brunswick, NJ: Transaction Publishers.

Russell, B., & Whitehead, A. N. (1962). *Principia mathematica.* Cambridge: Cambridge University Press. (Original work published in 1925)

Russell-Smith, E. (1974). *Modern bureaucracy: The home civil service.* London: Longman.

Rutter, M., Maughan, B., Mortimore, Ouston, J., & Smith, A. (1979). *Fifteen thousand hours.* Cambridge: Harvard University Press.

Salomon, G. (Ed.). (1993). *Distributed cognitions: Psychological and educational considerations.* Cambridge: Cambridge University Press.

Samelson, F. (1979). Putting psychology on the map: Ideology and intelligence testing. In A. Buss (Ed.), *Psychology in social context.* New York: Irvington Publishers/ Wiley.

Sapir, E. (1915). *The social organization of the West Coast tribes.* In D. J. Mendelbaum & E. Berkeley (Eds.), *Selected writings of Edward Sapir in language, culture and personality.* Los Angeles: University of California Press.

Sattler, J. M. (1992). *Assessment of children* (Rev. 3rd ed.). San Diego: Sattler.

Saxe, G. B., Guberman, S. R., & Gearhart, M. (1987). Social processes in early number development. *Monographs of the Society for Research in Child Development, 52*(2), (Serial No. 216).

Scardamalia, M., & Bereiter, C. (1991). Literate expertise. In K. A. Ericsson & J. Smith (Eds.), *Toward a general theory of expertise: Prospects and limits* (pp. 172–194). Cambridge: Cambridge University Press.

Scarr, S. (1981). *Race, social class, and individual differences in IQ*. Hillsdale, NJ: Erlbaum.

Scarr, S. (1985). An author's frame of mind: Review of *Frames of Mind* by Howard Gardner. *New Ideas in Psychology, 3*(1), 95-100.

Scarr, S. (1989). Protecting general intelligence: Constructs and consequences for interventions. In R. L. Linn (Ed.), *Intelligence: Measurement, theory, and public policy*. Urbana and Chicago: University of Illinois Press.

Scarr, S., & Carter-Saltzman, L. (1982). Genetics and intelligence. In R. J. Sternberg (Ed.), *The handbook of intelligence* (pp. 792-896). New York: Cambridge University Press,

Scarr, S., & McCartney, K. (1983). How people make their own environments: A theory of genotype→environment effects. *Child Development, 54*, 424-435.

Scarr, S., & Weinberg, R. A. (1976). IQ test performance of black children adopted by white families. *American Psychologist, 31*, 726-739.

Scarr-Salapatek, S. (1975). Genetics and the development of intelligence. In F. Horowitz (Ed.), *Review of child development research* (Vol. 4). Chicago: University of Chicago Press.

Schafer, E. P. W. (1982). Neural adaptability: A biological determination of behavioral intelligence. *International Journal of Neuroscience, 17*, 183-191.

Schaffer, H. R. (1984). *The child's entry into a social world*. London: Academic Press.

Schank, R. C. (1982). *Dynamic memory*. Cambridge: Cambridge University Press.

Schank, R. C. (1991). *The connoisseur's guide to the mind: How we think, how we learn, and what it means to be intelligent*. New York: Summit Books.

Scheibel, A. (1985, April). *Toward cortical substrates of higher brain function*. Paper presented at a conference on the neurobiology of extraordinary giftedness, New York.

Scheibel, A. (1988). Dendritic correlates of human cortical function. *Cortical Function Archives, 126*(4), 347-357.

Schlesinger, A. M. (1959). Walter Lippmann: The intellectual v. politics. In M. Childs & J. Reston (Eds.), *Walter Lippmann and his times*. New York: Harcourt Brace.

Schmidt, F. L. (1988). The problem of group differences in ability test scores in employment selection. *Journal of Vocational Behavior, 33*(3), 272-292.

Schmidt, F. L., & Hunter, J. E. (1981). Employment testing: Old theories and new research findings. *American Psychologist, 36*, 1128-1137.

Schmidt, F. L., & Hunter, J. E. (1992). Development of a causal model of processes determining job performance. *Current Directions in Psychological Science, 1*(3), 89-92.

Schön, D. A. (1983). *The reflective practitioner: How professionals think in action*. New York: Basic Books.

Scollon, R. (1976). *Conversations with a one year old*. Honolulu: University Press of Hawaii.

Scott, J. F. (1914). *Historical essays on apprenticeship and vocational education*. Ann Arbor, MI: Ann Arbor Press.

Scribner, S. (1984). Studying working intelligence. In B. Rogoff & J. Lave (Eds.), *Everyday cognition: Its development in social context*. Cambridge, MA: Harvard University Press.

Scribner, S. (1986). Thinking in action: Some characteristics of practical thought. In R. J. Sternberg & R. K. Wagner (Eds.), *Practical intelligence: Nature and origins of competence in the everyday world*. Cambridge: Cambridge University Press.

Scribner, S., & Cole, M. (1973). Cognitive consequences of formal and informal schooling. *Science, 182*, 553-559.

Scribner, S., & Cole, M. (1981). *The psychology of literacy.* New York: Harvard University Press.

Senge, P. M. (1990). *The fifth discipline: The art and practice of the learning organization.* New York: Doubleday.

Sharf, J. C. (1988). Litigating personnel measurement policy. In *Journal of Vocational Behavior, 33*(3), 235–271.

Shepard, L. (1993). Evaluating test validity. In L. Darling-Hammond (Ed.), *The Review of Research in Education, 19,* 405–450.

Sherman, M., & Key, C. B. (1932). The intelligence of mountain children. *Child Development, 3,* 279–290.

Shields, J. (1962). *Monozygotic twins brought up apart and brought up together.* London: Oxford University Press.

Siegel, M. (1991). A clash of conversational worlds: Interpreting cognitive development through communication. In L. Resnick, J. M. Levine, & S. D. Teasley (Eds.), *Perspectives on socially shared cognition* (pp. 23–40). Washington, DC: American Psychological Association.

Siegler, R. S. (Ed.). (1978). *Children's thinking: What develops?* Hillsdale, NJ: Erlbaum.

Siegler, R. S. (1991). *Children's thinking.* Englewood Cliffs, NJ: Prentice-Hall. (Original work published 1986)

Siegler, S., & Shipley, C. (1995). Variation, selection and cognitive change. In T. Simon & G. S. Halford (Eds.). *Developing cognitive competence: New approaches to process modeling.* Hillside, NJ: Erlbaum.

Simon, H. A. (1965). *The shape of automation for men and management.* New York: Harper & Row.

Simon, H. A. (1974). How big is a chunk? *Science, 183,* 482–488.

Simon, H. A., with Chase, W. (1979). The mind's eye in chess. In H. A. Simon, *Models of thought.* New Haven, CT: Yale University Press.

Simon, H. A., & Gilmartin, K. J. (1973). A simulation of memory for chess positions. *Cognitive Psychology, 5,* 29–46.

Simonton, D. K. (1984). *Genius, creativity, and leadership: Historiometric inquiries.* Cambridge, MA: Harvard University Press.

Simonton, D. K. (1988). Creativity, leadership, and chance. In R. J. Sternberg (Ed.), *The nature of creativity* (pp. 386–436). New York: Cambridge University Press.

Sizer, T. (1992). *Horace's school.* Boston: Houghton Mifflin.

Sloboda, J. (1991). Musical expertise. In K. A. Ericsson & J. Smith (Eds.), *Toward a general theory of expertise: Prospects and limits* (pp. 153–171). Cambridge: Cambridge University Press.

Snow, C. E. (1984). Parent-child interaction and the development of communicative ability. In R. Schiefelbusch & J. Pickar (Eds.). *The acquisition of communicative competence.* Baltimore, MD: University Park Press.

Snow, R., & Yalow, R. (1982). Education and intelligence. In R. Sternberg (Ed.), *Handbook of human intelligence.* New York: Cambridge University Press.

Spearman, C. (1904). General intelligence, objectively determined and measured. *American Journal of Psychology, 15,* 201–293.

Spearman, C. (1923). *The nature of "intelligence" and the principles of cognition.* London: Macmillan.

Spearman, C. (1927). *The abilities of man.* New York: Macmillan.

Spearman, C. (1961). The proof and measurement of association between two things. In J. J. Jenkins & D. G. Patterson (Eds.), *Studies in individual differences: The search for intelligence* (pp. 59–73). New York: Appleton-Century-Crofts. (Original work published 1904)

Spelke, E. S. (1988). The origins of physical knowledge. In L. Weiskrantz (Ed.), *Thought without language* (pp. 168–182). Oxford: Oxford University Press.

Spelke, E. S. (1991). Physical knowledge in infancy: Reflections on Piaget's theory. In S. Carey & R. Gelman (Eds.), *The epigenesis of mind: Essays on biology and cognition.* Hillsdale, NJ: Erlbaum.

Sperry, R. (1974). Lateral specialization in the surgically separated hemispheres. In F. Schmitt & F. G. Worden (Eds.), *The neurosciences: Third study program.* Cambridge, MA: MIT Press.

Starkey, P., Spelke, E. S., & Gelman, R. (1990). Numerical abstraction by human infants. *Cognition, 36,* 97–127.

Steel, R. (1980). *Walter Lippmann and the American century.* Boston: Little, Brown.

Stern, W. (1965). *The psychological methods for testing intelligence.* In R. J. Herrnstein & E. G. Boring (Eds.), *A source book in the history of psychology.* Cambridge, MA: Harvard University Press. (Original work published 1912)

Sternberg, R. J. (1977). *Intelligence, information processing, and analogical reasoning.* Hillsdale, NJ: Erlbaum.

Sternberg, R. J. (Ed.). (1984). *Mechanisms of cognitive development.* New York: Freeman.

Sternberg, R. J. (1985). *Beyond IQ: A triarchic theory of human intelligence.* Cambridge: Cambridge University Press.

Sternberg, R. J. (1986a). *What is intelligence?* Norwood, NJ: Ablex.

Sternberg, R. J. (1986b). Alternatives to the triarchic theory of intelligence. *Behavioral and Brain Sciences, 9*(3), 581–583.

Sternberg, R. J. (1988). *The triarchic mind: A new theory of human intelligence.* New York: Viking.

Sternberg, R. J. (1990). *Metaphors of mind: Conceptions of the nature of intelligence.* New York: Cambridge University Press.

Sternberg, R. J. (1995). For whom the Bell Curve tolls: It tolls for you. *Psychological Science.*

Sternberg, R. J., & Grigerenko, E. (Eds.). (in press). *Intelligence: Heredity and environment.* New York: Cambridge University Press.

Sternberg, R. J., Okagaki, L., & Jackson, A. (1990). Practical intelligences for success in school. *Educational Leadership, 48,* 35–39.

Sternberg, R. J., & Wagner, R. K. (1986). (Eds.), *Practical intelligence: Nature and origins of competence in the everyday world.* New York: Cambridge University Press.

Sternberg, R. J., & Wagner, R. K. (1993). The g-ocentric view of intelligence and job performance is wrong. *Current Directions in Psychological Science, 2*(1), 1–5.

Stevenson, H. W., & Stigler, J. (1992). *The learning gap: Why our schools are failing and what we can learn from Japanese and Chinese education.* New York: Simon & Schuster.

Stevenson, H. W., & Stigler, J. (1994). Psychological maladjustment and academic achievement: A cross-cultural study of Japanese, Chinese, and American high school students. *Child Development, 65*(3), 738–753.

Stigler, J. W., Shweder, R. A., & Herdt, G. (1990). *Cultural psychology: Essays on comparative human development.* Cambridge: Cambridge University Press.

Streufert, S., & Swezey, R. W. (1986). *Complexity, managers, and organizations.* Orlando: Academic Press.

Taylor, F. W. (1911). *The principles of scientific management.* New York: Harper & Brothers.

Taylor, H. F. (1980). *The IQ game: A methodological inquiry into the heredity-environment controversy.* New Brunswick, NJ: Rutgers University Press.

Terman, L. M. (1916). *The measurement of intelligence: An explanation of and a complete guide for the use of the Stanford revision and extension of the Binet-Simon intelligence scale.* Boston: Houghton Mifflin.

Terman, L. M. (1919). *The intelligence of school children.* Boston: Houghton Mifflin.

Terman, L. M. (1921). Intelligence and its measurement. *Journal of Educational Psychology, 12*(3), 127–133.

Terman, L. M. (1922). *Intelligence tests and school reorganization.* Yonkers-on-Hudson. NY: World Book.

Terman, L. M., & Oden, M. H. (1959). *Genetic studies of genius, Vol IV: The gifted group at midlife.* Stanford, CA: Stanford University Press.

Teuber, H. -L. (1964). The riddle of frontal lobe function in man. In J. M. Warren & K. Akert (Eds.), *The frontal granular cortex and behavior.* New York: McGraw Hill.

Thatcher, R. W., Walker, R. A., & Giudice, S. (1987). Human cerebral hemispheres develop at different rates and ages. *Science, 126,* 1110.

Thomson, G. H. (1939). *The factorial analysis of human ability.* Boston: Houghton Mifflin.

Thorndike, E. (1913). *Educational psychology* (Vol. 1–2). New York: Teachers College, Columbia University.

Thurstone, L. L. (1938). *Primary mental abilities.* Chicago: University of Chicago Press.

Thurstone, L. L., & Thurstone, T. G. (1941). *Factorial studies of intelligence.* Chicago: University of Chicago Press.

Tobin, J. J., Wu, D. Y., & Davidson, D. (1989). *Preschool in three cultures: Japan, China, and the United States.* New Haven, CT: Yale University Press.

Tomasello, M., Mannie, S., & Kruger, A. C. (1986). Linguistic environment of 1 to 2 year-old twins. *Developmental Psychology, 22,* 169–176.

Treffert, D. A. (1989). *Extraordinary people: Understanding 'idiot savants.'* New York: Harper & Row.

Turing, A. M. (1963). Computing machinery and intelligence. In E. A. Feigenbaum & J. Feldman (Eds.), *Computers and thought* (pp. 11–35). New York: McGraw Hill. (Original work published 1950)

Turing, A. M. (1986). Lecture to the London Mathematical Society on 20 February 1947. In B. E. Carpenter & R. W. Doran (Eds.), *A. M. Turing's ACE report of 1946 and other papers.* Cambridge, MA: MIT Press. (Original work published 1947)

Tyler, L. (1965). *The psychology of human differences* (3rd ed.). New York: Appleton-Century-Crofts.

Vernon, P. A. (Ed.). (1987). *Speed of information processing and intelligence.* Norwood, NJ: Ablex.

Vernon, P. A. (1990). The use of biological measures to estimate behavioral intelligence. *Educational Psychologist, 25*(3/4), 293–304.

Vernon, P. A., & Mori, M. (1989). Intelligence, reaction times, and nerve conductance velocity. *Behavior Genetics, 19,* 779.

Vernon, P. A., & Mori, M. (1990). Physiological approaches to the assessment of intelligence. In C. R. Reynolds & R. W. Kamphaus (Eds.), *Handbook of psychological and educational assessment of children. Vol. I. Intelligence and achievement* (pp. 389–402). New York and London: Guilford Press.

Vernon, P. A., & Mori, M. (1992). Intelligence, reaction times and peripheral nerve conduction velocity. *Intelligence, 16,* 273–288.

Vernon, P. E. (1950). *The structure of human abilities.* London: Methuen.

Vernon, P. E. (1956). *The measurement of abilities.* London: University of London Press.

Vernon, P. E. (1972). *Intelligence and cultural environment.* London: Methuen.

Vidal, F. (1994). *Piaget before Piaget.* Cambridge, MA: Harvard University Press.

Vogel, E. (1979). *Japan as number one.* Cambridge, MA: Harvard University Press.

Vuyk, R. (1981). *Overview and critique of Piaget's genetic epistemology 1965–1980.* London: Academic Press.

Vygotsky, L. S. (1978). *Mind in society: The development of higher psychological processes.* Cambridge, MA: Harvard University Press.

Vygotsky, L. S. (1979). The genesis of higher mental functions. In J. V. Wertsch (Ed.), *The concept of activity in Soviet psychology.* Armonk, NY: Sharpe.

Vygotsky, L. S. (1987). Thinking and speech. In R. W. Riever & A. S. Carton (Eds.), *The collected works of L.S. Vygotsky.* New York: Plenum.

Wachs, T. D., & Gruen G. E. (1982). *Early experience and human development.* New York: Plenum.

Waddington, C. H. (1966). *Principles of development and differentiation.* New York: Macmillan.

Wagman, M. (1991). *Artificial intelligence and human cognition.* New York: Praeger.

Wagner, D. (1980). *Learning to read by 'rote' in the Quranic schools of Yemen and Senegal.* Paper presented at the American Psychological Association, Washington, DC.

Wagner, R. K., & Sternberg, R. J. (1986). Tacit knowledge and intelligence in the everyday world. In R. J. Sternberg & R. K. Wagner (Eds.), *Practical intelligence: Nature and origins of competence in the everyday world.* Cambridge: Cambridge University Press.

Walters, J., & Gardner, H. (1985). The development and education of intelligences. In F. Link (Ed.), *Essays on the intellect* (pp. 1–21). Washington, DC: Curriculum Development Associates/Association for Supervision and Curriculum Development.

Wason, P. C. (1969). Regression in reasoning. *British Journal of Psychology, 60*(4), 471–480.

Watkins, M. H. (1943). The West African "bush" school. *American Journal of Sociology, 48,* 666–677.

Watson, J. B. (1913). Psychology as a behaviorist views it. *Psychological Review, 20,* 158–177.

Watson, P. (1980, May 25) Uncanny twins. *London Sunday Times Weekly Review,* pp. 1, 6.

Waxman, S., & Gelman, R. (1986). Preschoolers' use of superordinate relations in classification and language. *Cognitive Development, 1*(2), 139–156.

Weber, M. (1947). *The theory of social and economic organization.* New York: Oxford University Press.

Webster's new world dictionary of American English. (Neufeldt, Victoria ed.). (1994). New York: Webster's New World.

Wechsler, D. (1971). Intelligence: Definition, theory, and the IQ. In R. Cancro (Ed.), *Intelligence: Genetic and environmental influences.* New York and London: Grune & Stratton.

Weismann, A. (1889). *Essays upon heredity and kindred biological problems.* Oxford: Clarendon Press.

Weiss, A. (1973). The biosocial standpoint in psychology. In C. Murchison (Ed.), *Psychologies of 1930.* New York: Arno Press. (Original work published 1930)

Weizenbaum, J. (1976). *Computer power and human reason: From judgment to calculation.* San Francisco: Freeman.

Wells, H. G. (1956). *The time machine.* In H. Kuebler (Ed.), *The treasury of science fiction classics.* Garden City, NY: Hanover House/Doubleday. (Original work published 1931)

Werner, H. (1948). *Comparative psychology of mental development.* New York: Wiley.

Wertsch, J. V. (1978). From social interaction to higher psychological processes: A clarification and application of Vygosky's theory. *Human Development, 22,* 1–22.

Wertsch, J. V. (Ed.). (1979). *The concept of activity in Soviet psychology.* Armonk, NY: Sharpe.

Wertsch, J. V. (1991). A sociocultural approach to socially shared cognition. In L. Resnick, J. M. Levine, & S. D. Teasley (Eds.), *Perspectives on socially shared cognition* (pp. 85–100). Washington, DC: American Psychological Association.

Wheeler, D. L. (1992, June 24). An escalating debate over research that links biology and human behavior. *The Chronicle of Higher Education,* pp. A7–A8.

White, S. (1965). Evidence for a hierarchical arrangement of learning processes. In L. P. Lipsitt & C. C. Spiker (Eds.), *Advances in child development and behavior* (Vol. 2). New York: Academic Press.

Wiggins, G. (1989). A true test: Toward more authentic and equitable assessment. *Phi Delta Kappan, 70*(9), 703–713.

Willerman, L., Schultz, R., Rutledge, A. N., & Bigler, E. D. (1991). In vivo brain size and intelligence. *Intelligence, 15,* 223–228.

Willerman, L., Schultz, R., Rutledge, J. N., & Bigler, E. D. (1992). Hemispheric size asymmetry predicts relative verbal and nonverbal intelligence differently in the sexes: An MRI study of structure-function relations. *Intelligence, 16,* 315–328.

Wilson, E. O. (1975). *Sociobiology.* Cambridge: Harvard University Press.

Wilson, M. D. (1969). *The essential Descartes.* New York: New American Library.

Wilson, R. S. (1978). Synchronies in mental development: An epigenetic perspective. *Science, 202,* 939–948.

Wilson, R. S. (1983). The Louisville twin study: Developmental synchronies in behavior. *Child Development, 54,* 298–316.

Winner, E. (1982). *Invented worlds.* Cambridge, MA: Harvard University Press.

Winner, E. (1988). *The point of words.* Cambridge, MA: Harvard University Press.

Winograd, T. (1972). *Understanding natural language.* New York: Academic Press.

Wissler, C. (1961). The correlation of mental and physical tests. In J. J. Jenkins & D. G. Patterson (Eds.), *Studies in individual differences: The search for intelligence.* Appleton-Century-Crofts. (Original work published 1901)

Wood, D., Bruner, J. S., & Ross, G. (1976). The role of tutoring in problem solving. *Journal of Child Psychology and Psychiatry, 17,* 89–100.

Woodworth, R. (1941). *Heredity and environment: A critical survey of recently published material on twins and foster children. A report prepared for the Committee on Social Adjustment.* New York: Social Science Research Council.

Wundt, W. (1901). *Volkerpsychologie. Eine untersuchung der entwicklungsgesetze von sprache, mythus und sitten. Vol. 1. Die Sprache, 1900. Vol. 2. Mythus und religion:*

Part I, 1905. [Folk psychology: An investigation into the developmental principles of language, myth and custom. Vol. 1. Language, Vol. 2. Myth and religion.] Leipzig: Engelman.

Wynn, K. (1992). Addition and subtraction by human infants. *Nature, 358,* 479.

Yerkes, R. M. (Ed.). (1921). *Psychological examining in the United States Army. Memoirs of the National Academy of Sciences* (Vol. XV). Washington, DC: Government Printing Office.

Zaidel, E., Zaidel, D., & Sperry, R. (1981). Left and right intelligence: Case studies of Raven's progressive matrices following bisection and hemidecortication. *Cortex, 17,* 167–186.

Zajonc, R. B. (1976). Family configuration and intelligence. *Science, 192,* 227–236.

Zuboff, S. (1988). *In the age of the smart machine: The future of work and power.* New York: Basic Books.

Zuboff, S. (1995). The emperor's new workplace. *Scientific American, 273*(3), 202–204.

Copyright Acknowledgments

Figure and Table Credits

Box 1.1   From "Regression in Reasoning?" by P. C. Wason, 1969, *British Journal of Psychology, 60,* p. 471. Copyright © 1969 by The British Psychological Society. Reprinted with permission.

Box 1.3   From *Memoirs of the National Academy of Sciences, Vol. XV, Psychological Examining in the United States Army,* edited by Robert M. Yerkes, 1921, pp. 228–256, Washington, DC: U.S. Government Printing Office. Reprinted with permission of the National Academy of Sciences.

Figure 2.2   From *Hereditary Genius,* by Frances Galton, introduced by Professor H. J. Eysenck, 1979, p. 34, London: Julian Friedmann. Copyright © 1978 by Professor H. J. Eysenck. Reprinted with permission.

Figure 2.3   Reprinted with permission of Melissa Brand.

Figure 3.5   Reprinted with permission of Warren K. Wake.

Figure 3.6   Reprinted with permission of Warren K. Wake.

Figure 3.7   From *The Nature of Human Intelligence* by J. P. Guilford, 1967, New York: McGraw-Hill. Copyright © 1967 by McGraw-Hill. Reprinted with permission.

Figure 3.8   From *The Measurement of Abilities* by P. E. Vernon, 1956, London: University of London Press. Copyright © 1956 by Philip E. Vernon. Reproduced with permission of Hodder & Stoughton Ltd.

Figure 3.9   From *The Structure of Human Abilities* by P. E. Vernon, 1950, London: Methuen & Co. Copyright © 1950 by Philip E. Vernon. Reprinted with permission of Methuen & Co.

Figure 3.10   From *Standard Progressive Matrices* by J. C. Raven, 1938, figures A4 and A5, London: Lewis. Reprinted with permission of J. C. Raven Ltd.

Figure 3.11   From *Bias in Mental Testing* by A. R. Jensen, 1980, New York: The Free Press, a Division of Simon & Schuster. Reprinted with permission of The Free Press.

Figure 4.1   Reprinted with permission of Warren K. Wake and Mindy Kornhaber.

Figure 4.2   Reprinted with permission of Warren K. Wake.

Figure 5.1   From broadside entitled *Phrenological Chart* by N. Wheeler, (184?) Boston: B. W. Thayer. Reprinted with permission of Harvard Medical School Countway Library Rare Books Department.

Figure 5.2   From *Tarite' Complet de L'anatomie de L'homme* by J. M. Bourgery, 1844, Vol. II, plate 21. Paris: C. A. Delaunay. Reprinted with permission of Harvard Medical School Countway Library Rare Books Department.

Figure 5.3   From *Advances in the Psychology of Human Intelligence* edited by R. J. Sternberg, 1986, Vol. III, p. 21, Hillsdale, NJ: Lawrence Erlbaum Associates. Copyright © 1986 by

1994 by Daily Racing Form, Inc. Reprinted with permission.

Figure 9.1   From *The Lodging and Food Service Industry* by G. W. Lattin, 1989, p. 223, East Lansing, MI: Educational Institute of the American Hotel & Motel Association. Copyright © 1989 by the Educational Institute of the American Hotel & Motel Association. Reprinted with permission.

Figure 9.2   From *Handbook of Quality Tools: The Japanese Approach* by K. Ozeki and T. Asaka, 1990, p. 166, Portland, OR: Productivity Press. English translation copyright © 1990 by Productivity Press, Inc. Reprinted with permission.

Photo Credits

Chapter 1   p. 7, AP/Wide World Photos; p. 9, From *East Is a Big Bird: Navigation and Logic on Puluwat Atoll* by T. Gladwin, 1970, p. 14, Cambridge, MA: Harvard University Press. Copyright © 1970 by the President and Fellows of Harvard College. Reprinted with permission; p. 10, From *East Is a Big Bird: Navigation and Logic on Puluwat Atoll* by T. Gladwin, 1970, p. 129, Cambridge, MA: Harvard University Press. Copyright © 1970 by the President and Fellows of Harvard College. Reprinted with permission; p. 13, From *The Peoples and Politics of the Far East* by H. Norman, 1895, London: T. F. Unwin. Reprinted with permission of the Harvard-Yenching Library, Harvard University

Chapter 2   p. 32, The Granger Collection, New York; p. 34 (top left), Archives of the History of American Psychology; p. 34 (bottom right), Archives of the History of American Psychology; p. 36, Archives of the History of American Psychology; p. 40,

The Granger Collection, New York; p. 42, Archives of the History of American Psychology; p. 46, From *The Life, Letters and Labours of Francis Galton,* Vol. 11, plates by K. Pearson, 1930, Cambridge: Cambridge University Press. Copyright © 1930 by Cambridge University Press. Reprinted with permission; p. 48, Archives of the History of American Psychology

Chapter 3   p. 60, Archives of the History of American Psychology; p. 85, Stanford University

Chapter 4   p. 97, Archives of the History of American Psychology; p. 115, Reprinted with permission of Rochel Gelman; p. 118, Reprinted with permission of Robbie Case; p. 119, Reprinted with permission of Kurt Fischer; p. 131, Reprinted with permission of Annette Karmiloff-Smith

Chapter 5   p. 149 (bottom left), Reprinted with permission of Robert Plomin; p. 149 (bottom right), Reprinted with permission of Thomas Bouchard; p. 151, Drawing by Chas. Addams. Copyright © 1981 The New Yorker Magazine, Inc. Reprinted with permission; p. 153, Reprinted with permission of Arthur Jensen

Chapter 6   p. 170 (top left), Reprinted with permission of Marvin Minsky; p. 170 (top right), Reprinted with permission of Herbert A. Simon; p. 198, Reprinted with permission of Warren K. Wake; p. 199, Reprinted with permission of Mindy Kornhaber

Chapter 7   p. 200, Archives of the History of American Psychology; p. 201, Reprinted with permission of Warren K. Wake; p. 203, Reprinted with permission of Howard Gardner; p. 210, Drawing from *Nadia: A Case of Extraordinary Drawing Ability in an Autistic Child* by L. Selfe, 1977, p. 189, London: Academic Press. Copyright © 1977 by Academic Press. Reprinted with permission; p. 214, Reprinted

Name Index

Abel, L., 144
Acland, H., 313
Allen, C., 59, 92
Allen, R., 273
Altman, S., 135
Amabile, T. M., 258, 296-297
Anderson, M., 58, 70, 75, 84, 90, 92, 94, 95, 145, 196, 201, 202, 214-224, 227, 233-234, 237, 239, 243-245, 295
Angier, R. P., 19, 20
Ankney, C. D., 142
Anzai, Y., 271-272
Aoki, M., 285, 287-288
Argyris, C., 273-274, 298
Ariès, P., 105
Aristotle, 32-33
Arlin, P. K., 113
Armon, C., 305
Asaka, T., 284-287

Babbage, C., 164
Baillargeon, R., 115
Bane, M. J., 313
Barr, A., 178
Bashore, T., 307
Basso, A., 142
Bastian, A., 289
Bateson, M. C., 246-247
Bauer, N. F., 305
Bell, N., 198
Benditt, J., 150
Bereiter, C., 269, 272-273
Berry, J. W., 5, 7, 156
Bigler, E. D., 142
Binet, A., 18, 47-51, 196, 275, 299
Black, J. E., 157
Block, J. H., 311

Block, N. J., 88, 197
Bloom, F., 159
Blythe, T., 260
Bobrow, D. G., 175, 302
Boden, M. A., 173-175, 190
Boring, E., 37, 38, 47
Borke, H., 116
Born, R., 194
Bornstein, M., 155
Boster, M., 202
Bouchard, T. J., 59, 147-150, 152, 158
Bowen, J., 247
Brainerd, C. J., 112, 117
Brand, C. R., 258
Braudel, F., 11, 277
Brigham, C., 19, 20, 85
Brittain, W. L., 209
Broadbent, D. E., 168, 190
Broca, P., 36
Brody, N., 94, 142, 144
Bronfenbrenner, U., 5, 55, 198
Brooks, L. R., 204
Browning, H. L., 144
Brubacher, J. S., 17
Bruner, J. S., 252, 263
Bryant, P., 207
Buchsbaum, M. S., 144
Bullock, D., 308
Burt, C., 303
Butler, J. S., 279
Butterfield, E., 168

Caine, A. F., 246
Callahan, R. E., 17, 279
Campbell, J., 172, 177
Campbell, K. B., 318
Capon, N., 116
Capron, C., 303

Subject Index